THE CAMBRIDG[

LUC[

Lucretius' didactic poem *De rerum natura* ('On the Nature of Things') is an impassioned and visionary presentation of the materialist philosophy of Epicurus, and one of the most powerful poetic texts of antiquity. After its rediscovery in 1417 it became a controversial and seminal work in successive phases of literary history, the history of science, and the Enlightenment. In this *Cambridge Companion* experts in the history of literature, philosophy and science discuss the poem in its ancient contexts and in its reception both as a literary text and as a vehicle for progressive ideas. The *Companion* is designed both as a handbook for the general reader who wishes to learn about Lucretius, and as a series of stimulating essays for students of classical antiquity and its reception. It is completely accessible to the reader who has read Lucretius only in translation.

Mussenden Temple, Co. Antrim
An eighteenth-century architectural realisation of the Lucretian 'calm temples of the wise'
looking out over a storm-tossed sea (see p. 14 below)

THE CAMBRIDGE
COMPANION TO
LUCRETIUS

EDITED BY
STUART GILLESPIE
Reader in English Literature, University of Glasgow

PHILIP HARDIE
Senior Research Fellow, Trinity College, Cambridge

CAMBRIDGE
UNIVERSITY PRESS

CAMBRIDGE UNIVERSITY PRESS
Cambridge, New York, Melbourne, Madrid, Cape Town,
Singapore, São Paulo, Delhi, Tokyo, Mexico City

Cambridge University Press
The Edinburgh Building, Cambridge CB2 8RU, UK

Published in the United States of America by Cambridge University Press, New York

www.cambridge.org
Information on this title: www.cambridge.org/9780521612661

First published 2007

A catalogue record for this publication is available from the British Library

ISBN 978-0-521-84801-5 Hardback
ISBN 978-0-521-61266-1 Paperback

CONTENTS

CONTENTS

PART II: THEMES

PART III: RECEPTION

CONTENTS

ILLUSTRATIONS

Frontispiece

Plates

CONTRIBUTORS

ERIC BAKER is Assistant Professor in the Department of German, Scandinavian and Dutch, University of Minnesota. He has published articles on Kafka, Kant, Kleist, Schiller and Schopenhauer. He is currently working on a book dealing with Lucretius in eighteenth-century aesthetics, and an edition of Norbert Elias's unpublished manuscripts on humour.

REID BARBOUR is Gillian T. Cell Distinguished Professor in the English Department at the University of North Carolina, Chapel Hill. He is the author of *Deciphering Elizabethan Fiction* (1993), *English Epicures and Stoics* (1998), *Literature and Religious Culture in Seventeenth-Century England* (2001), and *John Selden: Measures of the Holy Commonwealth in Seventeenth-Century England* (2003). He is co-editor (with David Norbrook) of Lucy Hutchinson's translation of Lucretius (for Oxford). His current work includes an intellectual biography of Sir Thomas Browne.

JOSEPH FARRELL is Professor of Classical Studies at the University of Pennsylvania. He is the author of several books and articles, mainly on Latin poetry, including *Vergil's Georgics and the Traditions of Ancient Epic* (1991) and *Latin Language and Latin Culture* (2001). He is currently studying the representation of dissent in Augustan poetry, among other topics.

PHILIP FORD has taught since 1982 in the Cambridge University French Department, where he is now Professor of French and Neo-Latin Literature, as well as holding a Fellowship at Clare College. His current research, funded for two years by a British Academy Research Readership, is on the reception of Homer in Renaissance France.

MONICA GALE is Associate Professor in Classics at Trinity College, Dublin, with research interests in the poetry of the late Roman Republic and the Augustan period. She is the author of *Myth and Poetry in Lucretius* (1994) and *Virgil on the Nature of Things: the Georgics, Lucretius and the Didactic Tradition* (2000), and editor of *Latin Epic and Didactic Poetry: Genre, Tradition and Individuality*

(2004). She is currently working on a commentary on the complete poems of Catullus.

STUART GILLESPIE is Reader in English Literature at the University of Glasgow. He is the editor of the journal *Translation and Literature* and joint general editor of *The Oxford History of Literary Translation in English* (2005–). His other publications include *The Poets on the Classics: an Anthology* (1988), *Shakespeare's Books: a Dictionary of Shakespeare Sources* (2001) and *Shakespeare and Elizabethan Popular Culture* (2006). He is currently compiling an anthology of English Renaissance translations and an edition of the six volumes of Dryden's *Miscellany Poems*.

PHILIP HARDIE, formerly Corpus Christi Professor of Latin at the University of Oxford, is a Senior Research Fellow at Trinity College, Cambridge. He is the author of *Virgil's Aeneid: Cosmos and Imperium* (1986), *The Epic Successors of Virgil* (1993) and *Ovid's Poetics of Illusion* (2002), and editor of *The Cambridge Companion to Ovid* (2002). He is currently completing a commentary on Ovid, *Metamorphoses* 13–15, and writing a book on the history of fame and rumour.

YASMIN HASKELL is Cassamarca Foundation Associate Professor in Latin Humanism at the University of Western Australia. Her interests include neo-Latin poetry, the early modern Jesuits, and the interface between science and humanism. She is the author of *Loyola's Bees: Ideology and Industry in Jesuit Latin Didactic Poetry* (2003) and co-editor (with Philip Hardie) of *Poets and Teachers: Latin Didactic Poetry and the Didactic Authority of the Latin Poet from the Renaissance to the Present* (1999). She has co-edited Dufresnoy's *De arte graphica* (2005). She is editing (with J. Ruys) a collection on 'Latinity and alterity in the early modern period'. Her main current project is a book on 'hypochondria' in seventeenth-century Italy.

DAVID HOPKINS is Professor of English Literature at the University of Bristol. Among his recent publications are *The Poems of John Dryden* in the Longman Annotated English Poets series, and Volume III (*1660–1790*) of *The Oxford History of Literary Translation in English* (in both cases as co-editor). Recent essays appear in *The Blackwell Companion to Eighteenth-Century Poetry* (2007) and *The Blackwell Companion to Classical Receptions* (2007).

MONTE JOHNSON is Assistant Professor of Philosophy at the University of California San Diego, and a Fellow of the National Endowment for the Humanities (2006). He is the author of *Aristotle on Teleology* (2005), and of essays on ancient philosophy and the history of science.

E. J. KENNEY is Emeritus Kennedy Professor of Latin in the University of Cambridge, and was a Fellow of Peterhouse, Cambridge, from 1953 to 1991. His publications include a critical edition of Ovid's amatory works (1961); editions with commentary of Lucretius, *De rerum natura* III (1971), [Virgil] *Moretum* (1984), Apuleius, *Cupid & Psyche* (1990) and Ovid, *Heroides* XVI–XXI (1996); a translation with introduction and notes of Apuleius, *The Golden Ass* (1998); and *The Classical Text* (1974). He is at present working on a commentary on Ovid, *Metamorphoses* 6–9 for the series Scrittori Greci e Latini (Fondazione Lorenzo Valla), due for publication in 2009.

DONALD MACKENZIE is a Lecturer in English Literature at the University of Glasgow. He is author of *The Metaphysical Poets* (1990), editor of Kipling's *Puck of Pook's Hill* and *Rewards and Fairies* for World's Classics (1993) and co-editor of *The Fair Maid of Perth* (1999) for the Edinburgh Edition of the Waverley Novels.

DIRK OBBINK is University Lecturer in Papyrology and Greek Literature at the University of Oxford and a Fellow of Christ Church, Oxford. He is director and general editor of the Oxyrhynchus Papyri series, and has edited the Herculaneum papyrus roll containing Philodemus' *De pietate* (1996). He has edited the collection *Philodemus and Poetry: Poetic Theory and Practice in Lucretius, Philodemus and Horace* (1995) and published articles on Hellenistic philosophy, scholarship and *poetae docti*. He is currently engaged on a history of fragmentary literature, 300 BC–AD 800.

JAMES I. PORTER is Professor of Greek, Latin and Comparative Literature at the University of Michigan. He is author of *Nietzsche and the Philology of the Future* (2000) and editor, most recently, of *Classical Pasts: the Classical Traditions of Greece and Rome* (2006). He has just completed *The Origins of Aesthetic Inquiry in Antiquity: Matter, Experience, and the Sublime* (forthcoming), and is at work on a sequel volume, *Literary Aesthetics after Aristotle*.

MARTIN PRIESTMAN is a Professor of English Literature at Roehampton University. Major publications include *Cowper's Task: Structure and Influence* (1983), *Romantic Atheism: Poetry and Freethought, 1780–1830* (1999) and the selection and introduction of *The Collected Writings of Erasmus Darwin* (9 vols., 2004). In the field of crime fiction he has published *Detective Fiction and Literature: the Figure on the Carpet* (1990) and edited *The Cambridge Companion to Crime Fiction* (2003).

VALENTINA PROSPERI is Associate Professor of Classical Philology at the University of Sassari. Her publications include *Di soavi licor gli orli del vaso: la fortuna di Lucrezio dall'Umanesimo alla Controriforma* (2004), and articles on the reception of classical texts in English and Italian literature.

MICHAEL REEVE held from 1984 to 2006 the Kennedy Chair of Latin at Cambridge, where he is now a Director of Research in the Faculty of Classics. He has published editions of *Daphnis and Chloe* (1982), Cicero's speech *Pro Quinctio*

(1992), and Vegetius' *Epitoma rei militaris* (2004), and articles on the transmission of Latin and Greek authors, among them Lucretius. He is currently editing Geoffrey of Monmouth and studying the transmission of Pliny's *Natural History*.

ALESSANDRO SCHIESARO is Professor of Latin Literature at the University of Rome 'La Sapienza'. His research focuses on the intersection between Latin poetry, literary theory and Roman cultural history. He has written on didactic poetry, including *Simulacrum et imago: gli argomenti analogici nel De rerum natura* (1990); on Roman theatre (*The Passions in Play: Thyestes and the Dynamics of Senecan Drama*, 2003); and on several Latin authors and their reception. He is the co-editor of *Mega Nepios: the Addressee in Didactic Poetry* (1993) and *The Roman Cultural Revolution* (1997). Currently he is at work on the character of Dido in the *Aeneid* and beyond.

JAMES WARREN is a Senior Lecturer in Classics at the University of Cambridge and Fellow and Director of Studies in Philosophy at Corpus Christi College. His publications include *Epicurus and Democritean Ethics: an Archaeology of Ataraxia* (2002) and *Facing Death: Epicurus and his Critics* (2004). He is currently editing the forthcoming *Cambridge Companion to Epicureanism*.

CATHERINE WILSON teaches Philosophy at the Graduate Center of the City University of New York. She writes on the history and philosophy of the seventeenth-century physical and life sciences and is the author of *Leibniz's Metaphysics* (1989), *The Invisible World* (1995) and *Descartes' Meditations* (2003).

PREFACE

The editors have felt fortunate in being able to draw upon the expertise of scholars in a number of fields. We are extremely grateful for advice to Diskin Clay, Robert Cummings, Peta Fowler, John Henderson, Kit Hume, Doug Hutchinson, W. R. Johnson, Elisabeth Leedham-Green, Martin McLaughlin, Charles Martindale and David Norbrook. Several of our contributors have also ranged well beyond their briefs and responsibilities in assisting us, and Michael Sharp of Cambridge University Press has provided all the help we sought.

The generous support of two institutions should be acknowledged: the British Academy and the Faculty of Classics, University of Oxford, which together funded an essential conference that brought contributors, editors and others to Corpus Christi College, Oxford in June 2005. Participants in this event showed us not only that Lucretius can command attention across the disciplinary spectrum, but that sharing cross-disciplinary expertise is an especially fruitful, and pleasurable, way of approaching the *De rerum natura*. We hope the present volume demonstrates this equally successfully.

Abbreviations of ancient works follow those in the *Oxford Classical Dictionary* and the *Oxford Latin Dictionary*.

STUART GILLESPIE AND PHILIP HARDIE

Introduction

Lucretius' *De rerum natura* (hereafter *DRN*), together with Catullus 64 (a much shorter narrative mythological poem on the wedding of the parents of Achilles, Peleus and Thetis), are the first fully surviving examples of a hexameter *epos* in Latin. The Greek word *epos*, 'epic' in hexameters, includes both narrative poems on the deeds of heroes (in the line of the Homeric *Iliad* and *Odyssey*) and didactic poems that give instruction in some body of knowledge (in the line of Hesiod's *Works and Days* and *Theogony*). This formal link, through the shared metre, between what might appear to be two very different kinds of literary product is important: the *DRN* is both a poem of instruction and a celebration of the godlike achievement of Lucretius' philosophical hero Epicurus. Both the *DRN* and Catullus 64 were massively influential on later Latin poetry, not least because of the intense engagement with them on the part of the classic Roman hexameter poet, Virgil. Lucretius and Catullus are the two giants of Latin poetry at the end of the Roman Republic, without whose innovations and refinements in poetic technique and subject matter it is hard to imagine the works of Augustan classicism by Virgil, Horace, and the rest.[1]

For all the differences between Lucretius and Catullus in terms of themes and poetic *persona*, they share the status of major contributors to the naturalisation of Greek culture in Rome (the 'hellenisation of Rome'), a process coextensive with the history of Roman civilisation but which reaches a new intensity and sophistication in the late Republic, to feed into that blend of Roman and Greek that we know as Augustan classicism.[2] Both Lucretius and Catullus are major importers from the post-classical, Hellenistic, Greek world. Catullus is the chief representative of Latin 'Alexandrianism', the use of poetic techniques associated with Callimachus, Apollonius of Rhodes

---

[1] On the direct relationships between Lucretius and Catullus see pp. 69–70 below.
[2] For a perceptive study of the way in which Catullus 64 thematises the relationship of a Roman readership to a glamorous world of Greek culture see Fitzgerald 1995: ch. 6.

and other writers active in Alexandria and other Greek cultural centres in the centuries after the death of Alexander the Great. The *DRN* is an important monument in the history of the reception in Rome of Greek philosophy and science. That history was well under way in the second century BC; Lucretius and his contemporary Cicero mark a significant new stage of the large-scale adaptation and translation of Greek philosophical texts into Latin, so inaugurating a philosophical vocabulary for what would be the chief language of philosophy in the medieval and early modern periods.[3] Lucretius girds up his loins for the difficult task of 'shedding light in Latin verses on the dark discoveries of the Greeks' (*DRN* 1.136–7)[4] in an endeavour of both linguistic and cultural translation, the propagation of a Greek philosophical doctrine with the intention of changing radically the way that Lucretius' Roman audience thinks and lives.

That philosophy is Epicureanism, one of the two major dogmatic post-Aristotelian schools, together with Stoicism (the third major school being the sceptical continuation of Plato's Academy).[5] Like other schools of Greek philosophy, Epicureanism offered systematic coverage of the three major branches of philosophical thought: epistemology, physics and ethics. The purpose of philosophy is practical, to ensure the happy life. For Epicurus the highest good is pleasure, the *uoluptas* personified in Venus in the first line of the *DRN*. An enduring caricature of Epicureanism misrepresents this as a gross sensual hedonism;[6] in fact Epicureans maximise pleasure through the removal of pain, a goal achieved by the limitation of desires and the elimination of mental disturbance (*ataraxia*). In practice Epicurean ethics largely coincides with that of the other Hellenistic schools and is compatible with the conventional private virtues of Graeco-Roman culture. When Horace, for example, engages in popular-philosophical moralising, it is often difficult, and unnecessary, to specify whether he is drawing on Epicurean or Stoic platitudes. What sets Epicureanism apart from the other schools, as a lasting

---

[3] See pp. 19–20 below; Powell 1995a; and various essays on philosophy at Rome in Griffin and Barnes 1989, and Barnes and Griffin 1997.

[4] For discussion of Lucretius' famous protest at the 'poverty of the Latin language' see Farrell 2001: 39–51; on the details of his practice in translating Greek technical terms see p. 22 below.

[5] On Hellenistic philosophy in general see Long and Sedley 1987; on the wider history and reception of Epicureanism see H. Jones 1989, Warren forthcoming. For a detailed account of Lucretius' use of Epicurus see ch. 1 below; on the flourishing community of Epicureans in the Bay of Naples see ch. 2 below.

[6] Lucretius refers polemically to this distortion in his description of the unhappy, and un-Epicurean, life of luxury at *DRN* 2.24–8, alluding to features of the palace of the Phaeacian king Alcinous in the *Odyssey*, whose sensual delights were sometimes interpreted as an image of Epicurean pleasure: see D. P. Fowler 2002 ad loc.

scandal to conventional ways of thinking, is its physics, which includes theology (an account of the nature of the gods being a standard part of ancient philosophical doctrines on the nature, *physis*, *natura*, of the world). Adopting the atomist theories of the Presocratic philosopher Democritus, Epicurus teaches a radical and anti-teleological materialism. Everything is made up of indivisible (*a-tomos*) particles of matter moving, colliding, and congregating at random in an infinite void. The gods exist,[7] but they too are made up of a particular kind of atom, and they exercise no providential government of the sublunary world.

The *DRN* has the ethical goal of converting its readers to the Epicurean way of life, but its subject matter, as its title indicates, is for the most part physics, not ethics.[8] A true understanding of the nature of the universe is the precondition for Epicurean happiness, above all through the removal of the fear of the gods and of what happens after death (for the Epicurean merely annihilation). Another distinguishing characteristic of the Epicurean school was its near-idolisation of its founder, with the consequence that it was easy for Lucretius, working within the hexameter epic tradition as broadly defined above, to represent Epicurus as a uniquely great hero, engaged in a titanic struggle against the forces of superstition and darkness – 'titanic' in the sense that a recurring image of the poem is an assault, such as that of the mythical Titans or Giants, on the traditional Olympian gods, as Epicurus' mind (and Lucretius' and the reader's minds following after) ranges sovereign through the infinite void. The *DRN* is balanced between a sense of intellectual control of the mysteries of nature and a continuing wonder and amazement at the vastness and impersonality of the universe revealed by the power of Epicurus' mind. The poem is an important and hitherto inadequately recognised document in the history of the sublime, as James Porter shows in chapter 10 of this volume.

Docti furor arduus Lucreti[9]

The *DRN* is an unsettling poem whose aim is to produce in its reader a settled peace of mind. In his dogged and unswerving pursuit of a single truth Lucretius also emerges as a writer of paradox, although, arguably, some of the paradoxes are ones that later centuries have read into the poem. Statius in

---

[7] Or at least material images of the gods exist, from which we form our concepts of the gods: for the evidence for this now widely held 'idealist', as opposed to 'realist', view of Epicurus' gods see Long and Sedley 1987: I, 144–9; Peta Fowler in D. P. Fowler 2002: 239–40 n. 48.

[8] For an outline of the contents of the *DRN* see p. 81 below.

[9] Statius, *Silvae* 2.7.76: 'learned Lucretius' sublime frenzy'.

his one-line thumbnail of Lucretius juxtaposes the rationality of the doctrine of the *DRN* (*docti*) with the 'madness' (*furor*) of the poem's lofty inspiration. 'Learned' also points to the kind of poetry that is produced by art or technique (*ars*), as opposed to the untutored outpourings of genius or inspiration (*ingenium, furor*), an opposition central to the poetics of Lucretius' day, but which, Monica Gale argues in this volume,[10] Lucretius deliberately collapses in a poem that presents itself as *both* inspired *and* carefully crafted.

Another opposition which forcibly strikes the modern reader, that between poetry and science (or philosophy), would have been less apparent to the ancient reader: as a specimen of didactic poetry, the *DRN* belongs to a central genre in Graeco-Roman antiquity, and one which enjoyed a long life in the Middle Ages and Renaissance, both in Latin and in the vernaculars. Yasmin Haskell (ch. 11 below) traces some of the developments in neo-Latin didactic poetry of the early modern period, a tradition of considerable importance in the history of European culture[11] but to which little attention is usually now paid. Moreover, a strong scientific didacticism runs through some of the central monuments of the western canon. Although Dante could not have had direct access to the text of Lucretius, rediscovered in the early Renaissance,[12] one Dante scholar has developed an illuminating comparison between Dante and Lucretius in order to expound the connection between 'true knowledge' and 'poetry' that underpins the *Divina Commedia*.[13] Spenser's debt to Lucretius as well as (for his period) the more usual source of Ovid as a poet of physical law in *The Faerie Queene* has long been recognised.[14] Milton was a keen reader of Lucretius, and *Paradise Lost* is significantly indebted to the *DRN* as a poem that teaches its reader a sublime vision of a universe.[15] James Thomson's *The Seasons*, one of the most widely read poems of the eighteenth century, draws on the *DRN* in manner and structure.[16] This strain grows fainter after the eighteenth century, but around its end Erasmus Darwin, grandfather of Charles and a leading figure in the scientific culture of the time, wrote a number of strictly didactic poems with strongly Lucretian elements, pervasively influential on the Romantics.[17] Part of the Darwin legacy came down to Tennyson, whose copious scientific imagery led T. H. Huxley to call him perhaps the only poet since Lucretius to have

---

[10] See p. 72 below.

[11] And indeed American culture: on the Mexican neo-Latin poets Diego José Abad and Rafael Landívar see respectively Kerson 1988 and Laird 2006: 55–6, 59, 91 n. 68.

[12] On the medieval and early Renaissance transmission of the *DRN* see ch. 12 below.

[13] Boyde 1981 ('Introduction: Dante and Lucretius').

[14] See pp. 245–7 below.   [15] See pp. 177, 268–70 below.

[16] See p. 267 below.   [17] See pp. 291–2 below.

taken the trouble to understand the work and methods of the scientist, and whose poem *The Two Voices* has been called 'the closest thing to Lucretius in English Literature'.[18] The merely 'glancing engagements'[19] with Lucretius in twentieth-century poetry are one sign of a perhaps final divorce between science and poetry: as Nikolay Nikolayevich, uncle and intellectual mentor of Pasternak's physician-poet Dr Zhivago, expresses it, 'When modern man is vexed by the mysteries of the universe he turns to physics, not to Hesiod's hexameters.'[20] Recent studies of science and literature have tended to reverse the perspective: instead of looking at how poetry is used as a vehicle for the expression of scientific truths, the focus has been on the ways in which supposedly objective and value-free scientific discourse about the natural world and its history is unavoidably implicated in metaphorical and anthropocentric uses of language. The metaphors through which Lucretius builds his Epicurean universe can be analysed along the lines of Gillian Beer's investigation of Darwin's revolutionary theory as verbal construct.[21]

What might have struck the ancient reader as anomalous is the use of hexameter poetry to present the technical philosophy of one of the post-Aristotelian Hellenistic schools, and one whose founder, Epicurus, appears to have disparaged poetic uses of language.[22] In a calculated strategy Lucretius presents a modern philosophy in the vatic manner of an old-fashioned Presocratic philosopher, drawing specifically on the model of Empedocles, who had presented his thought in hexameter verse.[23] The *DRN* is a gospel of rationalist materialism, a manifesto of modernity in the sonorous voice of an Old Testament prophet. A defining generic feature of ancient didactic poetry is its careful attention to the relationship between poet and addressee, typically figured as a second-person singular, and often explicitly named (Memmius is the named addressee, intermittently present, of the *DRN*, probably to be identified with C. Memmius, a prominent politician, praetor in 58 BC, and patron also of Catullus).[24] Lucretius' didactic voice is highly distinctive, speaking from on high to a child afraid of the dark in a mixture of pity and scorn: *o miseras hominum mentis, o pectora caeca!* ('O pitiable minds of men, o blind hearts!', *DRN* 2.14). As Dryden puts it, Lucretius 'seems to disdain all manner of Replies, and . . . this too, with so much scorn and

---

[18] For both citations see Spencer 1965: 162.

[19] P. 312 below.   [20] *Dr Zhivago*, ch. 2.10.

[21] See Kennedy 2002: 70–2, discussing Beer 1983.

[22] See p. 94 below.   [23] See p. 64 below.

[24] Didactic addressee: see the essays by Obbink (Empedocles) and Mitsis (Lucretius) in Schiesaro, Mitsis and Clay 1993. On the identification of Memmius see Bailey 1947 on *DRN* 1.26; p. 54 below.

indignation, as if he were assur'd of the Triumph, before he enter'd into the lists'.[25]

In order to proselytise for his messages of scientific rationality Lucretius often uses the language and rhetoric of ancient religious revelation and initiation (in this continuing a practice found in earlier Epicurean texts). At the beginning of Book 3 Epicurus is the hierophant of the atoms and the void: the *diuina uoluptas . . . atque horror* ('divine pleasure and terror', 28–9) felt by Lucretius is a paradoxical combination of emotions at home in religious experience. Most notable is Lucretius' decision to begin the *DRN* with a hymn to Venus, which masterfully uses the full palette of ancient hymnic convention to produce a stunning picture of the power and beauty of the traditional goddess of love and her effects. Attempts to dissipate the religious afflatus of the passage by reducing Venus to an allegory of orthodox Epicurean physics and ethics have not persuaded all readers.

This and other episodes in the *DRN* where a non-Epicurean view of the world is presented with a vividness and passion beside which the Epicurean truth seems pallid have prompted some to detect anxiety and division behind the façade of confident certainty, an 'antiLucretius in Lucretius',[26] loath to renounce the beauty, mystery and variety of the world of illusion that most of us inhabit for the austere truth of a reality reduced to the 'third-person perspective' of atoms blindly colliding in the void – a poet of 'involuntary spirituality'.[27] Lucretius is a superb diagnostician of the discontents of civilisation: must he not really have suffered the ills for which he offers a cure? Particularly haunting are the description at the end of Book 3 of the rich man who cannot stay in one place because what he is really trying to escape from is himself, and the extraordinary account at the end of Book 4 of the insubstantiality and emptiness of sexual desire, as lovers strive violently to mingle in the impossible primal union which had afforded Plato matter for a myth in the speech of Aristophanes in the *Symposium*.[28]

The passage on sexual desire in Book 4 may have contributed to the invention of the story of Lucretius' madness, reported in the biographical notice in St Jerome's version of the *Chronicle* of Eusebius (under the year 94 BC): 'The poet Titus Lucretius was born. In later life he was sent mad by a love-potion; in the intervals of his madness he composed a number of

---

[25] Dryden 1956–2000: III, 10.

[26] The phrase is that of Patin 1868 (vol. I, ch. 7: 'Du poème de la nature. L'Antilucrèce chez Lucrèce'). For a recent discussion see W. R. Johnson 2000: 103–33.

[27] Patin 1868: I, 132.

[28] For a penetrating treatment of Lucretius the analyst of human anxiety see Segal 1990. For some modern responses to Lucretius on desire see pp. 322–3 below.

books, later edited by Cicero. He died by his own hand at the age of forty-four.'[29] Less is certainly known about Lucretius than about almost any other Latin poet;[30] in this gap the apocryphal story in Jerome has expanded to become the 'myth of Lucretius', a stimulus for versions of Lucretius as a tormented and suicidal individual driven by dissatisfactions not simply sexual. A gloomily melancholic figure replaced a pugnacious, blaspheming earlier one during the nineteenth century and threw a long shadow over twentieth-century readings, many of which are 'tinged with the sad legend of the saddest pagan who had cut himself off from cosmic comfort and paid the price'.[31]

An alternative response to these apparently un-Epicurean moments in the *DRN* has been to see them as part of a carefully controlled strategy of persuasion: know your enemy, allow him to present himself in his most alluring or most insidious form, before applying to the reader the unfailingly efficacious nostrums of Epicurean truth.[32] Lucretius is good at using his enemies' weapons against themselves: for example the metre and language of Ennius, the writer of the national epic celebrating the divinely favoured success of Rome, are deployed to teach that political and military ambition are misguided, that the gods are absent.[33] It is a strategy that could be used against Lucretius; Patin's term 'Antilucrèce' is an allusion to the title of the best-known neo-Latin poem in the Lucretian tradition, Cardinal Melchior de Polignac's *Anti-Lucretius, sive De Deo et Natura*, a defence of Christian orthodoxy that uses Lucretian tactics against Lucretius.[34] The adversarial nature of Lucretius' philosophical and poetic procedures makes for an unusually combative reception history, one of the best-known manifestations of which is Tennyson's poem depicting in his hour of madness and doom the arrogance and complacency of a Lucretius who fails fully to accept the doctrines of his Master, even calling in his despair to the gods he has cast aside: 'yet behold, to you | From childly wont and ancient use I call'.[35]

---

[29] At a later stage a wife by the name of Lucilia was introduced as the agent of the love-potion: see p. 208 below, and Canfora 1993b: 32–3.

[30] Canfora 1993b makes an ingenious attempt to expand what is known and to provide a detailed historical context, largely on the basis of the letters of Cicero. For an attempt to read autobiographical hints in the *DRN* see Wiseman 1974: 11–43.

[31] W. R. Johnson 2000: 133; see further p. 299 below.

[32] This unified reading of Lucretius now predominates, whereas 'two voices' readings of Virgil continue to be fashionable.

[33] See pp. 61–3 and 96 below.   [34] See pp. 165, 196 below.

[35] Tennyson, *Lucretius*, 208–9. For Tennyson see further pp. 301–3 below.

Poet of modernity: theology, science, politics

'The theses that reality consists exclusively of atoms and void, that atomic interactions are purposeless and reflect no plan, that there are no immaterial spirits, and that the gods do not care about humanity and produce no effects in the visible world'[36] – these teachings could provoke charges of impiety or even atheism in pagan antiquity, but there is little evidence that Epicureanism was ever regarded as dangerous in the way that it was in the Christian world.[37] Dante places the Epicureans 'who consider the soul mortal together with the body', in the sixth circle of hell (*Inf.* 10.15). Various expedients could be used to excuse an interest in the *DRN*, via what Valentina Prosperi calls the 'dissimulatory code':[38] an open acknowledgement of the error of Lucretian teaching, sometimes paired with a positive valuation of his poetic virtues,[39] or the enforcement of a division between content and form easy enough to make in a didactic poem on so technical a subject (but one that recent criticism has been at pains to qualify or even deny).[40] The honey round the rim of the cup could be enjoyed so long as one did not drink deeper; the medicinal wormwood had turned into poison. The *DRN*'s content was safer if it remained within the learned language of Latin: published translations into vernaculars appear late compared with many other classical texts, sometimes, as with Italian, demonstrably because of suppression of early attempts.[41] The anxieties of the forces of conservatism and reaction were not unfounded, since the *DRN* plays an important role in the several movements of libertinism and enlightenment in the seventeenth and eighteenth centuries.[42] Indeed the names of his more prominent eighteenth-century admirers – Voltaire and Kant, d'Alembert and Rousseau – are synonymous with the phenomenon we call 'the Enlightenment'.

The poem also plays no small part in the history of modern science, as a stimulus to the development of the corpuscularian and atomist theories that precede modern atomic physics.[43] One should not claim too much: the *DRN* was but one of a number of available testimonia for Epicurean physics, and, as is often the case when we are dealing with the reception of the doctrines contained in the *DRN*, it is more a general Epicureanism than a response specifically and solely to Lucretius that is at issue. Furthermore ancient and modern atomisms are very different animals; the former is the product of

---

[36] P. 131 below.

[37] Ancient charges of Epicurean atheism: Obbink 1989. For the 'Christian reaction' see ch. 4 of H. Jones 1989.

[38] Pp. 214–16 below.   [39] See pp. 215, 228 below.

[40] See ch. 6 below.   [41] See p. 215 below.

[42] See especially chs 9, 14 and 17 below.   [43] See ch. 8 below.

abstract reasoning about plurality, change, and the nature of first principles on the part of Presocratic philosophers of nature,[44] while the latter develops out of experimental and mathematical science. There is an important question here about continuity and discontinuity in the history of knowledge:[45] Lucretius' disconcerting modernity may be something of an illusion. On the other hand the *DRN* is the most detailed surviving source for many aspects of Epicurus' atomism. It was an important text for Newton[46] and continued to be a reference point in nineteenth-century controversies between theists and materialist naturalists.[47] Einstein pays tribute to Lucretius in a preface to a 1924 translation of the *DRN*, opining that the true goal of the poem is not so much Lucretius' expressed intention to free mankind from superstition and fear, but rather to convince his reader of the necessity of the atomic-mechanical world picture, although he could not openly say as much to the practically minded Roman reader. But Einstein stops well short of avowing any immediate scientific debt to a man who, he writes, could have had no inkling of the findings of modern science that we learn in our infancy. The modern child is by now wiser than the ancient teacher.[48]

Lucretius also plays a part in the history of anti-creationist reconstructions of the development of life on earth, with the account in Book 5 of the random and materialist origins of living beings, only the fittest of which survive. Thus far Lucretius may be said to anticipate Darwinianism, but his belief in the fixity of species runs counter to the theory of evolution proper.[49] Through his impact on Giambattista Vico, the Neapolitan historian of ideas whose *Principi di una scienza nuova* (1725) is the first comprehensive study of human society, descends a further line of Lucretius-influenced evolutionary thought.

The *DRN* is a text that impinges on politics, as well as religion and science. Its Epicurean message is that one should withdraw from political life to pursue the philosophical goal of happiness: the small circle of friends, rather than the larger structures of city and state, is the best context for this. The picture of a group of people in an idyllic landscape, content with the satisfaction of their natural and necessary appetites (2.29–33, 5.1392–6), is an image of a perfect society. Yet the *DRN*, despite its relative paucity of explicit

---

44 For a lucid account of the thinking behind ancient atomism(s) see Wardy 1996.

45 See Kennedy 2002: 2–3, 23–5.

46 See pp. 141–2 below. The Latin inscription on the base of Roubiliac's statue of Newton in the antechapel of Trinity College, Cambridge is taken from *DRN* 3.1043 (of Epicurus), 'The man whose genius outdid the human race' (*qui genus humanum ingenio superauit*).

47 See pp. 307–8 below.

48 Diels 1924: VIa-b. We are grateful to Niklas Holzberg for providing a text of this work.

49 See Campbell 2003: 1–8.

references to Roman history and society, is a political poem, informed by a deep concern about the problems of contemporary Rome. Gregory Hutchinson has recently used this as an argument for a downdating of the *DRN* to the beginning of the full-scale civil war between Caesar and Pompey, in 49 or 48 BC (as opposed to the traditional dating in the mid-50s BC).[50] Lucretius' anti-providentialist reconstruction of the prehistoric development of civilisation in Book 5 glances at the historical Roman experience at a number of points; he breaks off from his account of the role of astronomical and meteorological phenomena in the origin of religion to give a picture of a general embarked with all his forces at sea praying to the gods in the middle of a storm, a powerful image (whoever the general might be) of the interconnection of the religious, the military and the political at the heart of the Roman state.

Lucretius' version of Epicureanism is not atheist. The Epicurean view of the gods is in fact more traditionalist than the other Hellenistic schools of philosophy in that it holds up an image (and perhaps the reality) of anthropomorphic divinities, contemplation of and prayer to whom serves the purpose of bringing human minds closer to the *ataraxia* enjoyed by the gods. What Lucretius attacks without mercy is the superstitious belief in the intervention of angry gods in human affairs. As an attack on superstition rather than (valid) religion the *DRN* has spoken powerfully to thinkers and writers who identified perverted or misguided forms of religion as the source of political strife or repression, for example in the religious wars of late sixteenth-century France or among the more radical of the English Romantics (pre-eminently Shelley).[51] As a poem that conveys a strong sense of political crisis and was composed as the events that would lead to the 'Roman revolution' of Augustus were gathering to a head, the *DRN* has had a particular relevance in times of civil strife or revolution. Hence another paradox, whether apparent or real – that a poem which advocates political quietism has often found itself at the centre of heated political debates.

Lucretian episodes

The *DRN* is a tightly unified structure, deploying philosophical, poetic and rhetorical resources to the end of constructing an irresistible account of the Epicurean universe and the consequences that flow therefrom for maximising the welfare and happiness of the individual.[52] Commentators no longer agree

---

[50] G. Hutchinson 2001; see p. 124 below. See ch. 3 below on the Roman relevance of the *DRN*.

[51] See respectively pp. 154–5 and 295–8 below.

[52] Chs. 5 and 6 below explore the coherence of Lucretius' discursive methods and structures.

with Coleridge that 'whatever in Lucretius is poetry is not philosophical, whatever is philosophical is not poetry',[53] nor do they accept an older view of the *modus operandi* of didactic poetry, that the reader is kept sweet for long passages of technical instruction by the intermittent insertion of poetic 'purple passages'.[54] An intense power to visualise and vivify pervades the whole, and not only parts, of the poem. It is also true however that a number of striking passages and images recur with particular insistence in the Lucretian tradition; and it seems another sign of a lasting perception of the *DRN*'s ultimately episodic character that the most poetically ambitious and successful translation in English, by Dryden, is of a selection of passages.[55] We turn here to look briefly at some of the most memorable of these episodes and their reception.

The *DRN* is framed by, and throughout suspended between, visions of fertility and plenitude on the one hand, and on the other of destruction and emptiness. The opening epiphany of Venus as the driving force of generation in a serene but superabundant springtime is the poem's most famous image, as Lucretius perhaps meant it to be, often translated and adapted. To Montaigne, one of its first modern admirers, its power was a reflection less of Lucretius' verbal skill than his imaginative force, which 'does not so much please, as it fills and ravishes the greatest minds. When I see these brave forms of expression, so lively, so profound', Montaigne writes, 'I do not say that 'tis well said, but well thought.'[56] Lucretius contrasts the *uoluptas* of this vision with the horror of the *DRN*'s closing episode of the plague at Athens, where humanity and society are reduced to squabbles over the disposal of rotting bodies. More typical of Lucretius than this claustrophobic scene of a city crammed with death is the image of the ordered world breaking apart into atoms scattered through the endless void:[57] *horror uacui* is not a Lucretian phrase, but the terror and exultation aroused by the vision of the void, the womb and tomb of all that comes to be, is a quintessential Lucretian experience. As a visionary of the end of the world Lucretius is perhaps matched only by Leonardo da Vinci.[58] This creed of the mortality of the world and of personal annihilation may be meant to free mankind from fear – of the afterlife and of the unknown – but the terror has been

---

[53] For Coleridge see p. 295 below.

[54] See p. 88 below. [55] For Dryden's work see ch. 16 below.

[56] 'Upon some verses of Virgil', *Essays* 3.5, trans. Charles Cotton.

[57] See *DRN* 6.596–607. The language of the Epicurean revelation at 3.16–30 has points in common with the counter-factual description of the end of the world, the consequence of a false, rival, theory of nature, at 1.1102–10: Epicurean truth destroys the accepted view of the universe.

[58] For Leonardo see Gantner 1958.

more strongly felt by many readers than the consolation. Once, 'late over the midwinter fire', the Tennyson family read from Books 3 and 5. 'So carried away and overwhelmed were the readers by the poignant force of the great poet', wrote Tennyson's son Hallam, 'that next morning, when dawn and daylight had brought their blessed natural healing to morbid thoughts, it was laughingly agreed that Lucretius had left us last night all but converts to his heart-crushing atheism.'[59]

The 'poignant' and the 'heart-crushing' come together again in the passage W. B. Yeats described unqualifiedly as 'the finest description of sexual intercourse ever written'[60] at the end of Book 4. Introducing his translations from the DRN, Dryden acknowledged valid objections to 'the Obscenity of the Subject; which is aggravated by the too lively and alluring delicacy of the Verses'. To these he answers simply, and 'without the least Formality of an excuse', 'I own it pleas'd me'.[61] But voluptuous pleasure is, once again, one side of the coin only. Of the same passage the Victorian essayist J. A. Symonds noted: 'There is something almost tragic in these sighs and pantings and pleasure-throes, and incomplete fruitions of souls pent up within their frames of flesh.'[62] And the elderly George Saintsbury found the 'Day-of-Judgement contrast rung in by the terrible "nequidquam" ["in vain"] introduced *thrice* at the most voluptuous moments' had stayed with him from his teenage years to the end: 'I feel it as I felt it sixty years ago, and have felt it ever since.'[63]

The DRN provides powerful images not only for the processes of nature but also for the philosophical mind that understands those processes. Lucretius develops a commonplace with new expressivity in the description (DRN 1.62–79) of Epicurus' 'flight of the mind', and numerous later poets and thinkers have been celebrated in verse drawing on this model. One such is Milton, in Thomas Gray's *The Progress of Poesy* (1754):

> Nor second he, that rode sublime
> Upon the seraph-wings of Ecstasy,
> The secrets of the abyss to spy.
> He passed the flaming bounds of place and time:
> The living throne, the sapphire-blaze,
> Where angels tremble while they gaze,
> He saw; but blasted with excess of light,
> Closed his eyes in endless night.[64]

---

[59] H. Tennyson 1897: II, 500.   [60] Jeffares 1962: 267.   [61] Dryden 1956–2000: III, 12.
[62] Symonds 1875: 48.   [63] Saintsbury 1924: 129, 131.
[64] Ll. 95–102; Lonsdale 1969: 173–4.

Leopardi in his final moral testament *La Ginestra* (1836) uses the passage in another way, to celebrate the calling of the poet-philosopher rather than an individual exemplar:[65]

> Nobil natura è quella
> Ch'a sollevar s'ardisce
> Gli occhi mortali incontra
> Al comun fato, e con franca lingua
> Nulla al ver detraendo,
> Confessa il mal che fu dato in sorte
>
> (111–16)

He is a noble being | Who lifts – he is so bold – | His mortal eyes against |
The common doom, and with an honest tongue, | Not sparing of the truth, |
Admits the evil of our destiny

(trans. J. G. Nichols)

Abraham Cowley, imitating Lucretius' episode in his own eulogy of Francis Bacon (1663), emphasises the freedom fighter rather than the explorer:

> But 'twas Rebellion call'd to fight
> For such a long-oppressed Right.
> *Bacon* at last, a mighty Man, arose
> Whom a wise King and Nature chose
> Lord Chancellour of both their Lawes,
> And boldly undertook the injur'd Pupils cause.
>
> Autority, which did a Body boast,
> Though 'twas but Air condens'd, and stalk'd about,
> Like some old Giants more Gigantic Ghost,
> To terrifie the Learned Rout,
> With the plain Magick of true Reasons Light,
> He chac'd out of our sight[66]

Bacon is one of the founders of a modern science engaged in a continuing process of intervening in and transforming the world – knowledge as power. He felt some disquiet with the other great Lucretian set of images of mental attainment at the beginning of Book 2, the wise man's view from *terra firma* over the stormy seas of the unenlightened, the view of a great battle from a safe distance, culminating in the metaphor of the 'serene temples' from which

---

[65] For Leopardi and Lucretius see recently Timpanaro 1988 (for this passage 360–2).
[66] 'To the Royal Society', 35–46; Cowley 1905: I, 449.

the wise look down on mortals fretting and straying in the world.[67] For Lucretius, once the battle against ignorance has been won, the philosopher retreats from the world. A rendering of this passage contributes the beginning of Lucretius translation in English in the 1557 *Tottel's Miscellany*.[68] The image of the *templa serena* is projected into the real world when the Roman poet Statius identifies an embodiment of it in a rich Epicurean patron's seaside villa.[69] It is more eye-catchingly realised in Mussenden Temple, the library built in 1785 by Frederick Hervey, the idiosyncratic Earl-Bishop of Derry, on an Antrim cliff-top (see frontispiece). It is modelled on the Temple of Vesta at Tivoli and has the opening lines of *DRN* 2 inscribed around the frieze, the lines which Dryden translated: ''Tis pleasant, safely to behold from shore | The rolling ship, and hear the tempest roar.'

Since its early fifteenth-century rediscovery the *DRN* has never lacked for readers, critics and imitators. It is a text that has aroused unusual passions both positive and negative because of its philosophical and scientific content, and the uncompromising voice in which that content is delivered. The science has dated irreversibly in the last century and a half; the philosophy has received renewed attention because of the increasingly respectful appreciation in recent decades of the significance of the post-Aristotelian Hellenistic schools. Important new work continues on the *DRN*'s language, style and poetics, and also on intertextualities both with Lucretius' predecessors and followers. Major new commentaries have appeared.[70]

Quite recently there has been what may prove a major growth of interest in the reception of Lucretius and of Epicureanism more generally.[71] Reception studies are currently enjoying a boom in classical scholarship, but in this case much of the attention comes from the English literary side, notably for the period of Lucretius' first assimilation into English culture, 1650–1700. Today, following a generation's-worth of reassessment, the selective Dryden translation of 1685 is seen as a masterpiece.[72] There have been printings from manuscript of the John Evelyn and Lucy Hutchinson translations of the 1650s, with a further full-scale scholarly edition of the latter forthcoming.[73]

---

[67] On Bacon's unease with this passage see pp. 135–8 (Barbour) below. For other examples of the imagery see pp. 282–3 below.

[68] See p. 245 below.   [69] See p. 122 below.

[70] See the 'Further reading' for chs. 4–7. Of commentaries note esp. the major works of R. D. Brown 1987, D. P. Fowler 2002, Campbell 2003 and Piazzi 2005.

[71] For the latter see especially Gordon and Suits 2003; Warren forthcoming.

[72] For recent reassessments see esp. Hammond 1983 and E. Jones 1985.

[73] The recent printings are Repetzki 2000 and de Quehen (ed.) 1996a; forthcoming is David Norbrook's edition within Hutchinson's *Complete Works*.

Other contemporary Lucretians such as Aphra Behn and John Wilmot, Earl of Rochester, enjoy unprecedented levels of attention. Independently of this historical scholarship, one can point to contemporary responses in various media and emanating from various points of the compass. Chapter 19 below surveys literary Lucretianism post 1890; here might be added a different kind of example, the Canadian composer R. Murray Schafer's 1997 setting of the Latin text of *DRN* 4.549–95 (on human voice and vocal articulation) for the Tokyo Philharmonic Chorus.

This seems a good moment to offer a new *Companion to Lucretius*, then. In a departure from previous Cambridge Companions on ancient authors the volume is divided, in terms of bulk, more or less equally between Lucretius in his ancient contexts, and Lucretius' reception. The first and third sections obey the division between antiquity and post-antique reception; the second develops larger themes across conventional period boundaries. The aim is to provide a survey of the main areas of scholarship and criticism on Lucretius and his reception, but also, in the spirit of Lucretius' Epicurus, to range more widely in new or underexplored areas. Lucretius is usually quoted below from the Loeb edition (Smith 1992), which has a prose translation by W. H. D. Rouse. Other reliable translations are Latham 1994 (prose), Esolen 1995 (verse) and Melville 1997 (verse).

I

Antiquity

I

JAMES WARREN

Lucretius and Greek philosophy

Lucretius' relationship with earlier, Greek philosophy is determined by two principal factors. First, he is writing his work as a committed adherent to Epicureanism. He is confident that Epicureanism gives the correct answers to major philosophical questions such as the nature of the universe, the nature of a person and of the gods, and the goal of a human life. This commitment determines his presentation of all other philosophical ideas since any philosophy which is incompatible with the Epicurean truth is by definition false. Lucretius is also convinced that Epicureanism has been comprehensively described and elaborated by Epicurus himself. There is no further philosophical inquiry to be done; Lucretius' task is therefore expository and explanatory. He has merely to make clear the truth and make it palatable to his, as yet, uninitiated Latin audience. Any other philosophical views which appear in the work are always outlined against the background of this prejudicial Epicurean view. Alternative accounts of the world are offered as illustrations of the kinds of mistakes possible if the Epicurean truth is ignored. Second, Lucretius offers himself as a conduit and translator to Rome of Greek ideas. He is a translator not in the sense of merely rendering an original Greek text into Latin. Rather, he introduces, packages and explains Greek thought for a new audience and a new culture and time. Nor does he think it right to transmit all previous Greek philosophy to Rome. Rather, he acts as a filter of Greek thought, admitting and translating only those ideas which are conducive to the goal of understanding the universe correctly and passing over or disparaging those mistaken Greek ideas which might put obstacles in the reader's path.[1]

The relationship of Roman intellectual life, philosophical writing in particular, to its Greek predecessors is something made prominent by other writers

---

[1] Note the distinction made at 1.639–40 between 'frivolous Greeks' (*Graios inanis*) and 'serious Greeks' (*Graios grauis*).

of this period, most notably Lucretius' near-contemporary Cicero. Cicero's philosophical allegiance is to a brand of Academic scepticism which recommends the examination and discussion of rival philosophical theories as a road to showing the failure of all dogmatic systems to offer fully convincing answers, so he has a good philosophical justification for his detailed presentations and discussions of various competing Greek views in a way which would have struck Lucretius as unnecessary and distracting. But Cicero evidently shares with Lucretius the feeling that he needs to explain his decision to write philosophical works, dealing with predominantly Greek ideas, in Latin. The opening to *Tusculan Disputations* 1 tries to argue not that Romans can surpass the Greeks in philosophy, but that there is nevertheless a call for accurate and polished philosophical works for a wide audience of educated Latin readers.[2]

For Lucretius, his commitment to Epicureanism and the adoption of the verse form makes the relationship between his poem and Greek philosophical history quite different. On the one hand, Greece – and Athens in particular – is singled out for praise as the birthplace of Epicurus, that 'Greek man who first dared to lift up his eyes against superstition' (*religio*, 1.66–7).[3] Despite the poem's pointedly Roman opening and Lucretius' constant insistence on the relevance of the Epicurean message to his contemporaries, it is Greece which is the direct source of his inspiration and salvation.[4] Athens, Epicurus' city, is offered at the beginning of *DRN* 6 as the pinnacle of human achievement, the final and most promising stage in the chequered history of man's development which filled the later parts of *DRN* 5.[5] Lucretius' poem itself also pays homage to important Greek philosophical models. The poem's title, *On the Nature of Things*, is a nod to a title commonly given to early Greek philosophical works, themselves often in verse: *On Nature*, or *On the Nature of What Is* (in Greek, *Peri Physeōs* or *Peri Physeōs tōn ontōn*). Parmenides' hexameter poem was known by such a title at least in later antiquity, and Lucretius' most important source of inspiration as a poet-philosopher, Empedocles, also wrote a poem known by that

---

[2] Cic. *Tusc.* 1.1–8. Also see Cic. *Nat. D.* 1.7–14; *Fin.* 1.1–12. For more on the reception of Greek philosophy at Rome in this period see M. Griffin 1989 and, on Cicero in particular, Powell 1995a.

[3] See also the praise of Epicurus in 5.1–54.

[4] For the Roman opening note the invocation to Venus, 'mother of Aeneas and his descendants' (1.1), and see also Lucretius' hopes for Rome, e.g. 1.29–49.

[5] Athens is also the setting for the poem's climactic description of the plague of 430 BC (see 6.1138–1286). In so far as the plague is meant to illustrate psychological and ethical errors in the Athenian people, it is clear that these will be remedied by the imminent arrival of Epicurus, heralded in the proem of the same book.

name.[6] Of course, the title is also a gesture towards Epicurus' own monumental prose work *On Nature*, the source of much of the philosophical content of Lucretius' composition, but there is no doubt that Lucretius saw himself as part of a tradition of Greek philosophical poetry and as offering this tradition to a new Latin audience.

Lucretius follows the tradition of works *On Nature* and, most importantly, the scope of Epicurus' work by that name, in concentrating his attention on Epicurean natural philosophy to the comparative exclusion of other areas of Epicurean interest. Even accepting that for Lucretius 'natural philosophy' is broadly conceived according to the usual ancient categorisation to include discussions of, for example, theology, psychology, and the origin and development of species and human societies, there is in the *DRN* no dedicated discussion of, for example, the Epicurean distinction between 'kinetic' and 'katastematic' pleasure or the role and purpose of rhetoric. However, again like his Greek predecessors, Lucretius does not exclude ethics entirely. He is keen to emphasise points at which conclusions in natural philosophy bear directly on ethical issues (such as the discussion of the fear of death at the end of *DRN* 3) and notably uses the proems to the various books of the poem to introduce questions of more ethical interest.[7]

On the other hand, despite the clear and recognised Greek inspiration for his poem's form and content, there are many Greek ideas which in Lucretius' eyes are dangerously misguided. The consideration – let alone the adoption – of such confusions may prevent the reader from attaining the desired Epicurean goal of tranquillity (*ataraxia*) brought about through the sure understanding of the truth about the universe, the gods, and so on. There are therefore signs in Lucretius' work of another, more critical, attitude to Greek thought. Lucretius stands to his reader as someone who has already considered the available alternatives and is able to offer the correct view without unnecessary distractions. He has no interest in giving an account of Greek philosophical history or even a general survey of previously held philosophical views, and he will consider un-Epicurean ideas only if by doing so he can clarify the Epicurean truth or head off any dangerous misunderstandings. He himself makes clear that his innovations are confined to the method of expression of Epicurean ideas. In all philosophical matters he is merely following the path already marked by Epicurus' footprints

---

[6] See Diog. Laert. 8.77. For further discussion of Lucretius' poetic debt to Empedocles see pp. 61–4 below.

[7] On the fear of death see Segal 1990, Warren 2004. For other ethical themes in the *DRN* see, for example, D. P. Fowler 1989 and his 2002 commentary on 2.1–61. This combination of natural philosophy and ethics is prominent also in Empedocles and, of course, in Plato's *Timaeus*.

(5.55–90).[8] In this sense, Lucretius is an Epicurean (a 'follower of Epicurus') while Epicurus himself is not.[9]

This ambivalence is also signalled in Lucretius' handling of Greek philosophical terminology. He displays both a desire to find natural Latin equivalents for some Greek technical terms, those he wishes to 'naturalise' and recommend to his Roman audience, and also a willingness to declare certain other Greek terms alien, untranslatable, and therefore to be rejected. Famously, Lucretius consistently avoids using the Latin transliterated form of the Greek word 'atom' (*atomus* is used by Cicero)[10] even though a large part of his work is concerned with demonstrating that, according to Epicurean physics, the universe is composed of innumerable indivisible particles of matter, atoms, forever moving in a limitless void. Instead, Lucretius offers a range of Latin terms to capture what it is that atoms do. In just a few lines of *DRN* 1, for example (1.54–61), he uses the terms *rerum primordia* ('first beginnings of things'), *materies* ('matter'), *genitalia corpora* ('productive bodies'), *semina rerum* ('seeds of things') and *corpora prima* ('first bodies'). Later books occasionally also use *corpuscula* ('little bodies') and *elementa* ('elements'). This range of terms belies any complaints of the lexical poverty of Latin and allows Lucretius to express the importance of atoms by noting the various roles they play as the fundamental existents, components, and material substance, for all other things.[11] On other occasions, however, Lucretius opts to transliterate a Greek term and this occurs sufficiently rarely that it must be intended to be worthy of note. We shall see two prominent examples of such transliteration; in both cases, Lucretius is marking the Greek concept as alien and not to be accepted by his Latin audience. His lexical choices are therefore also designed to serve his didactic goals and to designate one Greek philosopher alone – Epicurus – as worthy of serious study and acceptance by a Latin audience.

Turning now to address one of the questions that drives much discussion of Lucretius in the history of philosophy: to what extent does Lucretius' work show signs of a knowledge of, or engagement with, philosophy from the period after Epicurus' own life? In his own work Epicurus had engaged with the philosophy of various Presocratic thinkers, as well as Plato, Aristotle and Theophrastus. But in the years between the death of Epicurus (270 BC) and

---

[8] Contrast his claim in 1.921–34 to be moving into uncharted poetic territory.
[9] See Furley 1978: 1–2; Clay 1983: 14–16.
[10] See, e.g., Cic. *De fato* 23. For more on Cicero's translations from Greek see Powell 1995b.
[11] For discussion see Sedley 1998: 38–9; Kennedy 2002: 76–8.

Lucretius' work (mid first century BC) there had been some important developments in philosophy, most notably the growth and elaboration of Stoicism and the revival of scepticism first in the Academy, and then, much closer to Lucretius' own time, the rise of a neo-Pyrrhonist school of radical scepticism under Aenesidemus. There are two general approaches to this question. One approach sees Lucretius' poem as thoroughly engaged with the more recent developments in philosophy. Some parts of the work, particularly the cosmological or anthropological sections, are seen to be informed by a variety of Hellenistic sources. Some arguments are interpreted as being aimed at Stoic rivals, others against various forms of Platonism or scepticism. Like other Epicureans such as Epicurus' pupil Colotes, Lucretius' contemporary, Philodemus, and the later Epicurean, Diogenes of Oenoanda, Lucretius is determined to point out the failings of much non-Epicurean philosophy of the later Hellenistic period after Epicurus' death. If this approach is correct, then Lucretius can be added to our sources for what is otherwise a poorly documented period in philosophical history. He might also be used as a barometer for discerning which of the newer philosophical ideas had permeated as far as Italy in the first century BC.[12]

The other approach sees Lucretius as an Epicurean 'fundamentalist'. The philosophical content of the poem is taken perhaps exclusively from Epicurus' *On Nature*, and shows no awareness of any developments in Epicureanism or other philosophical views from any later period.[13] This stance can take support from our increasing knowledge of Epicurus' work as the various papyri containing parts of that work found in the villa at Herculaneum are read and interpreted.[14] It seems that much of the organisation of material in the poem follows the order of exposition in Epicurus' work. If this hypothesis is correct then Lucretius becomes a much less useful source for the interesting period of philosophical history after Epicurus. Instead, he appears as a curious fossil even in his own day, and the lack of engagement with Stoicism seems extremely perplexing. The advantage, however, is that he can be used as a source for Epicurus' own philosophy, filling in the gaps in our knowledge of *On Nature*. Various forms of this line of thought are possible, varying in their readiness to grant to Lucretius some innovativeness in presentation, organisation and explanation of the material. But it is agreed

---

[12] See, e.g., Bailey 1947 *passim*; Asmis 1982; Schrijvers 1992 and 1999.

[13] See, e.g., Furley 1966, Sedley 1998. 'Fundamentalist' is the term used by Sedley 1998: 91–3. Campbell 1999, in his excellent review, rightly notes that this might unfortunately suggest that Lucretius distorts aspects of Epicurus' view.

[14] See ch. 2 below.

that the philosophical content, even the criticisms of other views, derives from Epicurus himself.

The debate between these two approaches has dominated much recent study of Lucretius as a source for philosophical history. One side offers a piece of text or some argument which is claimed to be a clear attack on, say, Stoicism, while the other rebuts it by pointing to some earlier or more general target, some inconsistency with orthodox Stoic thought, or some parallel in Epicurus' own work. This is not an irrelevant or uninteresting debate. And there is much at stake both for readers of Lucretius keen to set him in some sure context and also for those who would use Lucretius as part of a more general conception of the history of ancient philosophy. Nevertheless, the dispute is also to a degree conditioned by a disagreement over the proof required for the establishment of an object of philosophical attack. Is the fact that a particular view rejected by Lucretius is one to which, say, the Stoics adhere (e.g. that our world is unique) sufficient to show that when Lucretius rejects that view he does so in a deliberately anti-Stoic move? Or is it necessary for the view being criticised to be solely Stoic property before, in the absence of a named opponent, we can be sure of Lucretius' anti-Stoic intent? To some extent the decision will be guided by our starting assumptions. Some find it simply inconceivable, for example, that an educated and philosophically interested Roman such as Lucretius would not have read and been interested in Stoicism and have wanted to include his reactions in this poem. Others are less sure.[15]

No doubt such discussion will continue, but there are two means of side-stepping its often irresolvable disputes. First, if our interests are primarily philosophical then Lucretius' intent in writing a particular passage matters little. Whether or not he had some Stoic target in mind, we are at liberty to put Lucretius in discussion with Stoic philosophy ourselves. Where some Lucretian argument might provoke a Stoic or sceptical response, we can usefully put the two in dialogue and, in the process, hope to illuminate Epicureanism, its opponents, and also the philosophical issue itself. Second, in some ways the complicated debates about sources are in danger of overlooking the particular nature of Lucretius' work. Some readers may miss the heated tone of inter-school debate of this period. Those who come to Lucretius having read Cicero's philosophical works which pit Epicureans against Stoics or Stoics against Academics will miss the cut-and-thrust of that kind of dialectical

---

[15] For an analogous discussion of the possibility that Lucretius shows signs in Book 4 (see esp. 332–521) of knowing about later Hellenistic (even Aenesideman) scepticism see Burnyeat 1978, Vander Waerdt 1989, Schrijvers 1992, Lévy 1997, Sedley 1998: 85–90. The relative dating of Aenesidemus and Lucretius is itself controversial.

encounter played out between adherents of rival schools and be inclined to think that Lucretius must be ill-informed in comparison. But the *DRN* is not that kind of work. It is not concerned with carving out for the first time a particular philosophical theory by engaging in long and complex arguments with alternative views. Nor is it primarily a polemical work addressed to committed adherents of alternative philosophical schools, pointing out the failings in their own theory or answering criticisms launched by them at Epicureanism.[16] Nor is it a dialectical work whose purpose is to contrast and evaluate competing philosophies. Rather, it is concerned to explain an already completed philosophical system to someone who is as yet uncommitted philosophically. Lucretius' addressee, Memmius, is not himself, so far as we can tell, an adherent of any philosophical school. There is no reason to think that he has any knowledge of philosophy at all. He is therefore an appropriate pupil, as yet untainted by any other philosophy and ready to be disabused of any unfortunate false beliefs, about what to value or how the cosmos is organised, which he has acquired so far as part of his general education as an aristocratic Roman.

A further sign of Lucretius' relative lack of interest in inter-school dialectic, and indeed a cause of much uncertainty about the target of many of his criticisms, is his surprising reticence to name any other philosophers in the course of the poem. In fact, he names only four philosophers other than Epicurus himself, who is named only once (3.1042). Democritus, the early Greek atomist, is named on three occasions (3.371; 3.1049; 5.622) and he is generally treated with the respect one would expect for the person who came closest to the Epicurean truth without quite achieving the greatness of Epicurus himself.[17] The three remaining philosophers, Heraclitus, Empedocles and Anaxagoras, are all mentioned in a short section of *DRN* 1 and are all from the period of Greek philosophy before Socrates. Empedocles is clearly Lucretius' model for much of his poetry but he is nevertheless subjected to harsh criticism for his philosophical views, along with the other two.[18]

Let us now look more closely at two of the places where Lucretius discusses Greek, non-Epicurean, points of view: the rejection of the three Presocratic

---

[16] For a good example of Epicurean polemic see Plutarch's work *Against Colotes* for what it tells us about Colotes' work *That it is impossible even to live according to other Philosophers*.

[17] For discussions of Epicurean attitudes to Democritus see Warren 2002, esp. 25–6.

[18] For discussions of Empedocles as Lucretius' literary model see Furley 1970; Clay 1983: 22–3, 83–95; Sedley 1998: 21–34; Trépanier 2004: 38–44; Piazzi 2005, esp. 42–52; pp. 61–4 below. There may also be Empedoclean elements in the discussion of the origin of species in *DRN* 5.

cosmologies in *DRN* 1 and the rejection of the 'harmony theory' of the soul in *DRN* 3.

At 1.635–920 Lucretius offers the most concentrated discussion of named philosophical opponents in the entire poem. But it is remarkable that the three opponents, Heraclitus, Empedocles and Anaxagoras, would all have seemed antiquated in Lucretius' day. The most recent of them dates from some four hundred years before Lucretius' own time, and it is extremely unlikely that there were card-carrying followers of any of these early natural philosophers in the first century BC. In that case, it is a reasonable question to ask why Lucretius should be concerned to refute their views of the world at such length.[19] Two preliminary answers could be given, one according to each of the general views of Lucretius' relationship to non-Epicurean philosophy that I have already outlined. According to the first view, these three are intended to stand as proxies for contemporary opponents.[20] Following a common practice of avoiding direct reference to one's opponents, Lucretius here uses these venerable Presocratics as a means to attack his contemporary rivals. The most plausible case along such lines can be made for Heraclitus. His concentration on fire as the primary element might well be reminiscent of Stoic physics. But the others lack obvious contemporary analogues. Perhaps it could be allowed that Empedocles has featured heavily as a poetic model for Lucretius already, so that it is important for him to make clear that he diverges significantly from Empedocles' physical theories. Even then, on this model, the criticism of Anaxagoras is hard to explain.

An alternative interpretation would simply state that although these three are ancient in Lucretius' day, for Epicurus they would have been much closer and perhaps genuine rivals. There is good reason to believe that Epicurus included in Books 14 and 15 of his *On Nature* an extended discussion of these and other competing physical theories, and Lucretius has followed this source, although he has moved this section to a much earlier point in his exposition.

The debate between these two rapidly reaches a stalemate. But a further, promising, line of inquiry is opened when we ask what role the criticism of these three philosophers plays in Lucretius' own rhetorical and persuasive strategy. Even those who think he is working in the main from Epicurus' work must concede that he has decided to exclude a discussion of, for

---

[19] Diogenes of Oenoanda, writing some two hundred years after even Lucretius, still includes a refutation of the theories of Heraclitus, Empedocles, Anaxagoras and other Presocratics in his exposition of Epicurean physics (see fr. 7 Smith). He also includes the Stoics in his list of opponents, suggesting that for him, at least, they warrant a separate treatment.

[20] See Kleve 1978, Tatum 1984, Piazzi 2005: 4–7, 12–16, 25–42.

example, Plato's physical theory in the dialogue *Timaeus*.[21] So why these three and why at this point in the text? Lucretius has just introduced us to the Epicurean view that the universe is composed of two sorts of fundamental existents, the atoms and the void, and he has offered some discussion of the composition of atoms by extended but partless *minima*. Now he confirms the truth of this Epicurean position by refuting the most general possible alternative viewpoints. These three Greek philosophers between them exhaust the range of alternative conceptions of the fundamental elements of the universe (the *materies rerum*: 1.635) and are treated in order of ascending ontological complexity. Heraclitus stands for any monist view, that is, any view which holds that there is only one basic substance from which all other things are composed (for Heraclitus this is fire). Empedocles stands for a finite pluralist view, which holds that all things are composed from a combination or mixture of a number of elements (for Empedocles these are earth, air, fire and water). Anaxagoras is an interesting example of an extreme form of pluralism which holds that, in his famous slogan, 'in everything there is a portion of everything' (fr. B11 Diels–Kranz; cf. *DRN* 1.876–9). In Lucretius' interpretation, this amounts to the claim that the universe is composed of thoroughly intermingled 'homoiomerous' substances – that is, substances whose parts are the same in kind as the whole. (Lucretius explains the term at 1.834–42: gold is homoiomerous since if you chop up a piece of gold you create smaller portions of gold, but a person is not, since if you chop a person you do not create a number of smaller people.)[22] These three are also the leaders of their particular factions in this battle. Heraclitus heads the monists' charge (1.638). Similarly, Empedocles is in the pluralist vanguard (1.716; 1.734–41). We can now account for the antiquity of these thinkers, because Lucretius' aim is to mount an *a fortiori* argument against these standard-bearers for all possible competing ontologies. When each of them is criticised, the intention is that their failings should be common to all relevantly similar ontologies descended from a particular originator. So, when Heraclitus' view is rejected, this is meant to account for all monist views, whatever the substance chosen as the fundamental stuff (see 1.705–11). Lucretius therefore fortifies his reader with arguments sufficient – in his eyes, at least – to see off any alternative ontology. Nothing should now

---

[21] Epicurus discussed this in *On Nature* Book 14 (see *PHerc.* 1148).

[22] Compare Cicero's account at *Acad.* 2.118. The adjective 'homoiomerous' (*homoiomerēs*) does not appear in the extant fragments of Anaxagoras and is probably an Aristotelian coinage. The noun *homoiomereia* first appears in Greek in Epicurus (e.g. *Nat.* 14 xxxix.7 Leone; cf. Diog. Oen. 6.ii.6 Smith; Schofield 1975: 4–6; Piazzi 2005: 52–5). For more on Lucretius' sources for these philosophers see Rösler 1973; Sedley 1998: 123–6; Piazzi 2005: 8–10 and ad loc.

be able to tempt us away from the Epicurean truth of a universe composed of atoms and void.

Lucretius also uses this opportunity to reinforce directly the lessons he has already taught. Pluralists such as Empedocles, for example, find themselves in difficulties because they tend to say that the four elements somehow can be transformed into each other. They have to say something like the following: water evaporates to become air; air, if warmed, can become fire. But at the very beginning of *DRN* I Lucretius gave a long argument to show that no fundamental existent can come to be or pass away (1.146–264). This most basic metaphysical axiom, demonstrated by Lucretius before he then uses it to give his proof of atomism, has to be violated by these pluralists in saying that, for example, air *turns into* something else. Lucretius wastes no time in taking the opportunity to remind the reader of this axiom and show that Epicurean atomist theory has no trouble in explaining the transformation of one of these elements into another: air and water are both composed of something more fundamental – namely the atoms – and thus condensation and evaporation, like any other change, are to be explained by referring to alterations of the number, type and arrangement of atoms (1.782–829). Consideration of the failings of pluralism allows Lucretius to give a reminder of the basics of Epicureanism and also an example of Epicurean physical analysis in action.

Anaxagoras' 'homoiomeries' are a case in which Lucretius does not offer a natural Latin equivalent for a Greek philosophical term. Instead he draws particular attention to his need to resort to a simple transliteration and explanation (1.830–42). Here the 'poverty' of Lucretius' native language is perhaps a sign that Anaxagoras has himself needed to resort to far-fetched invention to generate his theory. It marks the alien nature of this particular philosophical concept: it cannot be rendered naturally in Latin, let alone comprehended or accepted by Lucretius' audience.

A similar point is made by Lucretius' second notable use of transliteration, when he comes to discuss the view that the soul is some kind of 'harmony' at 3.98–135.[23] It is also a case in which we are able to contrast Lucretius' and Epicurus' handling of the same rival theory. The two principal topics of *DRN* 3 are the nature of the soul and the fact that death should not be feared. Prior to our passage, Lucretius has just asserted his first significant claim about the nature of the soul, that no less than hands and feet it is 'part of a person' (3.96), a view which already rules out various competing views of the soul,

---

[23] See Sedley 1998: 48–9. See also Lucretius' handling of the Greek words *prēstēr* (6.424) and *magnētis* (6.908).

including Platonic notions of the soul as a separable incorporeal thing. But, immediately, Lucretius warns us against a related view, the 'harmony theory'. 'Some Greeks', he tells us, 'say that the sensation of the mind is not located in any particular part of the body but is a kind of living condition of the whole body' (3.98–9).[24] Why should Lucretius interrupt his exposition so abruptly? We have hardly begun to discover the true nature of the soul and already are being warned away from a Greek rival.

Again, Lucretius combines philosophical objections with a pronounced emphasis on the Greekness of the harmony theory. Not only does he claim that 'harmony' has no Latin equivalent,[25] but also, in completing his dismissal of the view, Lucretius emphasises its particular provenance. He notes that 'harmony' is originally a term from musical theory and recommends that it be excised from psychology and returned to the musicians, or, if they took it from elsewhere, to the original source. In any case, they are welcome to it (3.130–5). This completes a ring-composition: the theory was introduced as involving what 'the Greeks' call a harmony (3.100). Lucretius borrows the Greek idea and the Greek word for only as long as is necessary to demonstrate its misconception. Once this is completed, the word and the idea can be returned. He even goes so far as to recommend repatriation: it should be returned to the home of the Muses on the Greek Mount Helicon (3.132). It has no place in psychology and Lucretius has no further need for it in his Latin poem.

The harmony theory of the soul shares important traits with the Epicureans' own view.[26] Notably, they agree that the soul is mortal since the soul is a particular arrangement or condition of bodily elements, and, once that particular arrangement is disrupted, the soul too ceases to be. Both the harmony theory and the Epicureans also say that the soul is in some sense a kind of blending or mixture of material elements.

Lucretius gives three objections to the theory: the soul is not an arrangement of the elements of the body since it is possible for the soul to be healthy and well and the body not, or vice versa (3.102–11); the soul can be active when the body is motionless, as in sleep (3.112–16); the soul can function even in the case of extreme damage to the body. Also, sometimes a minor physical injury can cause major psychic malfunction (3.117–29). These interactions between body and soul are meant to be incompatible with the harmony theory and its assertion that the soul is not located in any

---

[24] For discussion of various forms of harmony theories in ancient philosophy see Gottschalk 1971, Caston 1997.

[25] Cicero uses *concentio* in his version of Plato's *Timaeus* (14).

[26] For Epicurean theories of the soul see Kerferd 1971, Annas 1992.

specific part of the body (3.101). No doubt a sophisticated harmony theorist might be able to answer some of these, but Lucretius' central concern is that some distinction must be made between body and soul to explain these phenomena of their mutual independence.

However, Lucretius also argues that the distinction between body and soul must not be drawn too radically since this will make it impossible to explain the various cases in which the body and soul interact. They should not be thought to be metaphysically different kinds of things. Much of this part of Book 3 is therefore devoted to various arguments demonstrating that the soul and body are both corporeal. In Plato's *Phaedo*, Socrates offers his own arguments against a similar 'harmony theory' (85e–86d; 91c–95a). Socrates agrees that any adequate account of the soul must give a reasonable explanation of the interaction between soul and body. One of his complaints is that the harmony theory fails to allow the soul to control or oppose the body and must admit that the soul and its affections are entirely directed by changes in the composition of the body (92e5–a13; 94b4–95a3). Socrates eventually settles on an account of an incorporeal and immortal soul. Lucretius, in contrast, uses considerations about the soul's ability to be affected by bodily changes to prove something decidedly uncongenial to Socrates, namely that the soul must be corporeal and mortal. For Lucretius, the discussion of the harmony theory is fully integrated into his positive exposition of the Epicurean theory of a material but distinct soul.

We are in the fortunate position of being able to compare Lucretius' treatment with Epicurus' approach. The sixth-century AD Neoplatonist Philoponus shows in his commentary on Aristotle's *On the Soul* that Epicurus, probably in *On Nature*, set about attacking not only the harmony theory itself but also Plato's attempts to refute the theory in the *Phaedo* (93c3–94a11).[27] Epicurus himself has no sympathy for Plato's account of the soul, nor for the harmony theory. But he nevertheless spends a lot of time showing how Plato's way of rejecting the theory is misguided, demonstrating its failings as well as the failings of the harmony theory itself. There is no sign of any such detailed engagement with philosophical history in Lucretius.

The harmony theory is a serious competitor with the Epicurean view since it shares its two major claims: the soul is mortal and corporeal or, if not corporeal itself, then a particular arrangement of corporeal elements. This proximity provokes not only the prominent rejection of the theory early in *DRN* 3 but also Epicurus' own evident interest in it. But we should notice their differing reactions. Epicurus was concerned to find the correct method

---

[27] See Philop. *in Arist. de An.* 142.5ff. For discussion see Gottschalk 1971: 196–8; Warren 2006.

for rejecting this dangerous alternative psychology, an emphasis missing from Lucretius' direct condemnation of the view. In *On Nature*, a work for committed Epicureans and those already interested in the finer points of philosophical detail, Epicurus offers a lengthy and detailed account of his philosophical system which throughout involves the discussion and rejection or modification of various alternative philosophical views. Lucretius, on the other hand, is writing a work addressed to those who have not yet declared an allegiance to Epicureanism and, quite possibly, are not well acquainted with philosophy of any sort. His concerns are primarily didactic and therapeutic; he wants to convince us of the truth that Epicurus has already discovered. Other views are worth refutation only if Lucretius believes that they are commonly held but misguided beliefs such as the doctrine that the gods will punish those they dislike and benefit those they favour, or else, like the harmony theory of the soul, they are philosophical theories which might be mistakenly adopted due to a slight misunderstanding of the Epicurean truth.

This therapeutic enterprise drives Lucretius' philosophical project and dictates his view and use of earlier Greek philosophy. Epicurus himself was famously reluctant to admit that he had learned anything from any other philosopher.[28] Lucretius happily admits that he learned the truth from Epicurus. This relationship of dogmatic master and accepting pupil leaves little room for further philosophical exploration of ideas outside the Epicurean orthodoxy, and it is a relationship which is replicated between Lucretius, now the instructor, and his readers. Lucretius thanks and praises Greece for its one significant philosophical gift to the world: Epicurus. But his Roman poem can ignore or refuse to translate and transfer any Greek ideas which do not agree with Epicurus' view. Lucretius is happy to pass over the historian's job of attributing ideas to particular philosophers, since it is irrelevant to the task at hand precisely whose false opinions these are. Similarly, he has no time for critical discussions which do not contribute directly to his goal of freeing us from false opinions and groundless fears. After all, nothing less is at stake than our chances of living a good life; and that, Lucretius is sure, is possible only through the acceptance of Epicurean truth.

Further reading

For an introduction to both Epicureanism and Hellenistic philosophy see the sources with commentary collected in Long and Sedley 1987. Algra, Barnes, Mansfeld and Schofield 1999 is a good introduction to the current

---

[28] See Sedley 1976.

understanding of much Hellenistic philosophy and will suggest avenues for further study.

Two recent, but different, treatments of Lucretius' use of Epicurus' works are Clay 1983 and Sedley 1998. Sedley argues for a position which makes Lucretius dependent for all his philosophical argumentation on Epicurus and excludes any later philosophical opponents. His approach follows the lead of Furley 1966, who dismisses many of the references to Stoic philosophy proposed by Bailey 1947 and other commentators. This view is opposed by others, notably Kleve 1978, Asmis 1982 and Schrijvers 1992. Sedley 1998 offers rejoinders to these and is a good place to begin for those wanting to trace the discussion. The essays collected in Algra, Koenen and Schrijvers 1997 explore the intellectual background to Lucretius' poem from various perspectives.

2

DIRK OBBINK

Lucretius and the Herculaneum library

> O ye, who patiently explore
> The wreck of Herculanean lore,
> What rapture! could ye seize
> Some Theban fragment, or unroll
> One precious, tender-hearted, scroll
> Of pure Simonides.
>
> That were, indeed, a genuine birth
> Of poesy; a bursting forth
> Of genius from the dust:
> What Horace gloried to behold,
> What Maro loved, shall we enfold?
> Can haughty Time be just!

Wordworth's poem 'Upon the Same Occasion' (1819) begins in sombre tones, a light lament on the passing of summer and time in the voice of an old man. Against this is held up the eternal energy of inspired poetry ('For deathless powers to verse belong', 25); and to this are called to witness Alcaeus, Sappho, and primitive (Gaelic?) poetry ('initiatory strains | Committed to the silent plains | In Britain's earliest dawn', 32–3). The final two stanzas, quoted here, challenge time's power to obscure even these, juxtaposing exuberant hopes for the rediscovery of lost poetic works, for example, of Pindar ('Some Theban fragment', 52) and Simonides.

Today these stanzas are often read ironically and pessimistically, as if to Wordsworth such wistful wishes for rediscovery would have seemed impossible. But this would not have been the case. He was a close friend and companion of Sir Humphrey Davy, whose experiments in unrolling the charred papyrus scrolls excavated in the eighteenth century from Herculaneum, one of the cities on the Bay of Naples buried by the eruption of Vesuvius in AD 79, held out great promise at that time. There is no reason to read the poem as doing anything other than wishing Davy well in his experiments.

As it happens, these were not a great success, although Davy did manage to recover the name of Sophocles from a fragment of one of the rolls he opened. Wordsworth would have had to wait more than a half-century for the find of a major lyric poet on papyrus from Egypt (Bacchylides, 1898; a scrap of Sappho containing fr. 3, was published in 1880). The Herculaneum library (of which Wordsworth did know) produced mainly prose, philosophical works. Although several centre on the philosophical criticism of poetry and contain a large number of quotations of the Greek poets, the treatises of Philodemus, Demetrius the Laconian, and Chrysippus, to name a few of the philosophical authors of the Herculaneum library, will not have fulfilled Wordsworth's wishes. But in 1989 the Norwegian classical scholar Knut Kleve, working in the Officina dei Papiri of the Biblioteca Nazionale in Naples, came across fragments of a roll broken open in the late eighteenth century, covered with a large Rustic capital script of a generation earlier than the poem on the battle of Actium copied in the early Augustan period (probably not long after 31 BC, the date of the battle), which is also preserved from Herculaneum.[1] Subsequent investigation seemed to reveal that the fragments came from several books of the *DRN*. In all, the tiny fragments contain remnants of sixteen hexameters from four or, more likely, two or three books of the *DRN*, from two or three different papyrus rolls.

More recently Mario Capasso (2003) has questioned Kleve's identification, casting substantial doubt on the identification of the exiguous fragments assigned to Book 2. But the identification of the others, if not entirely certain, may now be said to be compatible with the traces isolated by the new multispectral imaging techniques applied to the papyri by a team from Brigham Young University in 2002. A search for these strings of letters, separated into words by an interpunct by the scribe for the aid of the reader, even discounting those uncertainly read, in the corpus of Latin texts on the Packard Humanities Institute disk (currently the main computer-searchable CD of ancient Latin texts) produces matches only with the passages of Lucretius adduced by Kleve.[2]

The showpieces for the defence's case are as follows (see fig. 2.1):

Fr. A (P.Herc. 1829, pezzo 1a):
]tum·esç[
]cor[

= *DRN* 5.1301–2
[et·quam·falciferos·arma]tum·esc[endere·currus]
[inde·boves·lucas·turrito·]cor[pore·taetras]

---

[1] Kleve 1989.

[2] The identification is accepted by M. F. Smith 1992 and by Flores 2002: 19–20 and on *DRN* 1.874, 873; Kleve 1997 expands his explication of the papyrus fragments. See also Kleve; however, autopsy has confirmed no overlap of P.Herc. 395 with our text of the *DRN*, although it is certain from fr. 17C that this papyrus contains Latin verses. See also Suerbaum 1994 and Nünlist 1997. See also the response to Capasso 2003 by Delattre 2003.

Fr. A

Fr. B

Fr. C

Fr. H

Figure 2.1. Fragments of Lucretius from the Herculaneum Library.

Fr. B (P.Herc. 1829, pezzo 1a):

$$]ṇ[\cdot \cdot]ṛ[$$
$$]ṳehiḷọ[$$
$$]ṃ[$$

$= DRN$ 5.1408–10

[unde·etiam·vigiles·nunc·haec·accepta·tue]n[tu]r
[et·numerum·servare·genus·didicere·neq]uehilo
[maiorem·interea·capiunt·dulcedini·fructu]m

Fr. C (P.Herc. 1829, pezzo 1b):

$$]x:aḷio[.]c[$$
$$]ṣumṃ[$$

$= DRN$ 5.1456–7:

[namque·alid·e]x·alio[·]c[larescere·corde·videbant]
[artibus·ad·]summ[um·donec·venere·cacumen]

Fr. H (P.Herc. 1831, pezzo 1):

$$]igẹṇ[$$
$$]ḷueq[$$
$$]\; \cdot uir[$$

$= DRN$ 1.874, 873 + a new verse where modern
editors normally assume a lacuna:

[ex·alien]igen[is·quae·lignis·exoriuntur]
[praeterea·tel]lus·q[uae·corpora·cumque·nalit·auget]
       ]x·vir[

This gives us what is the earliest known manuscript of any part of Lucretius,
one contemporary with Cicero and a millennium earlier than the next surviving witnesses, the ninth-century manuscripts O, Q, and GVU.[3] Lucretius
scholars have been very slow in calling for full publication of the Herculaneum papyrus fragments: photographs of only several of these have been
published, while Capasso, though critical of some of Kleve's identifications,
does not produce new, corrected editions of them. Fr. H could show a text
of Lucretius, at a very early stage of its transmission, with a line present at
exactly the point where our medieval manuscripts are deficient and a lacuna
has long been suspected. But autopsy (May 2007) casts doubt on this, since
line 2 seems to read –ue, not –us· (as Kleve read). However, fr. B shows a

[3] See pp. 205–7 below.

rare and identifiably Lucretian word, *nequehilo*, so that frs. A–C place a copy of the most famous Epicurean poet of all time in a late Republican collection of books which included the works of the founder of the school himself, Epicurus, together with those of an older contemporary of Lucretius, Philodemus, who was born in Gadara in Syria about 110 BC and came to Rome in about 75 BC. Cicero's speech *Against Piso* reveals that he enjoyed the patronage of Calpurnius Piso, the father-in-law of Julius Caesar. Like Epicurus, Philodemus wrote philosophical treatises, including a *History of Philosophers* used by Diogenes Laertius a century later. Cicero also tells us that he wrote elegant poetry in the form of epigrams suitable for convivial occasions. Many of these are preserved in the *Greek Anthology*, and appear in a list of poems on a papyrus from as far away as middle Egypt. One of Philodemus' philosophical works, *On Piety*, was translated by Cicero, who by then had read and possibly even edited Lucretius.[4] The presence of all these books in a late-Republican private library would not in itself be matter of great note, except for one fact: this private library was probably in the palatial home of L. Calpurnius Piso, father-in-law of Julius Caesar and patron of the Epicurean Philodemus, as we know from one of Philodemus' epigrams (29 Sider), which invites Piso to dine at his own home on a simple meal while enjoying a philosophical and literary feast.

The identification of a Herculaneum papyrus as a text of Lucretius and the question of its significance among the books of the Herculaneum library have given rise to much speculation. It has been claimed as evidence for a personal intellectual connection between Lucretius and Philodemus (or Piso), and even for Lucretius' physical presence in the Villa of the Papyri (with or without Philodemus as a co-resident). But it has also been pointed out that the book may not have been part of the Republican-period library and could have been added later by another owner, and that it thus may not have formed part of the collection that contained Philodemus' books. Others have even doubted whether, if Lucretius' poem had formed part of Philodemus' library, he would have been able to appreciate Lucretius' Latin!

The very fragmentary text of the papyrus manuscript cannot give us anything more than a spot-check on the earliest stages of Lucretius' manuscript transmission. It cannot tell us anything certain about Lucretius as a person or his relations with others. Even the identification of the Herculaneum villa as Piso's, and of Philodemus' connection with the villa, rests solely on the slender grounds of the presence of a large number of Philodemus' books there (among over a dozen other authors thus far identified).[5]

---

[4] See p. 113 below.   [5] See Gigante 2002: 115–21, 'The books from Herculaneum'.

So what does it tell us? The first and perhaps most important aspect of the discovery of a text of Lucretius at Herculaneum is the archival context it provides for the earliest known stage in the life of the *DRN*. Its presence in Campania on the Bay of Naples, a hotbed of Epicureanism as we know from Cicero and the poets Horace, Virgil and Statius, all of whom studied there, is hardly a surprise. It dovetails nicely with evidence for a flourishing Epicureanism not just from literary sources and the Herculaneum library, but also from documentary sources, such as the Epicurean epitaph (*CLE* 961 = *CIL* 10.2971 = *ILS* 7781) from Naples:

> Stallius Gaius has sedes Hauranus tuetur,
>   ex Epicureio gaudiuigente choro.

> Gaius Stallius Hauranus watches this place,
> a member of the Epicurean chorus that flourishes in joy.

It marks the tomb of Gaius Stallius Hauranus, an entrepreneur who redeveloped the Odeon of Pericles at Athens after its destruction by Sulla, a wealthy landowner, like Cicero and Piso, whose epigram celebrates his vibrant Epicureanism with a Latin distich that is in its own right a bit of Epicurean poetry:[6] in the pentameter *Epicureio . . . choro* is a transliteration of a Greek phrase, and the compound adjective (*gaudiuigente*) follows Lucretius' own practice of forming Latin compounds on the model of Greek ones.[7] A date before the middle of the first century BC is guaranteed on metrical grounds.[8]

The Republican copy of Lucretius represented by the Herculaneum papyrus fragments from about the same period gives us a documentary, archival context for the earliest reception of the *DRN*: a large aristocratic villa belonging to a wealthy landowner who dabbled in Epicureanism, the setting for the same kind of patronage that Lucretius himself may have sought from Memmius. This is also the context for the Greek portion of the Herculaneum library, itself the product of the wholesale diaspora of philosophers and their books from Athens in the early first century BC. After Sulla's sack of Athens in 86 BC Greek philosophers and their books found shelter in other centres of learning (Rhodes, Alexandria) and in the west with wealthy Romans. Thus the Herculaneum library contained a complete set of Epicurus' *On Nature* (in no fewer than thirty-six books, some in duplicate copies) that had been brought from Athens, as we know from their subscriptions which carry Athenian archon-dates. The Latin books that accompanied them in the Villa at Herculaneum included Ennius' epic on Roman history, the *Annales*, and a comedy, *The Money-lender*, by Plautus' contemporary

---

[6] See Courtney 1995: 49–50, 241.   [7] See Sedley 1998: 24–5.
[8] Final *–us* before a consonant scanned as short, *Stalliu'* and *Gaiu'*.

Caecilius Statius, together with the works of Philodemus, who lived into the 30s BC. Of these the copy of the *DRN* conforms archivally and palaeographically with the bookrolls of Ennius and Philodemus, whose handwriting shows them to have been produced in the late Republic. Linguistically it conforms with Ennius, whom Lucretius admired as a model and imitated,[9] and thematically with Philodemus, with his Epicurean message and high regard for the school's founder.

It is even tempting to see the Herculaneum copy of the *DRN* as ancillary and exegetical to the Herculaneum copies of Epicurus' own magnum opus *On Nature*, offering both explanation, in an accessible poetic and Latin form, of Epicurus' technical Greek prose, and a naturalisation of it into a Roman context. The *DRN* would have provided important material and exercises for Epicurean study (*interpretatio*, exegesis, paraphrase), as well as the popular ancient method of setting one text beside another for comparison and contrast. For this is precisely what Lucretius' text, highly conscious of itself as a physical inscribed artifact, suggests. The proem to Book 3, for example, speaks of browsing on 'golden sayings', *aurea dicta*, in the pages of the Master, which seems to presuppose at least the possibility of access to them (despite Lucretius' rhetoric elsewhere that presents the *DRN* as offering illumination to those who find Epicurus' books too difficult, or do not have enough Greek). This at any rate offers itself as a tentative way of understanding the archival and cross-linguistic cultural significance of the presence of an early copy of the *DRN* in the Herculaneum library. And tentative it must remain: for we have no way of knowing for certain that the ownership of lavish and professionally produced books of coffee-table proportions had any value other than as a sign of social status, such as they might have had for Petronius' *nouveau-riche* freedman Trimalchio.

Would Wordsworth have been poetically satisfied with the appearance of a copy of the *DRN* from the dust of Herculaneum? Perhaps: because, in a very different genre from the lyric poems of Pindar and Simonides, it demonstrates an acute awareness of the poetics that informs those compositions.[10] Wordsworth himself responded profoundly to the poetry of Lucretius.[11] He would have had good reason to be pleased if the experiments of his friend Humphrey Davy had yielded such a find. And he might have found singularly appropriate to the self-fragmenting yet enduring condition of timeless poetry the state of preservation of the Herculaneum copy, returning as it is to dust at this very moment.

---

9 See pp. 61–4 below.
10 On Lucretius' awareness of early Greek lyric see p. 68 below.
11 See pp. 292–5 below.

Further reading

In general on the library of the Villa dei Papiri see Sider 2005, Gigante 2002. Philodemus' epigrams are edited with full commentary by Sider 1997; see 3–12 for an account of Philodemus' life and his relationship with Piso. On the significance of the remains of Philodemus' writings on poetics for contemporary Roman literary culture see the essays in Obbink 1995. On the relation between Philodemus and the *DRN* see Sedley 1998: 64–8; Milanese 1989: 134–9 argues for echoes of Philodemus' aesthetics at *DRN* 1.641–4. On the diaspora of Greek intellectuals in the first century BC see Sedley 2003. *Cronache Ercolanesi* is the official journal for the publication of the Herculaneum papyri of the Centro Internazionale di Papiri Ercolanesi in Naples. The Friends of Herculaneum Society, a University of Oxford Classics Faculty Research Project, is devoted to promoting research on and education about the World Heritage Site of Herculaneum. Its website at www.herculaneum.ox.ac.uk offers a regularly updated online bibliography 'The books from Herculaneum: a guide to editions and translation of the principal works discovered at Herculaneum and related texts'.

3

ALESSANDRO SCHIESARO

Lucretius and Roman politics and history

Lucretius' *de re publica*

Virgil provides an eloquent, if implicit, comment on the politics of the *DRN* when he inserts a recognisably Lucretian expression in Anchises' climactic speech in *Aeneid* 6 (851): 'remember, Roman, your task will be to guide peoples by your rule' (*regere imperio*). This engages dialectically with the very different attitude advocated by the Epicurean poet in his account of the development of societal structures: 'it is indeed much better to obey in peace than to desire to hold the world in fee (*regere imperio res*) and to rule kingdoms' (5.1129–30). The elliptic nature of the reference makes it impossible to judge whether Virgil is 'quoting' Lucretius in order to correct him[1] (the emphatic *tu* could suggest the contrast), or whether the Lucretian flavour of *regere imperio* questions *sous rature* the ostensibly imperial teachings of Aeneas' father.[2] Either way, Virgil identifies in the *DRN* a significant political dimension and seems prepared to read in the account of evolution in Book 5 a reflection on the Romans' philosophy of history and politics. The *DRN*'s ambition is indeed twofold: both to be involved (literally from the very first line) in the anxieties of a troubled age, and to teach eternal truths. Epicurean precepts possess transhistorical validity, but can also help here and now to make sense of Rome's stormy politics, rooted in the structural malaise of a society which has long lost any sense of 'what Nature barks for' (2.17) and of the natural *aequum* which in a distant past allowed communities to lead a carefree life. This stereoscopic vision, both local and global, both historical and transhistorical, is one of the defining features of the poem, and arguably one of the reasons why its political message was received with great interest centuries later.[3] Lucretius' 'politics' are never narrowly local, nor his

I am very grateful to the editors, and to Ingo Gildenhard, Gregory Hutchinson, Malcolm Schofield and Justine Wolfenden for criticism and advice.

[1] Pianezzola 1977: 612; Canfora 1993a: 300.
[2] Lyne 1994: 193–4.   [3] See esp. ch. 9 below.

prescriptions ephemeral, yet the *DRN* displays a sharper awareness of its historical context than is usually recognised. For Lucretius, as for Cicero, the very notion of politics encompasses philosophical, epistemological and religious considerations and therefore offers a privileged way into assessing the poem's position within its cultural *milieu*.

Lucretius' reconstruction of the vectors and causes of evolution in Book 5 provides simultaneously a long-term historical account, an outline of his philosophy of history, and, more indirectly, a commentary on contemporary Roman history. But even before we reach this section of the poem, Lucretius' treatment of cosmology and physics has included statements with momentous political implications:

(i) there exist, have existed, and will exist several worlds – all native and perishable (5.235–46), and potentially infinite in number – of which ours is but one; all are created by the chance encounter of atoms, surely not for men (5.195–234). More than one world can coexist at any given time (2.1048–89);

(ii) any man-made structure or artifact, great cities as well as social and political organisations, is destined to decay and destruction.[4] There is evidence that the peak in our world's growth and strength has already been reached, and decay has begun (2.1150–74; 5.826–7);

(iii) nothing survives the dissolution of atomic *concilia*, and the soul is as mortal as any other aggregate.

There is no need to wait for Anchises, or for Virgil's tantalising references to *imperium sine fine* (*Aen.* 1.279), to recognise that such a view of the cosmos entails a radical disruption of deep-seated assumptions about Rome and its position. A belief in the contemporaneous existence of multiple worlds destroys any illusion about the uniqueness, let alone the centrality, of our own, just as in a random world floating in a random universe Rome's pre-eminence must by definition be transient: neither its destiny nor that of the world is in the providential hands of a divine agent.

As he reiterates the mortal nature of the world in polemical terms (6.601–7), Lucretius' lexicon signals that destruction awaits both the world and men's political structures: *salus* (602) had previously been referred to political order (1.43),[5] and *ruina* (607), too, applies to violent political upheavals.[6] Even at its most general, however, Lucretius' position deserves to be read against the fact that during the second and first centuries BC the Romans assimilate and re-elaborate Hellenistic notions about the eternity of their

---

[4] See, e.g., 5.339–45; 5.1236–40; 6.588–90.
[5] Below, p. 54.   [6] *Oxford Latin Dictionary* s.v. 5a.

city,[7] and in spite of occasional expressions of concern[8] the belief in eternity (*aiōn*) gains wider and stronger currency well before Augustan times. Cicero's *De re publica* offers an articulate alternative to Lucretius' view of evolution, history and politics[9] as it asserts the uniqueness of our world (albeit small, and providing only transient glory) and its centrality in a balanced and geometric cosmos (6.17), regulated by providence. Rome was founded 'in the expectation of long life and power' (2.5), and, provided it keeps true to 'ancestral laws and customs' (3.41) and is not weakened by internal strife (*Rab. Perd.* 33–4), it is endowed with an 'immortality' which could be 'eternal' (3.41). The Roman *res publica* was born, grew, became adult and is now 'strong and well-established' (2.3), a testimony to the wonders of progress.

Within this general framework Lucretius elaborates in Book 5 his account of evolution, which is also ultimately rooted in the true understanding of the workings of nature:[10]

(i) evolution and progress are non-teleological and non-providential;
(ii) historical causation and events are mechanical and unpredictable: they reflect at the human and social level the unpredictable patterns of atomic aggregation made possible by *clinamen*;
(iii) since it obeys no predefined plan, 'progress' is inherently ambivalent: over time human life on earth improves in certain respects while worsening in others;[11] the ultimate goal of *ataraxia* is at times closer or more elusive.

These principles are finally put to work in the reconstruction of how men living *more ferarum* 'in the manner of beasts'[12] eventually develop distinctive forms of social organisation without any providential intervention (5.925–1160). This is not the place to review that important section in detail, but the observation of crucial junctures in Lucretius' innovative five-stage account of the process sheds direct light on his conception of politics and social life in general. A key point is represented by Lucretius' second phase (1011–27), when mating between men and women favours the recognition of children, the abandonment of nomadism for 'homes' (1011), and the formation of early communities. At this stage men experience the need to establish a social

---

[7] Mellor 1981: 1018–19.   [8] Such as by Scipio Aemilianus; see Hardie 1992: 59–61 at 60.

[9] The *Rep.* is dated to 54–51 BC; if the *DRN* is older (but see below, p. 124), the *Rep.* can be seen at least in part as a refutation (Andreoni 1979, qualified by Zetzel 1998; Minyard 1985: 75).

[10] On other Epicurean accounts see Cole 1990; Vander Waerdt 1988; Schofield 2000: 438–40.

[11] The development of war and seafaring are notable instances of negative development: 5.999–1001, 1430–5.

[12] Schiesaro 1990: 122–33.

contract aimed at defending the weaker members of society according to the principle of *nec laedere nec uiolari* (1020, 'to do no hurt and suffer no violence'). *Amicities* and *concordia* largely prevail: had they not, mankind would have been extinguished (1019–27).[13]

Lucretius inserts here a digression about the conventional origin of language and the equally unprompted discovery of fire and cooking (1028–104). Thus a third phase (1105–11) of intensified development opens up, in which natural leaders emerge and show how the *uita prior* (1105) can be transformed through the adoption of 'new ways' and – crucially – of fire. The beginning of this stage marks a strong caesura between the pre-urban, 'pre-civilised' – if to an extent organised – *uita prior* and the various stages of civilised, urban life which follow.[14] The men responsible for this development are 'pre-eminent in genius and strong in mind' (1107); now kings 'began to found cities and to build a citadel for their own protection and refuge' (1108–9). The structure of the passage suggests that kings are a sub-group of the alpha-men mentioned immediately before, who manage to increase their power through, arguably, even more remarkable personal characteristics. Kings are at the helm of what is effectively a natural meritocracy: they are the most gifted members of the community, and distribute cattle and lands according to 'strength and beauty and genius' (1111–12);[15] at this stage natural features remain the only cause of the increased differentiation among individuals. We must assume that the social compact established earlier for the protection of the weaker members of the community is not abandoned, but a social hierarchy begins to emerge. No negative consequence is shown to follow directly from this innovation.

It is only in a fourth phase (1113–42)[16] that the invention of 'property' and the discovery of gold, which are seen as two concurrent aspects of the same phenomenon, subvert these principles of social organisation, for men preferred (as they still do: lines 1115–16 are gnomic) to follow the 'party of the richer' (1115) rather than the most handsome and strongest among them. Significantly, the first systematic betrayal of nature and its teachings occurs with the discovery of the symbolic as a social factor: while the original function of kings was to regulate the allocation of material, natural goods, the abstract notion of 'property' – *res*[17] – is 'invented' (1113 *inuentast*); gold, too, is an arbitrary signifier of wealth, not an intrinsically useful element.

---

[13] Campbell 2003: 282–3.　　[14] Monti 1981: 50 and n. 6.

[15] As, e.g., among the Ethiopians: Hdt. 3.20.2; Strab. 17.822; Pomp. Mela 3.86. See also Schrijvers 1996: 224.

[16] Unlike D. P. Fowler 1989: 142, I take *posterius* at 1112 to mark the beginning of a new phase, the degeneration of the primitive monarchy (1105–11).

[17] *Oxford Latin Dictionary* s.v. 1. On the concept of *res*: Bretone 1998: 43–69.

The importance attached to *diuitiae* is thus based on an egregious misunderstanding, for, as Epicurus pointed out, 'man's greatest riches is to live on a little with contented mind' (1118–19).[18]

Once wealth becomes worth pursuing for its own sake, 'fame' and 'power' arise as attending social goals, on the equally false assumption that they are indispensable to the preservation of wealth itself and the possibility of leading a quiet life (1120–2). The breach occurring at this stage between natural needs and 'empty opinions'[19] is never overcome, and Lucretius concludes this section with a tirade against the futility of political ambition (1123–35), whose polemical target is timeless. It is because of this unreasonable perversion of social life that kings are killed, and anarchy prevails (1135–42), until 'there were some who taught them to create magistrates, and established law, that they might be willing to obey statutes' (1143–4). This transition to a state of law is explained in the same utilitarian terms already employed to justify the emergence of a rudimentary social contract: men were tired of living in violence, and therefore willingly submitted to 'statutes and strict rules of law' (1146–7: *leges artaque iura*).[20]

Lucretius' theory of social evolution is distinctive, and probably innovative even within the context of Epicurean doctrine. In his rigorously non-teleological and non-linear account he distinguishes sharply between an early phase characterised by kingship and a basic form of social contract, and a later one where the social contract is redefined, after a period of anarchy, thanks to a more elaborate set of laws. Kingship is thus seen as a natural form of social organisation which emerges early on and introduces social differentiation without scuppering the 'natural' social contract enshrined in *nec laedere nec uiolari* until society is corrupted by gold and the quest for wealth: anarchy is not the original state of mankind but follows a degeneration of this primitive model of society owing to unnatural assumptions. Lucretius' account is consistent with the heuristic model he adopts throughout this part of Book 5, the analogy between primitive men and animals: experience would have shown that the animal world is not 'anarchic', and that natural features such as strength and size (cf. 1007) justify the emergence of pack-leaders.

In his discussion of Lucretius' account, Momigliano concluded that 'magistrates and the laws, not kings, are able to ensure durable peace'.[21] In view of Lucretius' theory of 'natural' kingship, however, this statement holds true

---

[18] Cf. Democritus DK B 283.
[19] Cf. Epicurus 486 Usener.   [20] Cf. Tac. *Ann.* 3.26.
[21] Momigliano 1960: 388. His optimism is explicit: '[a] Republic is an advanced stage of . . . progress' (387).

only in the post-lapsarian society corrupted by *res* and *aurum*, where 'strict' laws are required. In a world where leadership is based on merit, leaders allocate resources according to natural criteria, and *concordia* prevails, there is no need for either magistrates or statutes, but a 'good king' can guarantee order and justice enough to allow his fellow-citizens to pursue the pleasures of friendship – hence the conclusion that obeying in peace is preferable to the exercise of power (1129–30). Kings, not the laws, characterise this Epicurean Golden Age,[22] to which men can return if they forgo their irrational desire for wealth, fame and power.[23]

Once again, a comparison between Lucretius and Cicero on the issue of evolution provides a clearer understanding of the disruptive force of the poet's position – and not just because of his rejection of any providentialist assumption. On two fronts the ideological conflict is especially acute: the utilitarian nature of the social contract and the origin of the *res publica*; and the origin and nature of laws.

Cicero's theory of the *naturalis congregatio* or *societas*[24] is pointedly at odds with the Epicurean position that 'human society does not exist'.[25] He strives to define and defend the existence of abstract principles which cannot be reduced to a utilitarian, contractarian basis. Men do not come together just because of weakness, but mainly through the natural instinct to seek the company of their fellow human beings (*Rep.* 1.39). No *foedus* naturally emerges from the collective efforts of an untutored community simply coming to experience the advantages of 'pitying the weak' (*De inuentione* 1.2). For Cicero, the very notion of *res publica* is grounded in natural law: ethics and politics cannot therefore be separated, and neither is based on evanescent man-made contracts.[26] Lucretius assigns no intrinsic value to any political organisation, while showing that a minimalist arrangement such as the one developed by the primitives can preserve the peace and allow men to pursue *ataraxia* – which is all political structures need to guarantee.

Laws, too, have a radically different status in Lucretius and Cicero. Cicero's 'natural law' springs from a natural metaphysical instinct, not the interplay of need, necessity and the pursuit of pleasure (*Rep.* 3.33). The aspiration to justice is a characteristic of all men everywhere – only the ways in which this can be attained may vary according to historical circumstances (*Off.* 2.42).

---

[22] Farrington 1939: 59–62.

[23] Cf. Diogenes of Oenoanda fr. 56 Smith, 1–12; Hermarchus fr. 24 Krohn.

[24] Cic. *Off.* 1.50, with Dyck 2004 ad loc. For Lucretius not even the bond between parents and children, the basis of Stoic *oikeiōsis*, qualifies as a transcendent *officium*: Lévy 2005: 63–4.

[25] Usener 523.   [26] On Cicero's definition of *res publica* see Schofield 1995.

For Lucretius neither the primitives' notion of equity (*aequum*) nor historical laws aspire in the abstract to justice and equability. While positing the existence of the notion of *aequum* from an early stage, he defines it in inductive and empirical terms. *Aequum* is the standard Roman term for *ius naturale* 'natural law', as opposed to the historical and variable *ius ciuile* 'civil law'. Lucretius, however, strips the notion of 'natural law' of metaphysical connotations by defining it as the desire to 'pity the weak' which arises once men begin to live with women and children. This is seen as a practical arrangement of self-evident – that is, natural – appeal, for its violation would lead to the early extinction of the human race (5.1023–7). Thus *aequum* – Lucretius' *ius naturale* – emerges as just another form of *utilitas*,[27] as historical, empirical and contractual[28] as any man-made law, but older and more basic. Historical laws, a relatively late and transient innovation setting out punishments for the violation of the pact of non-aggression, would not be needed in the ideal Epicurean world based on the respect for *aequum*.

While depriving laws of any metaphysical origin, Lucretius places them at the very heart of his atomistic cosmos as he constructs in the *DRN* a legal model for the universe.[29] A true understanding of the laws of Nature is consistent with the immediacy of the primitive social compact, itself based on self-evident truths – and both suffice to ensure peace of mind. In Lucretius' account of the universe, *nexus* 'bonds', *foedera* 'pacts' and *leges* 'laws' account for the behaviour of atoms and their combination into *concilia* 'unions', another term with legal and political implications, and thus form a coherent system for the rational understanding of nature.[30]

Lucretius' *foedera naturae* and *leges* possess a strong empiricist foundation;[31] 'laws of nature' are the projection into the infinity of time of the prevailing forms of association among compatible atoms that emerged at the beginning of the world and which natural reproduction has inherited.[32] As such, they are reliable, yet consistent with the indeterminacy and contingency of a mechanistic universe. Thus, for instance, when the soul is said not to be 'free from the law of death' (3.687), Lucretius is referring to the

---

27 Cf. Epic. *Kuriai doxai* 31, with Long and Sedley 1987: II, 129–30; Goldschmidt 1977: 27–8; Schofield 2000: 440 n. 11. Cf. Hor. *Serm.* 1.3.98 'utility, the mother almost of justice and equity', in the context of an ironic 'Epicurean' digression on justice, with Goldschmidt 1977: 150–65.

28 Cf. Epic. *Kuriai doxai* 33.

29 For (limited) Presocratic precedents see Schiesaro 2007. The behaviour of atoms, too, is described in terms borrowed from politics: Cabisius 1984.

30 More about the connection with Roman jurisprudence in Schiesaro 2007.

31 Long 1977, Droz-Vincent 1996.   32 Long 1977: 85.

perceptible truth that all material things come to an end as if obeying a 'law' of sorts. In Book 5 Lucretius explains that not all combinations of atoms are possible, but only those within specific *genera* 'kinds'. A young earth may have produced 'imperfect' human beings, but not centaurs, animals made up of different kinds of atoms. This fixity of each species is determined by the very nature of the atoms from which it originates, and as such is valid from the beginning:[33] from the 'absolute power'[34] of these impersonal laws stems the *certus ordo* 'regular order' which still is, and always will remain, the defining feature of the Epicurean universe. What we now perceive as abstract principles of aggregation arise in fact from the combinatory possibilities which atomic compounds established at the outset, and therefore 'laws' are yet another way in which we can describe, in Epicurean terms, the non-teleological order which governs the workings of Nature.[35]

Lucretius' laws of nature do not exist outside and above the physicality of atoms, do not answer an inscrutable teleological project and have not been promoted by a provident lawgiver. 'Natural laws' crystallise *post factum* the workings of nature, and embody a 'deeply fixed' (1.77) *terminus* for each creature, a limitation of possibilities which prevents anarchy in the physical world.[36] In this respect *foedera naturae* are at one with the *foedera* struck by primitive men in the earliest stages of their evolution, who do not have any metaphysical aspiration, but realise through experience that *foedera* (5.1025) are needed for survival. The Romans rightly connected *foedus* etymologically with *fides*, a 'horizontal', non-hierarchical bind which promotes pacts among equals while implying no superior lawgiver.[37] Again, the gradual evolution of Roman jurisprudence towards a systematic corpus of shared legal knowledge may be considered an enabling factor for Lucretius' strategy. But it should be noted that, in historical terms, laws at Rome had been seen from their first appearance as a means of preventing knowledge from being the secret preserve of the few, and a crucial step in the creation of a public, shared body of knowledge.

The plagues: politics and *religio*

A comparative analysis of Lucretius' and Cicero's positions on the origin, nature and function of the social contract and the *res publica* further highlights the disruptive potential of the politics of the *DRN*. Deprived of its

---

[33] 5.677–9 (cf. 2.707–10).   [34] Giussani 1896–8: IV, 172.
[35] The equivalence between *law* and *reason* is hinted at 2.718–19.
[36] Garani (forthcoming) rightly compares Lucretian *foedera* with Empedoclean 'oaths'.
[37] Maltby 1991 s.v. *foedus*.

metaphysical sanction, any constitutional form is nothing more than a purely historical, practical set of arrangements which must be evaluated on the basis of its ability to foster the attainment of *uoluptas* 'pleasure'. Contrary to Cicero's (and Sallust's) attacks against *uoluptas*, wrongly identified with vulgarian pleasures and wealth, Lucretius shows that it is precisely through embracing Epicurean *uoluptas* that men will understand which social values are essential for peaceful coexistence, and how society should therefore be structured. Judged against this unbending criterion, Rome's constitution and political life attract very harsh criticism – as indeed do all polities based on similarly distorted assumptions.[38] No aspect of Roman political life escapes condemnation: Lucretius turns squarely on its head the accepted wisdom of his times by showing that a notion of the public good based on *uirtus*, *pietas*, *nobilitas*, *honor* – in short, on the *mos maiorum* 'traditional ways' – is conceptually flawed and in practice disastrous, as recent and contemporary Roman events testify.

Lucretius attacks the follies of a political system predicated on the pursuit of honour, wealth and power in three distinct but connected sections: the proem to Book 2 (9–16); the syllabus of Book 3 (59–93); and the evolutionary account in Book 5 (1123–35). The three passages should be read together, as suggested by the repetition of key terms, some of which are connected with specific Roman practice,[39] and even of whole lines.[40] All three identify the root cause of perverse social pursuits in a misguided understanding of what is needed to attain a happy, natural life, which in Epicurean terms consists in the removal of mental anguish and of physical pain through the satisfaction of elementary needs. Epicurean *ratio* dispels the ignorance that spreads *terror* among men (3.87–93).

The central object of Lucretius' attack is political ambition *per se*, defined as the pursuit of wealth and power through *ingenium* 'talent' and *nobilitas* (2.11; 3.63; 5.1123), with its attendant complication of *inuidia* 'envy' (3.75; 5.1126) and concern for external recognition (3.78). This ambition runs counter to the pursuit of *uoluptas*, which entails a quiet life far removed from the *curae* of politics, and regards life in a 'well-balanced'[41] monarchy as the easiest way to secure its goal. In a society ordered according to Epicurean principles, moreover, there would be no political activity in which to participate. Laws themselves would disappear, since the principle *nec laedere nec uiolari* 'to do no hurt and suffer no violence' would be enough to guarantee stability and order. While the 'end of politics' remains the Epicureans'

---

[38] Pianezzola 1977: 615; Narducci 2004: 396.
[39] D. P. Fowler 1989: 143–4, with nn. 93–4.
[40] 2.12–13 = 3.62–3.   [41] Philodemus, *De bono rege* 4.

ultimate goal, they do allow that special circumstances (*tempus et necessitas*)[42] may at times force or advise political involvement, and not necessarily for a short span only. But political involvement is neither the aspiration of men who are 'political' by nature, nor an ideal lifetime occupation, but always only a necessity born out of the imperfect nature of a polity not yet converted to Epicureanism.[43]

In 3.59–93 Lucretius elaborates on this argument by positing that 'avarice and the blind lust of distinction . . . in no small degree are fed by the fear of death' (3.60–4). The passage is as intricate as it is eloquent, but the logical connection between fear of death and the worldly desires it 'feeds' (3.64) is not watertight.[44] A passage in Book 5 (1120–1), however, sheds fresh light on the issue, which Lucretius now tackles from a different angle as he remarks that the pursuit of unnatural pleasures is not innate: men want to become prominent and powerful once they identify wealth as a source of pleasure, and they wish to give it a 'firm foundation', make it last into the future. As an abstract entity, wealth demands the stability of the symbolic system which guarantees its role, thus making present happiness conditional on its continuation; and once *fortuna* loses a direct connection with material needs and their satisfaction,[45] it creates infinite desires whose satisfaction would be possible only if men were immortal. Shifting the satisfaction of pleasure into the future even at the risk of present anxiety[46] – a most un-Epicurean strategy – promotes the fear of death (note the figurative Tartarus at 1126–7), which pushes men into the 'blights of life' portrayed at 3.59–78 – greed, the desire for honours and the desire to attain the greatest wealth. The result is a vicious circle based on false projections and assumptions: infinite, non-natural desires are irrationally perceived as *egestas* 'lack' (3.65), the equally abstract opposite of *fortuna*, which has nothing to do with material need (1117–19) but, like *contemptus* 'ignominy' (3.65), defines an elusive obsession.

The way in which Lucretius articulates the negative consequences of an attachment to wealth *per se* differentiates his polemics from the standard diatribe attacks against wealth as the defining feature of today's 'iron age',[47] or the root, if relatively recent, cause of Roman decadence. 'Love of wealth' is neither an unavoidable curse nor the consequence of foreign conquest, much as Sallust's description of greed as 'always boundless' and 'insatiable'

---

[42] Cic. *Rep.* 1.10.

[43] Epicurus seems to allow political involvement under certain circumstances: D. P. Fowler 1989: 126–30; Schofield 2000: 441 n.13.

[44] Kenney 1971 on 3.65–73. Cf. Perret 1940, Desmouliez 1958, D. P. Fowler 1989.

[45] Cf. Epic. *Sent. Vat.* 25.   [46] Schofield 2000: 437–8; cf. Fallot 1977: 20–1.

[47] Ov. *Met.* 1.127–50.

(*Cat.* 11.3) sounds very Lucretian.[48] Rather, it is a form of mental unbalance which can be countered through an understanding of the workings of nature. Precisely because it is more radical, and grounded in Epicurean physics, Lucretius' pathology of wealth is unusually incisive. The landowner trying to 'flee from himself' as he moves from place to place is blinded by ignorance of the true 'cause of his disease', and therefore a more disturbing character than his Horatian counterpart (3.1067–70).[49] Lucretius' polemic against the lovers who expend all their energies and riches in vain pursuits, condemned to a total misunderstanding of reality (4.1120–4), goes beyond the 'Catonian' condemnation of conspicuous consumption now possible in a hellenising, affluent Rome. In this topsy-turvy society not only riches, but even names (4.1153–70) have lost their meaning.[50]

Both Lucretius and Cicero (not to mention the Stoics) attack the infinity of desire rooted in the pursuit of riches, especially financial ones. Wealth based on money is seen as wholly negative, detached from nature, a potentially boundless form of hoarding which either deprives the community of part of its wealth, or can be used against it in the fulfilment of personal ambition.[51] If diagnoses coincide, aetiology and prescriptions diverge radically. Cicero regards the centrality of *uoluptas* in Epicurean ethics, and the empirical cognition in its epistemology, as two formidable enemies for his conception of a subject free from the slavery of senses and projected towards metaphysical aspirations which are hypostatised in communal *uirtutes*, worth pursuing *per se*. He attacks Epicurean *uoluptas*, which he sees as indistinguishable from lust and luxury, as an unstable, fluid passion which engulfs the subject and removes him from any consideration of 'the common good': a wholly unsuitable foundation for the *mos maiorum* and its constitutive virtues. Cicero's polemical target is correct; his reconstruction of the Epicurean position, preposterous. Epicurus imposes upon *uoluptas* a firm natural limit by defining it as the removal of pain, not as the endless accumulation of pleasures – a radical distinction which Cicero decides to ignore even as he allows Torquatus to develop it in Book 1 of the *De finibus*.[52] But Cicero correctly surmises that assuming *uoluptas*, even in its correct Epicurean formulation, as an end rather than a means would destroy the very essence of the *res publica* as a community backed by metaphysical values. The attainment of *uoluptas* is a fundamentally private pursuit, which demands of society no more than the removal of obstacles such as anarchy or violence.

---

48 Cf. Liv. *praef.* 12.   49 Hor. *Serm.* 1.1.69.

50 As Sallust's philo-Epicurean Caesar observes: 'we have lost the true names for things' (*Cat.* 52.11).

51 Lotito 1981: 84–93.   52 1.42b–54, esp. 43–4.

Unsurprisingly, Lucretius reserves his harshest criticism for *religio*, especially in its social and political function, which Polybius (6.56) had so sharply identified as 'the foundation of Roman greatness'.[53] Early in Book 1 the story of Iphigenia insists on the truly impious nature of a belief in gods which turns into a violent tool of kingship. The political dimension of the tragedy which strikes the royal family (1.86, 94) is always much in evidence; the goal of the murder itself is couched in the language of Roman officialdom.[54] Iphigenia's sacrifice shows that all the values Greek citizens (91) seem proudly to assert are in fact just a perversion of natural values. Not even as fundamental a notion as that of paternity is safe from the destructive force of *religio*.

Religio fares no better in other contexts. The rites of the Magna Mater (2.600–60) offer another opportunity to underline, with a tinge of sarcasm, the connection between superstition and political and military power, the latter a frenzied, irrational activity. In Book 5 a section on the origins of *religio* and its diffusion (5.1161–1240) emphasises its negative role in Rome's political system.[55]

At a more fundamental level, the overall message of the *DRN* strikes at the heart of the expedient connection between religion and politics which characterises Roman practice throughout the Republic and is packaged theoretically by Varro's *Antiquitates rerum diuinarum* in the very same years. When Lucretius attacks the state of submission and ignorance in which men are kept by traditional accounts of the gods or of Etruscan books (6.381) and extols the virtues of a rational, Epicurean understanding of nature, he is attacking a system which relied on opacity and unintelligibility in order to further the predominance of the ruling classes (who are nonetheless in thrall to capricious gods: 5.1222–40). Cicero well knows that the epistemological dependency the *DRN* vows to eradicate is essential to the preservation of an ordered society,[56] while Lucretius' attempt to free men from religious superstition, and nature from *dominis . . . superbis* 'haughty masters' (2.1091), entails a formidable political message which Cicero's studied silence will only magnify.

The *DRN*'s ambition transcends limitations of space and time: rooted in the understanding of the eternal workings of nature, Epicureanism aspires to be

---

[53] Farrington 1939: 172–215. Cf. Pianezzola: 1977; Conti 1982: 36–7; Minyard 1985: 38–9.

[54] 1.100 *felix faustusque* echoes an official formula: see Pease 1920–3 on Cic. *Div.* 1.102; Appel 1909: 173–4.

[55] Note the polemical implications of 1226–35.

[56] Cf. Cic. *Leg.* 2.13, with Dyck 2004 ad loc.

a lesson for all people in all ages. Rome is but a transient *concilium*, political union, its pre-eminent position, like its eventual downfall, explicable through the vagaries of historical events (3.830–7). All kings and kingdoms share the same fate (3.1027–8). The lesson that any material compound is doomed to ultimate dissolution applies equally to great men such as Ancus Marcus or Scipio (3.1025; 1034–5). These brief references emphasise the absence of other prominent historical figures, first of all Romulus,[57] whose deification Cicero celebrates at length (*Rep.* 2.4–19): in the *DRN* Epicurus, not the man who decided to found Rome 'having taken the auspices' (*Rep.* 2.5), is deified. Not even Hercules' deeds compare favourably with the master's teachings (5.22–42).

If the *DRN* fails to assure its Roman readers that the destiny of the city can be any different from all others – a reasoned position which will cast a long shadow over all subsequent attempts to argue otherwise – it also offers a less than flattering account of its military prowess. The instinct to fight, rooted in nature, is a sort of bestial frenzy whose technical refinement can hardly be regarded as a sign of moral progress (4.843–7). In the confused slaughter which follows the attempt to exploit boars and lions as weapons (5.1308–49)[58] the boundaries between men and animals collapse. The connection between individual ambition, greed and violence established at 3.59–78, too, is deeply critical. If Stoicism emerged as a suitable conceptual infrastructure for imperialism,[59] Lucretius' Epicureanism taught a lesson of individual salvation and retreat which ran directly counter (in theory at least) to the imperialist ambitions of Rome.

Lucretius' own age comes under specific criticism.[60] In the syllabus to Book 3 the reference to the shedding of citizens' blood would have reminded readers of recent, if not current events.[61] In Book 5 the rejection of kings (1136–40) recalls the end of the Roman monarchy[62] but is also shot through with allusions to the dying days of the Republic (5.1123–35). The beginning of the poem mentions an emergency grave and specific enough to jeopardise Lucretius' engagement with his poem, and to confront Memmius with the kind of *necessitas* which would force even an Epicurean into politics (1.41–3). But precisely which *tempora* is Lucretius alluding to? Since the assumption that Lucretius was dead by 55–54 BC has now been plausibly

---

57 But cf. 4.683 *Romulidarum* (in a rather bathetic context).

58 Kenney 1972: 19–23; Schiesaro 1990: 159–68.   59 Shaw 1985.

60 References span from the 80s to the 40s BC: a list in Conti 1982: 45 n. 8.

61 D. P. Fowler 1989.

62 Sallust offers a comparable interpretation: see *Cat.* 6.7; 7.1–4; 10–11; *Jug.* 41; *Hist.* 1.10.

called into question,[63] it may be possible to connect this sense of impending doom with the imminence of the civil war in the latter half of 50 or, even better, with its first phase in 49–48, when the war has already gained an international dimension.[64]

Lucretius' party politics are no easier to pin down. His aristocratic education and ethos are normally assumed, but open political references are elusive. The preference for the old-fashioned monarchy which can be gleaned from Book 5, for instance, is hard to translate into a political programme, although Lucretius' ideal kings have limited functions: they are good keepers of the peace rather than expansionist warmongers. The ensuing mob rule is intolerable (1141–2), but again unlikely to refer specifically to *popularis* danger. The attack on ambition and greed, however, echoes aristocratic ideology, although not necessarily, at this chronological juncture at least, an *optimates* political stance.[65] Yet mention of *salus* 'security' at 1.43 is intriguing, since as a political concept *salus* is 'virtually Ciceronian property'.[66] The political implications of the term would not be impossible to reconcile with what we know of Memmius' shifting allegiances,[67] but would perhaps be more appropriate if the addressee is not C. Memmius L.f., praetor in 58, but the pro-senatorial C. Memmius C.f., tribune in 54 BC.[68] Then again, the hymn to *Venus genetrix* at the very beginning of the poem has been read as a strong indication of Lucretius' pro-Caesarian tendency.[69]

The target of Lucretius' attack is neither a faction nor an age: the very ideological and political superstructure of the Roman state itself, which Cicero strives to preserve by insisting on its metaphysical dimension, is shown to be an insurmountable obstacle to personal and social fulfilment. The *DRN* shows that a return to nature is the key not just to the happiness of the individual, but also to the salvation of the state. What Rome needs is a fresh social compact based on mutual respect, non-aggression, and, first and foremost, rejection of all false idols: fame, honour, armies, money, *religio*. Tinkering with party politics would not address any of these issues. Clearly, what is needed is not constitutional reform, but philosophical conversion.

---

[63] Canfora 1993b; G. Hutchinson 2001.

[64] *DRN* 1.29–30 may well refer to external conflicts: Grimal 1978: 237.

[65] Flores 1984–5: 1511–12.

[66] Dyck 2004 on Cic. *Leg.* 3.8.2. Cf. Winkler 1995: 30–5; Hellegouarc'h 1963: 412; G. Hutchinson 2001: 158–9.

[67] Pauly and Wissowa (1894–1963): XV.1, 609–16.

[68] G. Hutchinson 2001: 158–9. Cf. Pauly and Wissowa (1894–1963): XV.1, 616–18, and Cic. *Rab. Post.* 7.

[69] Grimal 1978: 240.

The politics of the plague

The final episode of the poem, where Lucretius does not limit himself to the reconstruction of a crucial episode of Greek history but offers a picture of the devastating effects of a life led according to non-Epicurean, or indeed pre-Epicurean, principles, offers important, if indirect, political lessons. This image of systemic destruction goes beyond Thucydides' original: Lucretius emphasises with particular bitterness the collapse of social structures and family bonds, while showing the ultimate 'bankruptcy'[70] of *religio* and attendant traditional values. An interpretation of the overall impact of this strategy cannot be attempted here, but there is merit in the view that much of the force of the section is proptreptic: by now suitably educated, the disciple of Epicurus and Lucretius should know that what he has been taught in the poem affords a very different way of life, and of death, from the philosophically challenged Athenians of the fifth century. The disciple will know that much of the misery they display is their own fault; and he will know, finally, that for all the seemingly conclusive disaster he has just witnessed, the cycle of life and death does go on – nature knows no permanent demise.[71]

The symbolic implications of Lucretius' description of the plague[72] allow for criticism of Athenian *mores* to reflect on the miseries of contemporary Roman life[73] – and, again, on the limitations of a political system structured around false values and aspirations. The chronological disjunction promotes the episode in Athens to the status of general truth. Key to the wider implications of this section is a set of established metaphorical associations upon which Lucretius builds his implicit argument: the identification of the body as a city is already Hippocratic,[74] and the equation of political *stasis*, civil strife, with disease dates back to Herodotus, Democritus and Thucydides.[75] The mechanics of the plague, too, parallel the deterioration of the body politic. All *concilia* perish because of blows from outside (2.1140), but this happens once they have become vulnerable;[76] thus, internal dissension jeopardises Rome's *salus* (1.43) just as the 'war' of *mundi membra* stirred against each other in 'impious [i.e. civil] war' paves the way for the dissolution of the world: 'again, since the greatest members of the world fight so hard together, stirred by most unnatural war, do you not see that some end may be given to their long strife?' (5.380–4).

The symptoms displayed by the victims of the plague turn into reality the metaphorical distress which characterises the struggle for political

---

[70] Minyard 1985: 59–61, at 61.   [71] Schiesaro 1994 and 1996.
[72] As pioneered by Commager 1957.   [73] Schrijvers 1970: 320.
[74] Vegetti 1983, Cambiano 1982.   [75] Cambiano 1982: 224; Cagnetta 2001: 7–14.
[76] Compare 2.1139–40 with 6.1162.

supremacy. *Anxius angor* 'torments of anxiety' and 'persistent retching' keep them awake day and night (6.1158–60), a detail which recalls both the distress caused by a political career (2.12–13; cf. 3.62–3), and the *anxia corda* 'anxious hearts' of men 'rolling in riches, mighty in honour and fame' but unenlightened by Epicureanism and thus doomed to perpetual unhappiness (6.12–16).[77] Diseased Athenians display the feverishness (6.1145) which, as the student of the *DRN* should know, cannot be cured faster if one lies on 'pictured tapestries and blushing purple' (2.34–6: note the senatorial implication).[78] 'Sweating blood' is the most striking parallel between the physical reality of the plague (6.1147–8) and the metaphorical disease of political ambition (5.1131). Overall, the plague brings about a state of lawlessness comparable to the effects of the civil war. Social bonds are broken (6.1239) just as when men, plagued by greed and blind desire for honours (3.60), descend into civil strife (3.72–3) and become oblivious to *pietas* (3.84). The collapse of *pietas* is a recurring feature in descriptions of the civil war,[79] as is the breaking down of familial ties.[80] The cumulative effect of the plague is thus the regression to a pre-social and pre-cultural state of life: 'without mourners the lonely funerals competed with one another in being rushed through' (6.1225).[81]

The internal connections with other parts of the *DRN* highlight an important aspect of Lucretius' strategy: the text suggests a similar aetiology for the plague's destructive impact on the fabric of society in pre-Epicurean Athens and for the social disease besetting contemporary Rome. The connection between the fear of death, ambition and greed,[82] and civil war established at 3.59–78, holds true as well at the end of Book 6, where the fear of death is more palpable. Indeed, the plague adds a final element to the causal chain established in Book 3 and developed, as we have seen, in Book 5: it shows that a body politic plagued by moral flaws can and will self-destruct given the circumstances, given, that is, *tempora* which are *iniqua* enough. Crucially, a similar aetiology can be found in Lucretius' Thucydidean model, where internal parallels, too, conspire to bring the political connotations of the epidemic into sharper focus. The excursus on the plague in Book 2 is paralleled, in Book 3, by the analysis of *stasis*, civil strife, at Corcyra. In

---

[77] Contrast the effort of Lucretius 'to watch through the calm nights' (1.142) in his mission to enlighten Memmius.

[78] Cf. 5.1423–4 and 1427–9.   [79] Jal 1963: 391.

[80] Jal 1963: 394–5. Cf. Thuc. 3.82.6, and Liv. 25.26.10, drawing on both Thucydides and Lucretius.

[81] On perverted funerals in civil war see Jal 1963: 394, and *DRN* 3.72–3 (above).

[82] Often portrayed as causes of civil war: Jal 1963: 378, but also one of the capital political vices since the second century BC: Flores 1984–5: 1510–11.

Athens the plague causes lawlessness and the destruction of ordinary habits, as Thucydides explains in a section which, interestingly, Lucretius does not 'translate' (2.53); in Corcyra, vying for power among groups leads to arrogance and ambition, and then, inevitably, to *stasis* (3.82),[83] which is regarded as the socio-political analogue of the plague.[84]

Even if, at the cosmic level, destructive motions have begun to prevail, and our world is inching towards dissolution, Lucretius outlines a general philosophy of existence which, through the radical elimination of false assumptions about wealth, honour and religion, will return men to natural values and, consequently, rational forms of behaviour. Internal strife, a form of social *discidium* 'splitting apart' will needlessly accelerate the decadence of our society. His are times when extreme measures must be taken if society is to be turned away from self-destruction, a fate which not even Athens at its peak managed to avoid: *tempore tali* 'at such a time' in the very last line of the poem (6.1251)[85] provides an emphatic connection with the opening *patriai tempore iniquo* 'in an evil time for the fatherland' (1.41), a reminder of how essential speedy moral renovation has become *now*.[86]

At many junctures in their history Romans would have had cause to see their current situation mirrored in Lucretius' reinterpretation of the plague, which thus acquires an important allegorical and political edge: in his extreme, and most impassioned, attempt to convert his readers, Lucretius offers a compelling example of the self-destructive neuroses of their society, which they should compare and contrast with the peaceful *uoluptas* guaranteed by an Epicurean Venus at the very beginning of the poem.[87] After all, all social problems spring from nurture, not nature.

The *DRN* questions the very foundations of 'civilised' society, of which both fifth-century BC Athens and first-century BC Rome are but specific instances. Only a radical change in the individuals' *Weltanschauung* and the creation of a social compact better suited to the attainment of *uoluptas* and *amicitia* will forestall the accelerated weakening and ultimate dissolution of the body politic and enable men to come closer to what the Epicureans would consider a true Golden Age. The sense of urgency – and pessimism – with

---

[83] Finley 1967: 159 n. 46.

[84] That the plague comes as punishment for men's evil is an established notion in Near Eastern, Greek and Roman thought: Woodman 1988: 32–3.

[85] P. G. Fowler 1997: 114–17. A connection should also be established with *in tali tempore* at 1.93 (G. Hutchinson 2001: 161 n. 26).

[86] Sallust confirms *post factum* that Lucretius' plague can be read with an eye towards Rome and its current politics: see P. G. Fowler 1997: 133; for a comparable strategy at the close of *Bellum Catilinae* see McGushin 1980 on Sall. *Cat.* 61.8–9.

[87] To which they should now turn again: Schiesaro 1994.

which Lucretius imparts this lesson advertises the vastness of the challenge ahead.

Further reading

The consensus on Lucretius' biography and dates is called into question by Canfora 1993b and G. Hutchinson 2001, if correctly then with notable consequences for our understanding of the poet's political and cultural contexts. Farrington 1939 and Fallot 1977 are both challenging points of departure for an exploration of Lucretius' politics. Nichols 1976 offers a preliminary account of its later influence. Grimal 1978 and, more extensively, Minyard 1985 offer useful overviews on the topic, but the most incisive overall treatment remains that of D. P. Fowler 1989. There is no systematic account of the dialogue (or lack of it) between Cicero and Lucretius: see recently Andreoni 1979 and Zetzel 1998.

Notwithstanding Algra, Koenen and Schrijvers 1997, a full account of Lucretius' broader, and specifically Roman, cultural background is still a desideratum. Promising avenues of enquiry include Cabisius 1984 on the social and political connotations of Lucretian atomology, and Nugent 1994 on the gender implications of the poem's physics. Schiesaro 2007 outlines a connection between the *DRN* and contemporary developments in Roman jurisprudence.

There is a vast bibliography on the evolution of human society in Book 5: see in general Furley 1978 and Manuwald 1980, and now the innovative commentary of Campbell 2003, which should also be consulted for further references.

Commager 1957 inaugurated a new line of thinking on the plague; see also Schrijvers 1970 and P. G. Fowler 1997. The argument sketched here is further developed in Schiesaro forthcoming.

4

MONICA GALE

Lucretius and previous
poetic traditions

Ennius . . . noster . . . qui primus amoeno
detulit ex Helicone perenni fronde coronam

(*DRN* 1.117–18)

Our own Ennius, who first brought down from pleasant Helicon a garland of ever-
green leaves

auia Pieridum peragro loca nullius ante
trita solo. iuuat integros accedere fontis
atque haurire, iuuatque nouos decerpere flores
insignemque meo capiti petere inde coronam
unde prius nulli uelarint tempora Musae

(*DRN* 1.926–30 = 4.1–5)

I wander through trackless places of the Muses, trodden by no foot before mine. It
is pleasant to approach untouched springs and drink, and pleasant to pluck fresh
flowers and seek a glorious garland for my head in places whence the Muses have
crowned no other brow.

These two closely related passages from Lucretius' first book suggest – when
taken together – a concern with literary filiation and poetic originality typical
of the poets of the first century BC. A cross-reference is implicit in the shared
image of the garland plucked on the mountain of the Muses: even as he
stakes his own claim as a literary innovator, the poet points us back to his
earlier acknowledgement of Ennius as literary forebear. Paradoxically, the
poet's originality is predicated on the existence of a prior tradition.

Lucretius' engagement with previous poetic traditions is intense and sustained, though largely conducted with a subtlety that has often led commentators to overlook its existence. The issue was a particularly pressing
one for an Epicurean poet: Epicurus himself appears to have held literary
pursuits in general to be trivial, if not positively dangerous.[1] The resulting need to justify the poetic form of the work will have combined with

---

[1] For Epicurus' views on poetry see Gale 1994a: 14–18; Asmis 1995.

contemporary preoccupations with poetic originality and artistry to make it inevitable that Lucretius should seek to distance himself from the misguided efforts of his literary predecessors. Yet Roman writers were always vividly aware of their literary heritage, and Lucretius is no exception. It is possible to trace through the *DRN* a process of negotiation between these conflicting stances: Lucretius represents himself at once as the literary heir of Homer, Empedocles, Ennius and others, and as their severe critic.[2]

Allied to this complex handling of literary tradition is an apparently ambivalent attitude towards the value of poetry in general. In the famous image of the honeyed cup, which follows the programmatic lines quoted above (1.936–50 = 4.11–25), poetry is overtly represented as a mere vehicle or adjunct to the philosophical message which it embodies: the 'honey of the Muses' is merely the sweetener which fools the patient/pupil into 'swallowing' the medicine of Epicurean doctrine. Lucretius takes a similar (and perhaps equally disingenuous) line in a sequence of passages where poetry and poets are implicitly downgraded in relation to Epicurus and his philosophy. In the history of civilisation at the end of Book 5, for example, poetry is briefly mentioned in the rapid catalogue of arts and luxuries which brings the book to its close (5.1444–7, 1451). In the proem to Book 6, however, Lucretius hammers home the message that technological and cultural advances have no power to make us happy: that is the preserve of Epicurus, whose philosophical discoveries should be seen as the true culmination (*cacumen*, 5.1457) of the historical process sketched in the previous book. Similarly, the brief catalogue of deceased Greek and Roman 'heroes' offered as a *consolatio* for the reader at 3.1025–52 includes both poets and philosophers in its ascending sequence: kings and generals give way to the 'companions of the Muses', of whom Homer is named as the doyen; but the climactic position is reserved for the philosophers Democritus and *ipse Epicurus*. Strikingly the simile used here to express Epicurus' superiority alludes to an epigram by Leonidas of Tarentum on Homer (*Anth. Pal.* 9.24). The Lucretian lines offer an implicit correction: it is not Homer but Epicurus who outshines the human race. A similar appropriation of metapoetic language can be observed in the proem to Book 3, where Lucretius disclaims any attempt to compete with his master: a swallow cannot vie with swans, nor a kid with a racehorse (3.6–8). This kind of comparison is elsewhere employed by writers paying tribute to earlier or contemporary *poets*: a rustic singer in Theocritus, for example, declares that he cannot compete with Sicelidas (Asclepiades) or Philetas, any more than a frog's croaking can surpass the

---

[2] See p. 112 below.

cicada's song (*Id.* 7.39–41).[3] For Lucretius, it is the philosophical model Epicurus who is inimitable; poets – even the great Homer – are a different matter.

Epic and didactic

As we have seen, Lucretius pays explicit tribute to his epic models in two places, the proem to Book 1 and the catalogue of great men of the past towards the end of Book 3. In addition to Homer and Ennius, a third poet mentioned by name and singled out for warm praise is Empedocles, whose role here is – at least in part – to represent the other main branch of the hexameter tradition, didactic poetry.[4] The praise lavished on Homer, Ennius and Empedocles in these passages suggests an act of homage on the poet's part: Lucretius implicitly represents himself as the heir to these three great predecessors. At the same time, however, Lucretius is explicitly critical of his literary ancestors: Ennius and, by implication, his 'source' Homer are condemned for propagating confused and misguided ideas about the afterlife, Empedocles for errors in his physical theories. More than declarations of allegiance, then, these programmatic passages can be read as putting forward a claim to transcend earlier works in the epic and didactic traditions – even those of Homer. Unlike that of his predecessors, Lucretius' poetic form is a vehicle for Truth.

Both Lucretius' self-representation as the heir of Homer, Ennius and Empedocles and his rivalry with them are borne out in various ways throughout the poem. Most obviously, aspects of Lucretius' language and style are modelled on those of Homeric epic, both directly and as filtered through the poetry of Empedocles and Ennius. The archaising style of Lucretian Latin[5] and the poet's pervasive use of alliteration are particularly reminiscent of Ennius, while other features such as the employment of extended epic similes (relatively rare in pre-Lucretian didactic poetry) and quasi-formulaic repetition appear to be derived more directly from the Homeric epics. Lucretius' practice here, however, owes much to that of Empedocles, who had already adapted the Homeric simile and the formulaic style of archaic epic as vehicles for philosophical argument. Repetition is exploited in Empedocles' *On Nature* as a means of structuring the argument and driving home key

---

3 Cf. also Antipater of Sidon, *Anth. Pal.* 7.173; Virg. *Ecl.* 9.35–6. Volk 2002: 107–12 interprets Lucretius' use of the comparison rather differently; see also Donohue 1993: 35–48.

4 That the doxographic section of Book 1 (635–920) is implicitly concerned with literary style as well as philosophical doctrine is persuasively argued by Tatum 1984.

5 See p. 96 below.

doctrinal points: Empedocles draws attention to this technique in fragment 25, 'it is good to say what is necessary even twice'. Similarly, the extended simile is transformed by Empedocles into an argumentative and heuristic tool. The surviving fragments include two justly famous examples: fr. 23, in which the combination of the four elements to form all the objects that make up the physical world is compared to the mixing of painters' pigments, and fr. 84, in which the construction of a lantern is used to illustrate the functioning of the human eye. In general, too, Empedocles' language closely resembles that of Homer, as Lucretius' resembles that of Ennius.[6] Like those of Empedocles, the similes in the *DRN* are carefully tailored to the demands of scientific argumentation,[7] and Lucretius' use of repetition serves a similarly functional end. Particularly noteworthy is Lucretius' tendency to compare things that are *essentially* similar – unlike Homer, whose similes generally bring together the realms of war and agriculture/peacetime activities, humans and animals, or human actions and natural phenomena such as fire and flood. The very first simile in the *DRN*, comparing the action of the wind to that of a river in flood (1.271–97), exemplifies this clearly: the wind affects solid objects such as trees and ships in the same way as the river just because it too is made up at the fundamental level of solid atomic matter, though this is not visible to the eye. Repetition, likewise, is made by Lucretius, as by Empedocles, to serve the didactic purpose of 'footnoting' connections between passages on similar themes. A good example is the brief reference at 2.167–83 to the imperfection of the world as a habitat for human beings, with the fuller development of the same theme at 5.195–234; the repetition of lines 2.177–81 at 5.195–9 acts – in conjunction with the explicit forward reference at 2.182 – as a footnote linking the two passages. Formulaic repetition – for example, of the lines called by Diskin Clay the 'Epicurean axiom of change',[8] 1.670–1 = 1.792–3 = 2.753–4 = 3.519–20 – can also function as means of fixing passages of doctrinal importance in the reader's mind.

But Lucretius maximises the poetological and philosophical opportunity presented by Homeric, Ennian and Empedoclean echoes by inserting obtrusive 'corrections' of the earlier poets' world-views. Naturally, the majority of such corrections remain implicit, as we would expect from a *doctus poeta* of the generation of Catullus; nor should we forget that Lucretius' original audience would have been steeped from schooldays in the epic tradition and thus much more familiar with the texts of Homer and Ennius than even the most highly educated of modern readers. To cite just one example for

---

[6] For Empedocles' 'Homeric' style see Bollack 1965, Wright 1997.
[7] See p. 122 below.   [8] Clay 1983: 191–9.

each of the three poets:[9] the programmatic first simile discussed above is modelled on lines from *Iliad* 5 (87–92), where the onslaught of Diomedes is compared to a river bursting its banks; but in the Homeric original, the flood is said to have been caused by 'Zeus's rain', whereas the only agents in Lucretius' version are the rain itself and *mollis aquae . . . natura*, 'the yielding substance of water'. The periphrasis *aquae natura* (more literally, 'the *nature* of water') seems particularly pointed in this context: not only is Zeus scrupulously excluded by the Epicurean poet, but he is in a sense replaced by Lucretius' own metaphorical 'deity', Nature. An implicit critique of Ennius and the themes of his *Annales* can be found in the triumphant lines that open the finale to Book 3: 'death', proclaims the poet, 'is nothing to us, since nothing will be able to affect us when we are no more' – any more than the world-shaking conflict of the Punic Wars could have an impact on those not yet born (3.830–42). The lines in which the cataclysmic effects of the war are evoked (834–5: *omnia cum belli trepido concussa tumultu | horrida contremuere sub altis aetheris auris*, 'when everything was shaken by the fearsome tumult of war, and trembled, shuddering, beneath the breezes of high heaven') draw on Ennius (fr. 309 Skutsch: *Africa terribili tremit horrida terra tumultu*, 'the land of Africa, shuddering, trembled with fearsome tumult'), implicitly making a metapoetic as well as a philosophical point: the historical subject matter of Ennius is ultimately of little importance, unlike that of Lucretius himself, which is – quite literally – a matter of life and death for every reader (3.1071–5).[10] Empedocles, finally, is implicitly corrected at least twice in the proem to Book 1, which draws extensively on the Presocratic philosopher-poet's *On Nature*.[11] The dualistic conception hinted at in the tableau of Mars in Venus' lap at 1.31–40 can be seen as a nod towards the alternating dominance of *Philotes* and *Neikos* (Love and Strife) over the universe in Empedocles' system – but, lest the reader should take the picture too literally, we are immediately told that *one and the same* nature (*natura . . . | . . . eadem . . . natura*, 56–7) combines the atoms to form the objects of the world around us, and dissolves those objects back into their constituent particles again. There are no separate forces of creation and destruction, attraction and repulsion: simply atoms, aggregating and disaggregating in space, in accordance with one natural law.[12] Similarly, the

---

[9] For further examples and discussion see Aicher 1992; Gale 1994a: 59–62, 106–14; Gale 2000: 235–8.

[10] Cf. 1.471–82, with Gale 1994a: 109–10.   [11] Furley 1970; Sedley 1998: 1–34.

[12] For Nature as *both* creator and destroyer, see also 2.1116–17 *donec ad extremum crescendi perfica finem | omnia perduxit rerum natura creatrix*, 'until Nature the creator which brings things to completion has brought them all to the furthest limit of their growth'. It may not be coincidental that these lines too come not long after a passage with strong Empedoclean

sardonic treatment of metempsychosis in 1.112–26 can be read as a sideswipe directed not just at Ennius but also at Empedocles, whose horrifying lines on animal sacrifice, in which a father unknowingly slays the animal in which the soul of his own dead son is now embodied (fr. 137 DK), form part of the complex of intertexts evoked in Lucretius' account of the sacrifice of Iphianassa (Iphigenia) at 1.80–101.

Empedocles, then, is treated by Lucretius not just as an important philosophical predecessor (and rival) but also as a representative of the didactic tradition, and the *DRN* is very much aware of its dual heritage from the Homeric and Hesiodic traditions of hexameter poetry. Intertextual engagement on both fronts is suggested not only by direct echoes of Hesiod's didactic poem on farming, the *Works and Days*, alongside the Homeric and Ennian allusions discussed above, but also – more pervasively – by patterns of imagery employed extensively throughout the poem. A particularly striking passage which lends itself to metapoetic reading along these lines is the illustrative ecphrasis at 2.317–32 of military manoeuvres and grazing sheep, both of which appear, when viewed from a distance, as stationary patches of light and colour. The two scenes are explicitly introduced as analogies for atomic motion within a composite body which appears stationary at the macroscopic level; the 'distant view' motif embodied in the lines has also been persuasively interpreted as a symbol of philosophical detachment, like that more explicitly constructed in the proem to the book.[13] Arguably, a third layer of meaning can also be found here: the contrasting scenes could be seen as emblems of military and pastoral life, or perhaps heroic and georgic *poetry*.[14] On this reading, the metapoetic implications of the lines would be very similar to those of the Ennian allusion in the finale to Book 3 discussed above: the Epicurean poet 'detaches' himself metaphorically from the worlds of Homer and Hesiod, just as the 'distant viewer' detaches himself physically from the troop movements and grazing animals which are the objects of his gaze.

Animal husbandry is somewhat marginal to the world of the *Works and Days (Op.)*: more central is the cultivation of crops, especially of vines and cereals. Images derived from plant growth are correspondingly frequent in the *DRN*, complementing the still more pervasive metaphors from warfare

---

resonances, 2.1081–3, which recalls fr. a (ii) 26–8 in the new Strasburg papyrus, as well as frs 20.6–7 and 21.10–12 DK.

[13] De Lacy 1964.

[14] For sheep in the *Works and Days* see 120, 234, 308, 516–18 and 795. Metapoetic interpretation of the Lucretian lines may be regarded as more plausible in the light of the Homeric echo in 325–7 (cf. *Il.* 19.362–3).

and navigation which serve to establish a connection with the heroic epic tradition.[15] If the atoms are engaged – like the warriors of the *Iliad* – in the perpetual struggles of a never-ending war (*uelut aeterno certamine proelia pugnas | edere*, 2.118–19), they are also 'seeds' (*semina*) from which the objects of the visible world 'grow'. Agricultural language of this kind is particularly prominent in the opening argument of Book 1, at 159–214, but it recurs at intervals throughout the poem. The sun 'sows' light on the earth or 'irrigates' the world with its radiance; the world itself 'grows' and 'ages' like a living thing; the multiplicity of atomic shapes and combinations is exemplified by the earth's capacity to bring all kinds of plants to birth and provide food for animals and humans; and so forth.[16] Of course, Lucretius repeatedly insists that all of this takes place 'without the help of the gods' (*opera sine diuom*, 1.158), and it is striking that explicit arguments to this effect appear rather frequently in conjunction with agricultural imagery. The phrase just quoted introduces the argument that 'nothing can come into existence out of nothing', with its intensive use of the seed metaphor; similarly, the Magna Mater digression, with its emphatic rejection of the idea that the earth is divine (2.600–60), arises out of the evocation of agricultural productivity at 2.589–99. This is a recurrent theme in Book 2 particularly: at the beginning and end of the book, Lucretius condemns the attribution of both agricultural success (2.167–83) and agricultural failure (2.1164–74) to the intervention of the gods in human affairs. The theme is resumed in Book 5, where the difficulties faced by the farmer are used as an argument *against* divine providence and teleology (5.195–234); and the 'invention' of agriculture is pointedly attributed to *natura creatrix*, with a punning allusion to the tradition that grain was the gift of Ceres/Demeter (5.1361–2).[17] This whole complex of ideas can be understood in part as a reaction to and refutation of Hesiod's insistence on the importance of ritual piety, in conjunction with the demand for hard and timely labour repeatedly enjoined

[15] Warfare: e.g. 1.62–79; 2.118–20; 2.569–76; 5.380–3; 6.96–101; navigation: e.g. 2.551–64; 5.10–12; 5.222–3; both together at 2.1–6. For further examples and discussion see Murley 1947; Hardie 1986: 193–219; Gale 1994a: 117–21.

[16] Sunlight: 2.211; 4.200–3; 5.281–3; 5.592–603 (for other planting and irrigation metaphors, see also 4.1107; 4.1272–3; 5.1290; 2.262); growth and ageing of the world: 2.1105–74; 5.821–36; earth's productive capacity: 2.594–9, 661–8 (and cf. 1.250–64, 803–22). On agricultural and biological metaphors in Lucretius see further Schrijvers 1978; Sedley 1997b: 46–51.

[17] The name Ceres is similarly derived from the verb *creare* ('create') by the ancient commentator Servius (on *Georgics* 1.7); for the extensive system of word-plays on the syllables –*cer*– and –*cre*– in the *DRN* see Snyder 1980: 136–42.

on his addressee, Perses. For Hesiod, agricultural success is, quite explicitly, a reward bestowed by the gods; famine and plague, conversely, are punishments inflicted by Zeus on the unjust city (*Op.* 225–47; cf. 298–301). Prayer and sacrifice will ensure a good harvest (335–41, 465–9), and grain 'belongs' to Demeter (e.g. 32, 597). This is precisely the view of the world attacked in *DRN* 2.

More specific allusions to the opening section of the *Works and Days* can be found in *DRN* 1, 5 and 6. The first part of Hesiod's poem consists of a series of mythological explanations for the nature of the world as it now is, and more particularly for the inescapable necessity of (agricultural) labour. Work and the hardship of the world in general are represented first as punishments inflicted by Zeus for Prometheus' theft of fire (42–105); then as part of a process of historical degeneration embodied in the Myth of Ages (106–201); and finally as punishments inflicted on the unjust through the agency of Zeus's daughter Dike (Justice; 213–64). Each of these myths is systematically refuted by Lucretius, in such a way that the passages in question, when taken together, can be read as a kind of 'anti-Hesiod'.

There is programmatic significance in the fact that this anti-Hesiodic theme makes its first appearance early in the poem, at the end of the first sequence of proofs. Lines 1.208–14 are marked off as a kind of footnote, following the 'conclusion' of 205–7. Like Hesiod, Lucretius seeks to explain the need for agricultural labour: the fantasy of a life without work, introduced here as an *adynaton*, is particularly reminiscent of the corresponding section of the *Works and Days* (*nostro sine quaeque labore*, 213, echoes Hesiod's *aergon eonta*, 'without working', *Op.* 44). But the Hesiodic model is subjected to a pointed rationalisation: ploughing and cultivation are necessary for the growth of crops not because Zeus has so decreed it, but because particles needed for nutrition are scattered through the soil (210–12). The Prometheus and Pandora story and the Myth of Ages are similarly rationalised in Books 5 and 6. The agency by which fire was 'brought down to mortals' was a bolt of lightning (*fulmen detulit in terram mortalibus ignem*, 5.1092), not Prometheus; the evils that 'fly' or 'wander' around the world are due either to nature (6.29–31; cf. 5.218–21), or to our own inability to limit our fears and desires (the soul is like a leaky jar, 6.17–23, recalling the jar of Pandora from which 'countless evils' fly out to wander amongst mortals in *Op.* 100–1); and there was never a magical Golden Age of peace and plenty – rather, the earliest human beings endured a primitive, bestial existence, without agricultural labour, but also without even the most basic comforts or any kind of communal life (5.925–1010). The subsequent metallic 'generations' are rationalised in Lucretius' account of the discovery of metals, in which the use of gold and silver gives way to that of bronze and finally iron (5.1269–96).[18]

An allusion, finally, to the 'ten thousand mist-clad spirits', which according to Hesiod roam the earth and act as the unseen guardians of Justice (*Op.* 253–5), can be detected in the memorable personification of fear and anxiety as insolent beings wandering boldly amidst the pomp and splendour of military and political power (*DRN* 2.48–52). Again, the message of the *Works and Days* is inverted: it is not Zeus but our needless fear of the gods and of death that inflicts suffering upon us; and not justice but *ratio* that will avert such sufferings (*DRN* 2.53).

Other genres in the *DRN*

To this point I have traced a pattern of engagement with works in the same genre as the *DRN* (Hesiod and Empedocles), or in the closely related (sub)genre of heroic epic (Homer, Ennius). In the genre-conscious world of late Republican literature, such poetic one-upmanship is less than surprising. But we also find Lucretius – more intermittently and opportunistically – evoking other literary genres, usually in such a way as to strike polemically at their underlying assumptions. Tragic intertexts, for example, are invoked in a number of places, most obviously the Sacrifice of Iphigenia episode (1.80–101), which recalls Aeschylus (and possibly Ennius)[19] as well as Empedocles. Lucretius cuts through the complex problems of overdetermination, divine causation and moral agency which are so central to Aeschylus' play: for him, there is only one culprit, *religio*, denounced in the epigrammatic concluding line *tantum religio potuit suadere malorum* ('such evils could religion incite', 1.101). Similarly, the memorable image of the 'sacred marriage' of Earth and Sky at 1.250–61 and 2.991–1001 recalls passages of Aeschylean and Euripidean tragedy;[20] as Fowler puts it, Lucretius is 'perverting to [his] own ends passages with an intrinsically religious point'.[21] These ends include demonstration of the fact that earth and sky are neither immortal nor divine (2.646–54; 5.91–415). Once again, polemical correction is inherent in Lucretius' evocation of tragic, as of epic, intertexts.

Other genres implicitly present at various points in the text include pastoral, lyric and (especially) epigram. The pastoral *locus amoenus* is

---

[18] See Gale 1994a: 164–78, 189–90.

[19] Aesch. *Ag.* 224–47; for possible Ennian echoes see S. J. Harrison 2002.

[20] Aesch. *Danaids* fr. 44 Radt; Eur. *Chrysippus* fr. 839 Nauck. A Latin paraphrase of the *Chrysippus* fragment, from Pacuvius' *Chryses* (fr. 86–92 Ribbeck²), also survives.

[21] D. P. Fowler 2000: 144.

appropriated as the setting for the 'Epicurean picnic' at 2.29–33 and its primitive forerunner at 5.1392–6. But while the simple pleasures of the *agrestis
musa* ('rustic muse', 1398) have a certain appeal for the Epicurean, Lucretius
is dismissive of pastoral's more fanciful aspects, in particular the supernatural
cast of nymphs and satyrs ridiculed at 4.580–94. Notable here is the personification of echoes as *uerba . . . docta*[22] *referri* ('words that have learned
to be echoed back', 579); can we detect a hint of mockery directed at the
hypersophisticated *doctrina* (learning, refinement) of Hellenistic pastoral, in
contrast to the simplicity of the true *agrestis musa*? The 'pastoral' passages
in Books 4 and 5 are linked by verbal echo (4.585 = 5.1385), and the later
passage explicitly makes the point that more sophisticated art is not necessarily a source of greater pleasure (5.1408–11). Sapphic lyric is subjected
to similarly cavalier treatment at 3.152–8, where Lucretius quotes Sappho's
celebrated evocation of the symptoms of love or sexual jealousy (fr. 31), in
as close and arguably as elegant a translation as that of Catullus (poem 51).
This version, however, is directed to the unromantic end of illustrating the
physiological effects of fear.

Epigrammatic *topoi* have a more extensive part to play in the *DRN*, particularly in the finales to Books 3 and 4. We have already seen how Lucretius
appropriates epigrammatic language in his praise of Epicurus: the rising
sun simile of 3.1043–4 is borrowed from Leonidas' epigram on Homer, and
Lucretius plays a similar trick at 4.180–2 (= 909–11), where the swan/cranes
comparison translates the closing couplet of Antipater of Sidon's epigram on
Erinna (*Anth. Pal.* 7.713.7–8). More satirical[23] are the hints of epigrammatic
language in 3.894–930 and the finale to Book 4. The fragments of imaginary laments quoted at 3.894–9 and 904–8 have parallels in both literary
and inscribed epitaphs; even more striking is the maudlin sentiment of 914–
15, which – in combination with the convivial setting sketched in 912–13 –
strongly recalls a perennial theme of sympotic lyric, elegy and epigram.[24]
Lucretius, of course, pours scorn on all these sentimental clichés: to mourn
the shortness of life or the curtailment of life's pleasures is for him foolish
and irrational. The *topoi* of erotic epigram – as well as New Comedy – come
in for similar ridicule, as Kenney has comprehensively demonstrated,[25] in
the finale to Book 4, where the language of love (Cupid's dart, the nets of
Venus, the fires of passion, love as a madness) is brutally deromanticised. The

---

[22] Lachmann's conjecture, for the MS *dicta*.

[23] On Lucretius and satire see Dudley 1965b, esp. 122–5 for possible echoes of Lucilius in the
finale to *DRN* 4.

[24] Cf., e.g., Theognis 973–8, 1007–12; *Anth. Pal.* 11.19 (Strato), 12.50 (Asclepiades). For the
'never again' and 'everlasting grief' *topoi*, see Lattimore 1962: 172–7, 243–6.

[25] Kenney 1970.

idea that the lover is wounded by the beloved, for example, is transformed in 1045–72 from a pretty conceit into a vividly concrete analogy for physiological processes (the man's semen is analogous to the blood which leaps from a wound and stains the enemy, 1049–51; the wound, if not treated, will fester and suppurate, 1068–72). The attack on romantic love culminates in a sketch of the lover locked out of his mistress's house – the *exclusus amator*, 1177 – straight out of Roman comedy.[26] The absurd – if not unsympathetic – Plautine *adulescens* is reworked as a wholly negative *exemplum*: his plight is not only ridiculous, but easily avoided (1188–91).

Here the controversial issue of Lucretius' relationship with his contemporary Catullus presents itself. The question is complicated by our uncertainty as to the dates of either writer:[27] datable references in Catullus' poems all fall within the years 57–55 BC, which would put their composition at around the same time as the conventional date for the publication of the *DRN*. It is also possible that the two men may have been closely enough acquainted to have seen or heard each other's work prior to publication (in any case a notoriously slippery concept in the ancient world). Intertextual links can, certainly, be identified, though it is impossible to be quite sure which text is the 'original' in any particular instance.

In the case of the finale to Book 4, it seems hard to resist the view that the cycle of idealisation, obsession, jealousy and disillusion sketched by Lucretius in 1121–92 satirises the relationship depicted in Catullus' Lesbia poems (though Catullus might equally be appropriating a negative stereotype *from* Lucretius or Lucretius' models, as he does in the case of the comic lover in poem 8).[28] Certainly the parallels are striking: like Catullus in the final stanza of poem 51, the Lucretian lover feels pangs of conscience for idling his life away (1135–6); like Catullus in poems 41, 43 or 86 he mocks other men's ugly girlfriends, while denying that his own has any imperfections (1157–9); he is tortured by jealousy (1137–40; cf., e.g., Catullus 8.15–18); he endows his mistress with superhuman qualities (1183–4; cf. Lesbia as 'shining goddess' in Catullus 68.70).

There are strong Lucretian parallels, too, in Catullus 64, though here it must be conceded that the *DRN* should probably be regarded as the source text (given that the common phrases occur in various parts of the latter poem, but are concentrated in a single locus – the Ariadne episode – within

---

[26] For pre-Lucretian examples (notably Plautus, *Curc.* 1–157) see Copley 1956: 1–42.

[27] For the date of the *DRN* see most recently G. Hutchinson 2001; for datable references in Catullus see, e.g., Quinn 1973: xiii–xiv.

[28] For the impact on later poets of Lucretius' satirical handling of (Catullan) *amor* see p. 120 n. 32 below.

Catullus' poem).²⁹ Particularly worthy of note from our point of view are the quite striking similarities between Catullus' description of the *thiasus* of Bacchus at 64.251–64 and Lucretius' lines on the procession of the Magna Mater at 2.618–23.³⁰ Both poets describe scenes of disturbing, even terrifying, supernatural power, though to rather different ends: for Catullus, Bacchus and his followers appear to embody the real and frighteningly uncontrollable force of irrational passion, whereas for Lucretius, the fear inspired by Cybele is explicitly false, and belief in the goddess' power is an unnecessary source of suffering and anxiety self-inflicted through ignorance of the true causes of natural and social phenomena. Whichever poet wrote first, a degree of antagonism between the values and world-views represented in their poems is evident.

Deconstructing generic hierarchies: *ars* and *ingenium*

The range of literary genres evoked at different points in the *DRN* is striking and invites us to view the poem as a kind of compendium of earlier literature.³¹ Homer was sometimes regarded in the ancient world as the source of all the literary genres; Lucretius, conversely, represents himself as subsuming and – in a sense – transcending them all. As we have seen, there is a marked tendency in the *DRN* towards a highly *critical* engagement with earlier literature: the poet hints repeatedly that the themes of his poetic ancestors – even those writing in the supposedly superior genres of epic, didactic and tragedy – are, in the last analysis, nugatory. From this determinedly Epicurean perspective, the traditional hierarchy of genres (an issue of intense concern to contemporary writers) becomes meaningless, and we can accordingly detect a tendency to collapse conventional oppositions between 'high' and 'low' styles of poetry. Notable in this connection is the programmatic passage 1.925–30, with its metaphors of untrodden path,³² untouched spring and garland of fresh flowers – all evocative of the much-imitated proem to

---

²⁹ For full lists of parallels see Bailey 1947: III, 1753–4; Giesecke 2000: 181–2.

³⁰ In addition to verbal echoes, *tympana . . . palmis*, Cat. 64.261 and *DRN* 2.618; *raucisono(s) . . . cornua . . . cantu*, Cat. 64.263–4, *DRN* 2.619, there is very pronounced alliteration on t, c and p in both passages.

³¹ This aspect of the poem can be related to Lucretius' presentation of his work as a *simulacrum* of the universe (see pp. 90–1, 126–7 below): if the *DRN* contains everything that there is, it must *a fortiori* encompass all literary kinds.

³² As Kenney 1970 and Knox 1999 point out, the path image is not exclusively Callimachean; the *combination* of path and spring in this programmatic context, however, along with the reference a few lines later to the rejection of Epicurean philosophy by the *uulgus*, makes it hard not to think of Callimachus. See also R. D. Brown 1982.

Callimachus' *Aetia*. This apparent declaration of allegiance to Callimachean ideals of innovativeness, refined artistry and abstruse learning sits oddly with the language of the preceding lines, 922–6:

> acri
> percussit thyrso laudis spes magna meum cor
> et simul incussit suauem mi in pectus amorem
> musarum, quo nunc instinctus mente uigenti
> auia Pieridum peragro loca

A powerful hope for praise has struck my heart with its piercing *thyrsus* and thrust sweet love of the Muses into my breast; goaded by it I wander ecstatically through trackless places of the Muses

The lines are problematic in themselves, both because of the (apparently un-Epicurean) desire for fame expressed in 923, and because the metaphors of Dionysiac possession seem so out of place in an Epicurean poem. Epicurus, quite to the contrary, suggests in his *Letter to Menoeceus* (132) that the disciple seeking after true pleasure needs to employ 'sober reasoning' in determining how best to live his or her life.

The clash between Epicurean sobriety and Dionysiac inspiration in Lucretius' programme can be linked to a related opposition between water and wine as symbols of inspiration in late Republican and Augustan poetry. The antithesis perhaps goes back to Callimachus himself,[33] though our earliest explicit reference is an epigram (*Anth. Pal.* 11.20) by Antipater of Thessalonica. Antipater rejects the precious, pedantic style of the 'thorn-gathering' poets who 'drink plain water from a holy spring', in favour of libations of unmixed wine poured in honour of Archilochus and 'manly Homer'. These 'thorn-gathering' poets, with their love of obscure glosses, are clearly practitioners of Callimachean *doctrina*.[34] Among Roman poets (especially the Augustans), references to Bacchus and Dionysiac inspiration are frequently associated with reflection on different poetic styles and hierarchical distinctions of genre. In the opening lines of *Epistles* 1.19, for example, Horace explicitly connects wine-drinking with Homer and Ennius, and elsewhere calls on Bacchus in self-consciously elevated contexts.[35] Closer to the date of the *DRN* is Catullus' apparently programmatic call for *calices amariores* ('more pungent cups', representing vigorous Archilochean invective?) and

---

[33] Cameron (1995: 364–7) and Asper (1997: 128–34) argue that the metaphor was not used by Callimachus himself; but cf. Gutzwiller 1998: 213; Fantuzzi and Hunter 2004: 448–9.

[34] See also *Anth. Pal.* 9.305, with Fantuzzi and Hunter 2004: 448–9.

[35] Esp. *Odes* 2.19 and 3.25; cf. Propertius 3.17.39–40 and 4.1.59–64.

dismissal of water (i.e. the 'milder' tone of Callimachean iambus?) in poem 27.[36]

By the first century BC at the latest, then, an opposition has developed between water-drinking and wine-drinking/Dionysiac inspiration, as symbols for, respectively, Alexandrian artistry and *doctrina*, and inspired, elevated, or robust, 'virile' poetry (especially epic and Archilochean iambic). To oversimplify only a little, we might equate the opposition with the familiar contrast between *ars* (artistry) and *ingenium* (inspiration). What is striking about Lucretius' deployment of the two terms is how he collapses any opposition between them. This is not just to suggest a kind of compromise or rapprochement between *ingenium* and *ars*, as Horace for example does in various ways in the *Odes* and *Epistles*, but to deny the distinction between learned and inspired poetry altogether. For Lucretius, the one actually *leads to* the other: the poet's wanderings in the 'trackless places of the Muses' are the result of his inspiration by the *thyrsus* wielded by 'the hope of praise'.[37] Lucretius, that is, lays claim *both* to the inspiration of the wine-drinkers, *and* to the artistry of the water-drinkers: the latter is represented as the effect of the former.

This somewhat startling and paradoxical claim is developed further in what follows. Lucretius goes on to explain that the pleasure he takes in composing poetry results from its utility: his poem aims to free the reader's mind from the 'tight bonds of religion', and to brighten its obscure subject matter with the 'sweet honey of the Muses'. This in turn is 'not without reason'; for as doctors induce their childish patients to take bitter medicine by coating the cup with honey, so the Muses' honey will help the reader to swallow the figurative medicine of Epicurean truth. A second, related opposition which was the focus of much debate in first-century poetry and literary theory comes to mind here, namely the opposition between utility and pleasure, or the *utile* and the *dulce* in Horace's terminology.[38] Here again, whereas Horace famously recommends a combination or mingling of the two ingredients, Lucretius can be seen to collapse the distinction altogether. The logic of his argument repays careful scrutiny (though it must be said that the poet himself does not make all the connections absolutely clear).

---

[36] For this interpretation of Catullus 27 see esp. Wray 2001: 169–76.

[37] The transition is facilitated by Lucretius' substitution of metaphors of Dionysiac *possession* for the sympotic language of the epigrammatists; cf. Horace, *Odes* 3.25, and see pp. 120–1 below.

[38] *Ars P.* 333–46; cf. 408–11 on *ars* and *ingenium*.

As already noted, lines 931–4 suggest that the pleasure derived by the poet from the composition of his poetry results from its beneficial effect on the reader; but the beneficial effect is shown in turn to rely on the pleasure the *reader* will derive from the work's poetic form. Poetry is pleasurable (for the poet) because it is beneficial (to the reader), and beneficial to the reader because the pleasure he or she experiences in the process of reading enables the salubrious philosophical content to take its effect. An important, if slightly obscure, connection is suggested by the phrase *id quoque enim non ab nulla ratione uidetur* ('for this too seems not unreasonable') in 935. The reference of *id* has been disputed, but it seems easiest to take it as referring back to the two previous lines generally: that is, there is a reason, in the sense of a rational, Epicurean explanation, for the course of action Lucretius follows in 'composing bright verse' and 'touching everything with the honey of the Muses'. This explanation must lie in the importance of pleasure as the ultimate goal of life for the Epicurean: Lucretius exploits our (instinctive) pursuit of sensual pleasure as a means to induce us to accept the ultimate pleasure of *ataraxia*, which will, ideally, be created in the reader by the poem's philosophical content.[39] To put it another way, utility and pleasure are *bound* to be the same thing for an Epicurean, for whom pleasure is the Good. Of course, as Epicurus himself emphasises, not all pleasures are 'choiceworthy': sensual enjoyment which brings greater pain in its wake is to be rejected, and moreover pleasure cannot be increased beyond the limit constituted by the complete removal of physical and mental pain. Here are two reasons why the Epicurean might find the aesthetic pleasure of poetry suspect: the value of pleasurable form may be negated by detrimental content; and aesthetic pleasure in itself might be thought to have relatively little value in that it does not satisfy any real need in the reader, or contribute to the attainment of *ataraxia* and *aponia*. This is in fact the line that Lucretius' contemporary Philodemus takes in *On Poems*: while accepting that poetry can give pleasure, he firmly denies that it can have any utility *qua* poetry.[40] If it happens to be beneficial to the reader, that must be entirely the result of its content, and the same effect could presumably be achieved just as well if not better by employing prose-form.

Lucretius appears, as I have suggested, to adopt a much more radical position. Though he hints elsewhere in the poem that the value of poetry is often vitiated by ethically dubious content, the implication of the present

---

39 Cf. 2.171–4, where pleasure and persuasion are explicitly linked.
40 Most explicitly in *Poem.* 5 col. IV Mangoni. On Philodemus' poetic theory see Janko 2000, esp. 8–9.

passage is that form and content *can* work together in such a way that poetry itself becomes wholly beneficial. The honey on the cup has a different function from the medicine inside, but both work together to ensure that the child gets better. Lucretius' poetry, similarly – and not merely its Epicurean content, but the form too – should actually aid the achievement of *ataraxia* in the very process of giving the reader immediate sensual gratification. Pleasure and utility are thus equated in an absolutely fundamental and extremely striking way.

Lucretius' exploitation of Callimachean language, then, need not amount to a declaration of allegiance to the Alexandrian poet's creed: rather, Lucretius implies that his own poem transcends the very distinction between Callimachean and anti-Callimachean poetics suggested by the conflicting images of Dionysiac inspiration and the draught of pure water from an unsullied spring. The *DRN*, with a wonderfully hubristic self-assertiveness, represents itself as the culmination not just of *one* poetic tradition but of *all* poetic traditions: the Epicurean epic, with its cosmic conflicts between battling atoms, is the ultimate successor to the 'kings and battles' of Homer and Ennius; but at the same time, Lucretius' celebration of the humble and mundane, as well as the emphasis he lays on aesthetic pleasure and careful, artistic polish seem indeed to give some grounds for his implicit claim to at least a partial adherence to Callimachean canons of style. Again, by collapsing the opposition between utility and pleasure, Lucretius can blithely dismiss the problem of the poet's role in society which so exercised Virgil, Horace and the elegists: simply by giving the reader pleasure (of the right kind), Lucretius can claim that he *is*, in Epicurean terms, contributing to the moral health both of the individual and of society as a whole.[41]

Lucretius' archaising style and his apparent neglect of developments in philosophy postdating Epicurus have sometimes led scholars to suppose that he wrote in a kind of literary and philosophical vacuum. This chapter has suggested that, on the contrary, the *DRN* is deeply engaged in contemporary debate about the proper function of poetry and the relation between style and content and is intensely aware of its place in not one but a number of poetic traditions. Artistic one-upmanship and philosophical polemic effectively coincide: through heavily qualified acknowledgement of a broad range of literary forebears, the *DRN* is able to present itself as at once critique and culmination of the Graeco-Roman literary canon.

---

[41] For the idea that social conflicts are caused ultimately by false values and failures of understanding on the part of the individual, see especially the proem to Book 3.

Further reading

On Lucretius' place in the didactic tradition, see most recently Dalzell 1996 and Volk 2002. On Lucretius and epic, see Murley 1947; West 1969: 23–34; Hardie 1986: 193–219; Mayer 1990; Gale 1994a: 117–21; and Gale 2000: 232–40. Lucretius' use of imagery has been much discussed: see especially West 1969 and 1970; Hardie 1986: 219–23; Dalzell 1996: 60–8; and Schindler 2000: 72–140. There is a good treatment of repetition as a didactic tool in Clay 1983: 176–85; cf. also Ingalls 1971 and Schiesaro 1994: 98–100. On Lucretius and Empedocles, see Furley 1970; Gale 1994a: 59–75; Sedley 1998; Campbell 2003, esp. 2–4, 101–9; Garani 2007. Lucretius' relationship with Hesiod has been surprisingly neglected: on his reworking of the Myth of Ages, see (not altogether convincingly) Beye 1963; also Gale 1994a: 164–74, 177–8 for fuller treatment of points made above, and Arrighetti 1997: 30–2. On Lucretius and tragedy, see Schiesaro 1990:111–22; S. J. Harrison 1990; D. P. Fowler 2000. Kenney 1970 includes a good discussion of Lucretius' relationship with Callimachus and Callimachean poetics, as well as the use of epigrammatic *topoi* in the finale to Book 4; on the former see also R. D. Brown 1982, on the latter R. D. Brown 1987: 132–5. For echoes of comic *topoi* in 4.1123–40 see Rosivach 1980. The problem of the relative priority of Lucretius and Catullus is addressed by Hermann 1956 and Giesecke 2000: 10–30 (with particular focus on poem 64); see also the good discussion of the relationship between the finale to Book 4 and Catullus' Lesbia poems in R. D. Brown 1987: 139–43. On wine-drinkers and water-drinkers see esp. Crowther 1979 and Gutzwiller 1998: 157–69.

5

JOSEPH FARRELL

Lucretian architecture: the structure and argument of the *De rerum natura*

Introduction

From the arrangement of individual phrases to the grand structure of the entire poem, Lucretius uses poetic form with economy and imagination to attract the reader's attention and to drive home his philosophical message. In their main lines, the structure and content of the poem's argument derive from earlier Epicurean and other philosophical models, and Lucretius' debts to some of his predecessors are quite detailed. But his handling of this material is distinctive, and his greatest originality lies in the reshaping of a philosophical exposition adapted from previous writers to produce a poem whose form instantiates the main points of its argument at every level and is aesthetically satisfying as well.

The order of argument and the question of Lucretius' source

A long-standing question is: to what extent was Lucretius an original thinker as opposed to a versifier of received wisdom?[1] For the purposes of this chapter, that question reduces to a related one: to what extent is the structure of the *DRN* Lucretius' own design as opposed to something borrowed from a previous work? The first scholars to address this issue simply assumed that Lucretius closely followed some particular source.[2] At length scholars started to leave this question aside, and the assumption that Lucretius worked without a single primary model in mind gained some appeal.[3] More recently, the Herculaneum papyri have provided enough evidence to reopen the question.[4] As of this writing, it is impossible to settle the matter. If the point is to understand the structure of Lucretius' poem, however, certain conclusions can be drawn.

[1] See ch. 1 above.   [2] The debate is summarised by Bailey 1947: 22–32.
[3] Clay 1983.   [4] Sedley 1998; see ch. 2 above.

It is likely that Lucretius borrowed the general structure of the *DRN* directly from the writings of Epicurus himself. Most nineteenth-century scholars identified the immediate model as Epicurus' *Letter to Herodotus*. Virtually every topic covered in the letter finds a place in the *DRN*. Conversely, Lucretius' treatment of these topics accounts for almost one-third of his poem – a substantial fraction. Within this fraction, the majority of topics (almost three-quarters) occur in the same order in both the letter and in the *DRN*. If we compare these totals with those found in other situations where we can measure a Latin poem's dependence on a surviving model, we find them comparable and, in fact, impressive. Nevertheless, Carlo Giussani set the tone for subsequent discussion by emphasising the differences between the two works and arguing that Epicurus' letter could not be Lucretius' model.[5] His goal was evidently not merely to identify a treatise that the *DRN* follows even more closely than it does the *Letter to Herodotus*; ideally the poet would have almost no role in determining the order of his argument but would merely have versified some treatise, following its sequence of topics and arguments as slavishly as possible.[6]

It is no wonder that this effort met with frustration. Of course it is possible that Lucretius simply translated and versified some now lost treatise; but if he did, he would have been behaving most unusually for a Latin poet. It makes better sense to assume that Lucretius started with a text that contained an argument of substantially the same form as we find in the *DRN*, but that he exercised freedom in reordering the sequence of topics, eliminating some of them and adding material from other sources. So, if we may relate to Lucretius what we have learned by studying other poets' handling of their models, the *Letter to Herodotus* could well be the principal model of the *DRN*.

That said, it would make sense if the letter itself – which is more a compendium than a definitive exposition – proved to borrow its own structure from the more authoritative treatise *On Nature*. Indeed, David Sedley remarks that the letter 'is almost certainly presenting itself as an epitome of *On Nature*'.[7] Since portions of *On Nature* have been found among the Herculaneum papyri, the possibility exists that new evidence will confirm Sedley's argument.[8] Among those portions that have been found,

---

5 Giussani 1896: 1–11.

6 Trenchant criticism of this attitude by Clay 1983: 13–53, especially 21–6.

7 Sedley 1998: 109.   8 See chs. 1 and 2 above.

however, the most explicit evidence proves that, if *On Nature* was Lucretius' immediate model, he reordered sections of it in fashioning the *DRN* just as dramatically as he would have done had the *Letter to Herodotus* been his actual model.[9] In the current state of our knowledge, then, since the structure of *On Nature* must in large part be inferred from that of the *Letter to Herodotus*, there is no point in arguing about which of these might have been Lucretius' immediate model; still less in the case of the *Great Epitome*, which must be presumed to have followed *On Nature* (the work that it was epitomising!) very closely indeed, but which is itself, in any case, utterly lost.[10]

The main point is that Lucretius' order of argument is anticipated in broad outline in Epicurus' own writings.[11] Whether Lucretius borrowed his argument directly from Epicurus, or copied the work of some lost intermediary or worked independently from first principles, he clearly fashioned an argument that is similar in broad outline to one that Epicurus and perhaps other Epicureans had produced.

Shaping the argument

If we pass from the murky issue of sources to the architecture of the poem that we have, we find substantially more agreement.[12] While each separate book possesses its own unity and integrity, the poem as a whole may be regarded as falling simultaneously into three pairs of books and into two halves consisting of three books each.[13] The general scheme is represented by the following chart:

[9] The most definite indication of such revision is Sedley's argument (1998: 123–6, 145–6) that Lucretius transferred his critique of the Presocratic philosophers from a late position in his source to an early position in his own poem.

[10] That the *Great Epitome* was Lucretius' model was Giussani's suggestion. We know of this text's existence only because it is mentioned three times in the scholia on the letter to Herodotus: see Bailey 1947: 24–5; Sedley 1998: 138.

[11] In places the order of Lucretius' argument pre-dates even Epicurus: see Sedley 1998: 166–85 and *passim*.

[12] I assume, with most scholars, that the text that we have is substantially complete and freer from disturbance than was formerly thought. Some have argued that the poem contains traces of a substantial change of plan undertaken in the course of its composition: see Townend 1979.

[13] The general scheme represented here is endorsed by Bailey 1947: 31–7; Boyancé 1963: 69–83; Minadeo 1965; Owen 1968–9; Kenney 1971: 12; Kenney 1977: 18–23; Sedley 1998: 144–5; Gale 1994b: 8.

Book	Topic	Organisation by thirds	Organisation by halves
1	elements	} atoms and void	} basic principles of atomic theory
2	compounds		
3	material soul	} psychology	
4	its affects		} ethical implications of atomic theory
5	the world	} natural history	
6	its wonders		

To understand these groupings of books and divisions of the poem, it will be useful to bear in mind a few principles that inform the structure of the poem at every level, from that of the individual sentence or paragraph to that of the poem as a whole. These principles are unity, sequence, balance, parallelism, and inversion.

Unity

Apart from the individual hexameter line, Lucretius' most clearly defined structural unit is the book-roll. This is an obvious but fundamental point.[14] Nothing about the length, internal articulation, or logical and rhetorical shape of the individual books is arbitrary or unplanned; each is conceived and designed as a unified whole.

Lucretius begins each book with a formal proemium and generally ends with a peroration in which various closural devices are evident. The proemia are brilliant epideictic performances, rhetorically charged, imagistically rich, and often informed by mythology in a way that seems incompatible with the poem's rationalistic tenor. Prominent in most of them (1, 3, 4, 5, 6) are images of birth and creation. Conversely, the majority of books (2, 3, 4, 6) end with images of enervation, death, diminishment or destruction. Book 6 illustrates the effect of this contrast. The proem celebrates Athens as a parent that gave 'fruitful progeny' (*frugiparos fetus*, 1) to mortals and that 'remade life' (*recreauerunt vitam*, 2) when it 'gave birth' (*genuere*, 5) to Epicurus. But the book concludes with the ghastly image of that city in the grip of plague. This contrast endows the book with an organic shape modelled on that of the human lifespan. The pattern is repeated for the poem as a whole, which begins with the 'Hymn to Venus', a celebration of the goddess as

---

[14] Kenney 1977: 18 makes the important point that 'Lucretius' is the earliest surviving Latin poem in which the "book" is handled as an artistic unit and plays an integral part in the literary architecture of the whole.' As such it is an important witness to the reception of Hellenistic aesthetic principles among Roman poets of the first century BC.

the life-force that brings everything to birth, and concludes with, again, the 'Plague of Athens'. These are classic opening and closural devices, tied to the natural rhythms of birth and death; but in the context of this poem, such devices powerfully reinforce one of Lucretius' basic philosophical themes, as we shall see.[15]

The individual books also share general features of internal articulation, but these are quite variable. Five of the six books are provided with a kind of secondary proemium, normally when the book is about three-quarters complete. These new beginnings add energy to the exposition, provide perspective on the lessons imparted so far and introduce the concluding argument of the book. Beyond this, all of the books can be understood as presenting arguments in either two (Books 1, 3, 5, 6) or three (Books 2, 4) major sections, the proportions of which vary. Table 1 outlines the individual books.

Clearly Lucretius relied on no single formula to shape each book. We see this as well in the occasional digressions, such as the famous 'Magna Mater' passage (2.598–643), which Lucretius seems to have deployed at just that point by following his poet's instinct rather than the specific needs of his argument or any abstract principle of poetic architecture.

Sequence

The most basic relationship among the six individual books is their sequence. Lucretius' argument develops in linear fashion from the simplest to the most complex aspects of the physical universe, taking the reader from insensible elements to sensible and, indeed, striking and even terrifying phenomena. Thus Book 1 deals with the axioms of Epicurean physics: that atoms and void are the irreducible elements of the physical world; that nothing is created from nothing; and so on. Book 2 expounds the ways in which atoms combine to produce more complex entities. Book 3 shows that the soul is no exception to the laws laid down in the earlier books, but is also made up of atoms and void. Book 4 goes on to address the passions of the soul. With Book 5 we enter the macrocosm, learning about the formation of our world, how the earth produced all the creatures that inhabit it, including human beings, and how humans came to live in societies and develop advanced civilisations without the help of the gods. Finally, Book 6 deals with unusual phenomena, such as thunder and lightning, earthquakes and plagues, and other seemingly capricious occurrences.

[15] On this topic see especially Minadeo 1969 and Penwill 1996.

Table 1

Book	Section	Passage	No. of lines
1	*Proem*: Hymn to Venus	1–145	145
	1. Atoms and void	146–634	489
	2. Doxography	635–920	286
	Second proem: Poetry and philosophy	921–50	30
	Peroration: Infinity	951–1117	167
2	*Proem*: Citadel of philosophy	1–61	61
	1. Atomic motion	62–332	271
	2. Atomic forms	333–729	397
	3. Atomic qualities	730–990	261
	Second proem: Hieros gamos	991–1022	32
	Peroration: Exhaustion of the earth	1023–1174	152
3	*Proem*: *A life worthy of the gods*	1–93	93
	1. Nature of the soul	94–416	323
	2. Mortality of the soul	417–829	413
	Second proem: Death itself is nothing	830–69	40
	Peroration: Diatribe against fear of death	870–1094	225
4	*Proem*: Poetry and philosophy	1–25	25
	1. Vision	26–215	190
	2. Sensation and thought	216–822	607
	3. Mind and body	823–1057	235
	Second proem: The real 'Venus'	1058–72	15
	Peroration: Love and sex	1073–1287	215
5	*Proem*: Epicurus a culture hero	1–90	90
	1. The earth	91–508	418
	2. Astronomy	509–770	262
	Second proem: Birth of the world	772–82	11
	Peroration: Anthropology	783–1457	676
6	*Proem*: Athens and Epicurus	1–95	95
	1. Meteorology	96–534	439
	2. Geology	535–1089	555
	Peroration: Plagues	1090–1286	197

Closely allied to this linear sequence is the tripartite segmentation of the argument by pairs of books. Thus the first third of the poem (Books 1 and 2) deals with the elements of atomic theory, the middle third (Books 3 and 4) with the nature of the soul, and the final third (Books 5 and 6) with natural history. Within each pair, the earlier, odd-numbered book establishes the relevant fundamental principles: Book 1 that everything consists of atoms and void; Book 3 that the soul is material and mortal; Book 5 that all of nature, including human societies, arose from the atomic interactions previously expounded. The latter, even-numbered books within each pair go on to state important corollaries of these principles, to explore various specific applications of them and to refute objections to them in some detail.[16] Thus Book 2 argues that the entire universe in all its diversity can indeed have been created from the simple, characterless particles discussed in Book 1; Book 4 examines the workings of the material soul described in Book 3; and Book 6 analyses various pathologies that afflict both the natural and the social worlds that were the subject of Book 5. The logical progression from the first to the second book in each pair enhances the general sense of forward movement that we recognised in the overall six-book sequence. Viewed as a whole, the three pairs of books are arranged in ascending tricolon (2291, 2381 and 2743 lines, respectively).[17]

Balance and symmetry

The poem's tripartite structure involves two further aspects which we may call 'balance' and 'symmetry'. These are closely related and serve to create an impression of unity for sections of individual books as well as for groups of books. At the same time, both principles are in creative tension with the forward movement implied by the sequence of books within each pair and across the poem as a whole.

Balance is exemplified within pairs of books: while the linear exposition leads the reader from the odd- to the even-numbered books, each pair stands as a well-rounded unit, of which each book forms half. Again, opening and closural devices come into play: the 'Hymn to Venus' in Book 1, with its powerful emphasis on creativity, ultimately gives way to the idea that the earth is nearing the end of its creative period, the note sounded at the end of Book 2. Books 3 and 4 end with lengthy diatribes against, respectively, the fear of death and sexual indulgence.[18] In this relationship one sees a strong ethical impulse towards *ataraxia* and against excessive terror of annihilation or false attachment to the pleasures of life. The unity and balance of Books 5 and 6 are especially impressive. Book 5 opens with praise of Epicurus as a culture hero. Then, in the relatively weak closure of that book, Lucretius observes that human nature alone, through experience and unaided by the gods, gradually advanced from its primitive state to the height of civilisation. Then the proem to Book 6 resumes the praise of Epicurus that had opened

---

[16] As noted by (e.g.) Gale 1994b: 4; Sedley 1998: 144.

[17] 'A pattern of crescendo is suggested by the appearance of Epicurus at the beginnings of the odd-numbered books as successively man (1.66), father (3.9), and god (5.8)' (Kenney 1977: 19; cf. Kenney 1971: 13).

[18] On Lucretius and the diatribe tradition in these passages see Wallach 1976; R. D. Brown 1987: 127–43.

Book 5, but this time locates his activity specifically in Athens. Lucretius praises Athens as, in effect, the pinnacle of civilisation alluded to at the end of the previous book, but especially as the place that made Epicurus' philosophy known to the world. The prominence of Athens here obviously looks ahead to the setting of the plague at the end of the book. But if these opening and closing passages underline the unity of Book 6, continuity between Books 5 and 6 is also very great. Book 5, then, may be said to begin an exposition that ends only in Book 6 about the rise and fall of civilisations. The unity of these two books is greatly reinforced by their midpoint: the last word of Book 5, *cacumen* ('pinnacle'), leaves the reader momentarily balanced, as it were, on a fulcrum between the rise of civilisation in the preceding book and its dissolution in the book that follows. The two perspectives balance one another within an expository relationship marked by logical and chronological progression.

The other aspect of balance is symmetry, which is most easily seen in groups of three. Typically Lucretius uses a symmetrical, triptych arrangement to throw emphasis on the central panel. In the poem as a whole, for instance, the discourse on atoms (1–2) and the discourse on natural history (5–6) surround an account of the materiality, the mortality and the passions of the soul (3–4).[19] There is a clear sense in which this is the central element of Epicurus' message as interpreted by Lucretius, who is relentless in his preaching against the fear of death.[20] Once Lucretius has proved that the soul is material and does not survive to experience the torments of the underworld, his case is won. What follows is important to a complete understanding of the world, but the main point has been made. The centrality of this point is reflected in the centrality of its position within the tripartite symmetry of the poem.[21]

This triptych structure is repeated at many levels of exposition. In some cases a central panel receives emphasis not only by its position, but by expansion as well. Book 2 consists of three major sections covering atomic motion (62–332 = 271 lines), atomic forms (333–729 = 397 lines) and atomic

---

[19] The idea that Books 1–2 and 5–6 constitute a kind of frame is established in other ways too. Kenney 1977: 19 shows that early in each of the four books (1.146–58; 2.167–81; 5.76–90; 6.50–79), but not in Books 3–4, Lucretius emphasises the idea that 'in the Epicurean universe the gods have no function', and that the earlier book in each of the framing pairs includes a verbatim repetition 'of the famous dictum about the fixed and limited (i.e. atomic) properties of all things: 1.76–7 = 5.89–90'.

[20] Boyancé 1963: 77; Kenney 1977: 19. Early in Book 1, Lucretius states clearly that the fear of death is the prime cause of religious superstition, and that this superstition arises from ignorance about the nature of the soul (1.101–57).

[21] On middles in Lucretius see Kyriakidis 2004.

qualities (730–990 = 261 lines). Here two shorter sections of nearly equal length surround a longer central section. On a smaller scale, the doxographic passage of Book 1 discusses three philosophers at varying lengths (Heraclitus, 635–704 = 70 lines; Empedocles, 705–829 = 125 lines; Anaxagoras, 830–920 = 91 lines). Again the middle section is the lengthiest, and it is also true that Empedocles is treated with much more deference than Heraclitus and Anaxagoras, as many have noted. Empedocles' prominence in this symmetrical arrangement seems clearly related to his importance as a poetic model.[22]

The triptych pattern informs even individual paragraphs and sentences. In the conclusion to the well-known passage on distant views, for instance, Don Fowler discerns the following structure:[23]

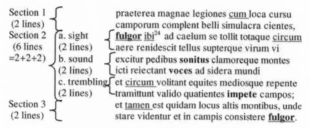

```
Section 1  ⎰       praeterea magnae legiones cum loca cursu
(2 lines)  ⎱       camporum complent belli simulacra cientes,
Section 2  ⎡a. sight ⎰ fulgor ibi[24] ad caelum se tollit totaque circum
(6 lines   ⎪(2 lines)⎱ aere renidescit tellus superque virum vi
=2+2+2)    ⎪b. sound ⎰ excitur pedibus sonitus clamoreque montes
           ⎨(2 lines)⎱ icti reiectant voces ad sidera mundi
           ⎪c. trembling⎰ et circum volitant equites mediosque repente
           ⎣(2 lines)   ⎱ tramittunt valido quatientes impete campos;
Section 3  ⎰       et tamen est quidam locus altis montibus, unde
(2 lines)  ⎱       stare videntur et in campis consistere fulgor.
```

Besides, when great legions fill the spaces of plains with
their manoeuvres as they practice war-games, a gleam
there raises itself to the sky and all around the earth
glows back with bronze and from below by the force of
the men a sound is raised and the mountains,
struck by their shouting, echo their voices to the stars,
and about them the riders fly and swiftly cross and
shake the plains between them with their powerful rush;
and yet there is a place in the high mountains, whence
they appear to stand and be a still sheen on the field.

The simple disposition of this passage, a steady march of paired hexameters, belies the complex movements that animate it. A single period is bracketed by two two-line cola, while the[24] six central lines divide into pairs. The first two lines (section 1) set the stage via a *cum* clause. Three succeeding couplets (section 2) elaborate the scene in terms of what the onlooker sees, hears and feels (a, b and c, respectively) as the armies practise their manoeuvres. But the elaboration is followed by a final pair of lines (section 3) – the main clause of this ten-line period – so strongly adversative that it negates the elaborations of the central three couplets. In a particularly nice touch, the final word

---

[22] On this passage see further Farrell 2001.
[23] Here I follow D. P. Fowler 2002: 397–8, with a few minor changes.
[24] Marullus' emendation of the mss. *ubi*: see D. P. Fowler 2002: 401 ad loc.

of line 332, *fulgor*, repeats the first word of the elaboration that begins in line 325, in effect undoing and even correcting that flight of epic pretension: while the sounds that reach hyperbolically to the stars and the shaking of the earth in couplets 1–4 are not even apparent to the distant onlooker in the final lines, the martial gleam of the weapons that, as in epic convention, was also said to rise to the heavens has been reduced to a vague sheen. Here again there is a productive tension between the symmetrical arrangement of the individual cola and the forward movement of the period as a whole. The emphasis – purely rhetorical, in this case – that is gained by the symmetrical placement of framing couplets around a longer central section is undone at the end in a clause that comes as a virtual enactment of Epicurean ethics.

Parallelism

A principle closely related to symmetry is parallelism. Here we may begin with the idea that the poem as a whole falls into halves. This bipartite structure is a more subtle matter, less closely tied to the logical structure of Lucretius' argument than is the division of the poem by thirds, and appreciation of it has been hampered by a perception of formal features intrinsic to it as problems of one sort or other, usually signs that the *ultima manus* was lacking. Most notably, the proem to Book 4 (1–25) repeats some twenty-five lines almost verbatim from Book 1 (926–50), as was noted above. Editors have generally regarded the repetition not as a scribal blunder but as an authorial stopgap, assuming that Lucretius would have replaced these lines with a new proem if he had lived to finish his poem.[25] But G. B. Conte has convincingly explained the repetition as an instance of the 'proem in the middle' that refocuses the reader's attention and, as it were, re-launches the poet towards his goal as he begins to approach the end of his task.[26] On this reading, repetition of a famous passage from Book 1 at the beginning of Book 4 signals a new beginning and divides the poem into halves.

Other features contribute to the same effect. For instance, the theme of death is treated most extensively in two places, at the end of Book 3 (the diatribe against the fear of death) and of Book 6 (the plague at Athens). Exactly what point Lucretius is making by drawing this parallel is open to discussion: is the poem's finale a kind of test for the reader, who after absorbing the lessons of Lucretius' poem should be able to read the concluding passage about the plague with equanimity?[27] Or is he making a historical

---

[25] See (e.g.) Bailey 1947.   [26] Conte 1992; cf. Gale 1994b.
[27] Commager 1957; Segal 1990: 234.

point about the benighted behaviour under duress of even the most civilised people on earth, prior to the arrival of Epicurus and his philosophy?[28] No matter how one answers these questions, it seems clear that the endings of Books 3 and 6 are designed to comment on one another and to stimulate such questions, even if they do not provide definite answers.

A broadly similar parallel can be found between Books 2 and 5, the central books of each half. Book 2 ends with the idea that our world had a beginning and will have an end, emphasising that it is already quite old and showing its age (1105–74). It concludes with the memorable image of the aged ploughman (1164) groaning and shaking his head at the earth's inability to produce crops comparable to those of his father's day. The idea of the earth's birth and inevitable senescence and death receives a great deal of emphasis from its position at the end of this book, but it is otherwise not very prominent in the first half of the poem. It is, however, a major subject at the beginning of Book 5, where it is developed at length and in great detail (91–508).

In these cases, when Lucretius deals with a particular theme or motif in both halves of his poem, he deploys the similar material in the analogous books of the respective halves (i.e. Books 1 and 4, Books 2 and 5, Books 3 and 6). This tendency greatly reinforces the sense of a bipartite structure. In addition, the analogies involved work in close cooperation with the principle of sequence, in that the earlier occurrence in each case announces a theme that will be developed with greater emphasis in the second half of the poem. A digression on Lucretius' poetic and philosophical mission in Book 1 is redeployed more prominently as the proem to the fourth book, and so to the poem's second half. In Book 2 the idea that the world was born and will die is introduced as the conclusion to a lengthy discussion of atomic compounds. This is, indeed, the logical conclusion to the kind of argument that is found throughout Book 2, but it goes well beyond the other issues with which that book deals, and it does not handle the topic of the world's birth or mortality in anything like a complete or even an adequate way. As such, the passage in Book 2 serves to prefigure the major discussion that is reserved for Book 5. Finally, the images of death that close Book 3, and so the first half of the poem, also prefigure, but pale in comparison to the plague of Athens at the end of Book 6, which closes the second half of the poem and so the poem as a whole. In this sense, the second half of the poem may be regarded as an ambitious rhetorical *amplificatio* of themes announced in the first half.

---

[28] Bright 1971. See also p. 55 above.

Inversion

Lucretius' argument, as we have seen, proceeds in linear fashion from the simplest things in the universe to the most complex. In the same way, it moves from things of which one can have no direct sense experience – atoms and void – to things that force themselves upon the senses – typhoons, earthquakes and plagues. This movement is linear and conforms to the principle of sequence; but at the same time, sequential movement from one part of the poem to another often involves some sort of change. For instance, movement between analogous passages from the first to the second half of the poem involves an element of *amplificatio*. In other cases the sort of change involved may be a complete inversion of the previous movement. In fact, this occurrence is so frequent that it deserves to be recognised as a principle of its own.

Inversion is not exclusively an architectural principle, but it is closely implicated with the poem's structure. The poem begins with an invocation of Venus, and the problem that this beginning presents is familiar.[29] After praising Venus as the generative force of the world and asking her to create conditions of peace in which Lucretius might compose and Memmius might read his poem, the poet suddenly states a general truth about Epicurean gods: they exist in conditions of perfect happiness and are untouched and unmoved by human affairs (44–9).[30] But if this is so, what is the point of invoking Venus and summoning her as an ally or patron? Then, in case we miss this paradox, Lucretius goes on to denounce *religio* at great length as the source of so many human troubles. Finally, as he concludes these preliminaries, Lucretius states the first general principle of his physical argument, that nothing is ever born from nothing through divine agency (*diuinitus* 150). In the space of these relatively few lines, then, Lucretius moves from the position of a conventional poet who petitions the gods for favours, to that of one who asserts that we live in a materialist universe in which the gods play no active role. The inversion of his original position is pointed and pronounced.

Another large-scale inversion that animates the poem's structure involves appeal to the senses. It is a canon of Epicurus' philosophy that all reasoning depends on the evidence of the senses (*Ep. Herod.* 38). But the basic components of the universe, atoms and void, cannot be perceived directly. So, in the earlier books, Lucretius appeals to the senses to explain the unseen by analogy.[31] The famous illustration of atomic motion by the image of dust

---

[29] The literature on the opening hymn is vast; see Gale 1994a: 208–23, with further references.

[30] On these lines see Clay 1983: 94–5; Sedley 1998: 26–7.

[31] The most comprehensive study of analogical argument in the *DRN* is Schiesaro 1990.

motes in a sunbeam (2.80–141) captures the basic method and attitude of the early books. At the end of the poem, however, Lucretius shifts his ground, using the unseen to explain the phenomenal world and proving that the most terrifying events are not acts of god but merely the result of those chance collisions of atoms discussed in Books 1 and 2. The reader's progress through the six books, then, takes him from the simple to the complex, but also to a new perspective on nature from which the intellectual spectacle of the simple but unseen is understood to be somehow more real and more sublime than the mere epiphenomena that are nature's grandest displays.[32]

Additions and digressions

For hundreds of years Lucretius' use of 'purple passages' – the six proems and a number of formal digressions from his strictly scientific exposition – has loomed large in the minds of his critics. These passages are in general either drawn from non-philosophical sources or freely composed, and they are used in such a way as to complement and shape argumentative portions of the poem.[33] In the proem to Book 1 Venus and Mars may be taken to represent the Empedoclean principles of Love and Strife, and David Sedley has argued persuasively that Empedoclean influence on the opening of the poem is very considerable indeed.[34] In a similar vein, Lucretius has borrowed from Homer's description of the gods' abode on Olympus in *Odyssey* 6 for the proem to his own Book 3.[35] And of course the poem concludes with the memorable account of the plague, which is famously borrowed from Book 2 of Thucydides.[36] None of these passages appeared in any previous Epicurean treatise of which we know. Each occupies a place of great structural significance, either beginning or ending a book and, in the case of the first and last passages cited, beginning and ending the poem itself.

A curious structural principle thus emerges. While the argument of the poem as a whole may well be borrowed from some previous Epicurean treatise, this argument is conspicuously framed by non-Epicurean material. We cannot say for sure exactly how Lucretius conceived of the relationship between this frame and the philosophical system that it contained, but the role of Homer here is notable. Not only is Homer himself imitated in the proem to Book 3, but the Empedoclean imagery of Love and Strife in Book

---

[32] See ch. 10 below.

[33] By now the idea that these passages represent an anti-Lucretian element is more a chapter in the history of the poem's reception than a credible interpretative position. On the stylistic issues involved see ch. 6, below.

[34] Sedley 1998: 1–34.   [35] With *DRN* 3.18–22 cf. *Od.* 6.41–5.

[36] With *DRN* 6.1138–1286 cf. Thuc. 2.47–52; see Commager 1957, Bright 1971, Penwill 1996.

1 is closely related to allegorical exegesis of Aphrodite's adulterous affair with Ares in the second song of Demodocus (*Od.* 8.266–369). Also in Book 1 Lucretius discusses Ennius' treatment of Homer, in which Homer appears explicitly as a philosopher.[37] It is hard not to infer from such passages that Lucretius' framing material and digressions are intended to mediate between the philosophical exposition that dominates the poem and the expectations of a readership that was either new to philosophy or accustomed to other kinds of poetry.

By the same token, passages that present themselves formally as digressions perform much of the same mediating work. Frequently such passages are explicitly linked to the framing material just discussed. For instance, Book 2 contains the passage on worship of the Magna Mater (600–60). These lines present themselves formally as a digression from the surrounding section (333–729), which concerns the multiplicity of atomic forms. The general thrust of the argument is that this multiplicity accounts for the enormous diversity of the things that the world produces; 'and this is why she is called great mother of the gods, mother of beasts, and parent of our body, all in one' (598–9). Lucretius then embellishes this point with a description of the ecstatic rites associated with the Magna Mater cult. He composes this passage in an elevated, agitated style that imitates the enthusiasm of the cult and that contrasts sharply with the more measured tone of the logical argument that surrounds it. Then he abruptly brings the reader up short, as he so often does, by stating an Epicurean doctrine that flatly contradicts any literal interpretation of the image that he has just presented:

> And yet all this, however well and skilfully composed in the telling, never-
> theless is very far removed from true reasoning. For of necessity the nature of
> the gods entirely and in itself enjoys immortality in utter peace, distant and
> far removed from our concerns. For, being free from any pain or hazard, and
> utterly self-contained, needing nothing from us, it is neither enticed by benefits
> nor touched by anger. (644–51)

The last six of these lines are repeated from a similar locus in Book 1, the Venus hymn. As such, they repeat in a new and more fully developed context a lesson that seemed more paradoxical at the very start of the poem; and they contribute to the unity of the argument in Books 1–2.[38]

---

37 *DRN* 1.126, where Homer expounds the nature of the universe (*rerum naturam expandere dictis*).

38 Repetition is much appreciated as an element of Lucretius' style (Minyard 1978), but examples such as this and the previously discussed proem of Book 4 show that it is an important structural principle as well. On the longer repetitions see Bailey 1947: 163–5, 602, and ad locc.

Analogical structures

Analogy is a major element in Lucretius' argumentative technique. In structural terms, the *DRN* presents itself as a linguistic simulacrum of the entire universe. This aspect is articulated in the argument from analogy in Book 1 concerning the arrangement of *elementa* – atoms or letters of the alphabet – in compounds and in the words of Lucretius' poem, respectively. As he draws to a close his critique of Empedocles' four-element theory, Lucretius presses home the point that an enormous variety of compounds can be created from mere atoms and void. The crucial point is that the very same atoms can be rearranged in different positions and motions relative to one another and can collide with one another in different ways, so as to produce different compounds (817–22). Thus Empedocles' 'elements', earth, air, fire and water, are not elements at all, but compounds formed of (let us suppose) the same atoms, variously arranged. He then continues, 'In fact, even in my own verses, here and there you see many *elementa* that are common to many words, though you have to admit that the verses and words are quite different in their significance and in their sonorous sound' (823–6). That is, the same atoms, differently arranged, produce compounds as different as fire and water, just as the same letters of the alphabet in different arrangements produce all the different words that make up the individual lines of Lucretius' poem. The argument is analogical, but the analogy is strengthened by the fact that *elementa*, the word that Lucretius uses here for 'atoms', is also the Latin for 'letters of the alphabet'.[39] This convergence lends the analogical argument a particularly compelling quality that Lucretius exploits when he returns to the idea a few lines later. In rebutting Anaxagoras' theory that everything consists of particles of the same substance – earth is made from particles of earth, water from water, and so on – Lucretius observes that, since our bodies are nourished by different kinds of food, plants grow from the earth, wood when burned becomes fire, smoke and ash, then the elements of which all these compounds are composed must be different from flesh, earth and wood (858–74). To answer the idea that wood, since it can burst into flames, must contain particles of fire, Lucretius again insists that what wood and fire, being compounds, share is the fact that each substance is a different configuration of the same atoms; and to drive the point home, he again refers to language: 'Now do you see, then, what I said not long ago, that it often makes a great difference with what and in what position atoms are contained and what movements they make and cause one

---

[39] OLD³ s.v. *elementum* 3; cf. Greek *stoicheion* (LSJ s.v. II.1 and 2). On this analogy see Aristotle, *Met.* A.4; *Gen. Corr.* 315b14; Cicero, *Nat. D.* 2.93.

another, and that the same atoms, if you change (their movements and positions) a bit, produce both wood and fire?' (907–12). Here the reader must be reminded that 'wood' is *lignum* and 'fire' *ignis* – similar-sounding words that, when written, share several letters (or, in Latin, *elementa*). Lucretius goes on: 'Just like the very words themselves, if the letters are rearranged a bit, when we denote "wood and fire" (*ligna atque ignis*) each by a different word' (912–14).

This argument subtends the structure of the poem in the largest sense. The *DRN* is to be read not merely as an exposition of the physical universe, but in some sense as its image as well. Similarly, the structure of the poem is cognate with the fundamental conceptual structures that the poet employs to reveal the structure of the universe, in which the simple, fundamental principles of atoms and void combine to produce ever greater and more complex phenomena. In this regard, the structure of Lucretius' exposition can hardly be regarded as a decorative appliqué or as an attractive container for some difficult lesson. The poem, specifically in respect to the most basic properties of its language and its inexorable movement from small to great, is itself a *simulacrum* of the universe; and the discovery of this homology is both a source of pleasure and one of the great lessons that the poem has to impart.

Further reading

The best guide to Lucretius' sources is Sedley 1998. For the view that Lucretius worked independently of any specific sources Clay 1983 is well worth reading. For Lucretius' shaping of the poem, see Bailey 1947: 31–7; Boyancé 1963: 69–83 (in French); Minadeo 1965 and 1969; Owen 1968–9; Gale 1994b. On analogies see Schiesaro 1990 (in Italian).

6

E. J. KENNEY

Lucretian texture: style, metre and rhetoric in the *De rerum natura*

The message

'Lucretius . . . is first and foremost a missionary.'[1]

Lucretius' mission was to convince his readers of the truth of the fundamental premises of the Epicurean philosophy, 'on which rests all of existence' (*fundamenta quibus nitatur summa salutis*, 2.863; 4.506). These basic doctrines were grounded on the application of reason and logic to the evidence of the senses, and what Lucretius aimed to achieve was enlightenment through intellectual conviction: to teach and to prove. Empedocles and Parmenides nowhere refer to themselves as teaching; Lucretius, exploiting the ambiguity of the word as signifying both 'teach' and 'prove' (*OLD* 3, 4), and conscious of the traditional moral authority of the poet as teacher, uses forms of *doceo* to refer to his exposition some forty times.

The task was a challenging one. Much of the argument was highly technical, and there was entrenched prejudice and superstition to contend with. To convince connotes winning a battle (*OLD conuinco*). When Lucretius writes that the behaviour of the moon 'is difficult to teach by reasoning and to prove by words' (*difficile est ratione docere et uincere uerbis*, 5.735) we detect an awareness that there was resistance to be encountered which logic and reason unassisted by force could not overcome. The reader may be brusquely adjured to admit that he has lost the argument, *uictus fateare necesse est* (1.624; 5.343); and Memmius himself is warned that resistance on his part to Lucretius' reasoning will be beaten down by an inexhaustible torrent of poetic eloquence (1.410–17).[2]

That Lucretius made sustained and effective use of rhetoric to enforce his arguments is not in dispute.[3] As a contemporary of Cicero and other eminent speakers and as (a reasonably safe inference from the tone and quality of his

---

[1] Bailey 1947: 13. [2] Schiesaro 1987: 47–50.
[3] Classen 1968, Asmis 1983, Schiesaro 1987.

writing) a man of education and family, he was exposed to the full force of Roman political and forensic oratory in its climactic efflorescence, and equipped to appreciate its techniques. Whether or not he had versed himself in rhetorical theory, he had every opportunity of hearing great speakers in action, demonstrating the three styles of oratory (*genera dicendi*) and their functions: the plain (*genus tenue, subtile*), which aims to prove; the middle or flowery (*medium, floridum*), which aims to charm and delight; and the grand (*grande, amplum, acre*), which aims to stir the emotions. As expounded by a great orator of an earlier generation, Marcus Antonius, in the *De oratore*, they constituted the speaker's basic armoury:

> ita omnis ratio dicendi tribus ad persuadendum rebus est nixa: ut probemus uera esse quae defendimus; ut conciliemus eos nobis qui audiunt; ut animos eorum ad quemcumque causa postulabit motum uocemus.　　　　(2.115)

> So the whole theory of oratory rests on three ways of persuading: by proving that what we are maintaining is true; by winning the favour of the audience; and by evoking in them whatever emotion the case we are arguing shall call for.

Similarly Cicero in his own person, citing Antonius as his authority:

> erit igitur eloquens . . . is qui in foro causisque ciuilibus ita dicet ut probet, ut delectet, ut flectat. Probare necessitatis est, delectare suauitatis, flectere uictoriae.　　　　(*Orator* 69)

> So he will be truly eloquent who, in forensic and political speeches alike, speaks so as to prove, to please and to move. To prove is necessary, to please is to charm, to move is to conquer.

Lucretius, as will appear, deploys all three styles[4] to impart maximum effect to his teaching.

In enlisting all the resources of contemporary rhetoric he was in step with his times. Later Epicureanism took a more tolerant view of rhetoric than the Master had done; and Cicero was both preaching and practising a style of philosophical writing that freely exploited rhetorical techniques.[5] The words in which he praises Zeno for speaking 'clearly, impressively, and decoratively' (*distincte grauiter ornate, Nat. D.* 1.59) correspond closely to the three *genera dicendi*. What Epicurus had objected to was 'any use of language which

---

4 The 'middle' or 'flowery' style plays as important a role as the other two, as is indeed suggested by Lucretius' emphasis on the 'sweetness' of his poetry at 1.935–50 (= 4.10–25); see pp. 101–3, 105–7 below. The 'expository'/'pathetic' dichotomy (Bailey 1947: 168; Kenney 1971: 16) does not do justice to the range of his rhetorical armoury.

5 Asmis 1983: 39, 48.

obscures the original, proper meaning of words'.[6] Lucretius' use of words is extremely precise, informing his employment of imagery and metaphor.[7] The decorative and 'pathetic'[8] passages which reinforce his argument are not, as they have been called, digressions; 'they are a continuation of the arguments by other means'.[9] This verdict, however, must be qualified by the admission that, as will be exemplified below, his use of these means to manipulate the reader's responses might sometimes have raised strict Epicurean eyebrows.

The medium

Quis potis est dignum pollenti pectore carmen
condere pro rerum maiestate hisque repertis?
(DRN 5.1–2)

Who is able with powerful mind to build a poem to match the grandeur of the subject and these discoveries?

That Lucretius should have chosen the epic hexameter as the medium for his message, in spite of the known hostility of Epicurus to poetry,[10] need not surprise us unduly. A renewed interest in didactic poetry coincided with the popularity of Epicureanism in the late Republic.[11] Lucretius was framed by nature to be a poet, and the superior antiquity of the medium itself, together with 'the time-honoured concept of the poet as teacher',[12] had invested the poetic form with an authority to which prose could not aspire. Moreover, poetry is memorable: the mother of the Muses is Mnemosyne. The repetitions of lines and passages which recur throughout the poem are intended to score fundamental principles on the reader's memory.[13] And in the opening lines of Book 5, as acutely remarked by Volk,[14] Lucretius comes very near to suggesting that Epicurus himself was a poet. Only the grandeur, *maiestas* (OLD 4), of this medium can do justice to the grandeur of the message.

Nothing, however, must be allowed to impair the clarity of that message. Clarity, σαφήνεια, Epicurus himself had insisted, was paramount.[15] Lucretius is heavily satirical at the expense of fools (*stolidi*) who

---

[6] Classen 1968: 111.   [7] West 1969, Catrein 2003.

[8] For the term see Russell and Winterbottom 1972: 602, Index s.v. Emotion (*pathos*).

[9] Classen 1968: 93. Cf. Schiesaro 1987: 31.   [10] Gale 1994a: 14–18.

[11] R. D. Brown 1982: 77–8.   [12] Volk 2002: 36.

[13] Epicurus had insisted on the importance of memorising the principal doctrines (*Epistle to Herodotus*, Diog. Laert. 10.35); cf. DeWitt 1954: 25, 112; Clay 1983: 77, 80, 176–85.

[14] Volk 2002: 111–12.   [15] Diog. Laert. 10.13.

> magis admirantur amantque
> inuersis quae sub uerbis latitantia cernunt
> ueraque constituunt quae belle tangere possunt
> auris et lepido quae sunt fucata sonore.
>
> (1.161–4)

rather admire and love anything which they see hidden in words turned on their heads, and take to be true whatever tickles their ears prettily and is meretriciously coloured with charming sound.

Cicero comments admiringly on the ability of Aratus, 'a man ignorant of astronomy', to write elegantly on the subject, and of Nicander, 'a man altogether remote from country matters', to write with equal brilliance about agriculture (*De or.* 1.69). The *DRN* is a concrete repudiation of the idea that a poet should be prepared to transmute any material, however technical, into polite literature on demand. Though Lucretius borrowed freely from Cicero's *Aratea* when it suited him, the superficial graces and cleverness for its own sake of Alexandrianising didactic must be rejected.[16]

For Lucretius it was the material that shaped the expression and metrical form of the message – 'his rhythm is to a great extent dictated by his vocabulary'[17] – and his vocabulary was in turn dictated by two fundamental imperatives: the vital significance of the doctrine and the need for complete clarity in imparting it. Where an Alexandrian or Augustan poet, having to refer repeatedly to the atoms, might have had recourse to elegant periphrasis, Lucretius uses whatever synonym or equivalent is metrically convenient[18] – *rerum primordia*, *genitalia corpora*, *corpora prima*, *semina rerum*, *principia* – not troubling to avoid repetition when a point is to be made or a distinction drawn:

> corpora sunt porro partim primordia rerum,
> partim concilio quae constant principiorum.
>
> (1.483–4)

Furthermore, 'bodies' are on the one hand the atoms themselves, on the other those that consist of a combination of atoms.

The sense would be the same with (e.g.) *quidquid generatur eorum*[19] (just as in English 'them' could replace 'atoms'), but Lucretius preferred to be

---

[16] Bailey 1947: 30; Kenney 1971: 21.   [17] Bailey 1947: 117.
[18] See 1.55–61; Bailey 1947: 606–7.
[19] Augustan and later poets used the oblique cases of *is* sparingly (Axelson 1945: 70–3); Lucretius has *eorum* thirty-five times.

explicit even at the cost of repetition and ending the verse with what to many contemporary ears would have seemed an ungainly pentasyllable.

The Latin hexameter as Lucretius inherited it was largely the creation of Ennius,[20] and Ennian characteristics such as the elision of final –*s* to create a short open syllable, or readiness, particularly in argumentative passages,[21] to admit 'irregular' word-division in the last two feet of the verse, must no doubt have seemed old-fashioned to ears attuned to Ciceronian elegance.[22] Lucretius' style however can rarely be termed uncouth, as Ennius' evidently seemed to some of his contemporaries.[23] Cicero's celebrated judgement is nicely balanced: the poem is 'sparkling with natural genius, but with plenty of technical skill', *multis luminibus ingeni, multae tamen artis*.[24] A century and a half later Quintilian was to bracket Lucretius with Ovid's contemporary Aemilius Macer as 'each elegant in dealing with his subject', *elegantes in sua quisque materia*.[25] That 'the most notable feature of Lucretius' style and diction' is archaism[26] is true in the sense that, when extracted and catalogued, his archaisms and departures from the norms of Augustan Latin – a natural though anachronistic touchstone – make an imposing show. Distributed through a poem of some 7400 verses, they do not obtrude themselves; such catalogues, as a compiler of them has acknowledged, can mislead by seeming 'to deny the integrity and authenticity of Lucretius' style'.[27]

To communicate his message in a way that left no room for misunderstanding, he was prepared to manipulate language freely, sometimes with a degree of violence: it was a short step from exploiting an existing prosodic ambiguity to creating one by the arbitrary lengthening of a syllable to accommodate an otherwise metrically refractory word.[28] Such licences, however, are not so frequent as to distract. What chiefly commands admiration is his lexical creativity. This is especially evident in his free use of expressive

---

[20] There is little evidence of substantial technical advance in the surviving fragments of hexameter poetry from the period between Ennius (d. 169 BC) and Lucretius (d. *c.* 55–51 BC, by the conventional dating).

[21] Kenney 1974: 29–30.

[22] Cicero's avoidance of such endings in the *Aratea* is almost total (Soubiran 1972: 103–4).

[23] Cic. *Tusc.* 3.45 *o poetam egregium! quamquam ab his cantoribus Euphorionis contemnitur.* Who these 'admirers of Euphorion' were is debated, but they were evidently influential enough to be worth slapping down.

[24] *Q. Fr.* 2.10 (9). 3 (14 S-B); tr. Shackleton Bailey 1980: 190.

[25] *Inst.* 10.1.87; Macer was the author of lost poems on birds (*Ornithogonia*) and snakebites (*Theriaca*). 'Elegance' is a slippery term. The *Rhetorica ad Herennium* defines it as 'what makes each and every topic seem to be expressed with purity and perspicuity', *ut locus unusquisque pure et aperte dici uideatur* (4.17). Cf. Douglas 1966: 25 on Cic. *Brut.* 35.

[26] W. E. Leonard and S. B. Smith 1965: 32.   [27] W. E. Leonard and S. B. Smith 1965: 156–7.

[28] Bailey 1947: 131–2.

compound adjectives, many of his own making.[29] Such formations, as Quintilian later remarked, 'suit the Greeks better; with us they are less successful' (*Inst.* 1.5.70). He adds that this is a product of prejudice: in a Greek poet κυρταύχενα 'with bulging neck' is admired, *incuruiceruicum* strikes us as comical. Naevius had given a cautious lead here, followed by the tragedians, notably Pacuvius; Lucretius went too far for his successors, whose usage was more restrained.[30] No less remarkable was his facility in forming nouns and polysyllabic adverbs: here Ovid can be seen taking a leaf out of his book, though less flamboyantly.[31] His often-quoted adversions on 'the poverty of our language', *egestatem linguae* (1.139) and 'the poverty of our ancestral speech', *patrii sermonis egestas* (1.832; 3.260) should be read in this context, not as an apology but as an implicit boast.[32] Cicero similarly complains of 'this poverty-stricken tongue of ours', *hac inopi lingua* (*Fin.* 3.51). That, ostensibly, is Marcus Cato speaking, but like Lucretius, Cicero is slyly drawing attention to the way in which he has risen triumphantly to the challenge of disciplining a still-developing language to the lucid exposition of unfamiliar and often highly technical subject matter. 'What Cicero did for Latin prose, in revealing the fertility of its resources, in giving to it more ample volume, and eliciting its capabilities of sonorous rhythmical movement, Lucretius aspires to do for Latin verse.'[33]

Two contrasting passages illustrate Lucretius' ability to shape the Latin hexameter to his purpose. The first concludes a series of proofs of the fundamental principle that nothing can be born from nothing, and the corollary, that whatever comes into existence does so because something else dies. The argumentative sequence that began at 1.155 is rounded off unexpectedly with a pastoral idyll:

> postremo pereunt imbres, ubi eos Pater Aether   250
> in gremium Matris Terrai praecipitauit.
> at nitidae surgunt fruges ramique uirescunt
> arboribus, crescunt ipsae fetuque grauantur.
> hinc alitur porro nostrum genus atque ferarum,

---

[29] Bailey 1947: 132–4; W. E. Leonard and S. B. Smith 1965: 135 n. 91.

[30] Kenney 1973: 121–2.

[31] Bailey 1947: 134–7; W. E. Leonard and S. B. Smith 1965: 134–5 and nn. 90, 92; Kenney 1973: 127. For the possibility that his predilection for innovative word-formation may owe something to the example of Nicander see Hollis 1998: 181–4.

[32] Farrell 2001: 41–3. Cf. Adkins 1977, suggesting that the apparently awkward metrical structure of 1.139 is a technically adroit demonstration of the problems.

[33] Sellar 1889: 273; cf. Munro 1886: II, 11. On the similarities and differences of the techniques employed by Cicero and Lucretius to render Greek philosophical terms into Latin see Sedley 1999: 233–5.

hinc laetas urbes pueris florere uidemus   255
frondiferasque nouis auibus canere undique siluas,
hinc fessae pecudes pingui per pabula laeta
corpora deponunt et candens lacteus umor
uberibus manat distentis, hinc noua proles
artubus infirmis teneras lasciua per herbas   260
ludit lacte mero mentes perculsa nouellas.
haud igitur penitus pereunt quaecumque uidentur,
quando alid ex alio reficit natura nec ullam
rem gigni patitur nisi morte adiuta aliena.

(1.250–64)

Lastly, the rains pass away when Father Aether has poured them down into the womb of Mother Earth. But there spring up bright crops and the branches become green on the trees, which grow themselves and are heavy with fruit. Hence too our race and the race of beasts is nourished; hence we see happy cities blooming with children and the leafy woods everywhere full of newly fledged birds; hence the cattle, weary with their fat, lay themselves down in the lush pastures and the white milk oozes from their swollen udders; hence the new brood with unsteady legs frisks in the fresh grass, their young minds drunk on the neat milk. Therefore nothing that we see passes away completely, since nature remakes one thing from another and does not allow anything to be born unless it is aided by the death of something else.

This delightful picture, Lucretius at his most graphic and playful, is introduced by an image reaching back into primeval myth that figures rainfall as the product of the *hieros gamos*, the sacred union of the Sky Father with the Earth Mother. For this he had both philosophical and literary precedents.[34] In other passages where the idea appears it is justified as metaphorical: 'in the light of these phenomena she [the earth] is rightly called mother', *quapropter merito maternum nomen adepta est* (2.998; cf. 5.795, 821). Here the demythification, so to call it,[35] of the image is more indirectly achieved through linguistic and metrical nuances. In contrast to the following twelve verses lines 250 and 251 end 'irregularly', and the archaism *terrai* reinforces the suggestion that what is described is fantasy born of ancient superstition. In respect of both technique and content the idyllic scenes that follow, notwithstanding the 'unAugustan' features noted below, have a 'modern' feel. Elsewhere 'demythification' may be effected by ridicule or flat denial.[36]

[34] Bailey 1947: 142 ad loc.

[35] Cf. Cucchiarelli 2003: 121–2 on the 'remythification' of it by Virgil in the *Georgics* (2.325–33).

[36] As in the next example and in the famous passage on the Great Mother (p. 106 below).

Here the myth is reinterpreted rather than refuted: it may illustrate by appealing to the imagination, but it cannot *explain*. This is a natural process governed by inexorable laws of cause and effect, of which the living proof is all around us if we care to attend to it in a scientific spirit. The prosaically expressed conclusion (262–4) drives the point home.

The central descriptive period is carefully structured. A distich picturing the resurrection of the 'dead' rain in the form of growth is built round four verbs of identical metrical shape arranged in pairs, each pair identically positioned in the line (252–3). There follows an eight-line period of parallel clauses increasing in length, the form conventionally termed tri- or (as here) tetracolon crescendo ('Gesetz der wachsenden Glieder'), articulated by the forceful anaphora of *hinc*. Emphasis is assisted by alliteration, a characteristic Lucretian feature,[37] especially appealing in the caressing *l*s of the charming picture of the newborn lambs capering unsteadily 'drunk' on the new milk (258–61).[38] Decorative epithets (252 *nitidae*, 255 *laetas*, 256 *frondiferas*, 257 *laeta*, 260 *teneras*) and ornamental periphrasis (258 *lacteus umor*) enrich the literary texture. In the conclusion discreet alliteration of *p* and *a* and the recurrent formula *alid ex alio* (also 1.407, 1115, 3.970, 5.1305, 1456) underline the inevitability of the conclusion to be drawn.

The *genus floridum* enlists charm to combat illusion and erroneous notions of causation nurtured by myth. The *genus acre* uses force:

> hoc etiam pacto tonitru concussa uidentur
> omnia saepe graui tremere et diuolsa repente
> maxima dissiluisse capacis moenia mundi,
> cum subito ualidi uenti collecta procella
> nubibus intorsit sese, conclusaque ibidem   125
> turbine uersanti magis ac magis undique nubem
> cogit uti fiat spisso caua corpore circum,
> post ubi comminuit uis eius et impetus acer,
> tum perterricrepo sonitu dat scissa fragorem.
> nec mirum, cum plena animae uesicula parua   130
> saepe ita dat magnum sonitum displosa repente.
>
>   (6.121–31)

In just this way it often seems, when there is a violent clap of thunder, that everything shakes and that the ramparts of the all-embracing firmament have been torn apart and leapt asunder; as happens when a mighty wind has gathered and twisted itself into the clouds, where enclosed in a spinning vortex it forces

---

[37] Bailey 1947: 150–2; W. E. Leonard and S. B. Smith 1965: 172–5.
[38] M. F. Smith 1992: 22–3n.; see *OLD*, *merus* 1b.

the cloud more and more on every side to form a hollow with a dense body all round it. When that has been weakened by the strength and fierce onset of the wind, it splits apart and explodes with terrifying sound. That is not surprising, seeing that a small bladder full of air likewise makes a big noise if suddenly burst.

The description is carefully organised to build up to the (literally) deflationary climax. Lines 121–3 picture the panic induced in the unenlightened by a huge clap of thunder, a feeling that the very fabric of the universe is being torn apart. Of course Lucretius cannot seriously have supposed that Memmius and his other educated readers thought that the end of the world was at hand every time there was a severe thunderstorm. What is described is the reaction of the ignorant savages whose irrational fears spawned the superstitions that still poison men's lives. Nevertheless the immediate impact of the rhetoric on the sensibilities of the reader is powerful, and thunder does terrify some people. The period is articulated by a series of interlocking hyperbata[39] carrying the reader on to the catastrophic denouement, accentuated by alliteration:

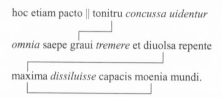

hoc etiam pacto ǁ tonitru *concussa uidentur*

omnia saepe graui *tremere* et diuolsa repente

maxima *dissiluisse* capacis moenia mundi.

There follows in lines 124–9 the explanation of what is actually happening. The tempo slows down as the tightly organised syntactical structure of the preceding verses gives place to a series of more loosely constructed sentences, with grammatically connected words juxtaposed: *ualidi uenti, collecta procella, turbine uersanti, spisso . . . corpore, impetus acer, perterricrepo sonitu.* Whereas in lines 121–3 the reader was swept irresistibly on by the rhetoric, here he is led step by step through the natural processes which result in the thunderclap; no room is left for misunderstanding. A picture is built up of relentlessly accumulating energy which finally detonates with thunderous effect, expressed in the fine onomatopoeic compound *perterricrepo*. It happens that Cicero, quoting from an unidentified poet, had condemned this epithet for its *asperitas* (*Orator* 164), precisely the quality for which Lucretius chose it here: a neat illustration of their differing conceptions of the style appropriate to didactic epos.

---

[39] Hyperbaton is a dislocation of normal word order, exemplified here by the wide separation of adjectives from their nouns.

There follows a further lowering of the stylistic temperature. 'What is there to be terrified about?' asks Lucretius: *nec mirum*, 'there's nothing to be surprised at', a recurrent signifier of the advent of reason into the discourse.[40] Thunder is nothing but a loud noise: think of a balloon and the disproportionately loud sound that it makes when popped. *Vesicula parua*, 'a tiny little bladder', the rare diminutive of a prosaic word, further qualified by *parua*, brings the scene down (again, literally) to earth. The noise made by a burst balloon is loud, *magnum*,[41] measured against the size of the balloon; how much more so with thunder, where the forces are huge. It is all a matter of scale. Illusion is dispelled by a douche of logical cold water expressed in homely language in a homely image.

The modes

cui lecta potenter erit res
nec facundia deseret hunc nec lucidus ordo.
(Horace, *Ars poetica* 40–1)

The poet who has chosen his subject masterfully will not be at a loss for eloquence or clear arrangement.

There is nothing mechanical about Lucretius' deployment of his rhetorical resources. His technique is fluid, but far from formless. He sought above all to shine the light of reason into the dark places of the human mind and heart by presenting a logically coherent case for the truth of Epicurean physics, to achieve both in and through his poem *lucidus ordo*. If ever a poet proved himself *potens* in his choice of subject and in the handling of it, it was Lucretius, not least through his supreme 'ability to focus intently on a single point without losing sight of his overall plan and direction'.[42]

It must, however, be admitted that, as was noted above and as will be illustrated below, his use of the power of rhetoric to charm or coerce the reader into acquiescence with propositions which, strictly speaking, turn out not to have been proved, may occasionally verge on the unscrupulous. The cards are to all appearances laid on the table in the famous and much-discussed *prise de position* at 1.926–50, repeated with minor variations at

[40] 2.87, 338; cf. 4.768 *non est mirum*; 5.192 *ut non sit mirum*; 5.748, 799, 6.615, 1012 *quominus est mirum*.
[41] *magnum* is the reading of one early sixteenth-century MS; cf. Isidore's paraphrase, *Orig.* 13.8.2 *cum uesicula quamuis parua magnum tamen sonitum displosa emittat*, where *quamuis . . . tamen* makes the paradox explicit. The rare *displodo*, 'burst apart', elsewhere in this sense before the fourth century only at Lucr. 6.825, reinforces the point.
[42] R. D. Brown 1987: 4.

4.1–26.[43] Here he sets out in order his reasons for aspiring to traverse ground untrodden by any poet before him:

> primum quod magnis doceo de rebus et artis
> religionum animum nodis exsoluere pergo.
>
> (1.931–2)

Firstly, because it is great matters that I treat of, seeking to release the mind from the fetters of superstition.

Only poetry is adequate to proclaim this mission of rescue:

> deinde quod obscura de re tam lucida pango
> carmina musaeo contingens cuncta lepore.
> id quoque enim non ab nulla ratione uidetur
>
> (1.933–5)

Next, because it is on a dark subject that I compose my luminous verses, touching all with the Muses' charm; and this too for a very good reason[44]

Epicurean physics is hard to swallow: the pill must be sugared, as children are beguiled into taking bitter medicine by smearing honey on the rim of the cup,

> ut puerorum aetas improuida ludificetur
> labrorum tenus, interea perpotet amarum
> absinthi laticem deceptaque non capiatur
> sed potius tali pacto recreata ualescat.
>
> (1.939–42)

so that thoughtless childhood may be deluded as far as the lips and meanwhile drink down the bitter wormwood and though deceived be not betrayed but in this way be restored and well again.

A sceptical reader encountering *ludificetur*, literally 'to be made game of', might wonder if he was to be led up the Garden path in more senses than one. However, no time for reflection is allowed:

> sic ego nunc, quoniam haec ratio plerumque uidetur
> tristior esse quibus non est tractata retroque
> uolgus abhorret ab hac, uolui tibi suauiloquenti
> carmine Pierio rationem exponere nostram
> et quasi musaeo dulci contingere melle,

---

[43] See p. 59 above.

[44] The double negative *non ab nulla* is emphatic: 'of course with very great reason' (Munro 1886: II, 103 ad loc.).

si tibi forte animum tali ratione tenere
uersibus in nostris possem, dum perspicis omnem
naturam rerum qua constet compta figura.

(1.943–50)

So now, since this philosophy is apt to seem somewhat repellent to those unversed in it, and the crowd shrinks back from it, I have decided to expound this doctrine of ours in sweetly-speaking Pierian song and as it were to touch it with the sweet honey of the Muses, if perhaps in this way I might be able to hold your mind to my verses while you perceive the whole nature of things, its shape and structure.

The emphasis in these lines on sweetness as the predominant characteristic of Lucretius' poetry recurs, there too with specifically Alexandrian overtones, in two identical passages in difficult technical contexts, the transmission of the 'idols' and the mechanics of sleep:

. . . suauidicis potius quam multis uersibus edam,
paruus ut est cycni melior canor ille gruum quam
clamor in aetheriis dispersus nubibus austri.

(4.180–2 = 909–11)

I shall explain in sweetly-sounding rather than many verses, as the brief song of the swan is better than the discordant cry of a flock of cranes in the clouds of southern skies.[45]

That is followed on its second occurrence (4.912) by an injunction to lend 'keen ears', *tenuis aures*, to the explanation, suggesting that critical appreciation of the poetry as well as comprehension of the argument would be required.[46]

What these passages would seem to suggest is that it was the middle style of oratory, that which sought to woo the hearer, that Lucretius envisaged as the spearhead of his rhetorical offensive. In fact the plain and the grand styles contribute in equal measure to inform the poetic texture. Many a simple expository passage is as 'poetic' in the sense of being as perfectly, indeed elegantly, shaped to its purpose as the most seductive description or impassioned diatribe. One example is representative of many:

praeterea nisi materies aeterna fuisset,   540
antehac ad nilum penitus res quaeque redissent

---

[45] Cf. the comparison of the song of the swan with that of the swallow at 3.6–7 (Kenney 1971: 75 ad loc.). 'The association of poetry with pleasure runs through the entire poem' (Volk 2002: 99).

[46] On *tenuis* as a stylistic marker see Clausen 1987: 3.

de niloque renata forent quaecumque uidemus.
at quoniam supra docui nil posse creari
de nilo neque quod genitum est ad nil reuocari,
esse immortali primordia corpora debent   545
dissolui quo quaeque supremo tempore possint,
materies ut suppeditet rebus reparandis.
sunt *igitur* solida primordia simplicitate,
nec ratione queunt alia seruata per aeuom
ex infinito iam tempore res reparare.   550

(1.540–50)

Moreover, if matter had not been everlasting, before this everything would have returned utterly to nothing and everything that we see would have been born again from nothing. However, since I have already shown that nothing can be created from nothing and that what has been born cannot return to nothing, there must be first beginnings of eternal substance into which, when its time has come, everything can be resolved, so that matter shall be forthcoming to renew things. It follows that the first beginnings are themselves solid and not compounds, and that there is no other way in which they can have been preserved through the ages from infinite time past to renew things.

The paragraph consists of three sentences occupying 3 + 5 + 3 verses, each introduced by a signposting particle. Within each sentence the syntax and the argument are articulated by the line-by-line structure, diversified by enjambement in the central sentence (543–4). To reiterate an earlier comment on a longer example (3.806–18): 'There is not a word or a phrase that can fairly be called superfluous, no merely ornamental epithets, nothing to fill out the line.'[47] This is literary craftsmanship of a high order: it cannot be too strongly emphasised that the ancients regarded poetry as a craft. *Poeta* (ποιητής) means 'maker'.

However, apparent simplicity can be deceptive. Exposition may be discreetly – one might almost say subliminally – reinforced by touches of descriptive charm or forceful expression. There is an interesting example of the latter ploy in the lengthy demonstration that the world itself is mortal: an expository paragraph is rounded off with a grandiloquent 'QED':

haud *igitur* leti praeclusa est ianua caelo
nec soli terraeque neque altis aequoris undis,
sed patet immani et uasto respectat hiatu.

(5.373–5)

---

[47] Kenney 1995: 29. Another striking example at 2.251–62, also overpunctuated by editors.

Therefore the portal of death is not closed off for the heavens or the sun or the earth or the deep waters of the sea, but waits yawning for them with huge and hideous gape.

This abrupt modulation into the pathetic is followed by an equally abrupt return to stylistic sobriety and the logical conclusion:

> *quare* etiam natiua necessumst confiteare
> haec eadem: neque enim mortali corpore quae sunt
> ex infinito iam tempore adhuc potuissent
> immensi ualidas aeui contemnere uires.
>
> (5.376–9)

Wherefore it is necessary to admit that all these also had birth: for it would not have been possible for things of mortal substance to defy the power of endless ages from infinitely long ago until now.

In invoking the image of Hades[48] as a devouring monster Lucretius suddenly pans the camera, so to say, from the cosmic to the human plane. The idea that the universe itself must perish, something that cannot be apprehended by the senses but must be grasped with the mind, is, as Lucretius had acknowledged at some length (5.91–109), unfamiliar and alarming. In the great diatribe against the fear of death in Book 3 the mythical terrors of hell had been emphatically exposed as born of illusion.[49] The echo of that passage here suggests that the cases are parallel, implicitly mocking the idea that there is anything terrifying about this prospect. Death is inevitable for anything created from atoms, large or small, cosmic or human.

Logic is likewise reinforced in subtle ways in such passages as 4.324–31 (ostensibly demonstrative but working on the reader's susceptibilities); 4.513–21 (the comparison of faulty logic to faulty housebuilding driven home by the metrically distorted line 517);[50] 5.261–72 (the profusion of words meaning water paradoxically underpinning the point that it is constantly perishing and being reborn). More overtly manipulative are the descriptions in which Lucretius lays himself out to charm. Nowhere is this more strikingly exemplified than in the depiction of the life of early man at 5.925–52. As throughout the whole narrative of which this is part, Lucretius had almost nothing that could be called scientific evidence to go on. It is by the sheer power of his imagination working through his rhetoric that he compels the

---

[48] On the connotations of *ianua leti* see Costa 1984: 75–6 ad loc.
[49] 3.978–1023 and Kenney 1971: 222 ad loc.
[50] Cf. Hinds 1987 on Lucretius' readiness to strain the language to the limits of its endurance to make a point.

reader to see that this is how it must have been.[51] The picture is liberally embellished from myth and literature: 'Thus, he presents the reader as if with a brightly coloured sugared pill, the outer coating of the myth [sc. of the Golden Age] intact and attractive, but with Epicurean medicine inside.'[52] Lucretius debunks even as he delights, as he had done more directly, even brutally, in the famous excursus on the worship of the Great Mother (2.600–43), where the whole splendid illusion celebrated by the poets is dispelled by the flatly prosaic assertion that these things

> quae bene et eximie quamuis disposta ferantur,
> longe sunt tamen a uéra ratione repulsa.
>
> (2.644–5)

But admirably well as all this is set out, it is far removed from true philosophy.

What he has just 'set out' is not only the false notions entertained by the worshippers of Cybele as imaged in her cult, but the magnificent descriptive *tour de force* which he himself lovingly built up.[53]

Charm may be deployed to steer the reader through – or round – a difficult technical problem. So discussion of the speed of the atoms in the void is prefaced by a lyrical description of dawn (2.142–9), offering an analogy which explains the whole thing in a nutshell to anyone prepared to use his eyes: *omnibus in promptu manifestumque est* (149). How many of his readers Lucretius might really have expected to grapple seriously with such technical questions we can only wonder. The pretty description of dawn develops a *topos* familiar in epic from Homer onwards, and readers conversant with and responding to the literary stimulus, and knowing nothing of modern distinctions between upper- and lower-case letters, may well have heard the *aurora* of modern texts as Aurora,[54] the goddess. The appeal to the evidence of the senses of course reflects basic Epicurean doctrine, as the argument from analogy reflects Epicurean practice. What is specifically Lucretian is the loving particularity of the description, reinforced by alliteration, a profusion of decorative epithets and synaesthetic metaphor subtly conveying the materiality of these phenomena.[55] The reader is lulled into acquiescence

---

[51] Kenney 1972.

[52] Campbell 2003: 182, q.v. for the full range of literary sources exploited.

[53] OLD, *dispono* 2b, *dispositio*; cf. Kenney 1981: 19–20, comparing 4.572–94. The same abrupt invocation of common sense at 5.42.

[54] So indeed printed by most editors down to the early nineteenth century.

[55] Catrein 2003: 170. See further D. P. Fowler 2002: 217–23 ad loc.

with the argument that follows – if indeed he is not tempted to skip it, as one wonders whether Memmius, to whom the passage is specifically addressed, may have been.

Practice in description was a standard part of rhetorical training. Persius is scornful of poets who cannot even 'describe a grove', *ponere lucum*, a familiar *topos* like the epic dawn.[56] Such descriptions are apt to be no more than technically adroit but lifeless variations on a trite theme. Lucretius' are in a class by themselves, truly embodying the precept of Cicero, echoed by Quintilian, that what is described should seem to be taking place before the eyes of the hearer, *quasi gerantur sub aspectum* (*De or.* 3.202 = *Inst.* 9.2.27).[57] So the famous description of sunlight striking through the awnings spread over the theatre (4.72–83) lavishly sugars a particularly indigestible Epicurean bolus, the explanation of the mechanism of vision and dreaming.[58] Lucretius' presentation of the argument here, 'half-way between analogy and example',[59] acquires persuasive force from the brilliance and accuracy of his depiction of a spectacle which must often have been the subject of admiring comment.[60] 'This imagery is put to vigorous logical work carrying a whole theory of optics.'[61]

Book 6 of the *DRN* is particularly rich in vivid description. In it Lucretius completes his mission to disabuse men once and for all of the fears that Epicurus had shown to be irrational. Not the least of these was fear of the gods as responsible for destructive, threatening, or mysterious phenomena such as thunderstorms, tornadoes, volcanic eruptions, 'marvels' of all kinds, and disease. He must have been alert to the danger that a mere catalogue accompanied by explanations, following on the long *tour de force* that ends Book 5, might bore his readers; and indeed, in spite of all, this book, apart from the very end, seems to have been regarded by posterity as something of an anticlimax, for it has certainly been less widely read and appreciated than the others. The unexpected appearance of the Muse Calliope near the beginning of the book evidently betokens awareness of this problem:

---

[56] *Satires* 1.70; see Bramble 1974: 120 and n. 1.

[57] This is 'the force that knows how to transform into sensory "evidence" the suggestion of things perceived' (Conte 1994: 16).

[58] On which see Catrein 2003: 114–27.   [59] Bailey 1947: 1186.

[60] The theatre is again invoked to illustrate the argument at 6.108–13, where the rumbling and crashing of thunderbolts is compared to the sound made by the awnings in a high wind.

[61] West 1969: 39; 'vigorous' is good. Cf. again Catrein 2003: 181–2 on Lucretius' use of synaesthetic metaphor to convey the materiality of these phenomena.

> tu mihi supremae praescripta ad candida calcis
> currenti spatium praemonstra, callida Musa
> Calliope, requies hominum diuomque uoluptas,
> te duce ut insigni capiam cum laude coronam.
>
> $\qquad\qquad\qquad\qquad\qquad\qquad\qquad$ (6.92–5)

Do you, as I speed towards the marked-out white line of my final goal, Calliope, cunning Muse, the repose and delight of gods and men, show me my course before me, so that guided by you I may win a garland with signal renown.

The appeal to Calliope is no more 'purely conventional' than that to Venus in the proem to Book 1,[62] which the words *requies hominum diuomque uoluptas* inevitably recall. In not only invoking Calliope (apposite as the Muse of epic) but also harnessing the image, familiar since Pindar, of the poet as charioteer, Lucretius is acknowledging that in this last lap of his poetic course he must deploy the full resources of his poetic art: the point is driven home by the pun *CALLIda CALLIope*.[63]

In what follows he rises triumphantly to the challenge. The first part of the book centres on violent natural phenomena and culminates in diatribe style[64] on the folly of supposing that thunderbolts betoken divine displeasure (6.379–422). From phenomena inspiring terror he then passes to those which occasion superstitious wonder, 'things unique or anomalous'.[65] Hence a modulation from the pathetic to the expository, diversified by ornamental descriptive touches drawing on the sometimes recondite literary sources from which his educated readers might have learned of these alleged marvels: the *doctus poeta* had a right to expect *docti lectores*.

The catalogue of marvels culminates in magnetism (6.906–1069), important as exemplifying a fundamental principle of Epicurean physics and a phenomenon that evidently interested Lucretius.[66] From magnetism he passes to disease, concluding with a graphic and gruesome account of the Athenian plague of 430 BC. The preceding discussion of the mechanics of infection (6.1090–1137), the scientific reason for including the subject, is relatively brief and dispassionate; nothing prepares for the abrupt transition to the

---

[62] Bailey 1947: 1567; see Kenney 1995: 11–15.

[63] On the large subject of Lucretius' use of etymology and wordplay see, e.g., Bailey 1947: 158–9; Gale 1994a: *passim*; Dionigi 1988: 65–70 and *passim*.

[64] The series of aggressive questions at 6.395–412 is characteristic of the hectoring style of the streetcorner preacher, the philosopher on the soapbox; cf. Kenney 1971: 17–19; Wallach 1975, 1976.

[65] Bailey 1947: 1661. Though they formally purport to illustrate the doctrine of the plurality of causes (6.703–11), the leitmotiv is the same: that the causes are not supernatural.

[66] Sedley 1998: 53–4.

picture of horror that now unfolds. The narrative is closely based on that of Thucydides (2.47–53), itself highly coloured and in scale and detail equally unexpected.[67] Vivid and grisly as Thucydides' descriptions are, Lucretius heightens them. Where Thucydides had described the breath of the infected as 'unnatural and evil-smelling' (2.49.2), Lucretius invokes the stench of corpses left to rot, 6.1154–5 *odorem,* | *rancida quo perolent proiecta cadauera ritu.* In Thucydides their 'inward parts burned' (2.49.5); in Lucretius 'a flame like a furnace raged in the stomach', 6.1159 *flagrabat stomacho flamma ut fornacibus intus.*

The climax of Thucydides' account is a powerful picture of progressive demoralisation. It began with the violation of traditional burial customs: people would appropriate the funeral pyres of others or throw their own dead on them (2.52.4). That, however, was only the beginning; much worse was to follow, a state of total moral anarchy, in which men thought only of pleasure, unmindful of divine sanctions or human laws (2.53). His description of the unceremonious treatment of the dead is comparatively low-key: having disposed of them as described, people simply 'walked away'. That is an effective (and one might think accurate) portrayal of the behaviour of people whose responses have been stunned by suffering and despair. It is this scene, not the picture of the following moral collapse, that ends the *DRN* as we have it:

> multaque res subita et paupertas horrida suasit:
> namque suos consanguineos aliena rogorum
> insuper extructa ingenti clamore locabant
> subdebantque faces, multo cum sanguine saepe
> rixantes potius quam corpora desererentur.
>
> (6.1282–6)

The suddenness of it, and poverty, prompted many shocking things. For they would lay their own dead with loud outcry on other people's pyres and light them, often coming to blows and bloodshed rather than abandon their dead.

Lucretius has not merely embellished Thucydides' picture; he contradicts it, replacing the silent departure of the mourners by a noisy and shockingly undignified brawl. This was not gratuitous. In fighting like this over the disposal of their dead they can be seen evincing all the irrelevant emotions that had been bitingly exposed as irrational in Book 3. If indeed this is how Lucretius intended the poem to end, he expected his readers to deduce the moral for themselves: that this scene was an image of the spiritual darkness

[67] Hornblower 1991: 316–18.

from which Epicurus had saved mankind.[68] The case for and against that interpretation must be argued elsewhere. Here it is pertinent to note that the foregoing analyses of Lucretius' rhetorical patterning of his arguments may lend support to an alternative view: that this highly charged manifestation of the grand style (which does not illustrate what precedes) was meant to be followed by a soberly expressed conclusion and final explicit restatement of the Epicurean message. Lucretius doubtless did not fear death himself, but it may have robbed him of the last word.

Further reading

The foundations of a truly informed appreciation of Lucretius' language and style for modern English-speaking readers were laid by Sellar as long ago as 1855 in *Oxford Essays*; see now Sellar 1889: 384–407. He was followed by Munro 1886: II, 8–20, acknowledging Sellar's account as 'by far the best' (20); both still repay study. The most comprehensive and detailed recent treatment of Lucretius' usage is that of Bailey 1947: 51–171; somewhat less ample but also useful is that of W. E. Leonard and S. B. Smith 1965; 129–86. Dudley 1965a offers contributions on a number of aspects; that of Maguinness provides pertinent selective discussions, coupled with a salutary warning against judging Lucretius by Augustan stylistic norms. On his standards of poetic craftsmanship as essentially Hellenistic see Kenney 1970 and R. D. Brown 1982. Dionigi 1988 brings together previously published essays in a stimulating demonstration of the organic relationship between words and things in Lucretius' poetry. On the technique of writing Latin hexameters Winbolt 1908 is still the best guide. The analyses of Lucretian imagery by West 1969 brilliantly illustrate his exactness in the use of words. Catrein 2003 breaks new ground in his examination of Lucretius' exploitation of synaesthetic metaphor to inform his imagery with Epicurean implications. On his rhetoric Classen 1968 and Asmis 1995 make important contributions; Wallach 1976: 1–10 had already pointed out that the widely held view that Lucretius' poetry was 'not rhetorical' was fallacious. Less specifically focused discussions of his poetic strategies are offered by Gale 1994a: 138–55 and Volk 2002: 83–118.

---

[68] The current orthodoxy: Gale 1994a: 224 n. 69; Gale *ap.* Kenney 1995: 46–7. Tentatively dissenting Kenney 1995: 19–20.

7

Lucretius and later Latin literature in antiquity

Parcus deorum cultor et infrequens,
insanientis dum sapientiae
    consultus erro, nunc retrorsum
      uela dare atque iterare cursus

cogor relictos: namque Diespiter   5
igni corusco nubila diuidens
    plerumque, per purum tonantis
      egit equos uolucremque currum,

quo bruta tellus et uaga flumina,
quo Styx et inuisi horrida Taenari   10
    sedes Atlanteusque finis
      concutitur . . .

I used to worship the gods grudgingly and not often, a wanderer, expert in a crazy wisdom, but now I am forced to sail back and once again go over, the course I had left behind. For Jupiter who usually parts the clouds with the fire of his lightning has driven his thundering horses and flying chariot through a cloudless sky, shaking the dull earth and restless rivers, the Styx and the fearsome halls of hateful Taenarus, and the Atlantean limits of the world.

(Horace, Odes 1.34.1–12, transl. West 1995)

Horace recants the 'madness' of Epicurean philosophy, which teaches that the gods take no part in the affairs of the world. The poet is forced to reverse his position after witnessing a thunderbolt from the blue, a display of the power that Jupiter wields throughout a universe whose limits are sketched in the panorama of the third stanza. That vision, based on a description by the early Greek poet Hesiod of the cosmic effects of the battle between Zeus and the monstrous Typhoeus (*Theogony* 839–41), implicitly corrects the vision at the beginning of *DRN* 3 of the peaceful and remote abode of the gods (itself modelled on another early Greek description of the divine, the calm of Olympus at *Odyssey* 6.42–6) and of a universe marvellously empty of all but the atoms eternally tumbling through the void.

'Lucretius is everywhere in this ode.'[1] Horace acts out a script written by Lucretius himself, when he warned (*DRN* 5.82–6) that 'if those who have learned well that the gods lead a life free from care (*nam bene qui didicere deos securum agere aeuom*) nevertheless wonder at the reasons for all that happens, especially in those matters which they see overhead in the heavenly regions, they are carried back again to their old superstitions (*rursus in antiquas referuntur religiones*)'. In his earlier *Satires* Horace had been a faithful pupil of Lucretius and scoffed at pious frauds: 'for I have learnt that the gods lead a life free from care' (*Sat.* 1.5.101 *namque deos didici securum agere aeuum*). Ancient literary imitation always tends to oscillate between hero-worship and violent antagonism: devotion and rebellion are intensified when the object of imitation is a poem about the ultimate truths of the universe.

Authority and belief

Horace's anti-conversion in *Odes* 1.34 purports to be a personal confession, but could almost be a blueprint for a dominant strand in the response to the *DRN* in later antiquity and beyond. Lucretius largely sets the parameters for the response to the *DRN* through his own statements about his relationship to his literary and philosophical predecessors.[2] Philosophically he is the faithful disciple, treading in the footsteps of Epicurus, and the relentless iconoclast when it comes to the false belief systems of others;[3] poetically he is the proud innovator, wandering over the untrodden paths of a mountainous landscape of the Muses.[4] Lucretius defines his relationship both to the Greek philosophical poet Empedocles and to the Roman epic poet Ennius through a bracing combination of homage (to their linguistic and mental powers) and repudiation (of their false doctrines about the nature of the world and of the soul). Later responses to Lucretius himself display a similar mixture of fascination and repulsion. The gravitational pull of this strongest of Latin poets is dangerous not just because it threatens the independence of those who fall within it, but also because Lucretius preaches an Epicurean gospel at odds with many of the core values and traditions of Rome. That danger should not, however, be exaggerated within the pluralist and relatively tolerant society of pre-Christian Rome, and the idea of a conspiracy of silence,

---

[1] West 1995: 163.
[2] On the methods and sources of Lucretius' own brand of polemical allusion see Hardie 1986: 233–7.
[3] See pp. 21–2 above.   [4] See pp. 70–1 above.

based on the fact that no Roman poet before Ovid actually names Lucretius, is to be rejected.[5]

In this section are surveyed the varying philosophical and literary responses to Lucretius' most distinctive claim, to be the master of truth. The history of Lucretius' reception begins with another great literary stylist who, like Lucretius, forged a Latin medium for Greek philosophy: Cicero. In a letter of 54 BC to his brother (*Q. Fr.* 2.10.3) he praises the *DRN* as a poem both of great genius (*ingenium*) and of great art. Jerome's report that Cicero edited the poem after Lucretius' death is unreliable,[6] but it is hard to resist the cumulative impression that, in the mainly negative reporting of Epicurean doctrines in his philosophical works, Cicero engages specifically and in detail with Lucretius.[7] When in *Tusculan Disputations* 1.48 (45 BC) Cicero scoffs at Epicureans who venerate as a god the discoverer and chief (*inuentor et princeps*) of a true knowledge of nature, the man who freed them from the most oppressive masters, the fear of death and the afterlife, he surely takes aim at Lucretius. Cicero concludes his earlier treatise *On the Republic* (54–51 BC) with a version of a Platonic myth, a dream in which the younger Scipio is taken up to the stars to meet the soul of his father, the elder Scipio Africanus, who reveals to him the rewards in the afterlife that await those who devote their lives to the public service of Rome. The younger Scipio begins by alluding to Ennius' account in the prologue to his epic on Roman history, the *Annals*, of his dream-vision of the shade of his poetic father, Homer, the passage to which Lucretius refers at 1.117–26 both to praise and criticise his epic predecessor. Cicero alludes to Lucretius' allusion to Ennius and implicitly corrects it, and he enlists Ennian archaising in the service of a doctrine about the afterlife and a message about the value of a life in war and politics, both of which the Epicurean Lucretius had rejected. The Ciceronian Dream of Scipio is thus the first 'anti-Lucretius'.[8]

Virgil also reworks the Ennian Dream of Homer in the meeting between Aeneas and the shade of Anchises in the Underworld in *Aeneid* 6. The following scene, in which the father first expounds to his son the nature of the universe and of the soul and then shows him a parade of future Roman heroes in order to spur him to strive for the glory of Rome, is indebted to the

---

[5] The idea goes back to Martha 1884: 22–3, romantically comparing the mystery surrounding the 'impious' poem to the ban imposed by Roman religion on entering those dread woods struck by lightning. The light of common sense is introduced by Traina 1975.

[6] *Chron.* (Helm) p. 149.

[7] See Pucci 1966 for a judicious survey; see also Novara 1983: 386–443; Schiesaro 1987; Zetzel 1998 (on Cicero's reversal of the Lucretian message in another carefully structured six-book work); pp. 46, 48–9, 51–2 above.

[8] So suggests Fontaine 1966.

Ciceronian Dream of Scipio. Here at the heart of the *Aeneid* Virgil lays out the core values of a vision of Rome, in a complex reworking of Ennius, Lucretius and Cicero's prior reworking of both Ennius and Lucretius.[9] Anchises is most Lucretian in the first part of his speech to Aeneas, an account of natural philosophy whose 'manner is constantly and pointedly Lucretian; the matter would have excited Lucretius' disdain.'[10] The use of a Lucretian manner to convey the matter of a Platonic-Pythagorean-Stoic account of a providentialist universe in which souls are punished or rewarded through a cycle of reincarnation enacts a pointed polemic with the *DRN*.

'The influence, direct and indirect, exercised by Lucretius on the thought, the composition, and the style of the *Georgics* was perhaps stronger than that ever exercised, before or since, by one great poet on another.'[11] The *DRN* inaugurates the line of Latin didactic poetry that extends down to the eighteenth century, and in his own didactic poem, the *Georgics*, Virgil unsurprisingly engages in a continuous dialogue with Lucretius.[12] Anchises slips easily into Lucretian mode in the largest panel of didactic poetry in the epic *Aeneid* but Lucretius is present throughout the *Aeneid* and already an important model for the *Eclogues*. It might, arguably, be stated simply that 'The influence exercised by Lucretius on Virgil was perhaps stronger than that ever exercised, before or since, by one great poet on another.'[13] From the beginning of Virgil's career this intertextuality, to use the modern term, extends beyond the narrowly textual to encompass a debate about world-views.

There is reliable evidence that in his youth Virgil spent time in Epicurean circles in the Bay of Naples. The simple pleasures of the pastoral world of his first major work, the *Eclogues*, have often been compared to the Epicurean ethical ideal.[14] The poetry book's opening picture of a music-making shepherd reclining beneath a tree owes something to Lucretian illustrations of the contented life of simple countryfolk in a tuneful landscape (*DRN* 2.29–33; 5.1392–8). But this is a poetic world from which the traditional gods have not been banished, and in which a rustic culture hero is literally elevated to a divinity ascribed only figuratively to Epicurus by Lucretius. 'A god he was, a god' (*DRN* 5.8 *deus ille fuit, deus*) says Lucretius of his master, the brute fact of whose mortality is acknowledged at 3.1042–4. 'A god, a god he is, Menalcas' (*Ecl.* 5.64 *deus, deus ille, Menalca*) sings the shepherd Mopsus of

---

[9] Hardie 1986: 75–83. [10] Austin 1977: 221. [11] Sellar 1877: 199.

[12] Gale 2000 is the fullest treatment.

[13] A fact symbolised in the ancient biographical fiction that Virgil assumed the *toga uirilis* on the day that Lucretius died (Donatus, *Life of Virgil* 6).

[14] On the affinity between pastoral and Epicureanism see Rosenmeyer 1969. *Eclogues* and Lucretius: Hardie 2006 (with earlier literature).

the resurrected Daphnis now installed on Olympus. The *Eclogues*' world is also one that the Lucretian therapy of desire does not reach, as the lovelorn Corydon discovers in *Eclogue* 2.[15]

Attraction to and rejection of the Lucretian message are combined in famous lines at the centre of the *Georgics*, a didactic poem ostensibly on farming but whose concerns extend to the largest questions about man's place in the world:

> felix qui potuit rerum cognoscere causas
> atque metus omnis et inexorabile fatum
> subiecit pedibus strepitumque Acherontis auari:
> fortunatus et ille deos qui nouit agrestis
> Panaque Siluanumque senem Nymphasque sorores.
>
> (2.490–4)

Blessed the man who was able to know the causes of things and trampled beneath his feet all fears and inexorable Fate and the din of greedy Acheron. Happy also the man who knows the rustic gods, and Pan and old Silvanus and the sisterhood of nymphs.

Lines 490–2, drenched in the language of the *DRN*, acknowledge the happiness awaiting the man who has successfully mastered the Lucretian syllabus and conquered ancestral superstition, but lines 493–4 express sympathy for an alternative and incompatible gnosis based on traditional religious and cultural values. Virgil borrows from Lucretius the positive imagery of a sequestered life of contented virtue in the countryside (*G.* 2.458–540: cf. *DRN* 2.20–36), but the god who, he prays in the prologue (1.24–42), will preside over an Italy restored is not Venus, the fructifying and maternal personification (but no more) of nature, invoked to bring peace to Rome in the Lucretian prologue, but the male cosmocrator Octavian, already set on the path to posthumous deification through his military impersonation of a thundering Jupiter (*G.* 4.560–2).

Thundering Octavian at the end of the *Georgics* paves the way for the grand epic themes of Virgil's *Aeneid*. Lucretius energetically destroys the belief in the divine agency of the thunderbolt (6.96–422), dethroning the mythological Jupiter. In traditional epic Jupiter and the Olympian pantheon are fully at home, but in the *Aeneid* it is often as if the gods have been redomiciled through a Virgilian 'remythologisation' of what Lucretius had

---

[15] See Clausen 1994: 74, quoting the Preface to Dryden's *Sylvae*: '*Virgils* Shepherds are too well read in the Philosophy of *Epicurus* and of *Plato*' (Dryden 1956–2000: III, 15).

demythologised.[16] The main narrative of the *Aeneid* begins with a violent storm motivated through an elaborate divine machinery, but whose language is largely a patchwork of passages in which Lucretius exposes the materialist reality of meteorological events.[17] Lucretius uses the imagery of gigantomachy (the battle between the Olympian gods and their chthonic enemies) in inverted form, to celebrate philosophy's destruction of the power of the sky-gods of traditional religion (esp. at 5.110–25). Virgil restores gigantomachy as a recurrent image of the successful struggle of Jupiter and his vicars on earth against their impious enemies. Virgil's epic world is once more full of gods, and the *religio* overthrown by Lucretius (1.62–79) is reinstalled at the heart of Rome (*Aen.* 8.349–50 *religio . . . dira loci* 'the fearful religion of the place', the sign of Jupiter's presence on the Capitol), but this is an indelibly post-Lucretian Rome.

At one point a character in the *Aeneid* goads Jupiter to respond to a prayer by suggesting that the Lucretian teaching about the thunderbolt might be true. Iarbas asks: 'Is it in vain that we shudder when you hurl your thunderbolts, Father? Are they blind, those fires in the clouds that terrify our spirits? Is it empty rumblings that they stir up?' (4.208–10) Within the fiction of the poem Jupiter is listening and immediately intervenes in the action. Yet the poem throws up enough hints about the uncertainty and unreality of events on the supernatural plane to make some readers suspect that Virgil had not entirely shaken off his Epicurean leanings.[18] Dido's Carthage, the city-foundation that both mirrors and threatens the future Rome, has been seen as the site for an alternative Epicurean set of values, filtered through Lucretian allusion.[19]

The links of poetry with science and philosophy had always been strong in antiquity, and this alone assured Lucretius a central place in the later history of Latin poetry. The *DRN* and Virgil's *Georgics* are the twin foundations of the tradition of didactic poetry in Latin. The kind of pleasure whose pursuit is the subject of Ovid's parodic didactic poem *The Art of Love* is very different from that advocated by Epicurus, but Lucretius had himself already given instructions in the management of *eros* at the end of his fourth book, and Ovid gives a hyper-Lucretian account of the origins of human society at *Ars amatoria* 2.467–88 when the Venus of sexual desire and union from

---

[16] Remythologisation: Hardie 1986: 178. On Lucretius' demythologising rationalisation of myth see Gale 1994a.

[17] Hardie 1986: 180–3, 237–40.   [18] See esp. Mellinghoff-Bourgerie 1990.

[19] Dido the Epicurean: Pease 1935: 36–8; Dyson 1996; Adler 2003. Kronenberg 2005 reads Aeneas' Italian enemy Mezentius as an 'allegorical Epicurean'.

the proem to *DRN* 1 is grafted onto the history of civilisation in *DRN* 5 to yield a version in which sex alone first civilises primitive man. Ovid is the first Augustan poet to break the alleged 'conspiracy of silence' and name 'sublime' (*sublimis*) Lucretius in a catalogue of poets in *Amores* 1.15. Despite initial appearances to the contrary, the thoroughly modern Ovid has an affinity with the old-fashioned Lucretius: both are poets of enlightenment and free-thinking, and 'Ovid, intelligent and impatient of the obscure, was temperamentally equipped to respond to the magnificent and unequivocal clarity of the Lucretian message.'[20] Ovid frames his epic *Metamorphoses* with two grand passages of didactic, the cosmogony in the first, and the Speech of Pythagoras in the last book. Pythagoras' mind flies freely through the skies (*Met.* 15.62–4), in the wake of the Lucretian Epicurus (*DRN* 1.72–7). Ovid's Pythagoras speaks with the stern superiority of the Lucretian voice, but teaches a doctrine about the soul diametrically opposed to the Epicurean. In this Ovid is true to the contrast-imitation programmed into the tradition of Lucretian didactic by Lucretius himself. The Lucretian freedom of the skies has particular relish for Pythagoras, a political exile from the tyranny of Polycrates in his native Samos. The path of the Lucretian Epicurus and the Ovidian Pythagoras will, finally, be the path of Ovid in the sky-soaring immortality in fame that he predicts for himself, out of reach of the anger of Jupiter and Augustus (*Met.* 15.871–9).

Looking further into the first century AD, contrast-imitation defines the relationship between the *DRN* and Manilius' *Astronomica*, a scientific didactic poem, of late Augustan and Tiberian date, which presents a Stoic account of astronomy and astrology in self-conscious opposition to the *DRN*'s Epicurean and anti-providential account of the world.[21] Virgil's incorporation of Lucretian scientific didactic into his epic narrative set a fashion for the inclusion of elements of natural philosophy in later Latin historical and mythological epic. Lucan narrates Roman civil war as cosmic catastrophe in a Stoic universe gone mad. Rome's self-destruction is compared to the final dissolution of the laws of nature at the collapse of the fabric of the universe (*machina mundi*), in a realisation of Lucretius' vision of the end of the world (*DRN* 5.93–6; cf. Lucan 1.79–80).[22] Lucretius uses multiple alternative explanations of phenomena in conformity with Epicurean orthodoxy to reinforce materialist certainty; Lucan and Statius use the form to highlight an inability

---

[20] Kenney 1973: 127–8, speaking of Ovid's use of language. Lucretius in Ovid's amatory works: Sommariva 1980, Shulman 1980/1, Miller 1997; in the *Metamorphoses*: Due 1974: 29–33.

[21] A. Wilson 1985: 286–9; Luhr 1969: 172 'The poem of Manilius is *the* "anti-Lucretius" [*Gegenlukrez*] of antiquity.'

[22] Lucan and Lucretius: Esposito 1996.

or unwillingness to learn the true cause of an event or phenomenon.[23] The monstrous worlds of Lucan's *Civil War* and Statius' *Thebaid* defeat attempts at rational explanation, a failure made the more abject through contrast with the confident certainties of Lucretius.

In late antiquity the use of Lucretius' weapons against himself takes on new ferocity in the service of a Christian zeal.[24] The African Church Father Arnobius (late third century AD), attacking the pagans, lists the benefactions for which Christ may justly be considered divine in terms that echo Lucretius' comparison of the 'divine' benefactions of Epicurus with the more dispensable benefactions of the traditional gods, Bacchus, Ceres, Hercules, and so forth (Arnobius, *Contra nationes* 1.38; cf. *DRN* 5.1–54). But Arnobius also polemicises with Lucretius: his divine hero, Christ, 'showed that which first brought mankind profit and salvation, what god is, how great, and of what nature', in contrast to Epicurus' revelation of a universe without gods. Arnobius' pupil Lactantius (240–320) frequently quotes Lucretius, sometimes enlisting him in the attack on traditional religious practice and superstition, but more often turning Lucretian scorn for the folly of non-Epicureans against what for Lactantius is the madness of Epicurus.[25] Lucretius' description of Epicurus as a guide to the *summum bonum* (*DRN* 6.24–8) is diverted to the praise of the Christian God (Lactant. *Div. Inst.* 7.27.6). Such attacks on the folly of Lucretius may have provided an impetus to the story in Jerome about the madness and suicide of the poet.[26]

Ways of seeing

In *Odes* 1.34 Horace gives a visionary account of his counter-conversion from Epicureanism (see above), in this faithful to the power of vision in the *DRN* as an intellectual and emotional instrument.[27] For Lucretius poetic vision serves the purposes of philosophical insight. In Epicurean epistemology sense perception is the foundation of knowledge; the *DRN* appeals continuously to the evidence of the senses, and of sight in particular, as the basis for correct judgements as to the nature of the reality that underlies the world around us. Lucretius offers us vivid pictures of the phenomenal world, and he finds ways of making us see into the invisible world of the atoms

---

[23] See Hardie forthcoming a. On the previous use of Lucretian multiple explanations by Virgil and Ovid see Perkell 1989: 166–72; K. S. Myers 1994: 140.

[24] Lucretius and the Church Fathers: Hagendahl 1958. Lucretius and early Christian poets: Prudentius: Rapisarda 1951; Boethius: O'Daly 1991: index s.v. 'Lucretius'.

[25] Brandt 1891.   [26] Canfora 1993b: 99–105.

[27] On the acuity of Lucretian visualisation see Jenkyns 1998: 275–8.

themselves, not least through a use of poetic simile that functions as scientific analogy. The philosophical 'action', as it were, of the poem is repeatedly focalised through viewing and spectating figures, beginning with Epicurus himself, who dares to lift up his eyes to outstare the gods at a time when human life lay oppressed by religion 'for all to see' (1.62–7). The *DRN* opens with a religious vision, an epiphany, of Venus, diverted to Epicurean ends.

This section examines aspects of the later response to the intense visualisings of the *DRN*: religious visions and the related experience of poetic inspiration, visions of the natural world sublime or otherwise, the use of poetic imagery to enable a vision of the truth.

The Lucretian visionary zeal is commandeered by the Stoic philosopher Seneca in his eagerness to peer into the secrets of the universe.[28] Earlier the poets Virgil and Horace had delighted in suddenly opening windows on a vision of the natural or supernatural worlds.[29] In *Eclogue* 5 the resurrected Daphnis stares with wild surmise on a re-divinisation of the vision, in the proem to *DRN* 3, of the dwelling-places of the Epicurean gods, and of the atoms whirling through the void beneath Lucretius' feet (*Ecl.* 5.56–7): 'Shining Daphnis marvels at the unfamiliar threshold of Olympus and sees the clouds and stars beneath his feet.' Another pointedly anti-Lucretian vision of what lies beneath results when Hercules violently tears open the cave of Cacus at *Aeneid* 8.241–2: 'there was revealed Cacus' cave, his vast palace was uncovered, and the shadowy caverns' recesses lay open', compared in the following simile to the sudden opening up of the mythological world of the dead, in defiance of the Lucretian denial of traditional eschatology. The lexicon of revelation (*detego, appareo, penitus, patesco, cauernae*) is heavily Lucretian. The most hallucinatory of the visions in the *Aeneid* comes in Aeneas' dark night of the soul in Book 2, when his mother, Venus, the goddess whose epiphany introduces the *DRN*, suddenly appears in all her divine radiance to cleanse the fog from her son's mortal sight so that he can see into the reality of things: an apocalyptic vision of the Olympian gods at work on the destruction of Troy. This is as far from Epicurean theology as possible, but derives much of its terror from an awareness that it alludes by inversion to a Lucretian vision of divinity. Whatever Lucretius meant when he summoned up all the resources of the ancient language of prayer and epiphany in his great opening hymn to Venus, the many imitations of

---

[28] E.g. *Quaestiones naturales* 6.5.2; *De otio* 5.6. See Mazzoli 1970: 206–9; G. Williams 2006: 124–46; p. 175 below.

[29] For fuller discussion of the Virgilian and Horatian passages discussed below see Hardie forthcoming b and Hardie 2008.

this passage usually serve a supernaturalist view of the presence of love and desire in the world.[30]

Closely related to the Venus proem, and itself the object of numerous imitations, is Lucretius' description of his Bacchic inspiration as he wanders over the mountain of the Muses (1.921–30).[31] Elsewhere he explains the atomic causes of the echoes in the countryside that have led the unenlightened to a false belief in a landscape populated by divine beings – satyrs, nymphs and fauns (4.580–94). Horace, in ironic awareness of the Lucretian disenchantment of the numinous poetic world, describes a vision of Bacchus in a remote mountain landscape teaching the nymphs and satyrs (*Odes* 2.18), the emotion of which still fills his breast: 'Euhoe, my mind quivers with fresh fear, and heart full of Bacchus I feel a troubled joy' (5–7). The oxymoron of the last two words (*turbidum laetatur*) recalls the mixture of *horror* and *uoluptas* that Lucretius experiences at the revelation of atomic reality (*DRN* 3.28–30). *Credite posteri*, says Horace in the second line: an earnest appeal to posterity for credence, or daring posterity to be credulous?

Lucretius' powerful analysis and evocation of the illusions of sense perception and desire in *DRN* 4 are nowhere put to more effective use than in Ovid's fable of the credulous boy Narcissus, duped both by aural and ocular illusions, and unable to cure himself of a desire incapable of satisfaction because it is aroused by sense perceptions that do not emanate from a substantial other. 'Credulous boy, why do you grasp in vain at fleeting phantoms?' asks the narrator (*Met.* 3.432), adopting the tone of the Lucretian didactic voice, but incapable of being heard by his fictional character. The whole of the Echo and Narcissus story may be read as a narrativisation of Lucretius' teaching on the subjects of sensory illusion and desire.[32]

In Horace's other major poetic vision under the influence of Bacchus, *Odes* 3.25, he compares his wonder at the crags and empty grove of the poetic landscape into which he has wandered to a sleepless Maenad's amazement at a snowy and mountainous Thracian landscape. Straying off the beaten track Horace yet follows in the traces of Lucretius: the 'empty grove' is a

---

[30] Imitations include Ovid, *Fasti* 4.1–18 (the poet in dialogue with Venus); Statius, *Theb.* 3.295–9; 8.303–38 (prayer to Earth); Apuleius, *Met.* 4.30, 6.6 (Venus), 11.5 (Isis).

[31] Imitated e.g. at Virgil, *G.* 3.291–3; Horace, *Epist.* 1.19.21; Propertius 3.5.19–22; Manilius, *Astronomica* 1.13–19.

[32] Hardie 2002: 150–63. Quinn's claim (1963: 144–7) that by destroying the idealising Catullan tradition of love Lucretius paved the way for the more realistic love elegy is overstated, but the powerful analysis of sexual desire registered with the elegists. On the relative priority of Lucretius and Catullus see p. 69 above.

lyric version of the atomist's vision of the void, and the snowy mountains invert the Lucretian vision of an Olympus where snow never falls (*DRN* 3.20–1).

Horace sums up the experience of *Odes* 3.25, in another oxymoron recalling the Lucretian *horror ac uoluptas*, as 'a sweet danger' (*dulce periculum*). The thrill of following Bacchus is also a way of talking about the temptation for the poet of the sublime. The *DRN* is an important document in the history of the sublime;[33] *sublimis* is the adjective used by Ovid to define Lucretius (*Amores* 1.15.23), and also by Fronto in a letter to Marcus Aurelius (*Ant.* 1.2), writing at a time when Lucretius was highly valued for his archaic manner.[34] Statius labels Lucretius a poet of learning but also of a lofty inspiration, *docti furor arduus Lucreti* (*Silv.* 2.7.76). The Lucretian sublime can be both a challenge and a danger. At *Epistles* 1.19.21 Horace boasts to his servile imitators of his own poetic originality, in language that echoes Epicurus' launch into the infinite, 'I first planted my footsteps freely in the void'. Elsewhere he warns of the danger of overambition, as in *Odes* 4.2 where he deprecates the attempt to take flight in the manner of Pindar, using language and imagery that also allude to Lucretius.[35] Deflation of a sublime often associated with Lucretius is a recurrent Horatian move: in *Odes* 1.28 this is projected onto an epitaph for the Pythagorean philosopher Archytas, who once took visionary mental flight through the universe like Epicurus, and who was able to measure the measureless grains of sand, but who now lies buried under a handful of dust. In *Odes* 1.3 Horace wishes his bosom-friend Virgil a safe voyage to Greece, and inveighs against the man who made the first ship, so embarking mankind on a hazardous and foolish journey into the unknown, in continuous allusion to Lucretius' description of Epicurus' daring launch into the void. The ode is really all about Virgil's hazardous embarkation on the perhaps madly ambitious *Aeneid*, a project which may founder as its hero Aeneas nearly founders in the highly Lucretian storm that opens the epic. At the end of Horace's *Ars poetica* the mad poet is exemplified in Empedocles who, in his wish to be thought a god, climbed to the top of Etna and hurled himself into the volcano's depths. Luciano Canfora suggests attractively that this is an indirect comment on the sky-reaching ambitions of the poet who haunts Horace's own hankering after the sublime, Lucretius, for whom Empedocles was a model of prime importance, and whom Lucretius

---

[33] See ch. 10 below.

[34] The fashion of 'reading Lucretius instead of Virgil', as a character in Tacitus' *Dialogue on Orators* (23.2) puts it.

[35] Hardie 2008; Ferri 1993: Indice degli argomenti principali s.v. 'Sublime'.

implicitly compares to Etna, the volcano of Empedocles' Sicilian landscape, in a passage of notable sublimity (1.722–33).[36]

Lucretius offers the reader a number of memorable landscapes, friendly and domesticated idylls as well as wild scenes of storm and volcano. A speciality is the distant view, whether as an exercise in cultivating philosophical detachment or to convey a synoptic grasp of an aspect of reality.[37] The view of the storm at sea from the elevated temples of wisdom at the beginning of Book 2 has become an emblem of the Lucretian message;[38] the image is turned into landscape reality in Statius' poem on the Epicurean Pollius Felix's villa on the Bay of Naples, *Silvae* 2.2.3 'a lofty villa that gazes out over the Dicarchean deep', a country seat whose owner 'looks down from the lofty citadel of his mind at our wanderings and laughs at human joys' (131–2).

The distant view alternates with the extreme close-up as Lucretius' eye penetrates to the microscopic structure of atomic reality. An exhilarating ability to switch between panorama and close-up is a trick that Virgil learns from Lucretius. But this kind of alternation serves a deeper purpose: Lucretius has an obsessive eye for the structural relationships between different objects and different scales of reality, in order to demonstrate that the whole of the phenomenal world, in all its parts and on all scales, is reducible to the same fundamental reality of invisible atoms moving in the void. Analogies are pursued in detail to show this underlying identity. For example at *DRN* 6.655–72 the terror of volcanic activity is removed through the consideration that these macrocosmic fits of shaking and burning are no more surprising than the fevers that assail the microcosm of the human body. This systematic working out of a correspondence is an important source for what has been called the Virgilian 'multiple correspondence simile', in which the tenor and vehicle of the traditional epic simile are interlinked in intricate detail.[39] Lucretius frequently draws an analogy between internal mental states and external events in the physical world, in the process often revitalising dead metaphors. Some people have a character marked by a tranquil breast and a serene countenance (3.293) *pectore tranquillo . . . uultuque sereno*: this is because in the physical compound of their soul there is a preponderance of air atoms, so that there is a literal calm weather in their breasts. When Virgil uses traditional elemental or meteorological imagery of mental states it is with an intensity and renewed physicality that owes much to Lucretian practice.

---

[36] Canfora 1993b: 100–3.

[37] Distant views in Lucretius: De Lacy 1964; exploited by Virgil: Schroeder 2004.

[38] Blumenberg 1997.   [39] West 1970; Hardie 1986: 219–33 'Levels and imagery'.

More generally the Virgilian sense of a spatio-temporal world shot through with echoes and correspondences and patterned by repetition can be read as a mystification of the Lucretian world where everything is connected by the omnipresent reality of atoms and void. The Virgilian notion of a sympathy between the natural and the human worlds, each subject to a providential ruler, is Stoic not Epicurean, but in the verbal and imagistic elaboration of this vision Virgil again looks to Lucretius, who often uses an analogy between city and universe, whether in the form of an image of the universe as a human construction (the 'walls of the world'), or of an image of the atomic order as a political or social structure, the 'laws of nature' (*foedera naturae*). Troy is destroyed in the space of a single night: 'an ancient city that had ruled for many years crashes to the ground' (*Aen.* 2.363 *urbs antiqua ruit multos dominata per annos*); Aeneas remembers Lucretius' teaching about the end of the world, which 'a single day will consign to destruction, and the massive fabric of the world, held up for many years, will crash down' (*una dies dabit exitio, multosque per annos | sustentata ruet moles et machina mundi*, 5.95–6). The *Aeneid* tells of 'a world destroyd and world restor'd', to borrow Milton's words (*Paradise Lost* 12.3). That equivalence of *urbs* and *orbis* will be crucial for Lucan's narrative of Roman civil war as an event that shakes the cosmos. Lucan's Stoicising nightmare of the dissolution of a Roman universe takes Virgil's epic of foundation as its immediate point of reference, but looks through Virgil to Virgil's own Lucretian models.

Lucretius the Augustan. History, politics, morality. The textual cosmos

In Lucan's epic, through a Stoicising recuperation of Lucretius' Epicurean vision of the world, the revolutionary and iconoclastic *DRN* is found to be useful for telling stories about Roman power. But Lucretius' manner and messages could be put more directly to use by late Republican and Augustan poets engaged with Roman politics and culture. We have learned not to regard Lucretius as an old-fashioned poet out of touch with the *avant-garde* literary movements of the 50s BC,[40] but the zealous voice of a poet out to reform the individual reader and his relation to society is readily adaptable to the *persona* of the '*uates*', 'bard, seer', the word used of themselves by Virgil, Horace and other Augustan poets when they turn away from the private and politically irresponsible pose of the neoteric poets to adopt a more serious role as spokesmen for the moral and political reform and education of the Roman citizen.[41] The Augustan reinvigoration of the traditional concept of the *Musarum sacerdos*, 'priest of the Muses' (Horace, *Odes* 3.1.3), owes

[40] Kenney 1970 is the important article.   [41] Hardie 1986: 17–22; Newman 1967.

something to a remystification of Lucretius' self-representation as a prophet or priest of rationalism. At the beginning of the *Georgics* Virgil replaces Lucretius' presiding 'divinities' Venus and Epicurus with Octavian, god to be, and invokes his aid in a manner programmatic for much that was to come (41–2): 'with me take pity on the country folk ignorant of the way, and enter on your path'; the ignorance, the pity called forth, and a path to be followed are all Lucretian, although the destination is very different.[42] Gregory Hutchinson has recently attempted to down-date the *DRN* to 49 BC or later, at the beginning of the civil war between Pompey and Caesar, in order to explain the urgent sense of a national emergency in the proem:[43] if this is correct, the impulse to write the poem may have more in common with the political motivations of poets writing in the triumviral and Augustan periods than has often been assumed.

On the face of it there might appear a contrast between an Augustan concern with historical achievement, energetic activity in the present guided both by the awareness of the long reach of the past and by the demands of the future, and the Epicurean philosophy of *carpe diem*. But the *DRN* has a very well developed sense of time, above all in the great culture history at the end of Book 5, determinative for most exercises in culture history in the Augustan poets as they try to make sense of the new order by reference to history and prehistory, with hopes of a better and more stable future.[44] The *Georgics* are concerned with the farmer's annual round, but they also register a far longer temporal perspective, looking back to a primal springtime of the earth (*G.* 2.336–45) suggested by Lucretius' account of a temperate 'infancy of the world' (*mundi nouitas*) favouring the birth of the first living things (*DRN* 5.780–820), and allusively charting the progress of mankind from a life in the woods to the arts and sciences of civilisation, in constant dialogue with the Lucretian reconstruction of human prehistory. *Aeneid* 8 marks a pause in the immediate epic action of the poem as Aeneas visits the site of the future Rome; what he hears there, and what he sees on the Shield given him by Venus at the end of the book, with its prophetic scenes of Roman history, taken together offer a panoramic sweep of Roman time, from the primitive inhabitants of Latium to the latest triumph of Augustus, and many of the building blocks are Lucretian.[45] One attraction for Virgil, here and elsewhere, of the Lucretian cultural history is its complexity and nuance, balancing as it does a story of gradual progress towards a summit of civilisation with a nostalgia for a primitive rustic life that approximated more closely to the Epicurean ethical ideal than does the discontented and anxious life of the

---

[42] For the Lucretian parallels see Thomas 1988 ad loc.   [43] G. Hutchinson 2001.
[44] Hardie 2006.   [45] Gransden 1976: 36–41; Hardie 1986: 213–19.

Figure 7.1. The so-called 'Tellus' ('Earth') relief from the Augustan Ara Pacis (9 BC), showing a female personification of fertility and peace in Italy

modern city-dweller: the mixture of optimism and pessimism in the Virgilian view of history is very Lucretian. Venus' sexual persuasion of her husband Vulcan to make the shield for her son is modelled on the Lucretian tableau of Mars and Venus: where Lucretius could only anxiously pray for peace, the sex goddess's softening influence now figuratively smooths the way to the final *pax Augusta*. The *DRN*, for all its power to visualise, does not have a major afterlife in the visual arts, but Karl Galinsky attractively suggests that the Lucretian Venus inspired the iconography of the 'Tellus' relief on the Augustan Ara Pacis (fig. 7.1), a powerful symbol of the emperor's claim to have brought peace and prosperity to the human and natural worlds.[46]

Lucretius is one of the great Roman satirists, in the diatribes against the fear of death and sexual infatuation in Books 3 and 4.[47] This kind of admonition, deriving from an ethical psychotherapy practised by all the Hellenistic schools of philosophy, feeds straightforwardly enough into the moralising discourse of the Augustan poets. A programmatic signal of the importance of the *DRN* for Horace's *Satires* is the simile at *Satires* 1.1.25–6 comparing the moralist who laughs even as he speaks the truth, to teachers who give pastries

[46] Galinsky 1969: 203–41.   [47] Murley 1939, Dudley 1965b, R. D. Brown 1987: 137–9.

to boys to induce them to learn their ABC (*elementa prima*, which could also be translated 'first elements of nature'), reworking Lucretius' honeyed-cup simile (1.936–42). The unflinching exposure of sexual mores in *Satires* 1.2 draws on the diatribe against love at the end of *DRN* 4. In *Satires* 2.4 the Lucretian voice is parodied in the person of an epicure who delivers a long didactic speech on the pleasures of the table, a *bon viveur* whose notion of the happy life corresponds to the popular caricature of Epicureanism. The Neronian satirist Persius, who writes as a committed Stoic, opens with a first line intriguingly redolent of Lucretius, *o curas hominum! o quantum est in rebus inane!* 'Oh the cares of men! How much vacuity there is in things!', the last three words applying the language of Lucretian physics to ethical comment.[48]

Horace transmutes Lucretian thundering into his more genial brand of moralising at various points in the *Odes*. The contrast between the simple life of contentment in the country and the discontents of urban luxury in the proem to *DRN* 2 is a recurrent point of reference, as in the *otium* Ode 2.16, largely a tissue of Lucretian reworkings, or in the first Roman Ode (3.1). The return in the first book of *Epistles* from lyric to the philosophical conversational manner of the *Satires* marks the most intensive engagement with Lucretian models in the Horatian œuvre, but with a further toning down of the strident Lucretian voice into an epistolary intimacy.[49]

Finally, the peculiar relationship of the *DRN* as a text to its subject matter, the nature of the universe, lent itself to Augustan appropriations. Lucretius exploits the two meanings of *elementa* to develop the analogy between the atoms that make up the universe and the letters of the alphabet that make up the *DRN*, so rendering the poem 'a linguistic simulacrum of the entire universe'.[50] The equivalence between poem and world is picked up by Virgil and Ovid in the use of ecphrastic images, the Shield of Aeneas in *Aeneid* 8 and the cosmogony in *Metamorphoses* 1, each of which alludes to cosmic images on the Homeric Shield of Achilles in order to hint that the poem of which it is a part is a cosmic icon, and that its maker is a *poeta creator*, the poet as creator of the universe that he describes,[51] and that as such the poet claims a kind of equivalence with Augustus who through military might has made of the world a Roman universe. Lucretius uses his own text and its production as examples of his subject in other ways: dreams are naturally

---

[48] The problem is that the scholiast says that this line is quoted directly from the early satirist Lucilius: for the issues see Zetzel 1977. On other Lucretian echoes in Persius 1 see Hooley 1997: 29.

[49] Ferri 1993 gives an outstanding account of Horace's use of Lucretius in *Epistles* 1.

[50] See pp. 90–1 above.

[51] Shield of Aeneas: Hardie 1986: ch. 8; Ovidian cosmogony as ecphrasis: Wheeler 1995.

explicable as a continuation of waking preoccupations, for example as I, Lucretius, continue writing *rerum naturam* in my dreams (4.969–70). An argument for the relative youth of the world is the fact that mankind is still developing the arts, as, for example, I, Lucretius, am only now the first to translate Greek physics into Latin (5.335–7). The *DRN* is the first Latin poem that self-consciously locates itself at the climax of a narrative 'from the first beginning of the world down to my own times', in the words with which Ovid defines the subject matter of his *Metamorphoses* (1.3–4).

As Monica Gale shows in this volume, the *DRN* also claims a universality of another kind, in its ambition to a generic inclusiveness.[52] In this too the *DRN* is a precursor of Virgil's encyclopaedic epic, which in a literary imperialism embraces not only the higher genres of epic and tragedy, but also more humble kinds, such as elegy and pastoral. The history of civilisation in *DRN* 5 describes the invention of music in the form of a 'rustic muse' (*agrestis musa*, 5.1398) recognisable as pastoral poetry: Virgil certainly recognises it as such when he alludes to this passage, and also to the passage on the echoic illusion of a music-making by rustic gods at *DRN* 5.580–94, in programmatic passages in the *Eclogues*.[53] It is almost as if at the beginning of his career Virgil intuits that Lucretius' capacious textual universe will provide space within which to develop the projects of all three of his major works.

Further reading

Alfonsi 1978 provides a detailed survey. Hadzsits 1963: chs. 4 and 9 is still useful. Poignault 1999 includes chapters on Cicero, Manilius, Ovid, Seneca and Lucan, Statius, Quintilian and Fronto, Servius, Lactantius and Jerome. Giesecke 2000 covers Catullus, Virgil and Horace.

For individual authors: CICERO: Pucci 1966, Zetzel 1998; VIRGIL: Hardie 2006 (*Eclogues*), Gale 2000 (*Georgics*), Hardie 1986: ch. 5 (*Aeneid*). HORACE: Rehmann 1969, Dionigi 1997; Ferri 1993 is palmary on Lucretius in the *Satires* and *Epistles*. PROPERTIUS: King 1998. TIBULLUS: Henderson 1969. OVID: Sommariva 1980, Shulman 1980/1 (*Ars* and *Remedia*); Miller 1997 (love elegy); Due 1974: 29–33 (*Metamorphoses*). LUCAN: Esposito 1996. SENECA: Mazzoli 1970, G. Williams 2006. APULEIUS: Zimmerman 2006. ARNOBIUS and LACTANTIUS: Hagendahl 1958. PRUDENTIUS: Rapisarda 1951. Canfora 1993b is suggestive on the theme of Lucretius and madness.

[52] See p. 70 above.   [53] See Hardie 2006: 276, 284–5, 288–9.

II

Themes

8

MONTE JOHNSON AND CATHERINE WILSON

Lucretius and the history of science

The central aim of the *DRN* was to demolish religious belief and banish superstitious fear. To that end Lucretius, following Epicurus' largely lost *On Nature*,[1] referred the production of all effects to the motion and interaction of atoms and denied all providential regulation of the universe: 'Nature is her own mistress and is exempt from the oppression of arrogant despots, accomplishing everything by herself spontaneously and independently and free from the jurisdiction of the gods' (2.1090–2). By way of accomplishing its aim, the poem addressed a range of scientific subjects: nutrition, perception and mental illness; cosmology, the seasons and eclipses; thunder, clouds, and the magnet; the emergence and evolution of animal and vegetable life; contagion, poisoning and plague.

Reintroduced into a Christian culture in which metaphysics and natural philosophy were dominated by a theory of providence and bolstered by Platonic-Aristotelian arguments against materialism, Lucretius' poem produced both fascination and alarm. The theses that reality consists exclusively of atoms and void, that atomic interactions are purposeless and reflect no plan, that there are no immaterial spirits, and that the gods do not care about humanity and produce no effects in the visible world were purged of some features and variously absorbed and reworked into the so-called 'new philosophy' of the seventeenth century. Thanks in large measure to their compelling presentation in Lucretius' poem, Epicurean ideas effectively replaced the scholastic-Aristotelian theory of nature formerly dominant in the universities. In place of continuous matter imbued with forms, qualities and active powers, immutable species differentiated by their unique, individual essences, and a single cosmos, in which order descended from higher entities to lower ones, the moderns came to acknowledge a phenomenal world of largely fleeting appearances and transitory entities, behind which there existed only tiny particles, deprived of all characteristics and powers

---

[1] For Lucretius' use of Epicurus see chs. 1 and 5 above.

except shape, size and movement, in constantly changing configurations and combinations. Both the atomic reality alleged to underlie the appearances and the self-sufficiency of nature forcefully asserted by Lucretius exercised a powerful influence on modern science, and his name was still being regularly invoked in scientific contexts as late as the nineteenth century, with his influence formally acknowledged well into the twentieth.

The undeniable influence of Lucretius' poem raises philosophical questions on the extent to which ancient ideas – about the discreteness of matter, the plurality of worlds, and the spontaneous adaptation of living things – are continuous with our own ideas about atomism, multiple universes and evolution. Readers should find it helpful to consider the continuities and differences on the basis of the intervening history of science.

Some knowledge of Epicurus, Lucretius and the existence of a pagan philosophy which held that all things including earth, air, fire and water (i.e. the elements), plants and animals, originate from atoms persisted in the medieval era.[2] There is mention of Lucretius in a work of William of Conches (c. 1090–c. 1154). Though William did not have access to the DRN, he mentions Lucretius, and he drew on Cicero, Virgil, Priscian, Isidore of Seville and possibly Seneca for his knowledge of his doctrines. In his *Dragmaticon philosophiae* the interlocutor says 'It seems to me, you are secretly falling back on the opinion of the Epicureans, who said that the world consists of atoms.' To which William's philosopher replies:

> When the Epicureans said that the world consists of atoms, they were correct. But it must be regarded as a fable when they said that those atoms were without beginning and 'flew to and fro separately through the great void', then massed themselves into four great bodies. For nothing can be without beginning and place except God.[3]

This compromise between Epicureanism and creationism, unlikely as it seems prima facie, was to have profound resonance throughout the development of the new philosophy and the scientific revolution.

Among the first scientists in the modern era to use Lucretius' text was the humanistic physician Girolamo Fracastoro (1478–1553).[4] In *On Contagion and Contagious Diseases* (1545) he developed a theory of contagion, proposing that some sicknesses are the product of exhalations of seeds or tiny living bodies. Although for Lucretius these contagious seeds are lifeless, the idea is Lucretian enough for words encapsulating

---

[2] See H. Jones 1989: 136–41. For knowledge of Lucretius generally in the Middle Ages see ch. 12 below.

[3] William of Conches 1.6.8–9, transl. Ronca and Curr 1997, modified.

[4] For Fracastoro's engagement with Lucretius see further pp. 191–2 below.

Fracastoro's idea to have been fabricated and interpolated into subsequent editions of Lucretius. These in turn were quoted in later medical texts on disease and bacteria until the late nineteenth century.[5]

Eventually other occult properties involving action-at-a-distance or mysterious communication or transmission were explained by natural philosophers in terms of minute bodies ('corpuscles'). Effluvia such as smokes, steams, fumes, vapours and scents were represented by Lucretius as types of particles, with specific effects (*DRN* 6.769–839), and this scheme was readily adopted by early modern chemists and physicians. The German physician Daniel Sennert (1572–1637) regarded the phenomena of fascination, plague and poisoning as proceeding from corpuscles or corpuscular effluvia. Walter Charleton (1619–1707) explained sympathies and antipathies in terms of a flow of atoms between the impassioned parties. 'Corpuscularians' – the term reflected agnosticism about the ultimate indivisibility of the particles and the existence of the void, and it implied dissociation from orthodox Epicurean atomism and thus from atheism and hedonism – were not applying a modern scheme to phenomena long deemed mysterious, but simply following Lucretius, who had explained dreams, ghosts, plagues and poisoning by the action of corporeal atomic effluvia.

Giordano Bruno (1548–1600) was the first philosopher in the modern period to revive the cosmological ideas of atomism.[6] Lucretius appears often in his writing, although Bruno was by no means an orthodox Epicurean. In *De l'infinito* (1584) the picture of an infinite plenum contained in an infinite void is attributed to Democritus and Epicurus. In his Frankfurt trilogy of Latin poems a kind of vitalistic atomism is elaborated as the explicit foundation of a cosmology embracing infinite worlds, and *De immenso* (1591) is devoted to the plurality and mutability of worlds.

This central Epicurean doctrine immortalised by Lucretius (*DRN* 2.1023–89) was consistent with the Copernican theory that the sun was merely another star, but it contradicted the Aristotelian teaching that our earth stood at the centre of the universe. It raised disturbing questions for Christians concerning the importance of the earth, its inhabitants and its allegedly sacred history. Fantasies of interplanetary travel and the discovery of new worlds nevertheless appeared throughout the seventeenth century, including John Wilkins's *Discovery of a World in the Moon* (1638), Pierre Borel's *New Discourse Proving the Plurality of Worlds* (1657), Cyrano de Bergerac's *States and Empires of the Moon* (1657), Bernard de Fontenelle's *Conversations on the Plurality of Worlds* (1686) and Christiaan Huygens's

---

[5] See Andrade 1928: xix n. 2.
[6] For Bruno's engagement with Lucretius see further pp. 192–5 below.

Cosmotheoros (1698). Leibniz took up the topic in his *New Essays* (written *c.* 1704). Contemporary astronomy takes the plurality thesis for granted, and few modern Christians appear to be troubled by the possibility that intelligent and morally meaningful life might exist in realms unvisited by the historical Jesus.

In *De minimo* (1591) Bruno treated the atom as a physical minimum corresponding to the geometrical minimum of the point and the ontological minimum of the unit or monad. But Bruno rejected the void in favour of a vital ethereal medium responsible for the motion and arrangement of the atoms, holding that the atoms have no gravity and hence cannot spontaneously move. A similar problem dogged atomists throughout the seventeenth century and encouraged Leibniz to invent a related form of vitalistic atomism expounded in his *Monadology* (1714).

Leibniz's return to vitalism came in response to the spectacularly successful revival of materialist atomism, in which the poem of Lucretius played an important part. But Lucretius was only one stream of influence on the development of corpuscular theories of matter in the early modern period. Others included the works of Aristotle (who directly opposed the atomism of Democritus), Hero's *Pneumatica*, and various sources in alchemy, iatrochemistry and metallurgy. Throughout the sixteenth century, natural philosophers worked on the problem of chemical mixtures, initially in response to the ancient controversy about whether in a mixture what is mixed retains its identity in the new substance, or rather takes on a new form. J. C. Scaliger (1484–1558) argued on the side of Aristotle that the mixed substance takes on a new form, and in this was later opposed by the atomist Sebastian Basso (*fl.*1550–1600), who discussed Lucretius in his *Natural Philosophy against Aristotle* (published 1621).

Bernardino Telesio (1509–88) had advanced a radically empiricist, anti-Aristotelian natural philosophy in *De rerum natura juxta propria principia* (1565; complete edn 1586). Telesio's influential views had been adopted at the academy of Cosenza; Francis Bacon (1561–1626) called him 'the first of the moderns' but took aim at him in a late essay, *De principiis atque originibus* (*c.* 1612), rejecting Telesio's system in favour of the atomistic philosophy of Democritus, citing many passages from Lucretius but referring to them as the words of Democritus. Bacon stated there that 'to me the philosophy of Democritus seems worthy to be rescued from neglect', echoing his earlier remark in the *Cogitationes de natura rerum* (written 1605): 'the Democritean doctrine of atoms is either true, or useful for demonstration'.[7] In the *Novum organon* (1620) Bacon recommended Democritus' method of

---

[7] Bacon 1857–74: III, 84; III, 15.

'dissecting nature' as against the Aristotelian method of 'abstraction',[8] and he appealed to the atomic doctrine in the later essay *Of the Dense and Rare* (1623), a subject well suited to atomistic treatment.

Bacon's enthusiasm for ancient atomism was nevertheless tempered and ambiguously expressed.[9] He rejected key tenets of Lucretian atomism such as the void and the swerve, the latter because he was committed to the view that all matter is ordered by divine providence. Although he described the formation of the cosmos out of chaos in terms of atoms, he rejected Copernicanism and the cosmology of infinite worlds. And his view of matter in the *Novum organon* relied as little on the atomic conception of matter as on what he called the 'abstract' Aristotelian one: 'People do not stop abstracting nature until they reach potential and unformed matter, nor again do they stop dissecting nature until they reach the atom. But even if these things were true, they could do little to improve people's fortunes.'[10] Bacon denied that rigid atoms in a vacuum were the 'true particles', replacing them with 'schematisms' resulting from the 'texture' of pneumatic matter. At the same time, the concept and even terminology of the *textura* owe much to ancient atomism in general and to Lucretius in particular.[11] The concept of material texture would later influence the first modern chemist, Robert Boyle.[12]

Daniel Sennert, professor of medicine at Wittenberg and a follower of Bruno's, had noted in an early work:

> everywhere amongst Philosophers and Physicians both Ancient and Modern mention is made of these little Bodies or Atomes, that I wonder the Doctrine of Atomes should be traduced as Novelty . . . All the Learnedest Philosophers . . . have acknowledged that there are such Atomes, not to speak of Empedocles, Democritus, Epicurus, whose Doctrine is suspected, perhaps because it is not understood.[13]

Atomistic ideas were indeed steadily gaining acceptance throughout the seventeenth century, in no small part due to Sennert's own defence of atomism in his *Thirteen Books of Natural Philosophy* (1618). He pointed out that silver atoms retain their individuality even after being combined with gold, reduced to invisibility with nitric acid and passed through a paper filter.[14] This

---

[8] Bacon 1857–74: I, 168–9.

[9] For Bacon's engagement with Lucretius see further pp. 155–8 and 251–2 below.

[10] Bacon 1857–74: I, 178.   [11] So Gemelli 1996: 196–7.   [12] See Clericuzio 1984.

[13] Sennert 1660: 446; the work quoted, the *Epitome philosophiae naturalis*, was first published in 1600; the section on atomism from which the above quotation was taken was included in the 1618 edition.

[14] See Michael 2001.

experiment would in turn be widely cited by other proponents of atomism, such as J. C. Magnenus in his *Democritus Revived, or, On Atoms* (1648). The Dutch physicist Isaac Beeckman (1588–1637) was another working chemist who inclined towards atomism.

Descartes (1596–1650), whose interest in the new physics was sparked off by Beeckman, formed the ambition of displacing the natural philosophy textbooks of the Aristotelians with his own system of the world. He drew not only on Galileo's Democritean analysis of sensory qualities, rejecting the Aristotelian conception of matter as imbued with active 'forms', qualities, and teleological principles, but directly on Lucretian cosmology. He elaborated a theory of the purely material animal and the self-forming cosmos in his suppressed treatise *The World* (written towards the end of the 1620s) and recapitulated his theories in his *Principia philosophiae* (1644). In the *Principia* (2.23) the original object of creation is 'extended substance' – matter that has no qualities apart from being measurable and extended. Corporeal substance, like Lucretian matter, is silent, uncoloured and unscented, but its parts can be moved around relative to one another. And what seems to begin as an undifferentiated block of matter divides into a collection of an indefinite number of particles, 'although it is beyond our power to grasp them all' or even 'exactly how it occurs'. Descartes denied however that there are atoms – least particles – on the grounds that their existence conflicts with God's power to do anything we can imagine. While mechanical statues were interesting to Descartes and his contemporaries, and while machine-animal analogies are not uncommon in baroque literature, Descartes's references to the 'machines of nature', which can grow, react, reproduce and generally display all the manifestations of life, and their operation, point to a specifically materialistic conception of life. The corporeal machine can, as Lucretius posited in *DRN* 4, account for some forms of sensation, dreaming and memory at least in animals. This less than original hypothesis was famously softened by Descartes's superaddition of an incorporeal soul (in humans alone), and by the claim that God is the only source of power, force or motion in the universe, being possessed of unlimited will and power by which he sustains the universe from moment to moment. Nevertheless, Descartes retained the Lucretian notion that from a chaotic state of distributed matter, planetary systems or 'vortices' form spontaneously and their numerous earths bring forth plants, animals and even men.

Sometimes known today as 'the French Bacon', and famous now for his criticisms of Descartes, Pierre Gassendi (1592–1655) was the most important reviver of ancient atomism in the early modern period. He undertook an ambitious project of editing, translating and interpreting an important Greek source for Epicureanism in his *Investigations into the Tenth Book of Diogenes Laertius* (1649), to which was appended his synoptic *Treatise on Epicurean Philosophy*. Although Gassendi's views were well known to his contemporaries through his extensive correspondence, the final version of his philosophy was not published until after his death, in the *Syntagma philosophicum* (1658). This work frequently quotes Lucretius at length and includes a complete philosophy according to the traditional Epicurean division of Canonic (i.e. Logic), Physics and Ethics. Its mechanical accounts of natural phenomena are, like those of his rival Descartes, Lucretian in tenor.

Gassendi was not just a philologist seeking to explicate an ancient philosophy. He intended also to revive atomism as a physical theory, and this required him to redeem atomism from the accusations of impiety and gross hedonism that had dogged it since late antiquity, through the influence of Cicero and the Fathers of the early Church, especially Lactantius. Gassendi, unlike Descartes, admitted least particles. He denied however that they were eternal and uncreated, observing in the *Syntagma*:

> To present at last our conclusion that apparently the opinion of those who maintain that atoms are the primary and universal material of all things may be recommended above all others, I take pleasure in beginning with the words of Aneponymus. After his opening remark that 'There is no opinion so false that it does not have some truth mixed in with it, but still the truth is obscured by being mixed with the false', he then continues, 'For when the Epicureans said that the world consisted of atoms they were correct. But it must be regarded as a fable when they said that these atoms were without beginning and flew to and fro separately through the great void, then massed themselves into four great bodies.' I say I take pleasure from these words for one can draw the inference that there is nothing to prevent us from defending the opinion which decides that the matter of the world and all the things in it is made up of atoms, provided that we repudiate whatever falsehood is mixed in with it.[15]

The words approved by Gassendi and here attributed to Aneponymus are those of William of Conches, the medieval philosopher quoted above. The view advanced is recognisable to the reader of the *Timaeus*, in which Plato presents his own version of atomism in the context of a creationist account of the formation of the world and its elements, plants and animals. This model for the reconciliation of theology with matter theory and this combination – both awkward and compelling – would become the dominant scientific world-view, developed by Gassendi, then Robert Boyle and Isaac Newton, among others. Gassendi's system preserved the notion that the entanglement, motion and interaction of invisible corpuscles are the basis of all

---

[15] Gassendi 1972: 398, transl. Brush, modified.

phenomena, even if it rejected the classical atomists' denial of divine providence. The atoms cannot move by themselves, but they have 'the power of
moving and acting which God instilled in them at their very creation'.[16] A
virtue of atomism was that, unlike Aristotelianism, it was compatible with
the prevailing voluntarist theology; atomism requires neither eternal forms
nor necessary essences. Against Lucretius and Descartes, Gassendi accepted
the appeal to final causes in explaining the parts and functions of plants
and animals. He also rejected the doctrine of the corporeality and mortality of the soul, responding to no less than twenty-seven arguments against
immortality drawn from Lucretius,[17] though his objections to Descartes's
Meditations might well lead the reader to wonder how much importance he
attached to the incorporeal human soul, by contrast with the corporeal souls
he thought men shared with animals, and whose powers included cognition,
language and experience.

Following closely on the continental developments was the growing inter-
est in atomism in England. In the early years of the seventeenth century,
Henry Percy, the 'wizard Earl', patronised an informal group of English
Copernicans and atomists, including Thomas Hariot, whose scientific
manuscripts were later studied by the mathematician Charles Cavendish.[18]
Charles, his brother William Cavendish and his sister-in-law, the writer Margaret Cavendish, were at the centre of an important intellectual circle in
Paris in the 1630s known as the 'Cavendish circle', which included Thomas
Hobbes.[19] Hobbes's stay in Paris for three years beginning in 1634 introduced him to the thought of Gassendi, Galileo and Descartes. Hobbes went
on to present his own materialistic system in terms of human ideation, not
fundamental ontology, even in his *On Body* (1655), as Locke was later to
do. But Hobbes nevertheless maintained that all was body, including God.
Margaret Cavendish alluded to the atomic construction of worlds in her own
cosmological poetry,[20] and she made little effort to award God a role in the
management of the atoms. A more conciliatory figure was Walter Charleton,
who referred to the 'pure and rich Metall' hidden amongst detestable doctrines in his *Darkness of Atheism* (1652). Charleton went on to expound
and develop long sections of Gassendi in his *Physiologia Epicuro-Gassendo-
Charltoniana* (1654). Other English philosophers influenced by Cartesian
and Gassendist corpuscularianism included Sir Kenelm Digby, the author of
Two Treatises, 1645 (on the nature of bodies and on the nature of the mind),

[16] Osler 2003.   [17] M. R. Johnson 2003.
[18] For the Percy circle see further Kargon 1966: 5–17 and p. 251 below.
[19] For the Cavendish circle see further Kargon 1966: 40–2 and Clucas 1994.
[20] See Rees 2000.

and John Locke, the author of the influential *Essay Concerning Human Understanding* (1690).[21]

Hobbes's enthusiasm for materialism did not help to polish the image of Lucretius, still regarded as the proponent of a dangerous and mostly unacceptable philosophy even in England. Robert Boyle (1627–91), in his essay *On the Usefulness of Experimental Natural Philosophy* (1663), repeated the old story that Lucretius' poem was written 'in one of the fits of that frenzy, which some, even of his admirers, suppose him to have been put into by a philtre given him by his either wife or mistress Lucilia'.[22] Under the title of an unpublished essay 'Of the Atomicall Philosophy' Boyle had written: 'These papers are without fayle to be burn't.' They were not, enabling us to read his observations:

> The atomical philosophy invented or brought into request by Democritus, Leucippus, Epicurus, & their contemporaries, tho since the inundation of Barbarians and Barbarisme expelled out of the Roman world all but the casually escaping Peripatetic philosophy . . . is so luckily revived & so skillfully celebrated in diverse parts of Europe by the learned pens of Gassendus, Magnenus, Descartes, & his disciples our deservedly famous countryman Sir Kenelme Digby & many other writers especially those that handle magnetical and electrical operations that it is now grown too considerable to be any longer laughed at, & considerable enough to deserve a serious inquiry.[23]

Boyle expounded corpuscularianism in his *Origin of Forms and Qualities according to the Corpuscular Philosophy* (1666) and in numerous other works, including the *Considerations about the Excellency and Grounds of the Mechanical Hypothesis* (1674) and the *Inquiry into the Vulgarly Received Notion of Nature* (1686), in which he described nature as 'the system of the corporeal works of God', consisting only of corpuscles moved according to laws imposed by the creator. If an angel were to work any change in the world, Boyle said, it would have to do so by setting matter in motion.[24]

Why was the theory of nature that Lucretius presented so appealing? Boyle suggested that both his experiments with the transformation and reintegration of chemical substances and the simplicity of the corpuscularian hypothesis recommended it. The doctrine of emergent qualities that atomism entailed perhaps appeared newly credible as a result of wider experience with chemical transformations and optical instruments. Yet methodologically Boyle seems to have interpreted his results – including his experiments with the air pump – in corpuscularian terms rather than effectively deriving the theory on

---

[21] For Locke see further pp. 275–6 below.   [22] Boyle 1999–2000: III, 255.
[23] Boyle 1999–2000: XIII, 227.   [24] Boyle 1999–2000: VIII, 104.

any experimental basis. One cannot say that physical or chemical phenomena really rendered the existence of atoms more likely. Rather the situation was reversed: the experimental philosophers sought specifically an ancient metaphysics upon which to declare their practices grounded in order to convey on them the dignity of philosophy, elevating chemistry from a merely mechanical practice. Meinel has argued that by the standards of any era, seventeenth-century arguments for and observations cited in favour of corpuscularianism were inconclusive, and that its reappearance and persistence in early modern science had as much to do with the charm of Lucretius' presentation, and its appeal to the senses and imagination, as it did with argument, observation and evidence.[25]

Boyle furthered Gassendi's project of detaching the science of atomism from its atheistic and hedonistic associations through his promotion of 'natural theology'. He insisted repeatedly that atomistic mechanism implied the existence and activity of a 'contrivance', one 'so Immense, so Beautiful, so well-contrived, and, in a word, so Admirable as the World cannot have been the effect of mere Chance, or Tumultuous Justlings and Fortuitous Concourse of Atoms, but must have been produced by a Cause exceedingly Powerful, Wise, and Beneficent'.[26] He named his version of the mechanical philosophy 'Anaxagorean', in order to distinguish it from classical atomism, and also from the Cartesian version which, though it introduced God as the cause and maintainer of corpuscular motions, nevertheless implied that the cosmos, and plant and animal life, had emerged spontaneously.[27] According to Boyle's doctrine of Anaxagorean mechanism, the frame of the world and its original plants and animals, or at least their 'seeds or seminal principles', had been intelligently and beneficently designed and created, though thereafter the laws of motion, the structure of objects and the dispositions of seeds sufficed for the production of all, or almost all, effects.[28]

This Anaxagorean system, one might think, reconciled religion and natural philosophy easily, provided one accepted the notion that the laws of nature could in some sense be prescribed to and obeyed by inanimate particles, and provided one was not troubled by the paradoxes of division and composition which militated against atoms. Yet Boyle was often troubled by his adoption of large parts of a pagan and arguably anti-theistic system. He believed himself to be living in an exceptionally dissolute age, and he considered the threat to religion and morals to be more serious and less easily

---

[25] Meinel 1988: 193.   [26] Boyle 1999–2000: XI, 299–300.

[27] The term 'Anaxagorean' appears in the suppressed sections of the *Inquiry into the Vulgarly Received Notion of Nature.*

[28] So Anstey 2002.

repulsed than other atheist and mortalist versions of Aristotelianism and pagan naturalism. 'Libertines', he says, 'own themselves to be so upon the account of the Epicurean or other Mechanical Principles of Philosophy',[29] and they fail to pay due regard to Aristotle, Scotus, Aquinas and Augustine. He complained of being taken for an Epicurean himself. Yet one cannot say that Boyle showed much deference to Aristotle or to his scholastic followers. By contrast, there are hundreds of references to Epicurus and Lucretius in his writings. If Boyle was sincere in maintaining that he had read little of Lucretius and was not conversant with Epicureanism in 1663,[30] he made up for his neglect later.

Isaac Newton was interested in atomism from his student days, attempting proof 'of a vacuum and atoms' in his Trinity Notebook.[31] He was influenced by both Gassendi and Boyle, but he also read Lucretius directly, even inserting his own line numbers into Fabri's 1686 edition.[32] Recent research on Newton's alchemical researches has revealed that they were far from being an embarrassing pseudo-scientific preoccupation; Newton was in the process of developing an atomistic chemical theory of matter.[33] His physics is also recognisably atomistic. Among his unpublished scientific papers is a 'fragment on the law of inertia' in which he attributes the first law of motion to the ancients, referencing Lucretius twice.[34] The notes of his disciple Gregory record him as saying that 'the philosophy of Epicurus and Lucretius is true and old, but was wrongly interpreted by the ancients as atheism'.[35] In a draft version of the *Mathematical Principles of Natural Philosophy* (1687), in which he set out to deal with the mechanical cause of gravity, Newton introduced the subject through an elaboration of Lucretius' discussion of the motion of atoms in the void.[36] And eventually, in the last query of the second edition of the *Optics* (1718), Newton published his belief that all things are composed of atoms:

it seems probable to me, that God in the Beginning form'd Matter in solid, massy, hard, impenetrable, moveable Particles, of such Sizes and Figures, and with such other Properties, and in such Proportion to Space, as most conduced to the End for which he form'd them; and that these primitive Particles being Solids, are incomparably harder than any porous Bodies compounded of them; even so very hard, as never to wear or break in pieces; no ordinary Power being able to divide what God himself made one in the first creation. While

---

[29] Boyle 1999–2000: VIII, 237.   [30] Boyle 1999–2000: II, 354.
[31] Transcribed in McGuire and Tamny 1983.   [32] See J. Harrison 1978 at H990.
[33] See Figala 1992.   [34] See Newton 1962: 309–11; Cohen 1964.
[35] Turnbull *et al.* 1959–77: III, 338.
[36] Newton 1962: 312–17; McGuire and Rattansi 1966.

the Particles continue entire, they may compose Bodies of one and the same Nature and Texture in all Ages: But should they wear away, or break in pieces, *the Nature of Things* depending on them, would be changed.[37]

This is one of the most influential pieces of writing in the history of science. And it occurred amidst what is essentially a paraphrase of certain arguments in *DRN* 1.540–98, fusing Lucretian doctrine with creationism and voluntarist theology. One sees here an extension of the line of thought articulated by William of Conches and later developed and propagated by Gassendi.

Magnenus, Charleton, Gassendi, Boyle and Newton all attempted to estimate the size of the smallest units of given materials, having conducted experiments on various substances such as smoke, incense, dust and flame. Theirs were the first attempts to quantify atomic phenomena. The mathematicisation of the atomic theory is notable in some sections of Newton's optical and chemical writings and in his *Mathematical Principles of Natural Philosophy*, which contain a mathematical derivation of Boyle's gas law: Newton assumed the existence of particles in his derivation, but refrained from mentioning the atomic hypothesis in this essentially mathematical work. Newton's results had in turn a major influence on John Dalton and contributed to the eventual success of a mathematical atomistic chemistry.

The threat posed by the revival of Epicureanism even in an officially Christian framework seemed to some metaphysicians to demand a more radical attack on the very notion of matter. Leibniz and Berkeley were not content with attacking the logical coherence of the notion of the least particle, but denied that there could be any purely material particle. The young Leibniz had been excited by material atomism, which he had encountered in Hobbes and Gassendi, but then turned away from it in favour of what he considered to be an improved version of the theory of substantial forms. He was much engaged (in unpublished writings), however, with the Lucretian notion of creation by combination and was evidently taken with the notion of a plurality of worlds.[38] Leibniz accepted the Lucretian argument that only the indivisible atom is indestructible and immortal, but he insisted in Platonic fashion that anything material is susceptible of division and destruction, and that only soul-like entities with experiences and appetitions can function in the role of eternal substances. Where the classical arguments are intended to show that, in order to be the elements of things, the atoms must be devoid of all qualities except size, shape and mobility, Leibniz drew the remarkable inference that the elements of things must be alive and infinitely complex.[39]

---

[37] Newton 1718: 375–6 (Query 31), emphasis added.
[38] C. Wilson 2003: 104–8.   [39] See further C. Wilson 1982.

Immanuel Kant (1724–1804) was perturbed by Leibniz and heavily influenced by Newton. He openly acknowledged his debt to Lucretius in offering a nebular hypothesis concerning the formation of the planets and solar system.[40] 'I will not deny', he admitted,

> that the theory of Lucretius, or his predecessors, Epicurus, Leucippus, and Democritus has much resemblance with mine. I assume, like these philosophers, that the first state of nature consisted in a universal diffusion of the primitive matter of all the bodies in space, or of the atoms of matter, as these philosophers have called them. Epicurus asserted a gravity or weight which forced these elementary particles to sink or fall; and this does not seem to differ much from Newton's attraction, which I accept.
>
> (*Universal Natural History and Theory of Heaven*, 1755)[41]

Despite his favourable attitude towards Lucretian cosmology, Kant rejected 'the mechanical mode of explanation' which, he said, 'has, under the name atomism or the corpuscular philosophy, always retained its authority and influence on the principles of natural science, with few changes from Democritus' (*Metaphysical Foundations of Natural Science*, 1786). Kant argued in the finale of his critical writings, the 'critique of teleological judgement' (Part 2 of *The Critique of Judgement*, 1790), that science required, conceptually, a teleological framework for the explanation of life, regardless of the basically unknowable nature of things. But atomistic and anti-teleological ideas were attracting a favourable reading in the rapidly developing life sciences. David Hume's *Dialogues Concerning Natural Religion* (first published 1779) contained a paraphrase of Lucretius' selection principle,[42] arguing that currently existing species of animals are those which, unlike their counterparts, had apt combinations of organs and were thus able to survive and reproduce, and this notion was common amongst the *philosophes*. Erasmus Darwin wrote a substantial Lucretian didactic poem, *The Temple of Nature* (1803), and his earlier *Zoonomia* (1794–6) explicitly endorsed the theo-mechanical version of atomism.[43] Lucretius did not technically elaborate a theory of evolution, since he held plant and animal species to be fixed.[44] But he did develop the older atomistic idea that extinctions play a key role in determining what life is now present on earth, a view developed by Erasmus' grandson, Charles Darwin, who became embroiled in theological controversies reminiscent of those of the seventeenth century.

---

[40] For Kant's engagement with Lucretius see also pp. 177–83 and 284–5 below.

[41] Transl. Hastie 1900: 24.

[42] Compare *Dialogues* Part 8 with DRN 4.823–57; 5.772–877.

[43] For Erasmus Darwin see further pp. 291–2 below.

[44] Campbell 2003: 6–8.

Historians have described a general 'victory of discreteness' in regard to the discovery of cells and genes, entities which, along with Darwinian evolution, are the bases of the modern life sciences. Lucretius represented the material units of heredity in a way that arguably anticipated later accounts. But the greatest victory for discreteness in the nineteenth century was the presentation of the first convincing experimental evidence for atoms themselves. In 1808 John Dalton asserted that 'observations have tacitly led to the conclusion which seems universally adopted, that all bodies of sensible magnitude, whether liquid or solid, are constituted of a vast number of extremely small particles, or atoms of matter bound together by a force of attraction, which is more or less powerful according to circumstances'.[45] The origin of Dalton's theory of the chemical atom is a highly contested episode in the history of science. Whether or not Dalton was directly acquainted with Lucretius, there are several clear indirect lines of influence. For example, he repeatedly copied Newton's derivation of Boyle's law into his notebook, and he wrote out Newton's Lucretian Query 31 (partially quoted above) from the *Optics*.[46] Dalton's mechanical atomism was perceived as successful in explaining the behaviour of heat and gas. He realised that gases combine to form compounds in definite ratios, and he inferred from this that they must consist of discrete particles, thus robustly joining speculative atomism with a quantitative and empirical methodology. The case for chemical and physical atomism was further strengthened by the successes of James Clerk Maxwell, celebrated for his work on electromagnetism and the kinetic theory of gases; Maxwell continued to evoke the spirit and letter of ancient philosophy, referring as late as 1873 to 'the atomic doctrine of Democritus, Epicurus, and Lucretius, and, I may add, of your lecturer'.[47]

Despite the affirmation of Maxwell, and despite Dalton's earlier claim that atomism was a universally accepted chemical fact, several doctrinaire empiricists rejected atomism. Towards the end of the nineteenth century Ernst Mach had advanced a form of positivism according to which only things directly perceived are real, everything else being a convenient heuristic for scientific thought, if not a figment of the imagination. Mach had many important disciples; they constitute the last bastion against atomism. As late as 1913 Pierre Duhem announced that the atomic theory was 'without a future'. 'Modern chemistry', he insisted, 'does not plead in favour of the Epicurean doctrines'.[48]

---

[45] Dalton 1808: 141.
[46] For the relevant parts of the notebook see Roscoe and Harden 1896: 124.
[47] Maxwell 1873: 437.　　[48] Duhem 2002: 93–4.

As the Nobel Laureate Steven Weinberg commented, it is somewhat odd that the atomic theory of matter did not win universal acceptance until the discovery of the constituents of the atom.[49] This is ironic because the discovery of subatomic particles seems to explode the idea of the indivisible atom. The recollections of the artist Wassily Kandinsky show how startling was this new conception of nature:

> The collapse of the atom model was equivalent, in my soul, to the collapse of the whole world. Suddenly the thickest walls fell. I would not have been amazed if a stone appeared before my eye in the air, melted, and became invisible. Science seemed to me destroyed.[50]

Kandinsky's language here suggests Lucretius' mention of 'the walls of the world fleeing at the destruction of the world' and of how 'the walls of the world part' (DRN 1.1102; 3.16–17). Kandinsky, like Lucretius and later Newton, decided that the division of the 'atom' implied there were no atoms, and anything could be destroyed or transformed into any other thing.

Of course, Kandinsky need not have worried that science was 'destroyed'. Physicists have acquired extensive knowledge of various 'elementary' particles with the help of electrolysis, accelerators, cathode ray tubes and other procedures and devices. There are now many ways to detect 'atoms': scintillation screens, Geiger counters, cloud chambers, photographic emulsions and scanning-tunnelling microscopes. As Erwin Schrödinger, the Nobel Prize-winning scientist, observed, 'The great atomists from Democritus down to Dalton, Maxwell, and Bolzmann would have gone into raptures at these palpable proofs of their belief.'[51] Atomism – understood as the theory of astonishingly small, active, and normally indivisible particles that underlie all appearances and change in the natural world – has moved from a hypothesis to a fact. Niels Bohr could state by 1929 that 'every doubt regarding the reality of atoms has been removed'.[52] Several models of the atom as a complex entity were advanced in the late nineteenth and early twentieth centuries, including J. J. Thompson's 'plum pudding' model, according to which electrons are embedded in a soup of positive charge, and, after the discovery of the nucleus by the resolute atomist Ernest Rutherford, Bohr's 'planetary model' in which electrons orbit the nucleus. Though the model is now discredited, a version of it remains the logo of the 'Atomic age'.

Also worth mentioning here are the experiments of Jean Perrin on Brownian motion. In his Nobel acceptance speech of 1926, entitled 'The discontinuous structure of matter', Perrin explicitly connected his work with

---

[49] Weinberg 1983: 3.   [50] Kandinsky 1955: 16; transl. Holton 1993: 105 n. 19.
[51] Schrödinger 1954: 87.   [52] Bohr 1934: 18.

the ancient theory. Lucretius, as was often noted, had called attention to the behaviour of dust motes in a sunbeam (*DRN* 2.114–28); the motes, he understood, must be moved by even tinier, invisible particles. It was on the basis of J. J. Thompson's work on the electron and Perrin's on Brownian motion that one of Mach's followers, Wilhelm Ostwald, virtually the last scientist to reject atomism, recanted.[53]

Erwin Schrödinger has argued that atomism has retained its appeal since the time of Democritus because it is a means of 'bridging the gulf between the real bodies of physics and the idealized geometrical shapes of pure mathematics'. 'In a way', he observes, 'atomism has performed this task all through its long history, the task of facilitating our thinking about palpable bodies.'[54] Nowadays children are taught that an atom is composed of 'elementary particles' – that it has a central nucleus, composed of protons and neutrons and surrounded by electrons. Werner Heisenberg, who preferred Plato's version of atomism to Lucretius', stated that 'it is obvious that if anything in modern physics should be compared with the atoms of Democritus it should be the elementary particles like proton, neutron, electron, meson'.[55] A so-called 'standard model' now offers to explain nature in terms of sub-subatomic particles – six quarks, six leptons and some 'force carrying particles', such as photons. Although there are major differences between this kind of model and what we find in the poem of Lucretius, Schrödinger was not wrong to say that 'all the basic features of the atomic theory have survived in the modern one up to this day'.[56] Similar thinking led the physicist Richard Feynman to remark:

> If, in some cataclysm, all of scientific knowledge were to be destroyed, and only one sentence passed on to the next generations of creatures, what statement would contain the most information in the fewest words? I believe that it is the atomic hypothesis (or the atomic fact, or whatever you wish to call it), that all things are made of atoms – little particles that move around in perpetual motion, attracting each other when they are a little distance apart, but repelling upon being squeezed into one another. In that one sentence, you will see, there is an enormous amount of information about the world, if just a little imagination and thinking are applied.[57]

What persists through all versions of atomism is the idea that macroscopic bodies and their qualities are ultimately composed of countable entities that do not possess most macroscopic qualities, and that retain their identity and characteristics throughout the changes we observe. The alternative is a concept of matter as infinitely divisible: the four elements of Empedocles and

[53] See Holton 1978: 82–3.   [54] Schrödinger 1954: 87.
[55] Heisenberg 1958: 69.   [56] Schrödinger 1954: 83.   [57] Feynman 1963: 1, 2.

Aristotle; the *pneuma* of the Stoics; any of the ethers and universal mediums that have been posited by those horrified by the vacuum. Although more recent fundamental ontologies based on fields, waves and strings appear promising, particles remain as indispensable to contemporary science as they were to Lucretius.

To summarise, the Lucretian conception of nature as 'accomplishing everything by herself spontaneously and independently and free from the jurisdiction of the gods' was a major driving force in the Scientific Revolution experienced in Western Europe beginning in the early seventeenth century. Over the following three centuries the theory of atoms was converted from a poetic fancy to a well-confirmed empirical hypothesis, the charm, consoling power, and provocation of Lucretius' poem contributing in no small measure to this result. In every field of inquiry, from chemistry and physiology to meteorology and cosmology, the Lucretian rejection of teleology, immaterial spirits, and divine and demonic intervention into the lives of men and the phenomena of nature provided an explanatory ideal, even when it was scorned as inadequate to the phenomena or rejected as a threat to morals, politics and religion.

There are nevertheless profound differences between ancient and modern materialism. With Boyle's and Hooke's experiments on air, the corpuscular theory assumed a quantitative and experimental dimension that would become the motor of the extraordinary successes of the physical sciences in the nineteenth and twentieth centuries. A subtler difference was occasioned by the move away from the attempt to understand some limited aspects of the natural world in atomistic terms for ethical purposes towards an effort – whether amoral or humanitarian – to remodel the world by manipulating its constituent atoms. The ethical significance of Lucretius' natural philosophy resided in its potential to remove, or at least reduce, the fear of death and anxiety over the consequences of offending the gods, and to free human beings from the compulsion to engage in repetitive, pointless religious observances. Acquiring power over nature and redirecting natural processes to serve human ends was not the aim of ancient philosophers; that branch of inquiry and practice belonged to magic and mechanics, not to science. The classical atomist regarded the atomic reality underlying the appearances and changes of the visible world as screened off from human perception and manipulation. By contrast, the moderns integrated materialism into a methodological theory of control, in which the transformation of nature and the application of technology was a guiding concern. If nature is purely corporeal, if all effects arise from the motion and arrangement of particles, and if human beings demonstrably can change arrangements and impart motions (as their success in carrying out chemical transformations shows), the possibility of generating effects is unlimited. This marrying of a Baconian programme of power over nature with a corpuscularian theory in the Royal Society programme of useful works was perhaps based on an accident: the publication in 1651 of Bacon's earlier atomistic writings, representing an ontology towards which the mature Bacon was ill-disposed. The resulting ambition is expressed in Descartes's claim that through the application of the new philosophy we may become 'masters and possessors of nature'. Lucretius' poem, by contrast, offered a contemplative view, reverential in its treatment of the spontaneous cycles of renewal and decline in nature, and at the same time deeply pessimistic in its estimation of the worth of much human exertion and agency.

Further reading

Robert Boyle, 'the father of modern chemistry', very concisely and persuasively articulated reasons for applying atomistic ideas to modern scientific questions in his essay *Considerations about the Excellency and Grounds of the Mechanical Hypothesis*, 1674. Andrade 1928 is another working scientist who, in a comprehensive overview, described the many contributions of Lucretius specifically to the history of science. But Lucretius' influence on science is, for obvious reasons, difficult or impossible to isolate from the revival of Democritean and Epicurean atomism, and thus the best histories discuss the revival of atomism generally. For the late medieval and early modern period see Lüthy, Murdoch and Newman 2001, an anthology which includes a complete and up-to-date bibliography. See also the important Meinel 1988 regarding the relationship between atomism and experimental science. The best general histories of materialism and atomism are Lange 1866, Lasswitz 1890, more recently Kargon 1966 (focused on English atomism) and Pullman 1998 (much wider in scope and written by a physicist). For the influence of ancient atomism on chemistry see Partington 1939, and of Lucretius specifically on the life sciences, Campbell 2003. Lennon 1993 deals generally with the philosophical debates between 'Epicurean' atomists and their Platonist opponents in the seventeenth century.

9

REID BARBOUR

Moral and political philosophy: readings of Lucretius from Virgil to Voltaire

The interpretation of Epicurean political philosophy as embodied in the *DRN* has rarely proved simple. The problem begins with the Epicurean repudiation of public life accompanied by a retreat into a small group of friends who cultivate tranquillity. Against this apparently straightforward backdrop, the dense, passionate verses of Lucretius have provoked the later transmitters of Epicureanism into engaging an astonishing range of political concerns and positions.[1] This chapter will consider four key historical moments in the interpretation of the *DRN*. For all their many differences, each of the four periods sponsors inventive and wide-ranging responses to the poem's moral and political tendencies. In each case, cultural arbiters are inspired and provoked by what they posit as the poem's tension between its passionate disruption of contemporary norms and its clarion call for a disengaged tranquillity. Construing their own age – sometimes approbatively, sometimes apprehensively – as a time of upheaval, they struggle to decide whether Lucretius offers recourse from or instigation to contemporary disorder, decadence and uncertainty. Finally, in each historical context, readers recognise that the poem's moral and political arguments are rendered the more complex by Book 5's extended account of civilisation.

First there is Virgil's emulation of Lucretius in the politically vexed but nonetheless Caesarean *Georgics*. Second, at the end of the sixteenth century and beginning of the seventeenth, Michel de Montaigne and Francis Bacon engage the moral and political dimensions of Lucretius in their efforts to make sense of religio-political turmoil, wanton civil bloodshed and philosophical impasse. Third, this chapter investigates ideological negotiations among Lucretian readers and translators in England during the mid seventeenth century. It ends with the Enlightenment in France and Prussia, when Lucretius was befriended by Frederick the Great.

[1] The several modifications of the Epicurean withdrawal from politics, the most notable of which are suggested by Diogenes Laertius, are presented in Inwood and Gerson 1994.

The late Republic

In Lucretius' poem the political values and implications of Epicureanism were transformed by a variety of literary and cultural factors, including especially the specific problems facing Romans in the late Republic. The political danger of Epicureanism to the institutions of the period involved far more than the drain of talent from the aristocratic pool – the disease, if the philosophy was one, could act with more virulence and aggression than that. Given that Memmius was 'a sophisticated senator', it is not surprising that Lucretius constructed the addressee of his poem 'as one who needed to be made interested in Epicurus' doctrines and was likely to think propagation of such doctrines damaging to the religious interests of the state'.[2] In the first century BC, any Roman would have known that when Lucretius rejected augury, with its division of the sky into *templa*, he was flouting something far greater: the power of Roman magistracy, law and empire. At the same time, however, Epicureanism was embraced by aggressive political figures in both Caesarean and anti-Caesarean circles.[3] Among these contentious understandings of Epicureanism and politics, Lucretius attempted to account for the ways in which Epicurean philosophy had interacted with societies, laws and rulers.[4]

In the *DRN*, assessments of the motives to political power and ambition are simply and scathingly negative; but, as has often been noted, Lucretius is far more complex on the political implications of his own philosophy within the history of civilisation. In effect, Epicureanism shared with Stoicism the need for casuistry on the circumstances under which a wise man might or should enter politics.[5] In marked contrast to the Stoics, however, 'what matters for the Epicurean is the chance to lead a quiet life; human societies are very imperfect instruments for attaining this end, but one has to do the best one can'.[6] This focus on a calculus of utility for constitutions does not indicate that Lucretius is indifferent to the current state of late Republican Rome. Far from it: his address to Venus, the ancestress of Rome; the longing for peace so that he can write his poem; his regular assaults on the vanity of militarism, with its bizarre and gory spectacles; the analogies he draws between civil war and atomic motion; his systematic critique of the civic values in the *mos maiorum*; and an animosity towards state religion that, according

---

[2] Jocelyn 1977: 361.
[3] See Momigliano 1960 for the 'heroic' Epicureanism of the tyrannicides.
[4] For the stages of civilisation in Book 5, the Lucretian critique of contemporary Roman values, and the reactions against his poem especially by Cicero, see ch. 3 above.
[5] M. Griffin 1989: 29–30, 32.   [6] D. P. Fowler 1989: 145.

to E. J. Kenney, is unorthodox even for an Epicurean: these elements corroborate J. D. Minyard's argument that the poem is 'the direct product of the genuine crisis of *civitas Romana*'.[7]

When Lucretius is featured posthumously and anonymously as a hero in Virgil's *Georgics*, the political circumstances of Rome have changed drastically from those of his own lifetime. Virgil's own controversial relationship to the triumphs of Octavian, the shifting tones and moods of the four books of the poem, and the alternative conception of heroism and happiness that the poet introduces side by side with the figure of Lucretius, all these factors heighten the elusiveness of the political message his readers may take from Virgil's revision of the *DRN*. Virgil epitomises his affection for Lucretius in heralding the happiness of the man who understands the universe and subdues his anxiety about destiny and hell (*G.* 2.490–2). But neither the relationship of these lines to their immediate context nor their contribution to the overall moral, political and philosophical thrust of the four books is entirely clear. In the immediate context of Book 2, Virgil has denounced the insanity of violence and then congratulated on his good fortune the farmer who lives far from the wars: this farmer's simple, peaceful life lacks nothing that a happy man needs (for he has no desire for the lavish accoutrements of the wealthy and powerful) except the *knowledge* that he is fortunate. This vision of the simple life owes a great deal to the impassioned moral pronouncements of Lucretius.

Nevertheless, Virgil ends up being divided between the philosopher who, knowing the nature of things, rebukes superstition, and the simpler farmer 'who knows the rustic deities' (2.493). Any 'synthesis' between the two 'sidesteps the central problems raised by Lucretius with regard to religion'.[8] Virgil allows that he will settle for the happy life without philosophy if he fails to gain access to the secrets of nature. But both happy lives embody a sense of justice that strikingly contrasts with the nightmare of Roman politics; indeed Justice's last earthly vestiges are found among simple husbandmen (2.473–4). The happy man, we learn further, cares nothing for courts legal or royal, nothing for war or wealth, and nothing for senatorial wrangling and oratory. As in the second phase of civilisation in Lucretius, the happy man's preferred society is his family, friends and neighbours.

The problem with this Lucretian rejection of Roman politics is that the hero of Virgil's poem, for better or worse, is Caesar Octavian. Critics are deeply divided over whether the poem's conception of its political context

---

[7] Kenney 1995: 12; Minyard 1985: 2.
[8] Hardie 1986: 50–1. Cf. Hardie's essay in this volume (ch. 7).

is optimistic or pessimistic.[9] In an optimistic reading of the poem, Llewelyn Morgan offers one point on which scholars agree:

> Perhaps the most striking 'external' feature of this poem is its date: 29 BC. This is one of the most significant dates in Roman history, a turning point for the nation, as it would come to seem, a crucial juncture for Octavian as it must have seemed at the time. Octavian had won another round of the Civil Wars. However, to ensure that this latest of many heralded 'ends' to the Civil Wars should not prove illusory, Octavian needed to follow up that military success with the creation of a stable political order in Rome.[10]

With this context in view, the poem offers a searching meditation on the traditions that Romans value, on the previous century of debacle and debauchery, and on the possibility, not yet realised, that Octavian might bring a new peace, harmony and prosperity to Rome. Some have seen in Virgil's Octavian 'the fulminating possessor of absolute power' while others have argued for the poem's propagandistic commitment to Caesar's 'mission of enlightenment to a generation that has lost its way'. Commentators largely agree that 'the influence of Lucretius, earnest and passionate', threatens to subvert the poem's political and religious pieties.[11] But the politics of Lucretius' heroism in the *Georgics* is only potentially, not necessarily, subversive: after all, the satire on the envy and the hostility of the *uulgus* in the *DRN* might be seen as in some measure congruent with Virgil's horror at the assassination of Julius Caesar, and the earlier poet's emphasis on quiet obedience might be read as an indictment of the bawling senators found later in the *Georgics* (2.508–10).

There is considerable complexity in the questions of how supportive of the new Roman hegemony Virgil's middle poem tends to be, and of how the presence of Lucretius contributes to its political and moral meaning. And the centrality of the Lucretian hero in the *Georgics* accentuates what is perhaps the poem's most deeply political aspect: its requirement that readers, including the Octavian to whom Virgil recited the poem, must exert an intellectual and moral labour in rethinking Rome's past, present and future. Roman readers must, that is, involve themselves in a rigorous, painful process that Francis Bacon would later characterise as a georgics of the mind.

---

[9] See variously, for instance, Gale 2000, Hardie 1986, Miles 1980, Morgan 1999, Putnam 1979 and Perkell 1989.

[10] Morgan 1999: 125.   [11] Putnam 1979: 15; Otis 1964: 38; J. Griffin 1986: 12.

Montaigne and Bacon[12]

In the last quarter of the sixteenth century and the first quarter of the seventeenth, Lucretius figures powerfully (though certainly not pervasively) in intellectual attempts to reckon with religious warfare between and within dynasties; with the moral and political dilemmas that accrue in a time of rampant persecution; and with the emergence of a scepticism perceived as both dangerous to and healthy for the advancement of learning. Montaigne and Bacon, their reading facilitated by great editions of Lucretius such as that of Lambinus, return time and again to the DRN for both positive and negative models of how to deal with contemporary religious, moral, political and epistemological problems and choices.

As a reader of Lucretius, Montaigne was exceptionally active, open and thorough. Now that his own copy of the Lambinus edition has been recovered, we know that he read and reread the book, notes and all, from cover to cover, annotating extensively.[13] Also striking is his engagement not just with the poetry of the DRN but with its network of ideas – Montaigne is apt to trace themes throughout the six books. He derives much personal comfort from Book 3's denunciation of the fear of death, and mines Book 4 for epistemological purposes, but his most intense interest is in Lucretius' critiques of religion and ambition. Although Montaigne's response is often simply 'contre la religion', he is clearly interested in the Epicurean notion that the gods do not care about our world, with the corollary that we should not fear them. Lucretius' anti-providentialism affords Montaigne a way of making the case that human arrogance creates fraudulent theologies to the detriment of our peace and happiness. It is this last point, the destruction of human well-being through the religious imagination, which guarantees the supreme relevance of the DRN to one of Montaigne's most pressing political concerns: the havoc of sixteenth-century religious conflict, in the shape of the conflict between the Catholics and Huguenots of early modern France.

Montaigne is thus apt to appropriate Lucretius in his writings about religious conflict and politics. In Essay 1.18, 'That we should not be deemed happy till after our death',[14] he appeals to Lucretius on the absurd weakness of fasces and axes, those Roman symbols of power, and taunts us with the argument that only in the scene of death are we ever revealed for the person we really are. In 1.26, 'That it is madness to judge the true and the

---

12 See for other aspects of Montaigne's response to Lucretius pp. 227, 236–8; for Bacon pp. 134–5 and 251–2 in this volume.

13 Screech 1998 presents all Montaigne's notes.

14 All essay titles are given in the versions of Screech 1987.

false from our own capacities', Lucretius' satire on the human preference for the new over the customary is thrice introduced to preface Montaigne's condemnations of arrogance and of the extremism – a belief too rash, a disbelief too feckless – that subverts order in contemporary France. Sometimes Montaigne writes in a spirit ironically contrary to the *DRN*: a number of the essays persist in citing Lucretius' clarion call for autonomy, his vindication of self, fearlessness in the face of death, and resistance to the desire for political power and conquest while offering guidance on obedience to monarchs.

In a series of essays – 'On solitude' (1.38), 'On the inequality there is between us' (1.42) and 'On one of Caesar's sayings' (1.53) – Lucretius serves Montaigne as antiquity's most brilliant critic of the ambition that cloaks itself in duty, as an exceptionally powerful advocate for individual freedom and autonomy, and as the therapist exposing those desires that make it so difficult for us to find true ease and legitimate pleasure as well as to avoid servitude to others and to our own fears. Hence he is invoked to question the equation of value with power, luxury, property and wealth; and to articulate the positions that without philosophical wisdom men are at bottom the same, that the powerful should avoid flattery, and that we should take care not to avoid slavery by leaping into anarchy. The boundaries Lucretius sets to human desire are reflected when Montaigne presents kings as pathetic, their prerogatives almost meaningless and their power far less genuine than that possessed by the autonomous philosopher-lord on whose life the king's authority rarely, if ever, impinges.

For Montaigne, Lucretius is urgently needed for guidance in the confusion and oppression of civil-war France. Ultimately, however, the Epicurean way proves insufficiently comforting to the sensitive philosopher facing the brutality of his countrymen. The longest of the essays, the 'Apology for Raimond Sebond' (2.12), shows both sides. Here Lucretius helps to generate a powerful satire on politico-religious warfare, but has far less to say about the way to human happiness. He contributes to Montaigne's demolition of human presumption; to the levelling of human nature with the creatures falsely supposed to be beneath man; and to the exposure of military spectacle as so much vanity. His portrait of Iphigenia centres Montaigne's bold rejection of religion – that is, religion understood as the inevitably faulty and corrupt human construction of the divine. Towards the end of the 'Apology' Montaigne quotes *DRN* 4.513–21, a passage stressing the importance of knowledge's being founded on the senses. But he heads off the hope of such a foundation, offering a revealing analogy for the epistemological shambles in which human beings find themselves. 'Who will be a proper judge', he asks, of the appearances of things? 'It is like saying that we could do with a judge who is not bound to either party in our religious strife, who is dispassionate and without prejudice.'[15] As Lucretius needs but can never really have the senses on his side, French Christians require that impartial judge but are never going to find him. For Montaigne, Lucretius is contemporary France's most astute diagnostic physician. But however capable he seems of ending the dispute, disappointment on this count is inevitable.

In England Francis Bacon was also contemplating the relationship between truth and utility in the Epicurean legacy. Understood as a hypothesis or framework, atomism would, he believed, contribute to the methodical and inductive advancement of natural philosophy, even if Democritus' account of the principles of nature was not strictly true.[16] But Bacon found it more difficult to determine whether the heirs of Democritus, Epicurus and Lucretius were useful or beneficial for civil polities, their religious guarantors and their social welfare.

Bacon realised how shocked Lucretius would have been at the atrocities of early modern religious violence. In a piece entitled 'Of Religion' for the 1612 edition of the *Essays* (then 'Of Unity in Religion' for the 1625) he disparages uncivil and inhumane methods of producing conformity with his citation of Lucretius' *tantum religio potuit suadere malorum* ('how powerfully religion directs towards evil', *DRN* 1.101). The slaughter of Iphigenia provoked the Roman poet's revulsion, and now there is the massacre of Huguenots in France and the Gunpowder Plot in England: Lucretius, had he known of these things, 'would have been, Seven times more Epicure and Atheist, than he was'.[17] The implications of this answer are that Lucretius is not really equipped to help Europe out of its difficulties, but ironically even atheism, for Bacon, is not so simple nor even so bad as one might expect. At the very least it allows Lucretius a moral revulsion Bacon believes exceedingly rare in early modern Europe; for, as Bacon claims in 'Of Superstition', atheism allows moral directives (it 'leaves a Man to Sense; to Philosophy; to Naturall Piety; to Lawes; to Reputation') often overridden by superstition.[18]

The question remains for Bacon, however, whether *uoluptas*, understood as a steady-state tranquillity of mind and as an austere cultivation of bodily health, is positively good for society. Lucretius figures prominently in Bacon's assessment of this concern, especially given Bacon's affection for the proem to *DRN* 2, which he quotes in the essay 'Of Truth' as well as *The Advancement of Learning*. Atheism is not simply bad for Bacon, but neither is the image of tranquillity at the outset of the latter simply good. For Bacon, at least two

---

[15] Montaigne 1987: 678–9.
[16] *Cogitationes de natura rerum*; Bacon 1857–74: V, 203 (for Latin); X, 287 (for English).
[17] Bacon 1985: 14–15. [18] Bacon 1985: 54.

questions disturb the tranquillity of the famous proem: whether its distance from turbulent affairs is in fact essential for the discovery of truth, and whether the motivations of the tranquil sage are morally legitimate. In the *Advancement*, the passage (*DRN* 2.1–10) is translated as follows:

> It is a view of delight . . . to stand or walke vpon the shoare side, and to see a Shippe tossed with tempest vpon the sea; or to bee in a fortified Tower, and to see two Battailes ioyne vppon a plaine. But it is a pleasure incomparable for the minde of man to be setled, landed, and fortified in the certaintie of truth; and from thence to descrie and behould the errours, perturbations, labours, and wanderings up and downe of other men.[19]

For his inductive method and in his opposition to the manifold delusions of human thinking, Bacon always insists that we attempt to remove ourselves from the world that we would perceive. At the same time, his image of the mind as a magical mirror illustrates that we are always tragically distant from the world that we would know. Even if we concede the value of the distance in the proem, however, the problem still remains for Bacon whether the tranquil mind is more desirable than the anxious and active one, for the latter is more likely to keep investigating the nature of things as Bacon always wishes. It is perhaps significant, then, that he adds the indecision about whether the viewer is standing or walking.

Bacon often argues that God expects far more from a moral life than private repose or the avoidance of perturbation, and that those who care only about their own calm (which they never really achieve anyway) 'retyre too easily from Ciuile businesse'.[20] But he is hardly ready to claim that Lucretius' distant repose is wholly without value. Far from it: Bacon's history of moral philosophy attempts to reconcile civil business and private peace. On the one hand, a 'preserver' aims at minimising what is ill about life; on the other, an 'advancer' attempts to maximise what is good. One is sincere and even; the other is vigorous and changing. There are men, he says, who delight in their pleasures even more than others, yet feel no trouble when they have to put them aside. Indeed 'most of the doctrines of the Philosophers are more fearefull and cautionary then the Nature of things requireth. For, when they would haue a mans whole life, to be but a discipline or preparation to dye: they must needes make men thinke, that it is a terrible Enemy, against whom there is no end of preparing.' Suddenly the attractions of that specific image of the wise man in *DRN* 2 are clearer: he has managed repose but is scarcely filled with dread or even caution. He can pay very close attention

---

[19] Bacon 2000: 52.   [20] Bacon 2000: 137–9.

to the vicissitudes of the world, whether political, military, social, moral, or natural.[21]

The question remains, however, whether the repose at the outset of the proem to Book 2 is legitimately motivated. In the essay 'Of Truth' Bacon quotes it again:

> The Poet, that beautified the Sect, that was otherwise inferiour to the rest, saith yet excellently well: It is a pleasure to stand in the window of a Castle, and to see a Battaile, and the Adventures thereof, below: But no pleasure is comparable, to the standing on the vantage ground of Truth: (A hill not to be commanded, and where the Ayre is alwaies cleare and serene;) And to see the Errours, and Wandrings, and Mists, and Tempests, in the vale below.[22]

The wise man does no walking here; but the space that matters most is the intellectually clear ground of truth (pleasure resulting from clarity and security) rather than the comforting window of the castle from which one stares in relief at battles and adventures. In Lucretius, it is true, there can also be found different levels of pleasure, but at the highest, fortified by philosophy, the sage looks at more specifically worldly wanderings, at those vain strivings after honour, wealth, power and the contestation of minds. Bacon's metaphors of storms, mists and errors remove the sage from a view of the specific follies of civil affairs into a realm more simply inward, morally and epistemologically.

So far in the passage, though, Bacon has omitted what for early modern students of Lucretius was the most significant point about the inwardness of the tranquil philosopher heralded at the outset of *DRN* 2, namely the poet's insistence that the happy man takes no delight in the misery of others. Bacon has not forgotten the modification. Having laid out the various levels of repose, he concludes with a more elaborate version: 'So alwaies, that this prospect, be with Pitty, and not with Swelling, or Pride. Certainly, it is Heaven upon Earth, to have a Mans Minde Move in Charitie, Rest in Providence, and Turne upon the Poles of Truth.'[23] Once again Bacon introduces intellectual motion, however regular, in the cause of truth; but motion also imports the moral criteria of charity and pity. The only rest included in Bacon's modification is settled on the very basis that Lucretius famously would exclude: providence. In short, Lucretius' distant repose is valuable to the extent that it remains intellectually dynamic (rather than self-satisfied) and concerned for human welfare at large (rather than gratified by public misery).

---

[21] Bacon 2000: 141–2.   [22] Bacon 1985: 8.   [23] Bacon 1985: 8.

Bacon suggests then that the distant sage of Book 2 is, on the one hand, poised better than the world's feverish participants to see clearly what is true, but on the other too removed from the tumult of life's quotidian business into the gratifying vanity of the self's cloistered and narcissistic theatre. In accusing the Epicureans of desiring a golden age of sameness and serenity without regard for ameliorating the horrible anarchy and violence of the world, Bacon posits that Lucretius was lying not to the world but, tragically, to himself.[24] To avoid this deception, Lucretius needs Bacon's modifications to his repose – charity, activity and an ongoing dissatisfaction with one's hold on the truth. In writing meant to subvert magisterial and rhetorical gratification, Montaigne and Bacon both tried to provoke early modern readers of the *DRN* into recasting its claims as a prolonged, painful, yet hopeful process of transforming the human mind and the world.

England 1640–1660

In the middle of the seventeenth century English intellectual culture began to welcome Lucretius into its mainstream for the very first time, a phenomenon embodied in the English translations of the *DRN* multiplying side by side with apologiae and commentaries (most of them deeply indebted to the French pioneer Gassendi). But the legitimisation of Lucretius in England proved contentious, not just because theologians and Cambridge Platonists feared its effect on orthodox convictions,[25] but also because his arrival coincided with the most turbulent twenty years in English history: the Civil War of 1642–8; the regicide of 1649; a series of new and controversial governments from 1649 through the 1650s; the bold disestablishment of the Church of England, the monarchy and the House of Lords, and their re-establishment (in altered forms) in 1660. As contemporaries were apt to point out, it was not very surprising that Lucretius would fascinate intellectuals working in an era that struck many as uncannily like the late Republic.

Indeed Walter Charleton's 1657 *Immortality of the Human Soul* might just as well be entitled *Lucretius our Contemporary*. Serving as a fictional persona for John Evelyn, whose translation of Book 1 had been published in 1656, Charleton's 'Lucretius' figures among the interlocutors in a garden dialogue as a highly sympathetic virtuoso. Set in the Luxembourg Gardens of Paris, the dialogue itself stresses its political context, for the discutants are cast as royalists in exile during the Interregnum, in need of a modified Epicurean

---

[24] Bacon 2000: 137–8.
[25] For two Cambridge Platonists on Epicureanism, John Smith and Henry More, see J. Smith 1978: xx, 46–51; More 1998: 261, 441, 611, 625–6.

philosophy to help overcome the melancholy of their banishment. A physician and a staunch royalist, Charleton was England's foremost transmitter and advocate of Gassendi's brand of Epicureanism at mid-century, purveying its natural philosophy in his *Physiologia Epicuro-Gassendo-Charltoniana* (1654) as well as its moral philosophy in *Epicurus's Morals* (1656), the latter with Charleton's own 'Apologie for Epicurus'. But *The Immortality of the Human Soul* outpaces his several other productions of the Interregnum period in emphasising the relevance of Lucretius to modern times. The use of dialogue suits Charleton's promotion of an eirenic, moderately sceptical, and sociable exchange among learned gentlemen. But it is Lucretius in particular who voices the loss of 'the dayes of youth, innocence and peace' resulting from 'so many troubles, dangers, and changes of Fortune, as the late Civill Warres in England hath driven us upon'. Ironically, whereas the ancient Lucretius writes during the death of a republic, Charleton's affection for a monarchy tragically supplanted by an English republic is perfectly clear. But in casting Evelyn as 'Lucretius', Charleton devises a persona whose 'Magazine of choice Morall Precepts' transcends the *DRN*'s own times. As Charleton presents him, Lucretius defines the perfect virtuoso, urges the need for a moderate scepticism in testing all positions and is willing to learn about immortality and providence, not least in the claim that the divine purpose of the Civil War involved a disenchantment with theology and law that has promoted the advancement of natural knowledge.[26]

But royalists were not alone in their mid-seventeenth-century engagement with Lucretius. The best verse translation of the *DRN* to come out of these years was written by the republican nonconformist Lucy Hutchinson, who, for all her eventual disdain for the poem's anti-providential materialism, identified with its powerful and rational opposition to violent superstition and tyrannical authority, authority of a kind that Charles I and his prelates epitomised for her. In her narrative of the Civil War and of her husband's leadership in it, as well as in her original poetry, Hutchinson reveals her solidarity with the *DRN*'s critique of ambition as well as its prescriptions for tranquillity, its support for the nuclear family, and its argument that at least in the fallen world, the rule of law is best equipped for securing human welfare, even if no one constitution offers a natural telos.[27]

Whatever their political affiliations, mid-seventeenth-century English students of Lucretius were attracted to the support he lent their retreat from a political world turned upside down by discord and ambition. Indeed, in

[26] Charleton 1985: 3, 13.
[27] For Hutchinson on Lucretius see R. Barbour 1998: 264–8; for her translation see ch. 16 below, and references there.

political culture during and after the Civil War, Lucretius was often positioned in the middle ground between factions: for instance, the moderate John Denham found in Lucretius a template for a constitutional monarchism.[28] The account of civilisation in Book 5 struck readers (as it had struck Gassendi) as harmonising completely with a moderate constitution according to which kingly sovereignty would be rectified with laws and compacts.[29]

For royalists such as Charleton as well as republicans such as Hutchinson, the atoms of Lucretius might represent the only guarantor of fixity and certitude in a world otherwise so fragile and obscure: after all, the *DRN* stresses that only they can never be broken and that their overall behaviour is predictable even if any one swerve or combination is not. But, more metaphorically, atoms also epitomised the very image of a state, a church and a society breaking into pieces. Thomas Browne intensified the dispersive tendency of atomic physics in the imagery of the first authorised edition of his *Religio Medici* in 1643.[30] From widely differing vantage points, writers such as Clarendon, Waller and Milton invoked Lucretius' analogy between civil war and atomic motion or between atomic compounds and human commonwealths, with Charleton working out the latter analogy in great detail and with considerable care.[31] Even the diction of Lucretius translations sometimes shows contemporary bias. Thus Evelyn speaks of Memmius as a 'loyal Cavalier', insists on the poet's intention to show 'that the Tyranny succeeded the overthrow of Monarchy' – the application of which (to Cromwell) he will 'leave . . . to the politicians' – and converts Lucretius' critique of ambition into 'a rare lesson for rebellious and turbulent spirits'.[32]

In direct as well as indirect ways, then, the English Civil War was contested by the mental and poetic means of an engagement with Lucretius. His atomism and hedonism figured frequently in mid-seventeenth-century assessments of both the causes of and the cures for internecine strife. With the aid of Gassendi, English intellectuals such as Charleton began more confidently and systematically to reconcile the mechanism of the *DRN* with a voluntarist natural theology which insisted that a harmony between providence and a particulate physics made good sense for the advancement of learning and its benefits for human society. Even so, theologians and moral philosophers feared that Lucretian enlightenment would bring with it not just a decadent atheism but also a Hobbesian tyranny with ancient roots

---

[28] For Denham see Scodel 2002: 122–7.   [29] For Gassendi see Osler 2002: 90–1.

[30] For Browne's atomic imagery see Wilding 1987: 91–3.

[31] For Clarendon, Waller and Charleton, see R. Barbour 1998: 266. Milton's treatment appears in *Paradise Lost* 2.890–900.

[32] Evelyn 1656: commentary, 101; translation, 5.1260–3; British Library Evelyn MS 33, 105^r, 106^r–7^r.

in Caesarean Epicureanism. In the following century this tension between imperialism and enlightenment was most clearly unfolded in Prussia.

Frederick the Great and Voltaire

One constant in the long and stormy relationship between Frederick II of Prussia and his sometime resident philosopher Voltaire was their mutual preoccupation with the moral, religious and political implications of the *DRN*. This is not to say that they responded to Lucretius in precisely the same ways. Whereas Voltaire's evolving understanding of Lucretius proved deeply ambivalent, Frederick's affection for the Roman poet was both simpler and more twisted.[33]

Lucretius inspired Voltaire to far more than merely a condemnation of the havoc wrought by priests and fanatics. The *DRN* incited him to assess and reassess the role of the solitary philosophical critic in the turbulent and often vicious political world at large, and the natural order in which human life is situated. Indeed, from very early in his writing career, Voltaire in Peter Gay's words 'introduces himself as a new Lucretius who will tear the mask from the face of religion, expose sacred lies, and teach his reader to despise the horrors of the tomb and the terrors of another life'. As adversity takes its toll on the happy, enlightened life, it becomes all the more heroic to 'uproot the noxious weeds of superstition, fanaticism, and cruelty before [people] can cultivate their garden with any prospect of a harvest'.[34]

As a relatively late work, Voltaire's imaginary correspondence between Memmius and Cicero, *Lettres de Memmius à Cicéron* of 1771,[35] summarises the Frenchman's complex response to Lucretius, for it seeks to reclaim the moral power and political clarity of the *DRN* even while repudiating its atomism and theology. In the first letter, which reports the suicide of the poet, Memmius complains that Lucretius had far more reason to embrace death than Cato, for if Cicero, Memmius and Brutus have survived the Republic, so might have Cato. In addition to settling for toleration and arguing for his version of divine providence, Memmius seeks to work out with Cicero the strategies for survival in an age of tyranny, a time when senators have nothing more to do than philosophise. But if Lucretius is admirable for his poetry and moral philosophy in the face of death, the poet is immortalised by his bolder attacks on superstition. What Memmius leaves unaddressed is just how this radical edge in the *DRN* can suggest anything other than suicide when tyrants rule.

[33] For Voltaire see also Redshaw 1980 and ch. 17 below.
[34] Gay 1966: 104, 202–3.   [35] Voltaire 1877–85: VII, 437–63.

Insofar as atheists are motivated to their disbelief in divine providence by human crimes and calamities, Memmius continues, Lucretius is excusable in the face of the nightmare through which he lived, during which time Romans swam in their own blood. And Memmius anticipates civil wars even more horrible than those already experienced, leaving the world a field of carnage. In the allegorical vein of Lucretius, Memmius notes that the fabulous monsters of the underworld are nothing in comparison to the Sullas and Mariuses of their own times. The only hope for Rome, Memmius concludes, is that tyranny will tire itself out with atrocities, and the savagery produced by superstition will not eclipse the principles of virtue natural to the human heart. In essence, the poetic project of the *DRN* is an enlightened and a noble failure, lovely, sometimes comforting, but often false and hapless, with no effective means of intervening in human affairs. The suicide of Lucretius has nothing to do with a love potion, but everything to do with the poet's meltdown in the face of senseless human misery.

Frederick's Lucretius is often emphatically different from Voltaire's. Among the powerful images of an emperor trying to reconcile despotism with enlightenment, and military-cum-political ambition with tolerance and tranquillity, at least two centre on the poet of the *DRN*. In one case, at Sans Souci, Frederick's retreat near Potsdam, a statue of Apollo holds a book with verses of Lucretius (fig. 9.1). In another, the great warrior Frederick carries a pocket edition of his 'friend' Lucretius into battle, no doubt mainly as a moral comfort in the face of death and in the atomic chaos of combat.[36] In these two versions of Lucretius lay the tension for Voltaire and Frederick within the relationship between wisdom and power: in one case, philosophy is static but lovely in presiding over tranquil retreat; in the other it is entrenched within the earthly battles from which it is supposed to offer relief. Verses engraved in marble and held by Apollo: here one finds the immortal wisdom of a poet whose advice necessitates passivity, quietude and disengagement, its bold assaults on the evil wrought by religion intended to make no trouble for the current government. A copy of the *DRN* as the imperial and despotic soldier's breviary in battle: here one finds the perverse, Caesarean militarisation of that relentless fervour with which the poet faces down chaos and hacks away at the enemies threatening the welfare of oneself and one's own community.

Whereas the individualistic Lucretius 'was too much of a rebel, too much an exponent of freedom to win the favour of Church or State', it was

---

[36] For Frederick's moral reliance on Lucretius see MacDonogh 1999: 271, and Lentin 1985: 254; on the 'breviary' Frederick took to war Gay 1966: 102; for the statue Fleischmann 1963: 632.

Figure 9.1. Statue of Apollo at Sans Souci. The book to which he points is inscribed with
DRN 1.24–5 'I long that you should be my helper in writing the verses that I am trying to
compose On the Nature of Things.' Apollo looks across to a statue of Celestial Venus on the
other side of the entrance to the vestibule

Frederick who gave Lucretius his best chance at hegemony in eighteenth-
century Europe, even if the Prussian emperor, in Voltaire's view, ended
up assuming the role of a Marcus Aurelius 'who combated the system of
Lucretius by moral reflections'.[37] In his *Posthumous Works* Frederick refers

37 Hadzsits 1963: 319–20; Aldington 1927: 305.

to Lucretius on several occasions. Of *DRN* 3 he asserts 'there are no better
remedies for maladies of the mind'. The same section of the poem affords him
'a very singular combat between ambition and philosophy maintained in my
mind'. Early in the Silesian campaign in 1741 he lambasts 'that ancient monster . . . Religion', with its fraudulence, persecution and fears, and heralds a
time 'when bold Lucretius' sword hung o'er her head'.[38]

It was in his long and stormy correspondence with Frederick, however,
that Voltaire teased out the connections between hedonism, government,
liberty of thought and religion, with Lucretius figuring as a persona who can
represent audacity and passivity in turn. The emperor and the philosopher
are in consistent agreement that superstition and fanaticism must be eradi-
cated. In 1736 theologians are said to 'claim despotic authority over men's
consciences'; a year later Voltaire quotes Lucretius' *tantum religio potuit
suadere malorum* for Frederick, 'the only prince in the world to whom I
would dare send it'. Letters back and forth decry religion as 'the idol of the
peoples'; as inimical to kings (though they rarely realise it); as destructive
of any 'love of the human race' and oppressive of any bold individual who
refuses religion's chains; as productive of both atrocities and 'all the innumerable daily little evils in society'; and as deeply entrenched in the weak
and foolish human mind.[39]

By 1770 the materialist philosopher d'Holbach's revival of Lucretian ideas
has prompted Frederick to impose severer limits on the tolerance that should
be extended to philosophers. In fact, Frederick's own stormy relations with
contemporary embodiments of Lucretius – with the philosopher La Mettrie
and with Voltaire himself – have incited him to attach conditions to intellectual tolerance itself: he will 'offer a refuge to the philosophers, so long
as they behave themselves and are as pacific as the noble title they assume
implies'. As Kant famously argued, Frederick meant that enlightenment –
understood here in the Epicurean terms of repose – requires philosophical
submission to political and military authority, even if Frederick fantasised
that this authority derives from an agreement of the people. For Frederick in
1766, philosophers are better off producing Epicurean peace than attempting
to arrive at the true nature of things.[40]

Writing from Potsdam in October 1770, Frederick summarised for
Voltaire the emperor's own philosophy, albeit curiously in the third person. Key tenets are deeply indebted to Lucretius and his legacy: that nothing
remains of us after death; 'that man is not a double being' but 'only matter
animated by movement'; that the divine nature is wholly unmoved by human

[38] Frederick II 1789: XII, 53–4, 221–2; X, 287–8.
[39] Aldington 1927: 31, 49, 77, 150, 270–1. [40] For Kant see Blanning 1990: 288.

events, services, injuries and wishes, with the corollary (of central interest to Montaigne) that human beings really have no reason to concern themselves with the gods; and that 'the animal kingdom' operates 'as an accident of nature, like the dust thrown up by wheels'. Politically and socially, the statement stresses the Epicurean principle of hedonistic relativism that law, custom and justice are contingent on the welfare of societies in their own place and time. It is not at all surprising that Frederick's personal philosophy would feature such debts to Lucretius. Attacking the modern paradoxes of Rousseau in 1762, he wrote to George Keith, Earl Marischal: 'I stick to Locke, to my friend Lucretius, to my good old Emperor Marcus Aurelius; those men have told us all we can know, (apart from Epicurus' physics) and all that can make us moderate, virtuous and wise.'[41] Lucretius, like Voltaire himself, was the dear friend with whom the emperor, embracing his own persona of Marcus Aurelius, was always apt to feud.

Often Frederick and Voltaire clearly coincided in their disdain for religion's anti-Lucretian backlash. As Cardinal Melchior de Polignac most famously captured in *Anti-Lucretius*, his nine-book Latin verse refutation of atheism, Lucretius anticipated the late-seventeenth- and eighteenth-century claim that society could manage and even prosper without religion, a claim on which Frederick and Voltaire agreed in an exchange of letters in 1766–7.[42] Early in Book 1 of his poem, Polignac reminds his reader that in Lucretius' day, ambitious Caesar was savaging the world. No state, power, or nemesis could stand once Caesar had decided to topple it. In this age of wild tyrannical force, human blood filled the Roman world while long-cherished values were trampled under foot. Polignac's point here is that the moral philosophy of Lucretius could do nothing to prevent these atrocities. How risible to think that the simple dictates of relaxation and inactivity could have stopped Caesar, who no doubt would have retorted to Lucretius: 'Rest then, if Rest's your Pleasure: our's is War.'[43] For the first time in the history of his reception, however – or so Polignac seeks to convince his readers – Lucretius was no longer simply the philosopher-poet who was irrelevant to Caesar: his legacy now inspired the wild rampages of contemporary Caesars in pursuit of godless ends. As Frederick the Great redefined and embodied his persona, Lucretius our contemporary came to play three irreconcilable roles: the incisive critic of the warfaring conqueror; the idle philosopher who sometimes yielded comfort but just as often represented an impossible leisure and wasted genius; and, strangely enough, the warrior himself, literalising the Herculean metaphor of the ancient poem (*DRN* 5.22–54) in a relentless,

41 Aldington 1927: 314–16; Lentin 1985: 176, 254.
42 For Polignac see also pp. 198–9 below.   43 Polignac 1757: 19.

bloody campaign to force purgation on his world. It is not surprising that contemporary observers were prone to confusion.[44]

Further reading

For Epicureanism and politics in the late Republic see Castner 1988, Griffin and Barnes 1989, Momigliano 1960 and Sedley 1997a. For differing interpretations of the political assertions and implications of the *DRN*, see D. P. Fowler 1989, W. R. Johnson 2000, Minyard 1985 and Nichols 1976. On Montaigne's direct responses to the *DRN* see Screech 1998. For an attempt to derive a coherent political philosophy from Montaigne's *Essays* see Schaefer 1990; for Montaigne's position in the Renaissance recovery of Lucretius see H. Jones 1989. For Bacon's extensive responses to Lucretius and atomism see R. Barbour 1998, R. Barbour 2005. For the revival of Epicureanism in mid-seventeenth-century England, see Kroll 1991 and Hadzsits 1963. For Frederick the Great and Voltaire see Fleischmann 1963, Gay 1966, Manuel 1959 and Redshaw 1980.

[44] Thus the translator of Polignac's *Anti-Lucretius*, William Dobson, was also the admiring author of *The Prussian Campaign, a Poem: Celebrating the Atchievements of Frederick the Great, in the Years 1756–57*.

IO

JAMES I. PORTER

Lucretius and the sublime

Is Lucretius a crucial link in the history of the sublime? The suspicion has been mooted in the past, though opinions vary as to where to place the accent (style and genre are the two contenders).[1] A fuller exploration of Lucretius' relationship to the sublime can shed light on much of his poetry, on his deepest insights into atomism and on his place in the ancient and modern worlds. To see how this is so, three kinds of connection need to be drawn: between Lucretius and Longinus; between both of these and their intellectual forebears; and between Lucretius and the greatest modern philosopher of the sublime, Kant. But as these connections are not commonly made, a few preliminary justifications will be necessary.

Defining the sublime

At any historical moment the sublime is hard if not impossible to define. After all, in the early modern period it was rebaptised as the *je ne sais quoi*, or 'I haven't got a clue', reflecting a sense of its ineffability or perhaps the sheer frustration of trying to pin down its ancient and modern meanings.[2] The only surviving author from classical antiquity to develop a language for naming and treating the sublime, known today as Longinus, wrote a treatise of uncertain date (usually placed in the first century BC) *Peri Hypsous – On Height*, or *On the Sublime*. However, Longinus was by no means the first to deploy the concept of the sublime, as he himself tells us. And for all his

Thanks to Philip Hardie, Stuart Gillespie, Peter Railton, Andrea Nightingale, Gregory Hutchinson and Ian Balfour for comments on earlier drafts, and to the participants in the Lucretius 'workship' held at Corpus Christi College, Oxford in June 2005.

[1] Style: Conte 1965, Conte 1966, Innes 1979. Generic and other criteria: Schrijvers 1970: 273 n. 49; Hardie 1986, esp. 171, and this volume; Segal 1990: 74–80; Conte 1994: 1–34; Ferri 1993, esp. 122–5; Schrijvers 2004.
[2] See Litman 1971; Brody 1958: 9–38, 54–6.

assurances about the meaning of the term, *hypsos* is in point of fact being disputed by him (1.1; 2.1). Thus, despite its alleged self-evidence (7.3–4), the very notion of the sublime is a matter of debate in antiquity. The point is significant for anyone interested in connecting developments in ancient philosophy to the tradition of the sublime.[3] The present inquiry into this tradition will limit itself to its potential relevance to Lucretius.

Both as philosopher and poet, Lucretius is naturally interested in the same kinds of sweeping topics that engage Longinus – nature, the soul and language. He also finds in each of these an element of sublimity, and often on similar grounds, despite the fact that Longinus' views are often coloured by Stoicism while Lucretius' are unrelentingly atomistic. Nevertheless, the sublime can be a remarkably unifying phenomenon, as will be shown. Given its potential variety of applications, a working definition of the concept is needed.

According to a contemporary analysis the sublime is to be found wherever 'a positive, material object [is] elevated to the status of [an] impossible Thing'.[4] Simultaneously fascinating and fearful, such an object resists integration into one's symbolic frameworks of understanding. The experience of the sublime is the gamut of responses one has in the face of such an object, although ultimately the experience one has is, on this view, of the contingency of one's own frameworks of meaning and understanding. Some of this complexity is seen at work in Longinus' text, for instance in his account of oratorical sublimity: 'produced at the right moment, [sublimity] tears everything up like a whirlwind, and exhibits the orator's whole power at a single blow', leaving the hearer momentarily stunned (1.4).[5] But the sublime is likewise to be found in the terrifying images of the gaping cosmos that Longinus (9.6) finds in Homer.

Atomism lends itself particularly well to the sublime, in at least two ways: through its glimpses of the void, which, in their radical negation of all that is and that has sense, unsettle conventional frames of reference and threaten to annihilate phenomenological meaning; and in the collision and confusion of the two incommensurable scales of the micro- and macro-levels, whereby the infinitesimally small can appear infinitely and forbiddingly large. Indeed, atomism seems practically designed to elicit feelings of sublimity, of fear and awe, again with the aim of realigning in a radical way one's view of oneself and the world, well beyond the mere replacement of mythological and theological awe with secular or scientific awe. The shudder of sublimity

---

[3] Cf. Wehrli 1946; Quadlbauer 1958.
[4] Žižek 1989: 71, developing Lacan 1986: 133. Cf. Stewart 1993: 140.
[5] Translations are from Russell and Winterbottom 1972.

that can be felt in all of Lucretius' verses is a symptom of this effort. The second section will trace some of the threads of the sublime that run through Lucretius' poem. The third will turn to the most striking parallels between Lucretius and Longinus. Armed with these two sets of readings, it will be possible to throw a glance back at antecedents, then forward to some later expressions and echoes in a similar vein.

The Lucretian sublime

> A puddle of water no deeper than a single finger-breadth, which lies between the stones on a paved street, offers us a view beneath the earth to a depth as vast as the high gaping mouth (*hiatus*) of heaven stretches above the earth, so that you seem to look down on the clouds and the heaven, and you discern bodies hidden in the sky beneath the earth, marvellously (*mirande*).
>
> (*DRN* 4.414–19)

What qualifications does it take to see gaping depths in a surface? None, which is surely the point: the image is an object-lesson in *prolēpsis* (natural primary concepts): anyone, potentially, can grasp the concept of void through native intuition. Lucretius' example appears in a list of optical illusions; but surely the greatest optical illusion is that presented by the world as it is perceived on a day-to-day basis. The senses continually read appearances (images, *simulacra*) off the surface of phenomena that reflection and science can serve to correct. But equally to the point, Lucretius' comment on perceptual fallacy here is deflationary in the extreme: grandeur, sublime heights and depths, vast expanses of heaven and earth, conjuring up beauties and horrors and reverential awe, are all vitiated here – voided – by a mere puddle. Lucretius' philosophical vision typically tends to evacuate the reality one intuitively knows and understands, even as it seeks to anchor this reality in the reassuring bedrock of physics (atoms and void). This gives us the true *maiestas*, the majesty or sublimity, of nature. But it is above all a majesty of *things* (*maiestas rerum*, 5.7).

Sublimity results from the sheer exhilaration that a glimpse of scientific truth affords. But it also draws its power from the fundamental discrepancy between such an insight into the nature of things and one's customary perspectives. The stark contrast of atoms and void presages this discrepancy in the very foundations of nature. In an atomist's hands, void in particular is a threatening concept and a rhetorical bludgeon, a source of philosophical argument and of never-ending anxiety. But it is also a source of endless fascination. Lucretius may display an even greater fascination with void than Epicurus. If so, then this is not only to be put down to Lucretius' superior attunement to the poetic potentials of void. The poetic meanings are tied to conceptual insights, and both are worth recovering.

Void and vacuity come to the fore in Lucretius in three areas; all three are productive of sublime sensations (of conjoined horror and fascination), and all three are interrelated. Void is poetically and philosophically active in the areas of:

(i) death, which signifies an absolute vacuity, in the sense that it is a vacancy we cannot represent to ourselves: being nothing, death is literally nothing to us (*DRN* 3.830; cf. 3.1046; Epicurus, *Ep. Men.* 124–5). Where the untrained fear death, an Epicurean's attitude is more complex and paradoxical, taking pleasure *in the very mortality of life itself* (Epicurus, *Ep. Men.* 124; cf. *DRN* 3.511).

(ii) the third-person perspective on nature that comes from viewing the world *sub specie physicae*. Subjectively speaking, the atomic constituents of nature map out a deep metaphysical absence, one the mind refuses to picture: here, we are nothing more than physical entities, mere fortuitous combinations of matter which reduce to their tiny and invisible elements upon disbanding, while the world is no different. The physical hypothesis of atomism is in this sense a very real threat to our conceptual livelihood, requiring a good deal of honey on the rim to be imbibed at all. Lying at the limits of representation, it presents a kind of conceptual death for a subject operating from a first-person perspective, but also a divine thrill and awe (*diuina uoluptas atque horror, DRN* 3.28–9).

(iii) the more palpable but also more emblematic evocations of void, which is to say, physically empty spaces that arguably stand in for cosmological void and bring some of the more extreme consequences of atomism into the immediate periphery of the viewing subject. Void, which in atomistic terms is invisible and intangible, here becomes, in its visible analogues, phenomenally apparent and sublimely so.[6]

It is this latter set of associations that will be of primary interest here, particularly as these are found in the final and in many ways culminating book of the *DRN*.

Apparently organised around ideas of prodigious earthly and cosmic marvels, Book 6 is in fact governed by a far subtler subtext. Its central theme is the porosity and voiding of sensible matter, and ultimately void as the absence (or unintelligibility) of matter itself. Hence the extraordinary frequency of terms for emptiness in this book: *caua, cauernae, uacuum, inanis,*

---

[6] Analogously, Schrijvers 1970: 270–1 and Hardie 1986: 191 on the sea as void in Lucretius.

fauces, foramina, barathrum, and so on. Hence, too, the focus of the book, namely bodies lapsing into emptiness, collapsing and caving in. Earthquakes, volcanic eruptions, vast cloud formations riddled with thunderbolts, empty spaces underground and overhead, and the boundless universe itself are all analogues for this emptying out of sensation's contents within the objects of sensation (this is the, as it were, *inane rerum* of 1.517). The focus, in other words, is on the dynamic function of void, whereby void is to be understood not simply as an agent or precondition of motion but also as an agent of commotion, terror and destabilisation (of change and death). Atomistic void is in this book the protagonist, and it is repeatedly presented in larger-than-life settings. But more than anything else, void, put centre-stage, comes to stand for itself and to gesture towards the nature of sheer vacuity and its irresistible compulsions.[7]

Earthquakes are a good example. As impressive as thunderclouds, earthquakes represent a more proximate danger: they are real gaps in matter. The language of celestial gaping from earlier in the same book is now repeated in subterranean fashion: *loca subcaua terrae, loca caua, magnum hiatum* (6.557, 580, 584), the last term particularly menacing as it conjures up the gate of death itself (cf. 5.375). But beyond death, earthquakes prefigure nothing less than the end of this world, its final wrenching expiration (as in 5.92–109).[8] But Lucretius is also making a psychological point about men's foreboding of the world's end whenever they behold the earth coming apart. For what they fear, without knowing it (Lucretius boldly claims), is precisely this catastrophe. Presumably they have a natural preconception (*prolēpsis*) of the end of the world, a preconception buried in their confused assumptions about natural disasters. Lucretius' language is carefully chosen: 'They fear to believe that a time of destruction and ruin awaits the nature of the great world', even when they see signs of its vulnerability and fragility all around (6.565–7). And this fear is in turn based on a deeper metaphysical fear that the world is not quite the way it is commonly known and experienced (as something more or less solid, permanent and secure), a fear which expresses itself psychologically as, one might say, a pervading *horror uacui*. Thus,

> let [common folk] believe as they will that heaven and earth will be indestructible, entrusted to everlasting safety; and yet from time to time the very present force of danger applies from somewhere this prick of fear, lest the earth should be snatched away suddenly from beneath their feet (*pedibus . . . subtracta*) and be borne into the abyss (*in barathrum*), and the sum of things, left utterly

---

7 See further Porter 2003 (from which this and the following two sections are drawn), foreshadowed by Porter 1992: 105, 106.

8 Cf. Hardie 1986: 190.

without foundation (*prodita . . . funditus*), should follow on, and the world
should end in a confused ruin. (6.601–7)

The phenomena picked out for description in Book 6 are emblematic of this
ultimate and primordial fear. As juxtaposed body and void, they represent
the physics of sensation; but as objects of fear they represent an untrained
response to the atomistic view of nature. Scenes of natural disaster are fearful
because they portend the unimaginable: the potential absence of a material
foundation in which one can securely place one's trust. If you have any
doubts about it, Lucretius says, just look down at the ground beneath your
feet: 'nor does earth stand as a barrier to all things being witnessed, all that
moves through the void beneath our feet' (*sub pedibus*) (3.26–7; cf. 1.1105–
8). But for an atomist it can be a sublime sensation to stand on nothing.

Lucretius and Longinus

DRN 6 contains a series of images that will become iconic in the sublime tradition from Longinus to Kant: storm-tossed seas, earthquakes, jagged mountains, impending clouds, the yawning abyss between heaven and earth. But
the book also contains a series of parallels between Lucretius and Longinus,
unique in the surviving literature of antiquity, and which seem to point to a
literary dependency going beyond a simple affinity of mind or spirit.

At 6.608–737 Lucretius runs through a list of geographical prodigies:
firstly the nature of the sea, then Etna, and then the Nile. These all have
their place in the thematics of atmospheric and geological void developed in
the previous passage and are a natural extension of their logic. That logic
leads to reflection about the nature of the universe, first in the terrifying image
just quoted of the world collapsing in ruin, and then in a more settled mood
of cosmic wonderment. The fear is one that atomism would allay; but it is
also one that atomism encourages in the mere presentation of the thought
of impending ruin. There is something sublime to the thought, which the
physicist entertains as he stands *à la* Kant on the edge of a precipice looking
down, safely detached, upon the turmoil below. All of Book 6 has this feel
of a detached spectacle about it.

Thus, the sea is wondrously capacious, so much so that it seems to defy the
laws of addition; it is a sum that cannot be added to (613–14). Etna's 'jaws'
open onto an 'exceedingly gigantic' furnace, but also onto subterranean
hollows that communicate again with the open sea (680–702; 698). And then
there is the Nile, 'the river of all Egypt', whose primary distinction seems to
be its fame for being famous. Lucretius' comparatively brief account of the
natural prodigy of the Nile (712–37) seems to belong here thanks to its sheer

size alone, and not as an emblem of the void. Nor is it found in Epicurus, probably Lucretius' immediate source in this section.[9]

Elsewhere in extant ancient literature these natural phenomena occur as a group only in *On the Sublime* 35.3–5,[10] which singles out as sublime and paradoxical wonders of nature the universe, the Nile, the ocean and the erupting craters of Etna. The examples are adduced by Longinus to illustrate how mankind is drawn to greatness; whence it occurs that 'our thoughts often travel beyond the boundaries of our surroundings'. Lucretius is making much the same point. The attraction to natural prodigies is irresistible, even erotic;[11] wonder comes naturally, as does the desire to transgress the limits of phenomena (Epicurus is a case in point). Lucretius' surface lesson, 'And if you kept my proposition clearly in mind, you would cease to wonder at many things' (6.653–4), is too easily understood as an injunction not to wonder at anything (*nil admirari*) in nature. But that is surely the wrong conclusion to draw. After all, even the reflection of the sky in a puddle is a 'marvellous' thing (*mirande*), both as an appearance of nature and as an index to the wondrous truths of physics.[12] Appearances can be admired and enjoyed *per se* so long as they do not conflict with atomistic truths, while their discrepancy with atomic realities can induce fear as well as fascination – a far more potent and complex form of 'marvel' – and (ideally) a supervening mental quiet. Sublimity can name all of these emotions, in their punctuality, intensity and rarity.[13]

The passage that is wedged between the account of Etna and the Nile in Lucretius (6.647–79) gives us some of the missing context here. Etna's blaze is 'exceedingly great' (673). But greatness is in itself both a perpetual fascination, and forever relative: each next greater thing puts us in mind of the gigantic (677 *haec ingentia fingit*), but the sum total of these greater things is 'nothing to the whole sum of the universal sum' (679), that is, compared to the universe itself. If Longinus is indeed quoting from some tradition of paradoxography, Lucretius might seem to be relativising it. In fact, he is working to outbid it,[14] as is clear from the beginning of this passage: 'Herein you must look far and deep and take a wide view to every quarter, that you may remember that the sum of things is unfathomable, and see how small,

---

[9] Sedley 1998, Mansfeld 1992: 326.

[10] The parallel has gone unnoticed. Other partial groupings: Sen. *Q. Nat.* 4a.2.20–1; 3.22.1; 2.30.1; Sil. *Pun.* 16.33–7; Luc. 10.194–267; Men. Rhet. 3:392.26 Sp.; Hyg. *Poet. astr.* 2.32.1; Cleom. 1.8.1–7 Todd.

[11] See Porter 2005: 113–24.   [12] Cf. 5.461–3 (echoed at 2.319) with Porter 2005: 141.

[13] Cf. Sen. *Dial.* 5.6.1 (claiming Democritus as his source); *Dial.* 7.4.5; Plin. *HN* 7.190.

[14] Cf. Sen. *Q. Nat.* 4b.11.2–5; [Arist.] *Mund.* 391a24–91b3.

how infinitely small a part of the whole sum is one single heaven – not so large a part as is a single man of the whole earth' (6.647–52).

For Longinus too the wonders of nature are mere outward emblems of a greater attraction – to a greatness that has no measure, because its grandeur is absolute and (literally) immense. 'The universe therefore is not wide enough for the range of human speculation and intellect. Our thoughts often travel beyond the boundaries of our surroundings. If anyone wants to know what we were born for, let him look round at life and contemplate the splendour, grandeur and beauty in which it everywhere abounds.' This cannot but bring to mind Epicurus, passing beyond the *flammantia moenia mundi* with his mind (*DRN* 1.72–3) or Lucretius' generalisation of this impulse to intellectual daring at 2.1044–7. The underlying thought is, to be sure, a commonplace,[15] but Longinus' use of ἐπιβολὴ τῆς διανοίας in 35.3 is not (cf. *animi iactus* at *DRN* 2.1047): this is a term of art in Epicureanism, meaning 'mental focusing' (Epicurus, *Ep. Hdt.* 51; 62). The idea of passing unconstrained beyond the limits of the world occurs earlier in *On the Sublime*, 9.5, in a cosmic image of divine winged steeds about to stride off into another dimension, and where the accent is laid upon the cosmic gap or void, the κοσμικὸν διάστημα, by which Homer has taken the world's measure. This image is juxtaposed with another glimpse of the cosmos gaping in its depths nearby. The image is gigantomachic: morally offensive on the surface, it can be salvaged as aesthetically and ethically sublime. Like Lucretius, Longinus prefers to see divinity represented 'as genuinely unsoiled and great and pure' (9.8).

Antecedents

These parallels suggest a common source, possibly in meteorological doxography (Longinus is unlikely to have drawn directly on Lucretius).[16] This latter may already have been drawn on by writers in a sublime literary tradition that now exists only in a few remnants and hints in various poetic and prose (rhetorical and natural philosophical) sources. Crates of Mallos would have been one of the links in this chain, especially if his theory of Homer's geography and cosmology (*sphairopoiia*) was a way of marking Homer's sublimity,[17] as is Aratus' *Phaenomena* (and its Latin versions), with its emphasis on grand heavenly orbits, Pliny's *Natural History*, and Varro,

---

[15] Russell (1964), ad loc.; Hadot 1995.
[16] See Mansfeld 1992, Runia 1997, Sedley 1998: 157–60.   [17] Porter 1992.

Manilius, the *Aetna* poet, the Younger Pliny and Seneca, not to mention the traces scattered in Augustan and post-Augustan poets.[18]

A clue that these texts point to the right vein, so to speak, is a passage from Seneca's *Natural Questions* (5.15.1–2), citing Asclepiodotus, a pupil of Posidonius and the author of a treatise on natural phenomena, on how men sent by Philip II of Macedon to explore an abandoned mine discovered not the riches he had hoped for, but something far more breathtaking: vast reservoirs of subterranean water, held in the generous embrace of the earth, which greeted the visitors 'not without a thrill of awe/horror' (*non sine horrore*). Seneca reads this 'with great pleasure' (*cum magna . . . uoluptate*) – evidently a smiling glance at *DRN* 3.28–9. Another source may be Theophrastus, whose *Metarsiologica* describes, among other things, the earth's inner hollow places. Theophrastus would in turn have been a relay for the first-generation atomists,[19] with their lavish use of the analogy of void.[20] Indeed, the motif of void appears to have been a veritable figure of thought and instrument of reasoning for Democritus (DK 68A128, 135(55); B191, 195). Whether the poetic emphasis on void originates with Lucretius is harder to determine: there are possible signs of an Ennian precedent (*Ann.* 558 Skutsch; *Trag.* 96, 319, 365–6 Jocelyn). And there was a Hellenistic epigrammatic tradition, which ranges over everything from volcanic eruptions to destructive floods to magnets to stranded monsters.[21]

Lucretius must be drawing on a tradition that had already blended natural speculation with poetic insight and in this way yielded a common set of *topoi* that lent themselves to the sublime. Common features would have been those signalled above – the casting of scientific speculations in poetic and rhetorical contexts, the emphasis on grandeur, wonder and paradox (which could locate grandeur in the particulars of matter and on an infinitesimal scale), but also the peculiar geometries of the celestial and meteorological sublime: the circular, the spherical, and gaping, empty spaces. The rich links between natural philosophy and poetry and their confluence in Longinus point us to a strange hybrid and still understudied tradition of sublime speculation in

---

[18] Landolfi 1992 (Varro, Cicero, Manilius); Mansfeld 1992: 328–31; Rosenmeyer 2000 (Seneca); Conte 1994: 67–104 (Pliny); Schrijvers 2004 (Silius). Cf. Ov. *Met.* 15.299–301; Sil. *Pun.* 7.371–2. Further, *Aetna* 94–119; Plin. *HN* 2.193–4; Sen. *Q. Nat.* 2.1.2, *Ep.* 79.5, *Oed.* 972; also K. S. Myers 1994.

[19] Aët. 3.1–4 proem. 1 and *DRN* 6; see Sedley 1998: 157–60.

[20] Theophr.: Daiber 1992 (e.g. p. 270); Sen. *Q. Nat.* 6.19.2 (*inania*) = DK 70A21 (Metrod.); 6.20.1 (*concaue*) = DK 68A98(1) (Democr.). Pl. *Phd.* 111c–112e may well reflect this early tradition too.

[21] Wick (forthcoming); cf. Runia 1997: 98.

antiquity. Central is what might be called an 'aesthetics of the gap'.[22] For 'gap' one might as well read 'void' (bearing in mind the atomistic term for void as a gap in matter, διάστημα). Even if Longinus had no direct access to the Roman tradition, he and Lucretius share a fascination with conceptual extremes and limits. A concept of the sublime not only pervades the concluding books of the *DRN*, but it also lies at the heart of the poem's conception. Lucretius has seen how atomism can be sublime, possibly in a way that Epicurus had not.

Later expressions and echoes: Kant and after

Lucretius' Latin successors respond to his sublimity. Ovid labels Lucretius *sublimis*, in a prediction of his canonical reputation that is underpinned, if not quite undermined, by allusion to the world's final destruction in *DRN* 5 (Ov. *Am.* 1.15.23 ~ *DRN* 5.95).[23] Virgil builds off the Lucretian sublime in various places to harrowing effect. There is the farmer at *Georgics* 1.493–7 who some day 'will strike empty (*inanis*) helmets with his hoe', and 'marvel', naïvely, 'at gigantic bones in the unearthed graves' (a nice Lucretian touch).[24] Or, in *Aeneid* 12, the stunned Turnus hurls at Aeneas a boundary stone, which 'whirls through the empty void (*uacuum per inane*) but does not cross all the space between', much like the flying javelin of Lucretius' thought experiment at the end of Book 1, which also has a parallel in Longinus: all three authors puzzle over the boundless nature of limits.[25] The phrase *uacuum per inane* appears only here and at *DRN* 2.202. Horace's indebtedness to the Lucretian sublime is an intricate story of ambivalent responses.[26] Later writers such as Lucan, Statius, Silius Italicus and Fronto all invoke or evoke Lucretius and the sublime.[27] To leap ahead a millennium and a half, in Italy beginning in the early seventeenth century all the themes mentioned so far enjoyed a revival in the writings of the *Umoristi*, the Jesuit natural scientists, and the Libertines, and then in the romantic landscapes of the Neapolitan Salvator Rosa (1615–73), which celebrated Lucretian and Longinian topoi (*cose brutte e horrende,*

---

[22] Porter 1992, Porter 2001.

[23] Lucretius himself uses *sublimis* or *sublime* only four times, always only in relation to the heavens.

[24] See de Saint-Denis 1966 ad loc., referencing *DRN* 2.1150–74; Gale 2000: 19; Farrell 1991: 167–8.

[25] *Aen.* 12.896–907; *DRN* 1.968–983; [Longinus] 9.5. Further, Hardie 1986 (esp. 157–240); Porter 2004.

[26] See Ferri 1993, Hardie 2008.

[27] Stat. *Silv.* 2.7.76 (*arduus furor*); Silius: Schrijvers 2004; Fronto, *Ep.* 1.2: *sublimis Lucretius* (a bare mention).

Figure 10.1. Illustration of Aetna erupting, from Athanasius Kircher, *Mundus subterraneus*

or *orrida belleza* and *orrore dilettevole*) and such Presocratics as Empedocles and Democritus. In the same line, Athanasius Kircher's *Mundus subterraneus* (1664–5) is a mystical continuation of the earliest paradoxography on *loca subcaua terrae* discussed above (fig. 10.1).[28] Across the Channel, Andrew Marvell, praising Milton's *Paradise Lost*, registers his reaction to 'Thy verse created like thy theme sublime', with a translation of the Lucretian *horror ac uoluptas*: 'At once delight and horror on us seize.'[29] Milton himself alludes to Lucretius' account of Phaethon as he tests his own capacity for sublime flight.[30]

But Kant is the most important milestone in the Lucretian-Longinian tradition, paving the way for the modern poetic and philosophical reading of it. It is perhaps surprising but no accident that Kant should pay greater tribute to Lucretius than to Longinus in his theory of aesthetics: Longinus, after all,

[28] See Langdon 2004.   [29] 'On Mr. Milton's *Paradise Lost*'; see Hardie 1995: 20.
[30] Quint 2004.

was the canonical representative in the aesthetic tradition, especially since Boileau's translation of Longinus (1674) and his *Réflexions critiques sur Longin* (1710), while Lucretius' contribution to this tradition was hardly obvious, and even less classical. Nevertheless, Edmund Burke's *A Philosophical Enquiry into the Origin of Our Ideas of the Sublime and Beautiful* (1st edn 1757; 2nd edn 1759) has foregrounded Lucretius in significant ways (see below); and Kant knew both Burke and Lucretius well.

Though launched as 'a mere appendix' to his theory of the beautiful in the *Critique of Judgement* (1790),[31] Kant's theory of the sublime has shaped every discussion of sublimity since. The parallels and points of contact between the Kantian and the Lucretian sublimes are extensive, but little discussed. In both authors the sublime emerges whenever the mind comes into bruising contact with nature. In Kant's terms, what the mind discovers in this encounter is purely phenomenal or material objects of vision (or perception), unboundedness, pure sensuality, objects of the senses construed as formless (which is to say, without the thought of their being bounded by form), chaos, abysses and a concomitant yearning for the supersensible. What the aesthetic subject experiences in the face of the sublime is a mixture of pain and pleasure, repulsion and attraction, impoverishment and enrichment, a momentary inhibition of the vital forces (*Lebenskräfte*), an expansion of the imaginative faculties, culminating in a feeling of release and freedom (or autonomy and superiority) and a certain sublimity of self (what later would be known, after Keats, as 'the egotistical sublime').[32]

For Kant, the sublime can be evoked by various means. The classic cases are terrifying scenes of nature that put us in mind of nothing so much as *DRN* 6:

> Bold, overhanging, and, as it were, threatening rocks, thunderclouds piled up the vault of heaven, borne along with flashes and peals, volcanoes in all their violence of destruction, hurricanes leaving desolation in their track, the boundless ocean rising with rebellious force, the high waterfall of some mighty river, and the like, make our power of resistance of trifling moment in comparison with their might. (*CJ* §28; Ak. 261)

Other examples include the limitless 'cosmos', Egypt (invoked for its pyramids, though not for the Nile), war, earthquakes, the distant made large

---

[31] *CJ* §23; Ak. 246 ("bloßer Anhang"). Translations are from Kant 1928; "Ak." = Akademie der Wissenschaften edition = Kant (1902), vol. v.

[32] Keats, letter to Richard Woodhouse, 27 October 1818 (Rollins 1958); see Weiskel 1976: ch. 6.

through telescopes, but also (as with Burke before him) the microscopically small (Ak. 256, 252, 263, 250).[33]

Lucretius had invoked similar sights and sounds in nature, not in order to label them sublime, but in order to point the way to something that is truly sublime and awesome in nature: its true rational order, which can be apprehended only with the mind. The thrill and awe that a sublime subject feels before nature is for Lucretius perhaps less one of admiration than of domination, which gives a possible if unexpected overtone to the expression *sub pedibus* in Book 3, where Lucretius looks down at what atomism reveals underfoot (3.27). If so, the echo of the proud supersession of religious superstition in Book 1 is inevitable: 'therefore religion in turn is crushed beneath our feet (*pedibus subiecta*), victory brings us level with the heavens' (1.78–9; cf. Virg. *G.* 2.490–2: *subiecit pedibus*). True to (atomistic) form, Kant makes an identical move in the sequel: 'We readily call these objects sublime, because they raise the forces of the soul above the height of vulgar commonplace, and discover within us a power of resistance [against the unwarranted fearfulness of nature] of quite another kind, which gives us courage to be able to measure ourselves against the seeming (*scheinbaren*) omnipotence of nature' (*CJ* §28; Ak. 261).

Kant goes on to connect these natural responses to the energies of nature with what he deems an improper reaction: the ascription to them of divinity, and especially of divine wrath. A reaction like this is not sublime; it is one of fear, based on 'submission, prostration, and a feeling of utter helplessness'. Besides, 'whoever is seized with fear cannot at all judge the sublime of nature' (*CJ* §28; Ak. 263; 261). The proper response, Kant argues, is not to lapse into cringing 'superstition' (Ak. 264), which would be an irrational and uncritical way of facing nature, but to rise up proudly and assertively against the natural world, discovering within oneself a power to assess the world independently of its allures and threats, and ultimately to discover within us a superiority (*Überlegenheit*) over nature (Ak. 261) – not a real superiority over nature, to be sure, which cannot be verified in any objective way, but rather an *a priori* one. In effect, Kant is urging us to take nature in as a mere phenomenon, and to see past its 'seeming' frights to its conformity with a hidden rational order, with which we are affined (whence our sense of pleasure and relief when we discover it in the end). Thus, in nature the mind discovers, not natural sublimity, but 'its *own* sublimity in its very determination [or 'vocation'], even over nature', which is to say, in the transcendental principles it uses to construe appearances (infinity, causality, law-like behaviour, and so on).

---

[33] Burke 1968: 72.

The mind thus discovers its own 'determination *as* exalted (*erhaben*) above [nature]' (Ak. 262; 264; emphasis added).

The parallels with Lucretius, echoes indeed, ought to be plain – so plain, in fact, that one has to suspect a certain awareness on Kant's part that he is working in a Lucretian, or at the very least atomistic, tradition.[34] The suspicion is an easy one. In his pre-critical work of 1755, the *Universal Natural History*, Kant had after all proclaimed that 'Epicurus has come to life again in the midst of Christianity, and an unholy worldly wisdom tramples faith under foot,' and he had boldly declared his affinity with the complete line of atomists from Leucippus to Lucretius (Ak. 1:212, 226). Here, in *CJ*, Kant is so to speak reliving a gesture from that earlier work. Kant's early and late affinities to atomism are perfectly intelligible. The entire thrust of the atomistic critique of nature was in a sense Kantian (proto-Enlightenment) in spirit: its aim was to demythologise nature, to liberate mankind from blinding superstition and to render nature susceptible of dispassionate scientific (rational) analysis. It is evident that Kant has Epicurus in mind when, in a striking concession, he acknowledges ('we must admit') that 'as Epicurus maintained, gratification and pain . . . are always in the last resort corporeal, since without the feeling of the bodily organ, life would be merely a consciousness of one's existence, but could not include any feeling of well-being or the reverse, i.e. of the furtherance or hindrance of the vital forces' (*CJ* §29; Ak. 277–8; transl. adapted).

Kant never sounded less Kantian than here – never more corporealist, more empiricist, even vitalist in his thinking, let alone Epicurean. Yet he is being perfectly consistent with himself in *CJ* and in his other critical writings. Let us simply note that the connection to the sublime is immediate in this passage, in so far as the sublime, unlike the beautiful, represents a threat to one's 'vital forces' (*CJ* §23; Ak. 244–5). This is the ground of 'fear' that one runs up against in the sublime, even as one is in no real danger but only in a notional or 'as if' danger, just as the fear is 'not [an] actual fear' but only a quasi-fear (*CJ* §29; Ak. 269; cf. Ak. 268). Exactly the same holds for Lucretius and Longinus, for whom the presentation of threatening natural wonders works to deflate a clichéd sublimity in favour either of a smaller, unexpected sublimity – whether dust motes or the atoms they metaphorically recall (*DRN* 2.112–24), or else syntactical particles crushed violently together, as in the Homeric phrase *hupek* (*Subl.* 10.6) – or of a grander, truer sublime that the commonplace sublimities put us in mind of and lead us towards. For what one experiences in the sublime is less fear than the presentation of

---

[34] See Fenves 2003: 8–31; see also Thouard 2003: 265–80 and pp. 143 above and 284–5 below.

fear in the form of an epistemological nuisance. The sublime, one might say, results from a subject's bumping rudely up against 'the narrow confines of sensibility (*die Schranken der Sinnlichkeit*)' (*CJ* §26; Ak. 255), which is to say, against the limits that comprise phenomenal materiality itself. Indeed, the various attributes of sublime objects simply *are* the attributes of raw materiality and unregulated heautonomy in the experience of them: chaos, formlessness, illimitability, the need for transcendental principles to inform these appearances, and so on (cf. *CJ* 'First Introduction', Ak. 20:209).

Whence Kant's pretty insistence on the flat materiality of vision in the face of sublime objects, which must be viewed, thanks to a kind of perspectival selection, 'just as one sees [them],' graced by neither concepts nor form. Thus, the starry heavens can be allowed no teleological existence if they are to be imagined *qua* sublime – they are not to be conceived as planets organised around some solar system or in some other rational way, but simply as phenomena occupying one's field of vision, immense and unfathomable. Similarly, the ocean becomes sublime whenever one 'regard[s] it, as the poets do, according to what the impression upon the eye reveals, as, let us say, in its calm, a clear mirror of water bounded only by the heavens, or, be it disturbed, as threatening to overwhelm and engulf everything in its abyss (*Abgrund*)' (*CJ* §29; Ak. 270).

To see the world in this way is akin to taking up the perspective of a materialist or an atomist who erases his or her humanistic view of things in the name of science and takes in the world from a distantiated perspective, which is in effect 'a view from nowhere'.[35] It is to view 'nature as [a] phenomenon (*Erscheinung*)' (*CJ* §29; Ak. 268) in all its flatness, and then to yearn to reach behind this to some further, concealed dimensions that one can only barely sense, what Kant will link up with the transcendental conditions of experience and what the atomists had linked up with their own version of the same (the hidden operations of the universe, which, however, and in contrast, have an objective reality). And so, in return for the 'negative pleasure' of the sublime, or else bound up with this, as one passes through and beyond the limits of sensation, one experiences a complex feeling of pleasure and pain, of horror and wonder: 'the astonishment (*Verwunderung*) bordering on terror (*Schreck*), the awe and thrill of devout feeling (*das Grausen und der heilige Schauer*), that takes hold (*ergreift*) of one' (*CJ* §29; Ak. 269). Is Kant thinking of the proem to *DRN* 3, where Lucretius describes his Epicurean revelation once he looks upon the face of nature afresh?

---

[35] Nagel 1986. For another perspective, see de Man 1996: 80.

For as soon as your philosophy, sprung from your divine mind, begins to proclaim the nature of things, the terrors of the mind fly away, the walls of the world part asunder, I see things moving through the void . . . The quarters of Acheron are nowhere to be seen, nor does earth stand as a barrier to all things being witnessed, all that moves through the void beneath our feet. Then from these things some sort of divine pleasure and a shuddering awe seizes me, knowing that by your power nature has been made so clear and manifest, laid bare in every way. (3.14–30)

Burke had already (mis)quoted *DRN* 3.28–30 in Pt. II, sec. v of his *Philosophical Enquiry* (1759), and Kant was intimately familiar with Burke's 'empirical' and often Lucretian-sounding view of the sublime's psychological impact (*CJ* §29; Ak. 277; see also Ak. 7:261). But there are other attractions in store here for Kant. The moment described by Lucretius is one in which the materiality of phenomena finally ceases to be an obstacle and a limit to the materialist – their scrim is lifted off the visible world – and the materialist in effect transcends appearances to become something like a transcendental materialist, someone who can take a holy and eerie pleasure in the unlimited appearances of matter and the world. Such a pleasure, being grounded in a paradox as it is, can only be described as sublime. One might, by the same reasoning, say that for Kant an aesthetic subject in the face of the initial shock of the sublime (represented by brute matter and appearances), as opposed to the blissful and harmonious beautiful, is fundamentally an Epicurean.

The real question is, when is Kant *not* an Epicurean in his dealings with sensation? The question is genuine, because there is every reason to think that Kant's theory of sensation is at its core a theory of the sublime, as well as a confrontation with Epicureanism in slightly cloaked guise. To see how this might be the case, one would have to look away from the classic instances of sublimity, familiar from the Third Critique, and turn instead to the First Critique (1781/7), in a chapter called the 'Anticipations of Perception' (B 208–25) where Epicurus is again explicitly invoked – this time as the eternal 'anticipator' of perception and sensation, so to speak (Kant's term, *Antizipation*, is an explicit calque on Epicurean *prolēpsis*, B 208) – and where Kant takes it upon himself to locate the 'real' of sensation. Here, it turns out that the real (or 'matter') of sensation can only be 'anticipated' *a priori* in an asymptotic approach but can never be known as such, and it thus poses the criterial limit between empirical and *a priori* knowledge; and that the very approach to this Real is sublime. This limit lies within *every* sensation, just as every perception contains an infinitely divisible synthesis of the manifold of appearances (one that, as in the mathematical sublime of the Third Critique, threatens to overwhelm the mind with its unsynthesisable

contents). Consequently, every moment of sensation is inhabited or inhibited, from the perspective of critical philosophy, by the sublime, in the form
of its anticipation.

This 'transcendentalist' urge within the sublime tradition helps to account
for one of its odder features. It is sometimes doubted whether nature, in
the last analysis, can be counted as sublime in Lucretius. Nature is finally
made banal, trivialised, no longer a fearful or wondrous object, but merely
an intelligible object. How can this deprecating gesture be squared with
sublimity? The same question can be posed with regard to Kant. For Kant
no object of the senses is properly speaking sublime: the sublime has to be
sought within one's mind and in one's ideas of nature (*CJ* §25; Ak. 250).
But in fact, this inward turn is a trait of the sublime tradition. 'Sublimity is
the echo of a noble mind,' Longinus famously writes (9.2). And Lucretius'
greatest praises are reserved for the sublimity of the mind of his master,
who transcended the limits of appearances, freed himself from his body
and embodied the position of a transcendental materialist (2.1047) – when
they are not aimed at cultivating the reflex of this model in what Weiskel
has called 'the "reader's" sublime' and what Conte has called 'the sublime
reader', though perhaps one ought to speak more broadly about a sublime
atomistic *subject*.[36]

The difficulty with this subjective, egotistical recuperation of the sublime,
which aggrandises a subject on a cosmic scale, is that the sublime is most
intensely felt where it most threatens to annihilate subjective identity. A view
from nowhere is in theory a view held by no one – or else by a 'vanishing
mediator' that disappears in the very instant that it founds the order that
sustains its symbolic existence.[37] In the hands of an atomist, a conception like
this can cut two ways: against the pretensions of subjectivity, and against the
pretensions of atomism itself. Lucretius, at least, is attentive to the potential
of atomism to unmask the desires of a subject to cling all too fervidly to
its own simulacral identity, whether conceiving itself as superior to nature
or, finally, trying to imagine its own death, which would have to count as
the greatest omnipotence fantasy available to any subject alive.[38] The trouble
with atomism is that it forces these recognitions willy-nilly whenever it *dares*
us to conceive of nature from a third-person perspective, which is to say, the
vast majority of the time. And that may be a test that no one can ever truly
pass.

---

[36] Weiskel 1976, Conte 1994: ch. 1.
[37] On the vanishing mediator, see Jameson 1973, Žižek 1991: 190–1.
[38] See Long 1997; Porter 2003: 201–2, 222; Nightingale 2007.

Readings of the atomistic or material sublime after Kant would draw out many of these consequences. Nietzsche and Bergson both found the very *idea* of atomism to be sublime.[39] And postmodernism, fond of deconstructing the subject (yet never quite managing to do so), has more recently shown a resurgence of interest around the conjunction of sublimity, materialism and atomism.[40] All of which, together with the present volume, bodes well for a renewed and broadened study of Lucretius in the fields of Classics and Reception studies.

Further reading

Some of the most stimulating thought on the sublime continues to be carried out by the French. Courtine 1993 contains a wide selection of recent French theory. Jankélévitch 1980 and Jankélévitch 1986 treat the problems of ineffability at the heart of the sublime in a philosophically reflective and literary way. Helpful for thinking about size at both ends of the scale is Stewart 1993. Žižek 1989 remains one of the most productive interventions in the theory of the sublime in recent years. For a useful survey of contemporary sublime theory in Kant's wake, and not only in musicology, see Brillenburg Wurth 2002.

[39] Nietzsche 1933–42: III, 332; Bergson 1884: 23 n. 7, *ad DRN* 1.945.
[40] Kristeva 1974, Derrida 1984, Lyotard 1991.

11

YASMIN HASKELL

Religion and enlightenment in the neo-Latin reception of Lucretius

The Renaissance bishop and poet Marco Girolamo Vida may have aimed a gentle rebuke at Lucretian imitators when he warned the aspiring Latin poet to avoid the example of those who 'pour out and pile up all things in their verses, without method, without art, especially if it is unknown, hidden, and not suitable for the ears of the crowd, such as the secret motions of the radiant heavens, or the inaccessible nature of the gods, or the uncertain origin of the impenetrable soul' (*De arte poetica* 2.194–9).[1] Many of the writers who composed Latin Lucretian poems in the early modern period did so wearing the robes of philosopher, physician, mathematician, even priest. Latin, the natural language choice for scholarship, science and theology from the fifteenth to the eighteenth centuries, brought challenges and opportunities of a different order from those facing Lucretius' vernacular imitators. Latin Lucretianists more frequently composed long philosophical poems, and engaged more freely with current and controversial topics in science and religion. To imitate Lucretius in Latin was perhaps a less risky business than it was in the vernacular, the learned language screening out unauthorised access by less educated readers, and many women. Thus a former Jesuit, Camillo Garulli, could publish, in Catholic Rome, a Lucretian poem endorsing the Copernican 'hypothesis' at a time when it was still officially proscribed by the Church (1777). On the other hand, neo-Latin poets were arguably in greater danger of being pulled into Lucretius' ideological orbit, if not sucked into the black hole of heresy.

This essay will explore some neo-Latin responses to Lucretius' thematics of religion and enlightenment. How did neo-Latin poets negotiate or exploit for their own purposes Lucretius' attacks on superstition? How did they represent both the enlightened individual and the cultural/intellectual progress of mankind? The primary focus on Italian poets, dictated partly by constraints

---

[1] Reference to Lucretius is suggested by R. G. Williams in Vida 1976: 155 n. 28. Translations are mine unless otherwise stated.

of space, is not arbitrary. Italy saw the earliest Renaissance imitations of Lucretius and some of the most poetically accomplished and influential. It produced the most intellectually audacious Lucretian poems of the sixteenth century. And in the age of Enlightenment, paradoxically, Catholic Rome was the scene of a Lucretian poetic movement unparalleled elsewhere in Europe. Lucretius would prove as useful a model for the defenders of Christian doctrine as for those who sought to undermine it.

Lucretius and the humanists

A copy of the *DRN* was retrieved from the saddlebag of the Greek mercenary and poet of exile Michael Marullus, who drowned while trying to cross the swollen river Cecina in 1500.[2] The 'great' Lucretius is named as poet of 'Nature' in one of Marullus' epigrams (1.16) and, unsurprisingly, most critics have looked for Lucretian influence in Marullus' *Hymni naturales*, a collection of hymns to the pagan gods that was conceived under the star of Florentine Neoplatonism. The syncretistic riddle of the *Hymni* has resisted complete solution by appeal to Neoplatonic, Orphic and Christian frameworks, and the not-so-shadowy presence of Lucretius throughout the work – significantly prominent in the opening, central and closing hexameter hymns – is intriguing. What place do the materialism and indifferent divinities of Lucretius have in a work in which the poet prays to the traditional gods with apparent fervour and sincerity?

The most didactic of Marullus' hymns is the longest and central hymn to the Sun (3.1). Marullus departs from Julian's hymn to King Helios, which was enjoying a vogue among the Florentine Neoplatonists, by affirming the *material* nature of the sun, in pointedly Lucretian terms. He praises the solar god as the principle of life (see especially 69–101 for rich parallels with Lucretius' hymn to Venus), who fills all with his 'sacred' light, giving sight to eyes and colour to all things (133–4). The joys of spring, nature's abundance and abiding vitality even as individuals pass in and out of the 'sweet breezes of light' (*dulces . . . luminis auras*) are celebrated in Lucretian terms, and 'if anyone believes there is room for death he wanders lost, having strayed far from the true path of Nature' (100–1). But this same life-giving and sometime providential Sun averts his gaze from the destruction of our greatest achievements. The 'piety' of the Greeks did not save them from capture by the Turks, so many 'golden temples of the gods' have succumbed to the flames. There are shades here of Lucretius mocking belief in a Jupiter

---

[2] Marullus had been preparing a commentary on the text, preserved in part in Pietro Candido's notes to his 1512 Florentine edition.

who strikes down his own temples and images (*DRN* 6.417–20), but for Marullus the realisation of divine indifference is more personal, more painful: 'and should I hesitate to admit that there is nothing sacred on the earth?' (266).

Marullus warns us in this hymn not to attempt to avert evil destiny through incense or prayers (253–4). Coppini is right to contrast such prayers, with which she compares the superstitious god-bothering of a certain Caecubus, satirised by Marullus in one of the epigrams (2.15), with the sophisticated poetry of the hymns themselves.[3] But if they are distinguished by a high degree of literary and philosophical knowingness, the hymns do not, in the end, advance a coherent natural philosophy. Despite the programmatic over-tones of the title *Hymni naturales* – which seems to promise *De rerum natura*, and to recall Menander Rhetor's designation of Parmenides' and Empedo-cles' scientific poems as *Hymnoi physikoi* – the consolations of Lucretius' science figure less in the hymns than his enlightened persona. Marullus main-tains a religious, even mystical, outlook, even as he adopts a Lucretian per-spective to reflect on the gap between ideal and material worlds, between the enlightened individual and the benighted mass of humanity.

The sighs of the soldier are never far below the surface of Marullus' poetry, and a Lucretian voice is often raised in the name of peace. Already in an epigram to his fellow-Greek exile Janus Lascaris (4.6), Marullus had con-trasted his own restless life of soldiering with his friend's philosophical con-tentment.[4] Lascaris stands aloof, like the Epicurean sage of *DRN* 2.1–19, devoted to the Muses and looking down with an easy heart on the things which we, the wicked mob, admire (*facili pectore despicis* | *Prave quae pop-ulus nocens* | *Miramur*: for *despicere*, cf. *DRN* 2.9; 3.26). Marullus grieves that man outdoes the beasts in wickedness, since even tigers and lions do not harm their own kind, killing only to sate their hunger (cf. *DRN* 3.68– 73, where fear of death is said to inspire unnatural fraternal violence). The remainder of this deeply Lucretian poem is a meditation on the mythological torments of *DRN* 3.978–1023, with pessimism prevailing over philosophi-cal hope. Like the epigram to Lascaris, it closes with a half-muttered death wish, a prayer to return to the heavenly fatherland, whence 'we can look down on (*despectemus*) so many futile cares of men'; and for wisdom not to 'admire empty and vain things' (*nil vanum, nil admiremur inane*, 104; cf. *miramur* in *Ep.* 4. 6). The *ataraxia* of the Epicurean sage remains a seductive but impossible spiritual goal for the soldier-poet – at least in this life.

The final hymn, to Earth (4.5), is eloquent of an internal conflict in the poet between his vocation as freedom-fighter and career as mercenary. As

[3] Coppini 1995: 25.   [4] See Dionigi 1985.

an *exemplum* of how much we owe our parents, Marullus revisits Lucretius' wailing infant, shipwrecked in this world, whose only good fortune is not to know how many labours are in store for him (44–8: cf. *DRN* 5.222–7). In the following lines he alludes to *DRN* 2.640–4, where devotees of the Great Mother brandish weapons to demonstrate their readiness to defend parents and *patria*. But where that Lucretian passage had culminated in *rejection* of the divinity of the earth, Marullus clings to the poetic fiction of her sacredness and sentience, even as he subtly references Lucretius' corrective coda: 'but what good is it to use nice phrases now if we pollute such holy names with foul deeds?' (picking up *eximie* in *DRN* 2.644–5). Then, in almost the same breath as he enjoins armed defence of the mother(land), he asserts that it is sacrilege (65) 'to dare to wound the common mother by dividing her', condemning war as the product of luxury and avarice, of 'false consciousness' Lucretius-style. Interestingly Marullus does not follow Lucretius in condemning superstition as a source of murderous error. In the hymns, old-time Greek religion and philosophical enlightenment coexist in an uneasy peace.

In the marriage proposal to Neaera, the longest of his epigrams (2.32), Marullus appeals to the other Lucretian 'enlightenment' mentioned above: the collective progress of the human race (vv. 103–16). The dispossessed Greek suitor reviews Lucretius' account of man's rise from savagery to civilisation in *DRN* 5: the first age was rough, lawless and ignorant; men lived in the forests with wild beasts, ate acorns, slept on the ground; they counted their flocks and herds with nuts, not on their fingers. It was *Greece* that first shaped our minds and showed us the power of speech (cf. *DRN* 6.1–8, the gifts of Athens, culminating in Epicurus). His share in the cultural capital of Greece affords Marullus a position from which to sue for the Italian Neaera's hand.[5] In his *Nutricia*, a potted verse history of classical poetry, the leading humanist of Medicean Florence, Angelo Poliziano, would also pay tribute to Lucretius' narrative of cultural evolution. Poliziano viewed Marullus as a rival, and it is quite possible that he wrote with a sideways glance at the upstart *Graeculus* who had encroached on his philological patch and poached his star pupil, Alessandra Scala: Poliziano credits an apostrophised 'Poetry', not Greece, as the patron of progress.[6]

Marullus' German editor, Beatus Rhenanus, regretted the poet's lack of faith in Providence, but flirtation with Lucretius was not yet a heretic's game in Italy. Naples was an early hub of interest in the *DRN*, and two

[5] For detailed discussion see Haskell 1998c.
[6] For another possible precedent for Poliziano's use of Lucretius in Lorenzo Bonincontri, see Gambino Longo 2004: 266–7 n. 42.

successive presidents of the Neapolitan humanist academy, Lorenzo Bonincontri (1410–91) and Giovanni Gioviano Pontano (1422–1503), both edited Lucretius and imitated the *DRN* in their astrological didactic poetry. Pontano, Marullus' one-time mentor, extolled Lucretius' rhetorical power towards the end of his influential dialogue on poetics, *Actius*: 'He drags the reader wherever he wants to go, he proves what he wants to prove, with the greatest subtlety and art, he exhorts, deters, stirs up, pulls back – all, finally, with elevation and ornament, when there is need of it, and this wonder (*admiratio*) we have been talking about.'[7] In the same context, however, Pontano declared that the purpose of poetry was to encourage virtue by teaching the immortality of the soul, raising the pious to heaven and condemning the wicked to Tartarus. We might well imagine Lucretius' atoms rolling in their grave, but Pontano's statement should not be read as preemptive self-censure. It speaks less of an anxiety of Lucretian influence than of the cheerful poetic opportunism of this generation, which found in the Roman poet a sweet-talking ally in the humanist project of uniting eloquence and wisdom, rather than a dangerous philosophical opponent to be engaged with on his own terms. Pontano heard Lucretius' critique of religion loud and clear, but used it selectively, for his particular purposes. Goddard shows how, in his *Urania*, Pontano cunningly exploits Lucretius' attacks on superstition to undermine Pico della Mirandola's strictures on judicial astrology.[8]

The first early modern Latin poet really to lock horns with Lucretius on the subject of religion was Antonio della Paglia (1503–70). 'Aonio Paleario' was executed for heresy in 1570 – not, to be sure, on account of his didactic poem on the immortality of souls, but of his later conversion to the cause of the Tuscan reformers. His *De animorum immortalitate* (1535) is the first of several early modern anti-Lucretian poems, culminating in Cardinal de Polignac's *Anti-Lucretius* of 1747. It is probably motivated less by the desire to set *Lucretius* straight than those who might be waylaid by the modern materialism of Pietro Pomponazzi (1462–1525), who denied the immortality of the soul. Paleario was the first neo-Latin poet to exploit the *DRN* as a continuous poetic foil, and he aimed to instruct but also delight humanist readers with his ingenious rehabilitation of Lucretius to prove the existence of a providential God, angels and immortal souls, true prophets, and the reality of posthumous rewards and punishments.

Paleario's anti-Lucretian voice is most strident at the beginning of his second book, where he contrasts the good *Graius homo*, Plato, with a caricature of Epicurus (2.18–21), 'who in his zeal for leisure dared to raise his mortal face against the gods, impotent idiot, and then to provoke the gods with

---

[7] Translation from Previtera's Latin text 1943: 238–9.   [8] Goddard 1991b.

words; busy looking into what might please the palate, he was never able to tear his mind away from loaded tables.' Paleario praises the civilising benefits of religion, which is the source of good faith, social bonds, compassion, peacefulness and sexual morality (contrast Lucretius' negative account in *DRN* 5). Without fear of God and eternal retribution, the vices 'have laid human life low in foulness' (*humanam foede vitam stravere iacentem*, 2.46; cf. *DRN* 1.62). The Christian poet uses Lucretian carrots and sticks throughout his poem to cajole the reader into religious faith. Those who follow God's law are portrayed as living the life of Lucretius' gods (1.217–19): 'Now the power and blessed seats of the heavenly ones appear to me, where there is true peace, and where a better sun radiates all with his lamp and the ether is always cloudless' (*Iam mihi caelestum numen sedesque beatae | apparent, ubi vera quies, ubi lampade lustrat | omnia sol melior semperque innubilus aether*: cf. *DRN* 3.18–22).

In his final book, Paleario assumes the role of poet-prophet to edify and terrify us with revelations of heaven, hell and purgatory, the senescence of the earth, and the Last Judgement. In those final times the earth will cease to be fruitful (3.400ff.; cf. *DRN* 2.1160ff.). Allusions to the meteorological and terrestrial terrors of *DRN* 5 and 6 (plague, earthquake, eclipse) are deployed here, ironically, to induce shock and awe in the reader. Paleario has no compunction about twisting Lucretian logic to prove the existence of an afterlife: 'It is indeed the case, but we ourselves cannot perceive it with our eyes (*non cernere quimus | ipsi oculis*: cf. *DRN* 2.837), ignorant as we are of things and uncertain of the future; but it is not false for that reason'. In Lucretius, the things not to be dismissed because we cannot perceive them are, of course, the atoms. To support his supernatural science, Paleario adduces marvels of nature and human technology, notably the magnet (199–216; cf. *DRN* 6.906–16, and *passim*) and gunpowder. He here recalls a famous Lucretian passage in which we are reminded that the heavens are no longer marvellous because we now understand them (3.246–51; cf. *DRN* 2.1026–43).

Paleario's application to the afterlife of Lucretius' argument from the marvellous is perverse indeed, accompanied as it is by a nod to modern scientific progress: 'it is clear, to be sure, that there are now many brilliant discoveries which earlier generations said could never occur' (*Multa quidem nunc esse liquet praeclara reperta, | quae fieri numquam dixere prioribus annis*, 252–3; cf. *DRN* 2. 1035–6).[9] Curiously, though, it resonates with a more

---

[9] He presents the magnet as ultimately inexplicable, quoting Lucretius' explanation of it (*DRN* 6.1031–2, 1037, 1085) as a *fabula nova* (2.211–16). While Paleario treats in passing the four element theory, and atomist and rival ancient theories of soul, natural philosophy takes a back

scientifically inflected didactic poem, published two decades later, on the venereal plague of the Renaissance: *Syphilis, sive de morbo gallico* (Verona, 1555). Lucretius is usually claimed to have exercised an influence on the science as well as the poetry of its author, the physician and humanist Girolamo Fracastoro (1478–1553).[10] Lucretius' description of the plague at Athens is an obvious model for Fracastoro's account of the origins of syphilis in Book 1. What has not yet received the attention it deserves, though, is the presence there of material from *DRN* 5, which feeds a poetics of wonder that Fracastoro cultivates throughout his poem.[11]

If Lucretius habitually uses formulae such as 'no wonder' (*nec mirum*) to rationalise the workings of the cosmos, and to combat superstitious belief in the gods,[12] Fracastoro, by contrast, insists on describing the venereal disease as 'unusual', 'strange', 'marvellous' in its genesis, transmission and bizarre symptomatology. In a 'wonderful' passage in the first book he undermines Lucretius' scepticism (*DRN* 5.837–924) about the earth's perennial capacity to bear monsters:

> Forsitan et tempus veniet, poscentibus olim
> Natura, fatisque Deum, cum non modo tellus
> Nunc culta, aut obducta mari, aut deserta jacebit,
> Verum etiam Sol ipse novum (quis credere possit?)
> Curret iter, sua nec per tempora diffluet annus.
> Ast insueti aestus, insuetaque frigora mundo
> Insurgent, et certa dies animalia terris
> Monstrabit nova, nascentur pecudesque feraeque
> Sponte sua, primaque animas ab origine sument . . .
> Quae quum perspicias, nihil est, cur tempore certo
> Admirere novis magnum marcescere morbis
> Aera, contagesque novas viventibus aegris
> Sydere sub certo fieri, et per saecula longa.
>
> (1.169–85)

Perhaps a time will come, at some future behest of Nature and the fates of the Gods, when not only the earth which is now cultivated will lie either covered by the sea or as a desert, but even the Sun himself (who could believe it?) will run a new course and the year will not flow according to its normal seasons. But unusual heat and unusual cold will rise against the world, and the day

seat to natural theology in his poem. Contrast Scipione Capece's *De principiis rerum* (Venice, 1546), on the elements, which is appended, with Paleario's poem, to the 1631 Frankfurt edition of Lucretius.

[10] See also pp. 132–3 above. Goddard 1993 queries whether Fracastoro's theory of disease 'seeds' is especially Lucretian.

[11] See Haskell 1999: 80–8.   [12] See Conte 1994: 20–1.

appointed will show forth new creatures on the earth, cattle and wild beasts
will be born spontaneously and take life from their primal source . . . When
you consider these matters carefully there is no reason why you should wonder
that at an appointed time the great expanse of air should grow languid with
new diseases and that new contagions should affect frail living creatures under
a destined star after the passage of long centuries.[13]

In a delightful and quite modern twist, then, Fracastoro exhorts us not to
wonder at the fact that there have been, and always will be, wonders. But the
physician-poet's attempt to put wonder back into Nature is, paradoxically,
more 'scientific' than Lucretius' attempt to remove it. Where Lucretius boasts
that his subject is difficult to write about (1.136–9), Fracastoro apologises
that his is difficult to write about because it is not fully understood (1.256–
60):

Yet I am in my mind under no illusion that it is difficult to tell of heaven's
actions or their order and to discover precise causes in everything: so long are
the periods of time over which they sometimes postpone their effects, and sometimes (which can lead one astray) chance and accidents, which vary according
to particulars, are intermixed.[14]

It is this long view of history which allows Fracastoro to claim that syphilis is
simultaneously wonderful *and* natural, to transform horror and alienation
into a form of admiration and acceptance: syphilis is an object inspiring
both curiosity and poetry not because it is supernatural and inexplicable,
but simply because it is new to the present generation. Where for Lucretius
natural philosophy is a *fait accompli*, for Fracastoro it is, implicitly, work
in progress. The poets in our next section may be more daring, but they are
also more dogmatic.

Lucretius and the heretics

Four Lucretian philosophical poets fell foul of the post-Tridentine Church in
Italy and are commemorated on the monument to Giordano Bruno in Rome's
Campo dei Fiori: Aonio Paleario, Scipione Capece, Marcellus 'Palingenius'
Stellatus and Bruno himself, who was burnt at the stake there in 1600. To
what extent was Lucretius implicated in the trials and tribulations of these
reformers and heretics? It is true that the DRN was never placed on the
Index of Forbidden Books and was read much more widely in Italy in the
second half of the sixteenth century than has traditionally been assumed.[15]

---

[13] Translations from Eatough 1984.   [14] See Gambino Longo 2004: 202–3.
[15] See Gambino Longo 2004; Prosperi 2004, esp. 97–117; ch. 13 below.

But the assumption of the mantle of missionary philosopher-poet would not have been without risk at a time when the Church was anxious to assert its univocal authority throughout the peninsula. At least two of our modern Lucretiuses seem to have imitated the wrong poet at the wrong time. Their mistake was less the (in any case selective) adoption of particular elements of the ancient poet's philosophy than of a defiant Lucretian *attitude*, which carried the threat of heresiarchy.

Both Palingenius and Bruno arrogate to themselves the almost godlike authority which Lucretius had imputed to Epicurus. In his great congeries of a poem, the *Zodiacus vitae* (Venice, 1534?–1538?), in twelve books, Palingenius attacks all the traditional sources of learning (humanist, medical, religious, etc.) to substitute his own highly idiosyncratic vision. It is telling that the poem opens with the words *mens mea*. The poet-narrator takes us on a personal journey through a world now physical, now allegorical. This is a work of multiple didactic and satirical voices, not all of them singing in concert. In the third book the poet meets and converses with Epicurus, but the ancient philosopher gets his comeuppance only after he has delivered a long, speciously convincing lecture on the pursuit of pleasure. We hear Lucretius in the passage on the mythological torments suffered by the victim of avarice (2.192–4; 506–14); the advice to seek a wife (or prostitute) rather than madly to 'desire and hope for what you cannot have, when you can dispel the disease with an easy remedy' (2.290–3); Epicurus' denial of life after death and posthumous punishment (3.125–77); the diatribe of *Mors* (6.76–114), whose consolations echo those of personified *Natura* in *DRN* 3. Throughout the poem we are frequently excoriated for our obtuseness (2.59–61): 'O mortal breasts full of blind shadows, and minds fenced in with the blackness of stupidity' (*O caecis mortalia plena tenebris | Pectora, et o mentes caligine circumseptas | Stultitiae*; cf. *DRN* 2.14–16.). Palingenius disingenuously declares his Catholic faith in the preface to the poem, but his denial of God's involvement in our world, his presumption of life on other stars, and his exhortation to commerce with the *coelicoli* – their delightful existence is extrapolated from that of Lucretius' intermundial gods rather than the Christian saints – are hardly orthodox. Add to this the unremitting satire of clerical corruption which endeared him to Protestant readers, and it is not difficult to understand why his corpse was exhumed and subjected to a posthumous auto-da-fé.

Palingenius had accepted the traditional Aristotelian configuration of the cosmos, with the opposition between celestial and terrestrial matter, but had projected an infinite light-world beyond the spheres (inhabited by *dii nobiliores*). Bruno quotes closely from Palingenius in the final book of his Frankfurt trilogy of philosophical didactic poems (1591), observing, with uncharacteristic generosity, that Palingenius is 'almost awake'; but Bruno is more daring in his physics. He was the first philosopher to combine the atomist theses of an indivisible minimum and an infinite physical universe of innumerable worlds with Copernican heliocentricism. He seeks to do for his own physics and metaphysics in the Frankfurt trilogy what Lucretius had done for Epicurus. But Bruno's 'Lucretian' style is far from the rhetorically polished one approved by Pontano in the *Actius*. It has an angry and icono-clastic edge designed to slice into the hallowed claims of Aristotelian physics and Catholic tradition (indeed, of the Christian religion). Bruno learned his anti-humanist Lucretian manner from the plain-speaking Palingenius, who programmatically warned against the seductions of lascivious classical poetry and professed a poetics of truth (e.g. in the proem to his sixth book).[16]

In his monumental Lucretian didactics, Bruno frequently mobilises a metaphorics of sleep and wakefulness, of chimeras and monsters, of rev-olution and revelation. In *De immenso* ('On the infinite universe') 4.1 he invokes the mutinous giant Enceladus, buried under Mount Etna, who is liberated from his burden by the realisation that the earth is not at the centre of the universe. Rather than the animal gods of the Nile, the gods of supersti-tion, Enceladus asks why we do not 'worship instead real men, who, relying on the strength of their intellect, have scoffed at the threats of heaven and found a world beyond worlds, beyond the painted ceiling?' (cf. *DRN* 5.117–21). Bruno himself is one of those 'real men', but also the rebellious giant; the painted ceiling is the firmament, the physical limit of the Aristotelian cosmos, but also the constraining power of the Christian religion. Bruno continues boldly: 'Where [now] is that feigned throne of the gods, where the harsh judgement seat?'

Bruno is more brutal than Lucretius in associating the philosophical errors of his opponents with their moral limitations. In the final (eighth) book of the *De immenso*, the professional philosophers are bearded, gloomy, fastid-ious types, who demand special garments, titles and praise. They are beset by the monsters impossible in the Lucretian universe: 'They think they are awake inasmuch as they follow their *simulacra*, and the idiots weave together these empty shapes, figments of madness, in their brains, wretches, and they weary the gods, the fauns and satyrs, the centaurs and half-beasts, half-men, who can do nothing, and have no existence' (cf. *DRN* 2.700–17; 4.580–1; 732–48; 5.878–924). The allusion to 'half-beasts, half-men' could well be a snide reference to Christ, who is the flouter of Nature and bringer of fear

---

[16] See Haskell 1998a: 120–3. Bruno's 'macho' Lucretian style differs radically from that of Paleario, Capece and Fracastoro.

in Bruno's most provocatively anti-Christian work, the *Spaccio della bestia trionfante*.[17] Earlier in the *De immenso* the phantasms are more specifically metaphors for the traditional physics (7.8): 'Therefore it is clear that the multiple spheres of the heaven are vain, the prime mover and proud motor have disappeared, and the [other] motors flourish under the false image of that God, which we can credit with no more existence than the figments of poets, Hell, the kingdoms of Rhadamanthus, the Gorgon, Centaur, Scylla, Geryon, Chimaera.'

Bruno's polemic against traditional religion and cosmology should not, however, distract us from the fact that he was a *religious* thinker before he was a martyr to science. The prose commentary accompanying the verses just quoted reminds us that the true motors of the stars are souls. In *De immenso* 4.15, Bruno endowed the earth with a *vis animai* which is not only co-ordinative but motive. Lucretius (*DRN* 5. 556–8) had used the *vis animai* which sustains the weight of our body as an *analogy* for the relationship between earth and space. Bruno *literally* animates the heavenly bodies, who dodge one another around space in a spirit of self-preservation![18] In *De triplici minimo* ('On the triple minimum') 3.1, Bruno mocks our fear of death, but co-opts Lucretian language on the indissolubility of the atom to prove the immortality of the soul.[19] It may be that it was his pantheist convictions that induced Bruno to ascribe to *all* atoms the spherical shape which Lucretius had reserved for the highly mobile spirit ones. Bruno was explicitly questioned about his attraction to Lucretius at his trial for heresy. The relationship between the two writers was more personal, more ideological, than strictly philosophical.[20] It is ironic that the Jesuits, Bruno's persecutors, were to produce some of the most accomplished Lucretian imitators of the following centuries.

Lucretius in the eighteenth century: religion and science

Less than twenty years after Bruno was burned at the stake, the Jesuit Famiano Strada, in his *Prolusiones academicae*, put a light-hearted Lucretian poem on magnetic telegraphy into the mouth of Cardinal Pietro Bembo.[21]

---

[17] There Bruno had adopted a frankly Lucretian stance on the evil consequences of the fear of death: see Ingegno 1985: 125.

[18] See Salvatore 2003b for Bruno's imitation of Lucretius on the impossibility of lovers' bodies merging (*DRN* 4.1105–16) to prove the impossibility of planets colliding (*De immenso* 6.5). I am grateful to Gabriele Dasso for apprising me of the contents of this article.

[19] Haskell 1998a: 130–1.   [20] Haskell 1998a: 132.

[21] Described by C. A. Gordon 1962: 303–7.

The best-known modern Lucretian poem in Latin was undoubtedly the *Anti-Lucretius* of Cardinal Melchior de Polignac, a product of Polignac's travels through Europe and discussions with leading intellectuals from Bayle to Leibniz, published posthumously and incomplete; Polignac's Latin education was courtesy of the Society of Jesus. It was the Jesuits who were the most prolific composers of Latin didactic poetry in the seventeenth and eighteenth centuries – including poetry about philosophy and science. Virgil's *Georgics*, to be sure, remained the primary model for Jesuit didactic poetry, even on scientific subjects, but one suspects that that choice was dictated as often by literary preference as religious scruple.

In the dedication to his *Philosophia novo-antiqua* ('New-Ancient Philosophy', 1704), the Milanese Jesuit and mathematician Tommaso Ceva (1648–1737) frankly acknowledged Lucretius as his model.[22] Ceva's curious title encapsulates his stated mission to reconcile the best of ancient and modern natural philosophy, incorporating some of his own more or less original reflections. The poem comprises six 'dissertations', with its centre of gravity in cosmology and mechanics, and engages with live issues for Catholic science (Copernican theory; Descartes's physics and denial of animal souls; Gassendi's atomism). A projected seventh and eighth book would apparently have treated arguments for the immortality of the soul and proofs of the existence of God, but these were never published (if ever begun).

The reviewer of the poem for the Jesuit journal of Trévoux (1728, 503–24) identifies Ceva's Book 3, in particular, as a sort of pre-Polignacian *Anti-Lucretius*. Ceva undertakes to snare his opponent just as insidiously as Lucretius had poisoned his readers with the honeyed cup, to wrap him up in a ball of thread, like a spider netting a drone with its slender thread. The book is in fact as rollicking and satirical as it is didactic and Lucretian, and while the ostensible target is ancient atomism, Lucretius and Epicurus serve as whipping boys for more contemporary 'freethinkers'. The poet has his sights on the conceited modern follower of Lucretius, who is secretly flattered when he overhears someone in the street whispering, in awe, that 'he does not care that his mind is composed of round atoms'. The book concludes with a drink and tête-à-tête between the poet and a delightfully self-important Epicurus, whose hopes of recruiting the genial Jesuit into his sect are brutally dashed on the last page.

---

[22] The poem, in successive editions, was to become something of an ideological football between the Jesuits and their enemies in eighteenth-century Tuscany. Its place in these polemics has been documented by intellectual historians, but the literary aspects of Ceva's poem have been largely overlooked. See Haskell (forthcoming b).

Ceva never lets the sublime Lucretius get off the ground. Throughout his poem he is careful to check human pretensions to absolute knowledge of nature as promised in the *DRN*. The proem to the final book warns against the proliferation of philosophical error, which is traced back, significantly, to Greece (to Pythagoras and Plato; cf. the Athenian Epicurus in the proem to *DRN* 6). The great diversity of opinions is 'due, no doubt, to the fact that the mind of man is buried in darkness'. Ceva offers an analogy of human ignorance worthy of Lucretius, except that he does not indicate a path to enlightenment through philosophy:

> Hinc, velut puer, cui vitta coercet
> Circumducta oculos, aequales inter ephebos
> Cursitat hac illac, si quenquam forte prehenset;
> Quem simul ac tenuit, subducto denique velo,
> Non illum esse videt, quem credidit: Haud secus atris
> In tenebris caeci discurrimus; ultima donec
> Obscuram ex animo nubem detraxerit hora.[23]
>
> (Ceva 1704: 96)

Hence it is just like the boy whose eyes are covered by an encircling blindfold, who rushes about now here, now there, among his young mates, in the hope of grabbing one of them; and as soon as he has taken hold of someone and the veil is removed, he sees that the one before him is not the one he thought. In just this way we blindly rush around in the darkness, until our final hour removes the obscuring cloud from our mind.

In a touching passage in the fifth book, the Jesuit geometer had looked forward to God's revealing the answers to all our natural-philosophical questions after death![24] For the present, we are to be content with a partial vision of nature – which is not to say a naïve and unscientific one, only that philosophical speculation should not conflict with Catholic teaching.

The *Philosophia novo-antiqua* was written at a moment of particularly lively Italian interest in the *DRN* – Alessandro Marchetti's translation was circulating, but not printed until 1717 – and of what Ceva bemoans as a perverted taste for 'novelty' and foreign books. The Jesuit did not want to render that forbidden fruit any more tantalising and so writes an anti-Lucretian poem in which allegory, fable, anecdote and invective dominate over the stylistic flavours of the *DRN*. It is not that Ceva pays mere lip-service to Lucretius: he is, rather, decentred, refracted through other poets, almost 'deconstructed'. In his *Anti-Lucretius* Polignac imitates the *DRN* more openly. From the outset he lectures and cajoles a named addressee,

---

[23] Ceva 1704: 96.   [24] Ceva 1704: 81.

a certain young 'Quintus', with atheist leanings.[25] Epicurus and Lucretius are ubiquitous in Polignac's poem, but, as for Ceva, they are only the thin end of a more dangerous modern wedge, which includes the philosophies of Gassendi, Hobbes and Spinoza.

Voltaire's early enthusiasm for Polignac's project gave way, after the poem's publication, to qualified public praise and withering private scorn (in a letter to Mme Du Deffand of October 1759). In 'Sur l'Anti-Lucrèce de Monsieur le Cardinal de Polignac' (1747/8) he regretted, more than the poem's style 'trop peu varié', its unjustified censure of Epicurus' personal morality.[26] Polignac deliberately misreads Lucretius' attacks on superstition (*religio*) as a wholesale rejection of 'religion', which he interprets as a recipe for hedonism, lawlessness and social disintegration.[27] Ceva's 'Epicurus', interestingly, had anticipated and rejected the familiar charge that his philosophy was a licence to sin: 'Pleasure must be decreed – not that pleasure which rumour attributes to us, but the kind to which the tranquil repose of the mind gives rise, and freedom from bodily pain.' Polignac leaves no room for doubt that the only 'enlightened' individual is the religious one. In Book 1 he provides starkly contrasting portraits of the lazy and selfish life of Epicurus, 'content with himself alone, totally devoted to himself' (*uno contentus se se, sibi deditus uni*), and the truly blessed life of the committed Christian, who comes to the aid not only of friends and relatives, but strangers, maintaining an inner tranquillity when duty dictates his participation in public affairs, and even war.[28]

William Mason opined in his biography of Thomas Gray that he had abandoned his Latin didactic poem on Locke's *Essay on Human Understanding* because of the 'little popularity which M. de Polignac's *Anti-Lucretius* acquired, after it had been so long and so eagerly expected by the learned'.[29] Polignac's endorsement of Descartes over Newton already drew criticism from Voltaire, and may have especially irked English readers, but reports of the poem's poor reception must be balanced against the spate of full or partial translations (into French, English, Italian, German and Dutch)[30] which followed its publication, and many reprints of the Latin text. Money

[25] See Tsakiropoulou-Summers 2004, who illustrates Polignac's thoroughgoing use of Lucretian language and rhetoric, but shows that the *philosophical* positions Polignac counters in his first book, in which *religio* is pitted against *voluptas*, are largely drawn from Epicurus' own writings rather than the *DRN*.

[26] Voltaire 1968: xxxc, 337–40.   [27] Tsakiropoulou-Summers 2004.

[28] On Polignac see also p. 165 above.

[29] Gray 1775: 157–8. I am grateful to Stuart Gillespie for this notice. Gray's fragment was also published in an Eton anthology of 'poems in the Lucretian style' (Eton, 1839). See Bradner 1940: 304–7 for three such specimens by Robert Percy Smith (1770–1845).

[30] See C. A. Gordon 1962: 300.

attributes Gray's abandonment of the *De Principiis Cogitandi* not to any 'malaise in neo-Latin didactic, so much as a reluctance in Gray to finish anything'.[31] Indeed, the early London printings of Polignac (1748, 1751) may have prepared the way for a really rather successful English neo-Latin poem in the anti-Lucretian tradition, the *De animi immortalitate* (1754) by Isaac Hawkins Browne (1705–60).[32] Browne's accomplished poem, in two books, inspired no fewer than five English translations, and the Latin text continued to appear in anthologies and separate reprints until 1833.[33]

Browne argues in his first book that our social institutions, arts and scientific achievements are evidence of a divine spark, of a 'living force of soul' (*vivida vis animi*). Our intimations of an afterlife must have a basis in fact, and, *pace* Lucretius, death *is* something to us.[34] Browne turns Lucretian *religio* on its head, finding evidence for the soul's immortality in 'primitive' cultural practices. All peoples expend care on the corpse and erect monuments to the dead; the Indian widow fearlessly mounts her husband's funeral pyre. In Soame Jenyns' translation: 'Grant these th'inventions of the crafty priest, | Yet such inventions never cou'd subsist, | Unless some glimm'rings of a future state | Were with the mind coeval and innate.' But Browne can still scoff at the animal-headed gods of antiquity, the leek god of the Romans: 'That there's a God from Nature's voice is clear, | And yet what errors to this truth adhere! | How have the fears and follies of mankind | Now multiply'd their gods, and now subjoin'd | To each the frailties of the human mind.' Reason must be our guide, and, even now that we have the benefit of Christian revelation, Nature can still help us discover the truth.

Browne praises Bacon and Newton as noble souls and bringers of light (Browne 1745: 7), but while there is much elevation in the *De animi immortalitate*, there is no science to speak of.[35] In Italy, meanwhile, a group of poets associated with the Roman College of the Society of Jesus were harnessing a sublime Lucretius to the triumphal chariot of modern science. Voltaire charged Polignac (as well as Lucretius and Descartes) with being a poor *physicien*, but no one could say of the poets of this Roman 'school' that

---

[31] Money 1999: 143.

[32] Browne's poem also connects with Paleario's, known in England through the anthologies of Atterbury (1684) and Pope (1740).

[33] Bradner 1940: 277.

[34] If we were nothing but dust and shadow, the criminal on his deathbed would have no concern about his posthumous reputation (*at nihil ad nos postera vox, erimus si nil nisi pulvis et umbra*. Browne 1745: 8; cf. *DRN* 3.830 *Nil igitur mors est ad nos*).

[35] Edmond Halley's Latin Ode to Newton, accompanying the first edition of the *Principia mathematica* (1687), served as a model for numerous eighteenth-century poems celebrating Newtonian science in English; Albury 1978 explores its debt to Lucretius.

they did not know their stuff.[36] They took their bearings from a Jesuit professor of philosophy, Carlo Noceti (1694–1741), who wrote 'hard' scientific
poems on the rainbow and the Northern Lights, and from the Croatian,
Benedict Stay (1714–1801), whose ecclesiastical advancement was assured
by the stunning success in Italy of his poem on the physics of Descartes,
a veritable Lucretius-by-numbers (*Philosophiae libri vi*, Rome, 1744). Stay
followed this work of his youth with an even more ambitious *Philosophia
recentior*, on Newtonian physics, published in ten books between 1755 and
1791; it was accompanied by notes and supplements by his compatriot,
Jesuit physicist, Roger Boscovich. Over the course of the next thirty years,
Jesuit poets such as Boscovich, Giuseppe Maria Mazzolari, Camillo Garulli,
Gregorio Landi Vittori and Bernardo Zamagna grappled in verse with the
most formidable subjects of the age: astronomy and meteorology, geodesy,
acoustics, optics, electricity and even aeronautics.

The aesthetic of this poetry was an unapologetically élite and Enlightenment one. Poets of the Roman school revel in their modernity, viewing out-
moded theories, and especially the errors of the ancients, with condescension.
The scientific wormwood is rarely palliated with ornamental myths, but readers are invited to wrestle with hexameter descriptions of the latest scientific
instruments and technological toys. Lucretian influence is ubiquitous, if not
always freely confessed.[37] The hymn to Venus becomes a hymn to the experimental method, or to gravity; modern scientific heroes (Copernicus, Galileo,
Descartes, Mairan, Newton, Boscovich) are praised, à la Epicurus; poets
reflect, like Lucretius, on the difficulty of writing scientific poetry. But what
Lucretius gains in coverage he loses in ideological power, and the Jesuits'
warm effusions about modern science are carefully insulated from the more
explosive aspects of Enlightenment thought.[38] The general absence of reference to Polignac is striking. It is indicative less of *campanilismo*, perhaps,
than of a reluctance to bring God too directly into the equation of scientific poetry. For the priest-poets of the eighteenth-century Collegio Romano,
the cultivation of science, including the laborious *versification* of science,
becomes a virtuous ascesis *ad majorem Dei gloriam*. They thus achieve what
might have seemed impossible at the beginning of this chapter, the apparent
reconciliation of religion and enlightenment in Lucretian poetry.

---

[36] Haskell 2003: 178–244.
[37] Mazzolari was somewhat peeved when his poem on electricity was described as Lucretian.
See Haskell 2003: 235–7 for his protestations of Virgilian faith.
[38] Gregorio Landi Vittori saves refutation of the errors of the 'polytheists', 'atheists', 'deists',
etc., for the twelfth and final book of his *Institutiones philosophicae* (Rome, 1767).

Further reading

Ludwig (1988) is a useful general introduction to neo-Latin didactic poetry. There are two recent studies of Lucretius in fifteenth- and sixteenth-century Italy: Prosperi 2004 and Gambino Longo 2004. For MARULLUS: editions by Chomarat (1995a) and Coppini (1995b), and especially the latter's commentary; Dionigi 1985; Boccuto 1984. POLIZIANO: Bausi 1996, Pizzani 1990. BONINCONTRI: Heilen 1999, Haskell 1998b. PONTANO: Goddard 1991a. FRACASTORO: Goddard 1993, Eatough 1984. PALEARIO: Sacré 1992, unfortunately printed without the rich commentary (in Dutch) accompanying his 1986 Leuven doctoral dissertation; Sacré 1999, Nüssel 1999, Gordon 1962. PALINGENIUS: Chomarat 1996, Nosei 1927. BRUNO: Monti 1991, Salvatore 2003a, 2000b; Haskell 1998a on Bruno and Palingenius. JESUITS: Haskell 2003 and forthcoming b (on Ceva); on STRADA, C. A. Gordon 1962. POLIGNAC: Tsakiropoulou-Summers 2004, A. Masson 2004, H. Jones 1991, C. A. Gordon 1962. Reinhold Glei is preparing a modern edition and commentary of the *Anti-Lucretius*: cf. Glei 1995 and forthcoming. GRAY, BROWNE: Money 1999, Clark 1991.

Among many other more or less anti-Lucretian poems of the early modern era are the *De sphaera* (1584) of George Buchanan (Gee forthcoming, Haskell 1998b, Naiden 1952); the *De contemptu mortis* (1621) of Daniel Heinsius; the *Mundus Cartesii* (1749) of the French Jesuit Pierre Le Coëdic (Haskell 2003); the *De deo uno* (1777) of the Polish Jesuit Ignatius Wilczek; and the epic-didactic *De deo deoque homine* (1769–80) of the Mexican Jesuit Diego Abad (Kerson 1988). From Fracastoro onwards, Lucretius was an important model for medical poets, including Claude Quillet (*Callipaedia*, 1655, on eugenics) (Ford 1999); Malcolm Flemyng (*Neuropathia*, 1740, on 'hypochondria'); Johann Ernst Hebenstreit (*De homine sano et aegroto*, 1753) (Haskell forthcoming a). Post-revolution, poets such as Hieronymus de Bosch (*Carmen de aequalitate hominum*, 1792) and Franz Hebenstreit (*Homo hominibus, c.* 1792) (Schuh 1974) discovered, for the first time, a socialist Lucretius.

III

Reception

12

MICHAEL REEVE

Lucretius in the Middle Ages and early Renaissance: transmission and scholarship

Where did the accent fall on *mulier* in the oblique cases? Medieval students were offered a hexameter that purported to tell them: *siue uirum suboles siue est mulieris origo*. The line scans if the *e* of *mulieris* is read as long, and it follows from the quantity that the accent fell on it. Most of the authors who quote the line attribute it to the tragedy *Orestes* by Statius, a double misapprehension not yet explained.[1] In fact, Lucretius wrote it (*DRN* 4.1232), and the manuscripts save him from the long *e*: they have *muliebris*. The true author was known to Mico of St-Riquier, who towards 850 compiled a work of a kind not attested in antiquity: an anthology of hexameters alphabetically arranged by keyword and labelled with the name of the poet, all chosen because they revealed the quantity of a vowel.[2] It includes sixteen lines from Lucretius, and *muliebris* has already lost its *b*. Even if, as an overlapping anthology suggests, it was not Mico himself who picked the lines out, the task was accomplished no earlier than about 825,[3] and the source was almost certainly a text of Lucretius, because the lines could not have been assembled from other ancient works now extant. The longest passage of Lucretius that a medieval writer quotes, 1.150–6, occurs in a letter written about 850–5 to his abbot by a monk at St Gallen concerned with the quantity of *ri* in *uiderimus*;[4] and another anthology of hexameters, preserved in St Gallen 870 (s. IX²), includes twenty-eight lines with no attribution.[5] So much for atoms and fear of death.

Though the writer in the ninth century who quotes Lucretius most often, Hrabanus Maurus, could have found all nine of his quotations in ancient sources, the availability of Lucretius at the time is proved by manuscripts still extant: O (Leiden Voss. Lat. F 30), Q (Leiden Voss. Lat. Q 94), and GVU (Copenhagen Gl. Kgl. S. 211 2° + Vienna 107 fos. 9–14, 15–18), the last related to Q and probably fragments of one manuscript. About the

---

[1] Sivo 1988.　　[2] Leonhardt 1989: 81–6.　　[3] Munk Olsen 1979: 57–64.
[4] *MGH Epist.* V 1899: 554.6–13.　　[5] Stephan 1885: 266–9; Munk Olsen 1979: 73–4.

origin and history of OQGVU not enough is known. In 812 the Irish scholar Dungal wrote to Charlemagne about an eclipse, and Bernhard Bischoff, who identified him as Lachmann's *corrector Saxonicus* in O, at first assigned O to 'the palace school'; but later he broadened this to 'north-west Germany or thereabouts'.[6] Neither origin, however, readily fits the career of Dungal, who left St-Denis for Pavia about 820 and bequeathed manuscripts to the nearby monastery of Bobbio.[7] O received other corrections and glosses up to 1.827 'ca. s. X^2',[8] and in 1479 a librarian entered in it an *ex libris* of Mainz Cathedral, where it may already have been in 1417 if it was the manuscript that has left over fifty Italian descendants by way of a lost copy made for Poggio during the Council of Constance[9] – the copy that restored Lucretius after half a millennium to what he would have called 'the realm of light'. Q, though annotated in the fifteenth century by an Italian hand, reached Paris between 1544 and 1559 from St-Bertin and was assigned to north-east France by Bischoff, who assigned GVU first to south-west Germany but later to 'probably northern Italy (Bobbio?)'.[10] Copies of Lucretius are recorded in the ninth century at Bobbio and Murbach and in the twelfth at Corbie and Lobbes.[11] The one at Corbie may have been Q, and the one at Lobbes may explain how Sigebert of Gembloux (†1112) came to write 'Lucretius *naturam clandestinam*' (1.779) beside a hexameter of his own that included *clandestina*.[12]

In the absence of extant manuscripts written between the ninth century and the fifteenth, scholars have naturally combed medieval works for evidence that Lucretius was nevertheless read. When Ettore Bignone surveyed their efforts, he concluded that the only writers who knew him at first hand were Mico and the monk at St Gallen;[13] but the copy recorded at Bobbio has since led his countrymen to detect Lucretian influence in north-Italian writers of the ninth to eleventh century, in the Paduan prehumanists about 1300, in Dante, and in Petrarch and Boccaccio.[14] There is more to be said for reversing

---

[6] Bischoff 2004: 50 no. 2189.

[7] Ferrari 1972. She had found no trace of Lucretius in Dungal's works (38).

[8] Bischoff 2004: 50 no. 2189. In Reeve 2005: 157–61 I discussed the corrections in O and argued that Dungal restored from the exemplar lines that the scribe had omitted by *saut du même au même*.

[9] Reeve 2005; see 156–7 for new evidence.

[10] Bischoff 2004: 61 no. 2231; Bischoff 1998: 411 no. 1184.

[11] For references see Reeve 2005: n. 114, and add Tosi 1984–5: 135–61 for a better text of the catalogue from Bobbio; 'Lib. Lucretii I' is his no. 386 on p. 143. I owe the reference to Fiesoli 2004: 6 n. 10. The copy of Lucretius is not among the books *quos Dunghalus praecipuus Scottorum obtulit beatissimo Columbano* (Tosi 1984–5: 144).

[12] Manitius 1931: 340.   [13] Bignone 1913.

[14] For references see Solaro 2000: 93–122 'Testimonianze medievali'.

their arguments: as we have no evidence that anyone was in a position to read Lucretius, we see what kinds of resemblance might arise by accident. Certainly accident seems a likely enough explanation for the recurrence in Mussato of such phrases as *camposque uirentes* or (in a different sense) *fructum . . . dulcedinis*.[15] Similarly, Lucretius' argument for a temporary vacuum when contiguous surfaces move apart (1.384–97), much debated by medieval philosophers without reference to him, could have occurred to someone else independently.[16]

Had OQGVU and their descendants perished, it would still be possible to form some conception of Lucretius' poem from ancient references and quotations. A modern scholar could do so by putting together the *testimonia* assembled in Diels's edition,[17] the passages listed in the indexes of Keil's *Grammatici Latini* and of Lindsay's Festus, Nonius, and Isidore,[18] the passages that Servius in his commentary on Virgil and Macrobius in *Saturnalia* 6.1–5 give as the models for passages of Virgil,[19] and the passages or views that Lactantius contests or applauds; not many quotations or references would slip through this net. A medieval scholar would have found it much harder, not just for want of indexes but also because several of the works in question were themselves scarce. Three of the earliest *testimonia*, for instance, occur in a letter from Cicero to his brother Quintus, in Nepos' *Life of Atticus*, and in the history of Velleius, which hardly anyone could have tracked down even if they had had the strange idea of looking.[20] The richest source of quotations, 116 in all, is Nonius' dictionary, which like Lucretius' poem had a dormant transmission between the ninth century and the fifteenth.[21] Indeed, enough traditions surface or resurface in the fifteenth century to cast doubt on the common notion that Christian scruples were to blame for the neglect of a poet who preached the mortality of the soul and the unconcern of the gods.[22]

Interest in Lucretius was perhaps most likely to leave a mark in biographical dictionaries or in glosses on works that mention him. Jerome's entry on

---

[15] Billanovich 1958: 188–90. [16] Grant 1981: 86–7.

[17] Diels 1923: xxxv–xlii 'De uita et arte Lucreti testimonia'.

[18] These too appear in Diels's edition, between the text and the main apparatus; Martin 1934 adds little. An inaccuracy in Diels's second entry misled me, Reeve 2005: 163, when I reported P. Thiermann's contention that Bruni must have known 1.3 from Lucretius himself: in fact Nonius quotes not just 1.4 *concelebras* but 1.3 too.

[19] Pieri 1977 argues that Macrobius bolsters his case by quoting some passages of Lucretius in versions closer to Virgil than they should have been. Gellius 1.21.7 had recognised Virgil's debt to Lucretius.

[20] Reynolds 1983: 135–7, 247–8, 431–3. [21] Reynolds 1983: 248–52; Milanese 2005.

[22] Reynolds 1983: xli–xliii.

him, the source of the notorious allegation that he composed between fits of insanity and killed himself when driven mad by a love potion, lent itself to expansion, but the encyclopedist Vincent of Beauvais in the thirteenth century (*Spec. hist.* 5.95) and the anonymous author of a work *On the life and habits of philosophers* composed early in the fourteenth[23] merely copied it out, and Guglielmo da Pastrengo (†1362) adjusted it only by adding *comicus* to Lucretius' name.[24] In an epigram ascribed to him by medieval scholia on verse 419 of Ovid's riddling *Ibis*, Lucretius addresses Asterion in the person of a frustrated admirer Almenicus,[25] and a wife Lucilia came on the scene when someone identified Lucretius as the husband she poisons with a love potion in Walter Map's work *On fripperies in courtly circles*.[26] Readers of poetry were most likely to meet him in Ovid, at *Amores* 1.15.23–4 and *Tristia* 2.425–6, and the latter passage would hardly have been transparent ('and prophesies that the threefold fabric will collapse'); but whether glossed manuscripts give further details I do not know, nor whether anyone identified the poem 'whose first words are *Aeneadum genetrix*' (*Tr.* 2.261), which could have been done with the aid of Priscian, *Institutio* 7.9, just as the name of its addressee, Memmius, could have been recovered from Servius' introduction to the *Georgics*, or its subject identified as physics and philosophical teaching by anyone with access to Quintilian (1.4.4; 3.1.4) or as *rerum natura* by anyone with access to Vitruvius, who treats Lucretius as an authority on it (9 pr. 17).

When Poggio's copy reached Florence, his friend Niccoli did not write the copy known as L (Laur. 35.30) till the 1430s, just when Traversari's Latin translation of Diogenes Laertius was opening up an easier route to Epicurus' life and thought.[27] The first copy of Poggio's copy may well have been not L but instead the lost source of the earliest dated manuscript, A (Vat. Lat. 3276), written in 1442 probably at Naples.[28] Two unemended relatives of A (one of these, Madrid Nac. 2885, is cited below as S) best illustrate the difficulties that confronted Italian humanists: non-existent words, erratic word-division, unmetrical lines, strange forms. The remedies adopted in A, probably devised by the poet Antonio Beccadelli (Panormita) or associates of his, concentrate on producing recognisable words and metrical lines, often in defiance of sense and syntax. The same approach recurs in other manuscripts, for instance at 1.487–8, where the faultless reading of OQ had given way to an unmetrical corruption:

[23] Knust 1886: 334 no. CI.   [24] Bottari 1991: 139.   [25] Solaro 1993: 60–2.
[26] Solaro 1997; Solaro 2000: 14–16.   [27] Sottili 1984, Gigante 1988.
[28] On the Italian tradition see Reeve 1980, Reeve 2005, Reeve 2006.

– etsi difficile esse uidetur credere quicquam
in rebus solido reperiri corpore posse

even if it seems hard to believe that anything in objects can be found with a
solid body

credere *OQG*: forsitan *LSA, Harl. 2554*

forsitan et quicquam et si difficile esse uidetur *Harl. 2554 mg.*

Nevertheless, modern editors rightly accept a number of conjectures that first
appear in A. By recourse to Nonius and other ancient material, readers found
preferable variants and defences for strange forms such as 1.71 *cupiret*, and
in mid-century someone impressively overhauled the text by starting from
a good copy of Poggio's manuscript, drawing on a fresh copy or collation
of O, consulting a wide range of indirect evidence, and applying thought
and a sense of style; the results of this editorial endeavour are best known
from F (Laur. 35.31), but its relatives shed more light on the process. Sadly,
the editor, who probably worked at Rome, has not been identified.[29] Here
are two examples of his work from Book 3. Exiles lead a life of tribulation,
'and yet wherever they arrive they sacrifice to the dead and slaughter black
sheep . . . and in their distress turn their minds far more intently to religion':

> et quocumque tamen miseri uenere parentant
> et nigras mactant pecudes et manibus diuis   52
> inferias mittunt multoque in rebus acerbis
> acrius aduertunt animos ad religionem.

52   et *(e V)* manibus diuis *QV, Nonius*: manibus diuis *O*: manibusque diuisque
LS: manibus diuisque *A*: quas manibus diuis *F*   53   inferias mittunt *Q²*, *LF*:
inferiamittunt *OQ¹V*: inferri amittant *SA*

So adversity is the true test of a person, 'because only then are true utterances
coaxed from the depths of their heart, the mask snatched away':

> nam uerae uoces tum demum pectore ab imo
> eliciuntur eripitur persona manare.   58

58   eripitur *OQVS*: et eripitur *LAF*   manare *OQVLA²*: manere *SA¹*: manet res
F: minaci *Morel*: mala re *Heinze: an* manu *(cf. 4.843)* a re ? *Martin*

In 52 Poggio's copy must have had *manibusque diuisque*, a still unmetrical fudge (since the first syllable of *diuisque* is long) devised by someone

---

[29] In Reeve 2005: 150–1 I tentatively suggested that he might have been Lorenzo Valla, though
Valla worked mainly on prose.

confronted with the reading of O who took *manibus* as 'hands' and saw that the metre then went awry; A improves on this by reducing *manibusque* to *manibus*. Whether by drawing on a collation of O or by applying thought, the editor behind F saw that the word required was *mānibus*, 'shades', which scanned if the *s* was ignored as it sometimes is elsewhere in the poem (a phenomenon remarked on by ancient grammarians). In 58 S is free from the conjecture *<et>* but like A has at the end of the line the commoner word *manere*, which unlike *mānare* scans; neither, however, can be construed or interpreted, whereas the conjecture *manet res*, 'the reality is left behind', satisfies metre, sense, and syntax, so well indeed that it puts the modern conjectures to shame.

By the time that Iohannes Baptista Pius brought out the first commentary on the poem (Bologna, 1511),[30] more conjectures were circulating, many of them recently made by Marullus, who ventured transpositions and deletions.[31] Open discussion of its arguments or literary merits, however, had not kept pace with textual work. In the late 1460s, after spending a fortnight copying out the 7381 lines *ad dei optimi maximi laudem sempiternam*, a scholar who later became a bishop and crossed swords with philosophers, Pietro Barozzi, put a request to fellow-Christians – not that they should take the work with a pinch of salt, but that they should blame on the exemplar any errors of sense and metre, which they would find marked; 'if instead you blame me, then I shall consider you (to quote [Martial 2.8.6]) insensitive'.[32] Apologising again for the state of the text, the first editor (Brescia, *c.* 1473) assures *studiosi* that they will be better off emending it than going without it altogether,

> especially since Lucretius steers clear of stories that in the words of the poet entertain unoccupied minds [*Georgics* 3.3] and instead tackles thorny questions of physics, with such intellectual sharpness and such literary flair that all his poetic successors, especially the prince of poets Virgil, model their descriptions on him, to the point of borrowing not just his very words but sometimes three whole lines or more.

When Basil's work on profiting from secular literature had been circulating in Bruni's Latin translation for half a century, even shielding Lucretius behind Virgil might have seemed unnecessary. Thirty years or more of study

---

[30] In 1492 Ficino claimed to have burnt *commentariola* that he composed in his youth, probably about 1457–8, when he used Lucretius for a sketch of Epicureanism; but the term surely means 'essays'. See Ficino 1576: 933; Kristeller 1937: II, 9–10, 81–7; Vasoli 1997: 381.

[31] Deufert 1999.   [32] Padua Capit. C 75 fo. 148v; Reeve 2005: 141 n. 79.

by Pomponio Leto, who wrote a manuscript in 1458 and contributed to the annotation in a copy of the second edition (Verona 1486), are not reflected in anything more discursive than brief remarks on the nature of philosophy, its arrival in Rome, the life and reception of Lucretius, the significance of Venus, Vulcan, and Mars, and Cicero's misrepresentation of Epicurus as a voluptuary when his mistake was actually unawareness of God and resurrection.[33] In Vat. Ottob. Lat. 2834, however, a member of Leto's circle wrote this note on the proem:[34]

> If a god is not susceptible to favour or anger, why are you appealing to Venus, who in your opinion is deaf? That suits not you but people who say that the gods are moved by the prayers of mortals. Perhaps, if he had opened with something that other mortals recoiled from, no one would have read him. Writers make a habit in their proems of giving the reader uplift and encouragement. Here, though, he speaks as a human being, later as a madman. If we grant that Venus is the cause of generation, thanking her by paying her compliments would be more rational than being charged with ingratitude, and indeed one might suppose that she can do harm just as she has done good.

In a copy of Niccoli's manuscript that he wrote in the 1470s Bartolomeo Fonzio annotated the section of Book 3 on hellish passions and the death of the great, the section of Book 4 on love, and the section of Book 5 on the early life of man. The deepest appreciation shown of Lucretius in the second half of the fifteenth century is also the hardest to pin down: emulation by poets of the day, above all Bonincontri, Pontano, and Marullus.[35]

Unless the strange assemblage of garbled verses at the end of the second and third edition (Verona 1486, Venice 1495) was meant to have a programmatic function, it was Aldus who first commended Lucretius editorially (Venice, 1500), as a learned and stylish exponent of Epicurean doctrine and a Latin follower of the innovator Empedocles, whose philosophical verse had survived only in quotation.[36] Aldus' editor, the able critic Hieronymus Avancius, introduced an emended text, badly needed after the editions just mentioned, with a snappy account of Lucretius' style. From a Platonic standpoint close to Ficino's, Raphael Francus published apparently not in many

---

[33] Solaro 2000: 25–30.

[34] Reeve 2005: 148 n. 95; I now think the unusual abbreviation *pōa* stands for *postea*, not *poeta*. On Leto see Reeve 2005: 144–7, 148–51. An article is forthcoming by Helen Dixon on the annotated incunable Utrecht Univ. X 2° 82, the incunable can be viewed online (http://digbijzcoll.library.uu.nl/index.php?lang=en&letter=d, 'De rerum natura').

[35] Goddard 1991a: chs. 2–4; Goddard 1991b. On Pontano and Marullus see further pp. 186–9 above.

[36] For the place of the edition in Aldus' output see Davies 1995: 40–3.

copies (only four have been reported) a *Paraphrasis in Lucretium* of Books 1–3 with an appendix on the immortality of the soul (Bologna, 1504); the work has been described as 'a model of clarity, to the point of tempting the reader to suspect that his disagreement was by no means as deeply rooted as he wished it to be thought'.[37] Then, from a surprising quarter, came a fully fledged commentary: previously, Iohannes Baptista Pius had taken to extremes Beroaldus' crusade for the archaic, flowery, and uncanonical, but he now set Lucretius' poem, which he represented as bristling with difficulties, in a painstakingly documented and largely unpartisan context of ancient and medieval philosophy dominated by the Presocratics, Aristotle, Albertus Magnus, and Aquinas.[38] His introduction avoids explicit controversy: Lucretius aimed at dispelling ignorance, leading his readers to the intellectual bliss described by Virgil at the end of the second *Georgic*, and serving the common good (1.43), for instance by freeing minds from the bonds of *religionum hoc est superstitionum* (a gloss that Lucretius would have rejected if it implied that there were acceptable *religiones*).[39] A typical note accompanies Lucretius' tirade against the notion that the gods made the world for the benefit of the human race (5.156–80): labelled in the margin 'Why people were created', it surveys the answers given by Origen, Augustine, and Aquinas, but does not adjudicate. Pius displays many other interests. His note on hermaphrodites (5.839) passes from Pliny, Ausonius, and an epigram (*Anth. Lat.* 786 Riese), to an ancient inscription that he has recently seen near Bologna, and from that to Quintilian, Varro *De re rustica*, Horace with Porphyrio's commentary (which he emends in passing), Albertus Magnus, and an epigram by Palladas that has been misunderstood.

Incongruously alluding to Apuleius' *Golden Ass*, Pius ends his frontispiece by promising the reader enjoyment; but at the end of his introduction the Gothic type of the frontispiece returns in a declaration, *Omnia ortodoxe fidei subiicio*, 'I submit everything to orthodox belief.' A copy now in Cambridge (CUL Adv. a 25.6) has jottings by an early reader, perhaps Mario Maffei, whose sons and heirs owned it. Underneath *Omnia ortodoxe fidei subiicio* he wrote *Omnia ergo retractanda*, 'Everything, then, needs revising.' For this reader, as for many another, the sting was not so easily taken out of the poem.

---

[37] Pizzani 1986: 333; for details of copies see p. 322 n. 43 (only two complete: Tolbiac; Florence Bibl. Naz.).

[38] Del Nero 1985–6, a fine appreciation; Raimondi 1974 is more concerned with the place of the commentary in Pius' chequered career.

[39] Solaro 2000: 43–8 reprints the introduction.

Further reading

On transmission generally see Reynolds 1983: 218–22. On ancient testimonia: Diels 1923: xxxv–xlii and apparatus of *testimonia*, Pieri 1977, Milanese 2005. NINTH CENTURY: Stephan 1885, Finch 1967, Munk Olsen 1979, Leonhardt 1989, Ganz 1996, Bischoff 2004. MIDDLE AGES: Bignone 1913, Billanovich 1958, Grant 1981, Sivo 1988, Solaro 1993, Solaro 1997, Solaro 2000: 93–122. FIFTEENTH CENTURY (1417–1511): Lehnerdt (1904), Bertelli 1964, Raimondi 1974, Reeve 1980, Del Nero 1985–6, Pizzani 1986, Goddard 1991a, Goddard 1991b, Deufert 1998, Deufert 1999, A. Brown 2001, Reeve 2005, Reeve 2006.

13

VALENTINA PROSPERI

Lucretius in the Italian Renaissance

The dissimulatory code

There are two critical moments for the reception of the *DRN* in the Italian Renaissance. The first is 1417, the year in which Poggio rediscovered the text of Lucretius;[1] the second comes in the early decades of the sixteenth century, when religious conflict led to the rigorous censorship of secular culture. The cultural and political circumstances of Counter-Reformation Italy created a threat that the *DRN*, 'restored from death to life' by Poggio,[2] might once more be consigned to oblivion because of its Epicureanism and its anti-providential materialism. In the event, as witnessed by its uninterrupted influence on Italian literature of the fifteenth and sixteenth centuries, readership of the *DRN* showed no falling off after the Counter-Reformation. This is because, when faced with a text as risky and as alluring as the *DRN*, Lucretius' admirers spontaneously adopted measures of self-censorship which collectively can be called a 'dissimulatory code', in order to head off the far more threatening censorship of the Church. The self-imposed cautiousness of its readers had two main consequences for the reception of the poem. In the short term this provided a defence against the risk of an official condemnation of Lucretius; but, in the long run, the dissimulatory code brought about a change not only in the nature of the response to the *DRN* but also in the perceptions of later centuries, leading sometimes to the assumption that there is little to report of sixteenth-century responses to the *DRN*.[3]

Concretely, there are many signs of the success of the dissimulatory code in assuring the poem's circulation, chief among them the absence of Lucretius from the Index Librorum Prohibitorum, a phenomenon underlined by the many favourable mentions of the poem at the highest levels of the

---

[1] See p. 208 above.
[2] So Francesco Barbaro in a letter of July 1417 to Poggio (Barbaro 1999: 72).
[3] Alfonsi 1978 is simply silent on the sixteenth century in a review of the reception of Lucretius.

ecclesiastical hierarchy. Even at the end of the sixteenth century the Jesuit Father Antonio Possevino, whose *Bibliotheca selecta* provided a bibliographical survey of texts acceptable to Counter-Reformation orthodoxy, expressed his admiration for the literary and moral value of the *DRN*, while condemning its Epicureanism.[4] It is true that the number of printed editions of the text in Italy from its rediscovery to the end of the sixteenth century is considerably lower than those of other Greek and Latin classics of comparable literary importance.[5] But the recurrent presence in these editions of 'warnings to the reader', in which printers or publishers distance themselves from and denounce the Epicurean impiety of the poem, should not be taken as a signal of the work's lack of success. On the contrary: given the times, every edition of the *DRN*, the poem that proclaimed the indifference of the gods, the mortality of the soul, the infinity of worlds, is in itself a sign of the extraordinary status it had acquired, and the 'warning to the reader' was a modest nod to official morality, one of the forms taken by the dissimulatory code. Yet the possibility of censorship remained none the less real, as is shown by the reaction, as late as the mid seventeenth century, to Alessandro Marchetti's Italian translation of the *DRN*. The likelihood of vastly increased circulation in the vernacular led to a hardening of attitudes, with the result that Marchetti's translation did not see the light of day, despite the vehement protestations of his religious conformity in the prefatory material, and it ended up on the Index.[6]

A chronological sample will illustrate the pervasive operation of the dissimulatory code. An early and extreme example of the tension between a committed reading of Lucretius and the constraints on the wider circulation of his poem is the *Paraphrasis in Lucretium* (1504) by the Florentine professor of philosophy Raphael Francus.[7] No mere paraphrase but a genuine exegesis, Francus' work evinces a profound affinity between the commentator and the object of his analysis. Yet despite this, Francus – a notorious unbeliever and 'philosophus Lucretianus'[8] – felt impelled to add an appendix 'De animi immortalitate', in which he deployed Platonic and other arguments explicitly to refute the Epicurean doctrine of the mortality of the soul. As censorship grew stricter over time, precautions intensified. A man such as Vincenzio Borghini, directly involved in cultural policing as a leading member of the Congregation of the Index (he was the official reviser of Boccaccio's works),

---

[4] Possevino 1595: 148–51.
[5] See C. A. Gordon 1962: 29. On early editions and commentaries see ch. 12 above.
[6] On this episode see Saccenti 1966. [7] For Francus see also pp. 211–12 above.
[8] Verde 1998: 128 n. 35.

did not conceal his knowledge of the *DRN*, but was anxious to make clear the ideological limits of his appreciation of Lucretius, even in a private note-book of 1560.[9] The mechanism of the code is clearly visible in the work of another eminent scholar of the sixteenth century, Pietro Vettori. Impassioned declaration of Catholic orthodoxy is one, but only one, of the forms his repudiations of Epicureanism take, depending on context and addressee. Thus his ire is kept to a minimum when addressing his friend Giovanni Della Casa; he is succinct but prudent when addressing his readers; and he waxes indignant towards the reckless Girolamo Mercuriale, a physician who made no secret of the fact that he 'held the greatest regard' for the authority of Lucretius.[10]

Anyone tempted to conclude that the innumerable condemnations of Lucretius reveal an excessive pusillanimity on the part of Italian men of letters might reflect on the fate of the Paduan Sperone Speroni. In the 1540s, throwing caution to the winds, the young Speroni had liberally sprinkled his *Dialogo d'amore* with quotations from the conclusion to *DRN* 4. A few decades later and in a changed cultural climate, that recklessness proved costly, when in 1575 he was anonymously denounced to the Inquisition. Thereafter the traumatised Speroni did not fail to obey the code. It is hard to say whether the prudence displayed in one of his late works is more comical or pathetic, when he cites the proem to *DRN* 4 only after making crystal clear that Lucretius is impious; that the impiety of his doctrine is such that to commit to memory lines from the *DRN* 'almost appears to be a sin'; that the citation from the *DRN* will be used for the morally unexceptionable purpose of praising a Christian poet, Dante; that to make extra sure, the citation will be altered to give a religious sense;[11] and finally, that the opening of Book 4, thus modified, can thereby be read as a 'prophecy' of Dante's great Christian poem.[12]

Doctors, poets and painters

In Speroni's *Dialogo d'amore* the offending portion of Lucretius was the end of Book 4, damned not only by the specific prohibition of the code, but also by a more general Roman Catholic sexophobia. Yet this twofold dissuasion did not prevent a kindling of interest in Lucretius' lines on love

---

[9] See Borghini 1971: 112.   [10] Vettori 1586: IV, 146.

[11] By replacing *exsoluere* with *compescere* at DRN 4.7 *religionum animum nodis exsoluere pergo.*

[12] Speroni 1988: II, 273–4.

and sex as early as Marsilio Ficino,[13] who cited the passage several times in his *Libro dell'amore* (1469),[14] albeit with some embarrassment, as an authority on the physiology of love. Ficino's coyness was perhaps partly due to an awareness of the ambiguous effect of the episode, whose cautionary message is more than a little obscured by the intensity of the description. An inverted reading of *DRN* 4 as a hymn to the ineluctability of desire is found a few decades later in the popular *Libro de natura de amore* by the humanist Mario Equicola,[15] and then again in Speroni. By the end of the sixteenth century the celebration of the joys of sex was, as we have seen, far from acceptable, and later treatises on love allude to Lucretius without including direct quotations from the *DRN*.[16]

Yet one class of readers in Italy enjoyed relative freedom in the discussion of bodily matters: medical doctors. The story of Lucretius' suicide on account of love had revived interest in his poem's comments on the passions. Furthermore, Aristotle's distinction between poets and non-poets on the basis of whether their subjects were or were not imitative, had the effect of classing Lucretius among the *physici*, natural scientists like Empedocles. Without diminishing interest in Lucretius on the part of men of letters, this attracted the attention of other types of reader, including the doctors. Thus the sixteenth century saw not only examples of outstanding physician-poets, modelling themselves on Lucretius (most famously Fracastoro),[17] but also scientific readings of the *DRN* as a source of medical ideas. Girolamo Mercuriale, for example, cites the text several times in his *Variae lectiones* of 1588, in confirmation of claims made in ancient medical texts. The description of the plague at the end of the *DRN* was a great favourite, and long extracts, sometimes in translation, are cited in sixteenth-century treatises on the disease. The poem's medical authority lasted in Italy until well into the seventeenth century, when one published commentator on the *DRN* was in fact a physician, the Florentine Giovanni Nardi. His *Paraphrastica explanatio* of 1647, an ambitious work ignored, or worse, by later Lucretian

---

[13] Ficino later repented of his adherence to Epicureanism in his youth (see p. 210 n. 30), but he never renounced an admiration for Lucretius, evident throughout his works. On the influence of Epicureanism in Ficino see Kristeller 1943.

[14] The *Libro dell'amore* is Ficino's own translation of his *Commentarium in Convivium Platonis*, a work widely acclaimed throughout much of the sixteenth century; see Ficino 1987: vi.

[15] Equicola 1999: 101^r–102^v.

[16] E.g. Gabriele Zinano's *L'amata seconda*; Benedetto Varchi's *Cinque quistioni d'amore*; Torquato Tasso's dialogue *Il Cataneo, overo de le conclusioni amorose*.

[17] See pp. 191–2 above.

exegetes,[18] examines the text from the point of view of content rather than form; and in his own scientific treatises Nardi not infrequently resorts to Lucretian quotations in the course of scientific demonstrations.[19]

In a debate on the role of poetry, which once more became a burning issue in the sixteenth century, the *DRN* acquired iconic status for its image of the honeyed cup, which presents poetry as the sweet vehicle of a bitter truth, and the poet as the wise physician who restores health (*DRN* 1.933–50). Not that the imagery itself was unknown before 1417, since it had been used repeatedly by many other ancient writers, becoming a veritable *topos*,[20] and all the non-Lucretian occurrences had already been exploited in the debate between those, on the one hand, who wished to deny poetry any autonomy and to subordinate it to pedagogical ends, and on the other hand those who, while in general allowing the educational role of the intellectual, rejected any interference in the creative process. But among the numerous sources for the image, Lucretius had the advantage of poetic form and memorability. Already Lorenzo Valla's little *De arte grammatica* in verse (1443) commenced by presenting a version of the image as a programmatic declaration of how to combine the theory and practice of teaching. By the middle of the sixteenth century the Lucretian simile made an appearance in every theoretical or literary work that sought to contribute to the debate, and it figured prominently in the work of two authors who combined poetic theory and practice at the highest level, Bernardo Tasso and his son Torquato. Torquato ensured the Lucretian image's popularity by using it for the proem of his 1581 masterpiece *Gerusalemme liberata* (1.3).

The presence of Lucretius is marked in all Tasso's works, and nowhere more so than in the Lucretian passages woven into his greatest poem. The fabulous island of Armida, where the hero Rinaldo abandons everything for love, is a tissue of poetic reminiscences concerning in particular the internal freedom the individual may attain through the teachings of Epicurus, and the less abstract spaces of the *intermundia*, the abodes of the Epicurean gods. The palace of Armida rises up undisturbed by the elements, the pleasures of its stable repose heightened by contrast with what is troubled, 'just as it is sweet to gaze out from land at a ship that wanders on a troubled sea' (*Ger. lib.* 15, *ottava estravagante;*[21] cf. *DRN* 2.1–2). Sea and sky are calmed as at the appearance of the Lucretian Venus (*Ger. lib.* 15.9; cf. *DRN* 1.7–8).

---

[18] See C. A. Gordon 1962: 75 for the scornful comments by Tanneguy Lefevre and Thomas Creech on Nardi's work.

[19] For example, in the treatise *De igne subterraneo* (1641) passages from *De rerum natura* are utilised to support Nardi's arguments.

[20] See Prosperi 2004: ch. 1.   [21] Tasso 1979: 605.

The garden of Armida flowers in an eternal springtime, like the abodes of the Lucretian gods (*Ger. lib.* 15.54; cf. *DRN* 3.18–22):

> Not as elsewhere now sunshine bright, now showres,
> Now heat, now cold, there enterchanged weare,
> But euerlasting spring milde heau'n downe powres,
> In which nor raine, nor storme, nor cloudes appeare,
> Nursing to fields, their grasse; to grasse, his flowres;
> To flowres, their smell; to trees, the leaues they beare.
>
> (transl. Fairfax)

Rinaldo and Armida lost in a mutual amorous gaze repeat the attitudes of Mars and Venus (*Ger. lib.* 16.18–19; cf. *DRN* 1.32–6):

> Ore him her lookes she hung, and her soft breast
> The pillow was, where he and loue tooke rest.
>
> His hungrie eies vpon her face he fed,
> And feeding them so, pinde himselfe away;
> And she, declining often downe her hed,
> His lippes, his cheekes, his eies kist, as he lay.
>
> (transl. Fairfax)

Almost a century earlier the humanist and poet Poliziano, who also applied his philological skills to the text of the *DRN*, had made striking use of the Lucretian descriptions of Mars and Venus and the home of the gods in the *Stanze per la Giostra*. But while Tasso had to live with the grim reality of the Counter-Reformation and its censorship, Poliziano wrote in the golden age of Lorenzo il Magnifico. While Tasso shares the fate of his hero Rinaldo, prevented from following an ideal different from the Christian, Poliziano is unencumbered by ideological anxieties as he sprinkles antique ornaments over his new poem:

> e ginne al regno di sua madre in fretta,
> ov'è de' picciol suoi fratei lo stuolo;
> al regno ov'ogni Grazia si diletta,
> ove Biltà di fiori al crin fa brolo,
> ove tutto lascivo, drieto a Flora,
> Zefiro vola e la verde erba infiora.
>
> (*Stanze* 1.68)

[Love] went in haste to the realm of his mother, the home of his thronging little brothers: to the realm where every Grace delights, where Beauty weaves a garland of flowers about her hair, where lascivious Zephyr flies behind Flora and decks the green grass with flowers. (transl. David Quint)

Figure 13.1. Sandro Botticelli, *Primavera*

This stanza, modelled on the pageant of the arrival of Spring at *DRN* 5.737–40, has attracted attention through its connection with Botticelli's *Primavera* (fig. 13.1). It is above all in the visual arts that modern scholarship has recognised the influence of Lucretius on the vernacular culture of the Italian Renaissance. Aby Warburg's suggestion that Lucretius, via Poliziano, was the source for Botticelli's painting was contested by Ernst Gombrich, who interpreted the painting as an illustration of the moral virtues addressed to the young Lorenzo di Pierfrancesco de' Medici.[22] But today, thanks to new documentary evidence and a new dating, the Lucretian description of the arrival of Spring itself is once more seen as the most important of several ancient sources of Botticelli's *Primavera*.[23] In the second of the two paintings Botticelli made for Lorenzo, *The Birth of Venus*, critics have unanimously recognised the influence of Lucretius' Hymn to Venus, mediated via Poliziano's *Stanze*:

> A young woman with nonhuman countenance is carried on a conch shell, wafted to shore by playful zephyrs; and it seems that heaven rejoices in her birth. You would call the foam real, the sea real, real the conch shell and real the blowing wind; you would see the lightning in the goddess' eyes, and sky

[22] Gombrich 1972: 37–64.   [23] Dempsey 1968, 1992.

Figure 13.2. Sandro Botticelli, *Venus and Mars*

and elements laughing about her . . . and where the strand was imprinted by
her sacred and divine step, it had clothed itself in flowers and grass.

(*Stanze* 1.99–101, transl. David Quint)

The iconography of Botticelli's painting of *Venus and Mars* (fig. 13.2) may
derive immediately from an astrological interpretation of the myth by
Marsilio Ficino, but the pose of Mars may be inspired by Lucretius' description of the war-god's 'shapely neck thrown back' (*DRN* 1.35).[24]

In the years before the expulsion of the Medicis from Florence the reception
of Lucretius' Epicureanism was filtered through the dominant Neoplatonism
of Marsilio Ficino, and thus it is reflected in Botticelli's paintings. Later, in the
years of the Florentine Republic, attention focused above all on the account
of the evolution of culture in *DRN* 5, a passage which Poliziano had already
imitated in the history of poetry in his *Nutricia*, but in positive and optimistic mode. The 'hard primitivism' that characterises the Lucretian vision
of the history of mankind (as opposed to the 'soft primitivism' of a Golden
Age view of man's remote past) was particularly congenial to the restored
leader Lorenzo di Pierfrancesco de' Medici and his circle of friends, including the poet Michael Marullus and the Florentine Chancellor Bartolomeo
Scala, both fervent admirers of Lucretius.[25] The 1490 Scala family palazzo
in Florence is decorated with bas-reliefs of hunting and fighting between men
and animals which, via Scala's collection of fables, the *Apologi centum*, draw
their inspiration from *DRN* 5.[26] And a Lucretian primitive state of nature
ignorant of laws and customs, in which the strong (whether man or beast)

[24] Gombrich 1972: 215 n. 133.   [25] A. Brown 2001: 45–53; on Scala see A. Brown 1979.
[26] A. Brown 2001: 42–3. The palace has two names: Palazzo Bartolomeo Scala or Palazzo
della Gherardesca.

Figure 13.3. Piero di Cosimo, *The Forest Fire*

Figure 13.4. Piero di Cosimo, *A Hunting Scene*

prevails, is represented in the *Early Man* panels by Piero di Cosimo. Erwin Panofsky in the late 1930s identified the source of this complex pictorial cycle as the last part of *DRN* 5.[27] Panofsky also hypothesised a Lucretian source for the Piero di Cosimo paintings known as the *Stories of Vulcan*, now thought to derive from elsewhere. But there is no doubt that *The Forest Fire* and *A Hunting Scene* (figs. 13.3 and 13.4) are very close to the Lucretian description of primitive mankind.

The hymn to Venus

In sixteenth-century Italian poetry imitation of Lucretius tends to stay closer to the original than is the case with many other classical texts, perhaps because of the recent rediscovery of the poem, or perhaps because of its highly distinctive character. This is true even in genres far removed from

[27] Panofsky 1962: 36–67; qualifications: Fermor 1993: ch. 2. S. Campbell 2003 argues for Lucretian influence in Giorgione's enigmatic *Tempest* but fails to convince.

that of the *DRN*, and nowhere is it more striking than in adaptations of the hymn to Venus that opens the *DRN*. Humanist scholars had pondered the meaning of the hymn and its relation to the poem's anti-providentialist Epicurean message. Generally they arrived at one of two conclusions: either the hymn should be taken as a celebration of the universal force of sexual desire (*hominum diuumque uoluptas*), or Venus was invoked as the ancestress of the Roman race (*Aeneadum genetrix*). This scholarly difference is also reflected in the practice of the poets, with the result that in the programmatic reuses of the hymn to Venus, in whatever genre – epic, lyric or didactic – context reveals the author's interpretative choice.

As early as the end of the fifteenth century Boiardo had composed a lyric *Ad amorem*, in which the soothing and life-giving virtues of the Lucretian Venus, viewed as a figure of sensual love and universal generative force, are transferred to the god of love:

> Alto diletto, che ralegri il mondo
> e le tempeste e' venti fai restare,
> l'erbe fiorite e fai tranquillo il mare,
> et a' mortali il cor lieto e iocondo.

Exalted beloved, you who gladden the world and make still the storms and winds, make the meadows flower and the sea calm, and give to mortals a heart happy and joyful.

Two other early examples are the exordium of Luigi Alamanni's *Della coltivazione* (1530) and Francesco Berni's proem for Book 2 of his reworking (*rifacimento*) of Boiardo's *Orlando Innamorato* (completed early 1530s). Both are faithful renderings of the original and they answer respectively to the two opposed interpretations of the Lucretian hymn. Alamanni's Venus is the universal generative force, in keeping with the context of his poem, a modern didactic in the manner of the *Georgics*. Alamanni's version begins:

> Alma Ciprigna Dea, lucente stella
> De' Mortai, de gli Dei vita e diletto;
> Tu fai l'aer seren, tu queti il mare,
> Tu dai frutto al terren, tu liete, e gai
> Fai le fere, e gli augei, che dal tuo raggio
> Tutto quel ch'è fra noi raddoppia il parto.
>
> (268–73)

Cyprian Soul, Goddess, shining star of mortals, life and delight of the gods; you make the air serene, you calm the sea, you make the earth bear fruit, you make the animals and birds happy and joyful, since by your rays all that is on earth gives birth with doubled force.

Alamanni follows Lucretius almost word for word, though omitting the apostrophe *Aeneadum genetrix* as an inappropriate generic marker of epic. Berni, contrastingly, composes a proem for a chivalrous epic, and correspondingly includes the opening address to the 'Holy Mother of Aeneas':

> Madre santa d'Enea, figlia di Giove,
> Degli uomini piacere e degli Dei,
> Venere bella, che fai l'erbe nuove
> E le piante, e del mondo vita sei;
> Da te negli animal virtù si muove,
> Virtù che nulla fôran senza lei;
> Vincol, pace, piacer, gioia del mondo,
> Spirto, foco vital, lume giocondo.

Holy Mother of Aeneas, daughter of Jupiter, delight of men and of the gods, fair Venus, who makes new the meadows and the plants, and who are the life of the world; from you power stirs in the animals, power such that nothing would exist without it; binding force, peace, pleasure, joy of the world, spirit, fire of life, joyful light.

The epic appropriation of the Lucretian proem was no less successful, fuelled in part perhaps by the favourable reception of Berni's reworking of the *Innamorato*.

Bernardo Tasso's principal work, the epic poem *L'Amadigi*, was published posthumously in 1587. In this influential poem the invocation, in markedly Lucretian language, of the goddess in the third stanza is given an epic slant in the fourth stanza, making clear Venus' role as the guardian of soldiers:

> Santa Madre d'Amore, il cui bel raggio
> serena l'aria, e 'l mar turbato acqueta . . .
> Tu, c'hai sovente sospirare udito
> Arsi dal foco tuo gli alti Guerrieri;
> Che spesso visto gli hai col ferro ardito
> Difender regni, et acquistar Imperi;
> Tu Dea, col tuo valor raro, infinito,
> Tu muovi la mia lingua, alza i pensieri;
> E dona a l'opra mia favor cotanto,
> Ch'ogni futura etade oda il mio canto.

Holy Mother of Love, whose beautiful beam calms the air and quietens the turbulent sea . . . You who have often heard the sighs of lofty warriors ablaze with your fire; who have often seen them with bold steel defending kingdoms and conquering empires; you, goddess, with your incomparable and infinite power, I beg you to move my tongue, raise my thoughts; and grant to my work such favour that every future age shall hear my song.

More succinct and freer than Berni's version, and shorn of the final plea to Mars to intervene, Bernardo's verses reveal an ongoing formularisation of the Lucretian hymn, a process the more marked the fewer the artistic pretensions of the modern writer. Thus in an anonymous and pedestrian mid-sixteenth-century poem in *ottava rima* the invocation to Venus is reduced to the stylemes of sparkling light and a smiling earth.[28] By contrast, Giovan Battista Marino's ambitious *Adone* of the early seventeenth century flaunts its erudite memory of the model.

Later incarnations of the hymn can seem distant indeed from the original, for example Ferdinando Donno's novel *L'amorosa Clarice* (1625), where the solemn Lucretian invocation is transformed into the prayer of a woman suffering unrequited love, and the rich verbal tapestry of the poem becomes mannerist decoration.[29] Yet even as late as the end of the eighteenth century Ugo Foscolo found inspiration in the Hymn to Venus. Foscolo's interest in Lucretius is attested in his letters and an abandoned project for a critical study of the *DRN*,[30] and a Lucretian presence is diffused through the richly classical texture of his poetry. In this mosaic of materials the hymn to Venus is not simply another piece of ornament, but condenses one of Foscolo's central ideas, the cathartic power of beauty in the midst of the ills of humanity. In one of his most famous sonnets, 'A Zacinto', the apparition of a Lucretian Venus casts a light of otherworldly comfort over the tormenting memory of his lost fatherland:

> Né più mai toccherò le sacre sponde
> Ove il mio corpo fanciulletto giacque,
> Zacinto mia, che te specchi nell'onde
> Del greco mar da cui vergine nacque
> Venere, e fea quell'isole feconde
> Col suo primo sorriso.

Never again shall I touch your sacred shores, where as a small boy I laid me down, Zacynthos mine, who mirror yourself in the waves of the Greek sea from which Venus was born, virgin, and made fertile those islands with her first smile.

Further reading

Fleischmann 1971 is a succinct but comprehensive point of departure for the fortunes of Lucretius in the early modern period, cataloguing all the

---

[28] 'O Vener bella il cui fulgido raggio | adorna il ciel e fa rider la terra', Anon. 1988: II, 545.
[29] Donno 1979: 1.29.   [30] See Foscolo 1990.

principal sixteenth-century editions and commentaries. C. A. Gordon 1962 is still useful, although, like Hadzsits 1963 and Alfonsi 1978, he underestimates the importance of Lucretius in the later Renaissance. Kristeller 1956 reconstructs the cultural environment of the circle of Marsilio Ficino, with numerous references to Lucretius. In recent years research on Lucretius in the Renaissance has intensified: studies on individual periods or authors include A. Brown 1979 on Bartolomeo Scala; A. Brown 2001 on Medicean Florence; Basile 1984 on the philosophical doubts of Tasso's later years. Recently Prosperi 2004 and Gambino Longo 2004 trace different aspects of the Italian Renaissance reception of Lucretius.

14

PHILIP FORD

Lucretius in early modern France

Thanks to a large extent to Montaigne's interest in Lucretius as well as the strong tradition of rationalism in French philosophy which developed towards the end of the sixteenth century, the role of the author of the *DRN* in early modern French literature and thought has been generally recognised by scholars, though it has not been explored as fully as it deserves. Fraisse 1962 establishes the main areas of influence but is very often forced to admit that direct allusions to the Roman poet are rarer than might have been expected. Essays and articles have subsequently concentrated in particular on Lucretius' place in Montaigne's *Essays*, where he is the second most frequently cited poet after Horace.[1] However, because of his association with the ideas of Epicurus, Lucretius was throughout the early modern period treated in France with a mixture of admiration and caution. It is no doubt a tribute to his poetic powers that he is to a large extent exempted from the more general climate of hostility towards Epicureanism.

Sixteenth-century French readers of Lucretius tended to view him in one of two ways. On the one hand he could be seen principally as a poet, whose archaising style and rugged hexameters provided a model for the increasingly popular genre of scientific poetry,[2] or whose famous *topoi* might be taken out of context and used and reused by poets in a range of genres.[3] On the other hand, he was also seen as a philosopher, a mouthpiece for a form of rationalism which would contribute to the rise of libertinism

---

[1] See, for example, Moore 1967, Hendrick 1975, Ferreyrolles 1976, and Ménager 1989.

[2] For an overview of this genre see Schmidt 1970.

[3] These *topoi* include in particular the personification of Nature as Venus, the image of the philosopher as one who serenely views a shipwreck from afar (on which for this period see Delon 1988), and the poet treading unknown paths as an image of poetic originality (respectively from the start of *DRN* 1, 2 and 4).

in the early seventeenth century, when Lucretius served as a literary and philosophical source for many of the theories which the *libertins* embraced. This chapter, then, will focus on the two sides of Lucretius from the early Renaissance to the time of Molière, in order to describe his position in French letters.

Judging by the number of French editions of Lucretius, there was a considerable demand for his works throughout the sixteenth century.[4] The first French-printed edition was published a century after Poggio's discovery of the manuscript, in 1514 by Josse Bade and Jean Petit. This elegant folio text contains a dedicatory letter by Nicolas Bérault, who recommends Lucretius both for 'the traces of learned antiquity which are apparent in him' and 'the inexplicable delightfulness of the poetry and the inimitable sweetness and pleasantness of those ancient times'.[5] This double endorsement, which brushes aside all question of Lucretius' atheism, is perhaps slightly called into question by the Jerome-based biography also included, which very much coloured the way in which sixteenth-century French readers viewed him: 'having lapsed into madness as a result of a love potion, after he had written during respites from his insanity a number of books, which were subsequently corrected by Cicero, he committed suicide at the age of forty-three'.[6] Here we have the various elements which made up the legend of Lucretius for French readers as for others.[7]

In terms of the history of the text, the most significant event was the Lambinus edition of Lucretius, first published in both Paris and Lyon in 1563, then reprinted in France in 1564, 1565 and 1570. Denis Lambin (1519–72) was a renowned humanist who held successively, from 1561, chairs of Latin and Greek at the Collège royal. His 1561 edition of Horace was justly esteemed and prepared the way for his work on Lucretius. Here, in addition to the careful establishment of the text, Lambin adds a detailed commentary and a compendious index, which would have considerably facilitated the use of the *DRN*. Unlike Josse Bade, he also faces up directly to the problems posed by the text to sixteenth-century readers. He highlights four unacceptable aspects of Lucretius' philosophy: Lucretius 'attacks the immortality of the soul, he denies divine providence, he does away with all forms of religion, and he assigns the highest good to pleasure'. However, argues Lambin, the poem itself is 'beautiful', 'magnificent', 'adorned, distinguished and embellished

---

[4] For the bibliographical history see further Fleischmann 1971, C. A. Gordon 1962.
[5] Fo. Ai^v; my translation.   [6] Ibid.
[7] On the biographical tradition see further the Introduction to this volume.

with all the merits of genius',[8] and he feels that the reader is perfectly capable of rejecting the more extreme and absurd ideas of Epicurus, while accepting those which conform with Christian views.

The other format in which Lucretius was read is that of the seven Sebastian Gryphius editions produced in Lyon from 1534 to 1576. Here the text alone is presented, based on the Aldine version of 1500. In whatever light Lucretius was read, there appears to have been a constant demand for editions of the *DRN* in France, particularly from the 1560s onwards, though fresh editions are infrequent in the seventeenth century. On the other hand, it is in the seventeenth century that we see vernacular translations of the whole of the *DRN* emerging, the first by Michel de Marolles in 1650 (reprinted, revised, and versified from 1659 on), with others following in the final decades of the century. We also see the emergence of a tradition in illustrated frontispieces to these editions, as Marolles's draws upon Jansson's and is echoed in Evelyn's a few years later (see figs. 14.1–4).

As we have seen in both the Bade and the Lambin editions of the *DRN*, there was general agreement about the quality of Lucretius' poetry. Moreover, as a model for scientific poetry, the *DRN* provided a framework which vernacular poets could follow, although in practice there are fewer close links between French writers and Lucretius than might be anticipated, with Virgil's *Georgics* often providing an alternative template for didactic verse. In the case of Maurice Scève (*c.* 1500–?1560), one of the first authors of scientific poetry in sixteenth-century France, it is acknowledged that the *Microcosme* owes a general debt to the *DRN*, particularly in the depiction of Adam and Eve after the Fall (2.101–204), which is loosely modelled on *DRN* 5.925–87.[9] At most, however, Scève draws a few commonplaces about primitive man from the Roman poet, and many other sources feed into this poem. Similarly, two poets associated with the Pléiade, Jean-Antoine de Baïf (1532–89) and Remy Belleau (1528–77), also make a limited use of Lucretius in their scientific poetry,[10] while Guillaume de Saluste Du Bartas (1544–90), in *La Sepmaine*, despite his own Calvinist rejection of Epicurean ideas, nevertheless uses Lucretius as a poetic resource.[11] For example, he asserts (2.149–53) the traditional idea of *nihil de nihilo* in terms which recall *DRN* 1.155–64, while at the same time rejecting Lucretius' statement at 1.150 that 'nothing can ever be created *by divine means* out of nothing':

---

[8] My translations from the 1570 edition, fo. a2[v].

[9] On Lucretius and Scève see Schmidt 1970: 155–8.

[10] On Baïf and Belleau see Fraisse 1962: 136–41.   [11] See Kany-Turpin 1991: 31–9.

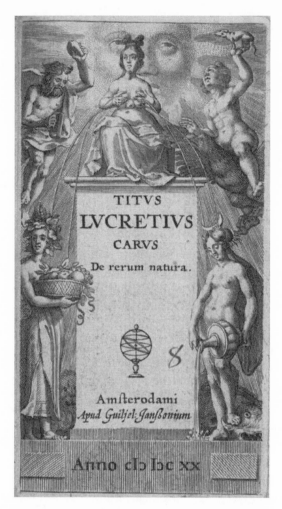

Figure 14.1. *De rerum natura* apud G. Janssonium (Amsterdam, 1620), frontispiece.
Apparently the earliest printed illustration to the *DRN*. In the background is the Sun,
composed of atoms, as the source of light and life. Nature is given the place of honour,
surrounded by the four Empedoclean elements (clockwise from bottom left) Earth (Demeter),
Fire (Prometheus or Deucalion), Air (Ganymede) and Water (this figure doubles as Venus).

> Car tout ce qui se fait, se fait de la matiere,
> Qui dans l'antique rien fut faite la premiere.
> Tout ce qui se resould, en elle se resould.
> *Depuis que l'Eternel fit de rien ce grand Tout,*
> Rien de rien ne se faict: rien en rien ne s'escoule.[12]

---

[12] Du Bartas 1994: 44, my translation.

Figure 14.2. *Le poëte Lucrece, Latin et Francois de la traduction de M. D. M[arolles]*
(Paris, 1651), frontispiece
The design draws on Jansson's frontispiece, again personifying Nature and the four elements,
but Vulcan now takes the part of Fire and Neptune that of Water.

For everything which is made is made out of the matter which was made
initially in the ancient void. Everything which dissolves dissolves into this. Since
God eternal created this mighty universe out of nothing, nothing is created out
of nothing, and nothing decays into nothing.

None of these poets, however, demonstrates an extensive debt to their Roman
predecessor.[13]

[13] For further details of their transactions see Fraisse 1962: 133–42, 155–68 and Whitaker 1936.

Figure 14.3. John Evelyn, *An Essay on the First Book of T. Lucretius Carus* (London, 1656),
frontispiece
Adapted from Marolles's frontispiece by Evelyn's wife Mary, this design was mocked by
Evelyn's rival translator Lucy Hutchinson for substituting the translator's head for Lucretius'.

With Pierre de Ronsard (1524–85) a much deeper appreciation of
Lucretius' poetry enters into his works, at times in quite unexpected contexts.[14] Even so, it is clear that the leader of the Pléiade was not in any

---

[14] Ronsard, like Montaigne, owned a copy of Lambin's edition of the *DRN*; it is discussed by
Morrison 1963.

Figure 14.4. Thomas Creech, *T. Lucretius Carus . . . his Six Books* (2nd edn, Oxford, 1683),
frontispiece
Lucretius sits surrounded by animal species and points to a sky in which atoms can be
discerned behind the appearances of things, descending from a sphere labelled
'CASUS', 'chance'.

way attracted to Epicureanism. In the 'Prosopopée de Louis de Ronsard son
pere' he writes: 'Vous qui sans foi errés à l'aventure, | Vous qui tenés la
secte d'Epicure, | Amandés vous, pour Dieu ne croyés pas | Que l'ame meure
avecques le trespas' (You who wander aimlessly without any faith, you who
follow the Epicurean sect, amend your ways, for God's sake do not believe

that the soul perishes with death).[15] Nevertheless, this does not prevent him from including elements of Lucretius' thinking in his poetry.

An early example is found in a love poem addressed to Cassandre in Ronsard's 1552 collection *Les Amours*, whose opening quatrain alludes to the Epicurean theory of atoms and the concept of the *clinamen* (*DRN* 2.292):

> Les petitz corps, culbutans de travers,
> Parmi leur cheute en byaiz vagabonde
> Hurtez ensemble, ont composé le monde,
> S'entracrochans d'acrochementz divers.[16]

The little atoms, tumbling topsy-turvy, by their obliquely wandering fall, clashing together, brought order to the world, hooking up with each other in diverse patterns.

In a movement which immediately distances us from Epicurean thought, the poet goes on to compare these clashing atoms to the various emotions he experiences, and the 'amoureux univers' (world of love) which they have created in his heart. Similarly, in another sonnet in this collection, Ronsard uses as his starting point the Epicurean theory of sight expounded by Lucretius in *DRN* 4.42–128:

> Si seulement l'image de la chose
> Fait à noz yeulx la chose concevoir,
> Et si mon œil n'a puissance de veoir,
> Si quelqu'idole au devant ne s'oppose . . .[17]

If the image of the object alone causes our eyes to conceive that object, and if my eye has no power to see unless some simulacrum strikes it . . .

He then goes on to regret that God failed to give him large enough eyes to take in the greatness of his beloved. Lucretian science, then, may be the starting point for some of Ronsard's love poetry, but it is put to purely poetic purposes in these poems and does not imply any intellectual commitment to it on the part of the poet.

Elsewhere Ronsard draws on the famous image at the start of *DRN* 2 of the man safe on shore, watching a ship in trouble at sea:

> Ainsi que fait cettuy-là qui du port
> Voit enfondrer en mer, bien loing du bord,
> Quelque navire, il se resjouist d'aise,
> Non, pour autant que la vague mauvaise

[15] Ronsard 1924–75: VI, 40–1.   [16] Ronsard 1924–75: IV, 40.
[17] Ronsard 1924–75: IV, 70.

La fait perir, mais pour autant qu'il est
Loing du danger, qui de la nef est prest . . .[18]

Just as one who sees from the harbour a ship sinking at sea, far from the shore, rejoices, not because the malicious wave is causing it to perish, but because he is far removed from the danger which looms over the ship . . .

Ronsard's poetry is full of similar Lucretian reworkings, indicating a thorough knowledge both of the poem itself and of the philosophy which underlies it. The passages to which he most frequently turns for inspiration are the opening invocation to Venus[19] and Lucretius' evocation and rejection of the torments of the Underworld in *DRN* 3.978–1023.[20] While not subscribing to Lucretius' view of the world, Ronsard nevertheless exploits for poetic purposes Epicurean ideas as well as Lucretian topoi. One passage, taken from the poem addressed 'A Monsieur de Belot' and modelled on *DRN* 1.10–20, is typical of the way in which Ronsard adapts the Roman poet, in this case incorporating metonymically the description of the rutting animals to suggest Apollo's desire for Admetus:

Qui çà qui là vagabonds d'aventure
Poussent dehors cette flame si dure,
Dont trop d'amour espoinçonne leur flanc
Quand le Printemps fait tiedir nostre sang.
Ny les torrens, ny les hautes montagnes,
Taillis ronceux, sablonneuses campagnes,
Rocs opposez, n'empeschent point leur cours:
Tant furieux est l'aiguillon d'amours![21]

Wandering here and there at random, they exhale that harsh flame with which an excess of love pricks their flanks when springtime warms our blood. Neither torrent nor lofty mountain, brambly copse, sandy plain or opposing rocks hinder their course, so frantic is the goad of love!

Ronsard here creatively takes the well-known Lucretian description out of its original context in order to suggest the madness of desire.

Paradoxically, then, Lucretius makes some of his most interesting appearances in poetry which exploits the ideas of the *DRN* in non-scientific texts,

---

[18] Ronsard 1924–75: VIII, 102.
[19] Further examples are Ronsard 1924–75: V, 225; VIII, 252; IX, 112; X, 110; XII, 30, 164; XIII, 106, 218; XV, 32, 284; XVI, 128. Ronsard's friend and fellow poet Joachim Du Bellay was also attracted to this passage, which he translated into French alexandrines; see Du Bellay 1908–31: VI, 403–4, 425.
[20] See VIII, 100, 172; X, 14, 317; XI, 122; XVI, 287.
[21] Ronsard 1924–75: XV, 32; ll. 357–64.

while French didactic poetry from this period owes a far smaller debt to the Roman poet. The hostility towards Epicureanism which has been noted in the poetry of Ronsard and other writers continued in some quarters until the end of the sixteenth century, though Lucretius himself tends to escape this general condemnation.[22] Moreover, in the closing decades of the century there commences a period characterised by a radical sense of doubt with regard to previously unquestioned certainties in both the philosophical and the religious spheres. The optimism of the neo-Platonic view of the universe, which overlay the thinking of many Christian humanists, was being called into question as a result of discoveries in the realm of astronomy; the French wars of religion had seriously undermined religious harmony and divided the country; and interest in philosophical systems such as Stoicism and Scepticism was fuelled by the rediscovery and printing of the writings of Epictetus (1528), Marcus Aurelius (1558) and Sextus Empiricus (Henri Estienne's Latin edition, 1562). As already noted, it is Montaigne who leads the way in showing how Lucretius' philosophical views could be exploited in vernacular works, in particular in his longest essay 2.12, 'L'Apologie de Raimond Sebond'.[23]

One issue which would become central to the whole course of French philosophy is the relationship between sense perceptions and the outside world, which Lucretius deals with in *DRN* 4. Lucretius, of course, defends the Epicurean principle of direct realism, that our senses do provide us with an accurate representation of the external world, and that, if we are at times deceived by them, this is because our minds distort these representations. Lucretius does not avoid this problem (cf. *DRN* 4.387–8, 391–4), and he gives examples of a number of optical illusions – jaundice sufferers see everything in yellow, square towers can appear round from a distance, oars placed in water appear bent. However, he concludes that 'there is nothing harder than to separate the facts as revealed from the questionable interpretations promptly imposed on them by the mind' (*DRN* 4.467–8), thus calling into question our interpretation of what we perceive rather than the perceptions themselves. The reason why Lucretius can embrace this position is, of course, because he believes there is a direct physical connection between the objects which surround us and our sense organs. Everything emits *simulacra*, composed of atoms, which strike our eyes or our other organs to create an image, or *phantasia*, of what we perceive in our minds. Depending on the

---

[22] As is pointed out by Ménager 1989: 25; 36–7 n. 4. The author sees the Lambin edition as responsible for separating Lucretius from the teachings of Epicurus.

[23] Screech 1998 shows how fully Montaigne read and appreciated Lucretius. On his response see also pp. 153–5 above.

shape of these atoms, the sensation will be more or less pleasurable (*DRN* 4.551–2).

When Montaigne comes to consider the whole question of the senses in the 'Apologie', although Lucretius very often forms the basis of his discussion, he invariably draws precisely the opposite conclusion. He starts off, as so often in this paradoxical chapter, on a promising note with regard to Epicurean theories: 'La science commence par eux [i.e. the senses], et se résout en eux' ('knowledge begins with them and can be reduced to them').[24] But like so much of the *Apologie*, the position which Montaigne appears to be supporting in his opening statement is swiftly countered by a whole series of arguments and examples – drawn mostly from Lucretius himself. After citing at length Lucretius' conclusion that it is absurd to deny the evidence of the senses (4.499–510), Montaigne establishes what will be his own position, reinforced by many of the examples to be found in Lucretius. Man, he says, 'cannot avoid the fact that his senses are both the sovereign regents of his knowledge, and yet, in all circumstances, uncertain and fallible'.[25] On the other hand, other Lucretian ideas mentioned by Montaigne are not rejected with the same insistence. For example, the plurality of worlds appears to him possible, despite its heretical nature,[26] and he appears to share Lucretius' scepticism about the survival of the soul after death.[27] He also sees religion as an accident of birth, rather than as divinely revealed, and he fiercely opposes the religious divisions which have grown up in Europe.[28] Despite concluding the *Apologie* by affirming the existence of God, Montaigne's arguments have all tended to the opposite conclusion, helped not a little by Lucretius, who is cited more than seventy times in this chapter (out of a total of 147 Lucretius quotations in the *Essays* as a whole).

Elsewhere in the *Essays*, Montaigne draws on *DRN* 3.830–977 to persuade himself that death should not be a source of terror. In particular, the closing pages of Essay 1.20, 'That to philosophise is to learn how to die', are punctuated by quotations from Nature's words on death (*DRN* 3.933–62), which seek to assure the reader that death is natural and desirable. Similarly, in the final chapter of the *Essays*, 'De l'experience', although Lucretius is not actually cited, his presence is felt in the generally Epicurean conclusion that 'il n'est rien si beau et legitime que de faire bien l'homme et deuement, ny science si ardue que de bien et naturellement sçavoir vivre cette vie' ('there

---

[24] Montaigne 1978: 909.   [25] Montaigne 1978: 915; my translation.
[26] Montaigne 1978: 524.   [27] Montaigne 1978: 549–52.
[28] Cf. Montaigne 1978: 445: 'Nous sommes Chrestiens à mesme titre que nous sommes ou Perigordins ou Alemans' ('We are Christians in the same way that we are natives of Périgord or Germany').

is nothing so fine or right as acting the man well and fitly, nor so difficult a science as knowing how to live this life well and according to nature').[29]

Montaigne's legacy in the seventeenth century can be seen in many aspects of French thought, but it was his objections to the veracity of our sense perceptions which would have an immediate impact on Descartes (1596–1650) in the *Discours de la raison* and the *Meditationes*, leading, of course, to the dualism of Cartesian philosophy. Descartes temporarily rejects the conclusions of Lucretius in the build-up to the *cogito*, though, having established the existence of a God who can act as a guarantor of clear and distinct ideas, he is prepared again to rely on sense perceptions, but without subscribing to the Epicurean notion of atomism as an explanation of how they function.

Although Lucretius' ideas were often considered dangerous by French writers unless clearly signalled as belonging to a 'pagan' world-view, one group which developed in the early years of the seventeenth century, the so-called *libertins*, embraced them wholeheartedly.[30] Of their number was the original and eccentric author Cyrano de Bergerac (1619–55). *L'Autre Monde, ou les états et empires de la lune* was first printed, in a badly bowdlerised form, in 1657, two years after the author's death, though the work circulated in a more complete manuscript version during Cyrano's lifetime. Although, even in this manuscript form, it is a highly elusive work, characterised by a deliberately destabilising form of irony, certain Epicurean themes are nevertheless evident, used in support of Cyrano's rationalist and atheist view of the world. This is particularly the case with the senses, where he takes over many of the ideas to be found in Lucretius, but without Montaigne's scepticism. For example, one of the principal characters on the moon, the Jeune Homme, expounds a theory of the senses based on atomism.[31] The narrator exclaims at the end of the Young Man's exposition: 'Un grand poète et philosophe de notre monde . . . a parlé après Epicure, et lui, après Démocrite, de ces petits corps presque comme vous' ('A great poet and thinker in our world . . . spoke, following Epicurus, and Epicurus following Democritus, about these atoms in almost the same terms as you'). Cyrano also subscribes to the Lucretian idea of the link between the shape of atoms and their pleasurable or disagreeable effect on the individual.

Thus, like Lucretius, Cyrano embraces a form of direct realism based on an atomistic theory of the senses and an essentially empirical view of knowledge. It is clear in the course of this narration that he accepts Galileo's theories of astronomy based on observation of the heavenly bodies. However,

---

[29] Montaigne 1978: 1110.
[30] For the influence of Lucretius on the *libertins* at large see Spink 1960.
[31] Cyrano de Bergerac 2000: I, 128–32.

in his desire to undermine religion and in particular Christianity, Cyrano puts forward as an ideal a view of the senses as a source of pleasure which goes beyond the Epicurean notion of pleasure as the *summum bonum*. For Epicurus and his followers there were two essential categories of pleasure, katastematic and kinetic. Katastematic pleasure is associated with a stable state of mind, caused by the absence of mental or physical pain, *aponia* and *ataraxia*. Without rejecting the importance of kinetic pleasure, Lucretius, like Epicurus, seems to privilege katastematic pleasure, which is less likely to destroy the tranquillity of soul necessary for happiness (*DRN* 4.862–9). Cyrano's moon-dwellers, on the other hand, require considerably more sophisticated kinetic pleasures, and the Young Man is quick to defend sexual gratification and to condemn celibacy. He argues that sexual stimulation is no more sinful than emptying the bowels, or than the contemplation of God by the devout, all of which activities involve pleasure.[32] Cyrano tends throughout to reduce all forms of pleasure to the same basic kind of *chatouillement* or titillation, in order to subvert any notion of nobility or greatness in human actions. For him, religious mysticism, the sexual act and defecation all come to the same thing. Thus he inverts the traditional hierarchy of the senses, in which sight was the highest form, by reducing all pleasure to a variation of the sense of touch. Cyrano embraces precisely those areas of Lucretian thought that Lambin had seen as most pernicious: the denial of the immortality of the soul, divine providence and religion; and the promotion of pleasure as the *summum bonum*.

How far this view deviates from more mainstream thinking in France can be shown by turning to Marolles's translation of Lucretius. Commenting on the section of *DRN* 4 which deals with sex, Marolles writes:

> J'auouë que i'ay eu de la peine à me resoudre à faire la traduction de la dernière partie de ce Liure, parce qu'elle contient vne matiere assez mal-aisée à exprimer de bonne grace, & honnestement dans le sens de l'Autheur.[33]

> I admit that I found it hard to determine to translate the last part of this book, because it contains material which is quite difficult to express decorously, and honestly according to the author's meaning.

In fact his translation glosses over many of the more contentious points, such as the possibility of homosexual desire, where he translates Lucretius' reference to the lover struck by 'a boy's effeminate limbs' ('siue puer membris muliebribus hunc iaculatur', *DRN* 4.1054) with deliberate vagueness – 'soit qu'il ait esté blessé de quelque Beauté rauissante, par des membres délicats'. Moreover, unlike Montaigne, Marolles feels uncertain about the whole of

---

[32] Cyrano de Bergerac 2000: I, 109.   [33] Marolles 1659: 475.

Book 3 on the nature of the soul, and he comments relatively little on it, excusing Lucretius by saying that even the finest minds are subject to error, 'and that it is in the most important matters that they often make the most serious mistakes'.[34]

Nevertheless, in making Lucretius available in the vernacular, Marolles may have helped to fuel the heterodoxy of other readers, including Molière, who is said to have embarked upon a verse translation of the *DRN* based on Marolles's prose version. Eliante's speech in the so-called 'Portrait scene' in *Le Misanthrope* (1666), II.iv.711–30, which offers a version of *DRN* 4.1149–65, provides us with an idea of how this might have turned out. But it is likely that Molière's debt to Lucretius, or at least to Epicureanism, went further than this.[35] In one of his darkest and most controversial plays, *Dom Juan*, the hero is presented not so much as an obsessive womaniser as a rationalistic Epicurean. Questioned by his inept and comic servant, Sganarelle, the nearest thing the play has to an apologist for traditional values, he exposes his views in Act III, Scene i, rejecting any belief in heaven, hell or the afterlife. This rejection of religion, and his devotion to a life based on pleasure, coupled nevertheless with a certain intellectual honesty, all ensure that he appears at the end of the play in a similar light to the Young Man at the end of Cyrano's *Voyage dans la lune*, who, having won the argument about the non-existence of God, is nevertheless carried off by 'un grand homme noir tout velu'.[36]

It is, then, the *libertins* in France who come closest to the spirit of Lucretius, both in their acceptance of empirically based knowledge and in their rejection of religion. The increasingly intrusive censorship of the period, however, meant that their ideas were largely confined to their own intellectual circles, and that lip service had to be paid in their published work to religion. However, Lucretian rationalism would remain a potent, if underground, force in France until the 1789 Revolution allowed it to come into its own.

Further reading

The general survey of Lucretius in sixteenth-century France by Fraisse 1962 systematically examines French poetry of the period, in particular Lucretius' influence in the second half of the century (a first chapter on the period from the twelfth to the fifteenth century precedes). For the following century Spink 1960 and Lennon 1993 usefully assess Gassendi as a purveyor of Epicureanism. For French scientific poetry, Schmidt 1970: 155–8 and 280–3 complements Fraisse. On individual authors, by far the most work

[34] Marolles 1659: 444.   [35] On Molière and Lucretius see further Calder 1996.
[36] Cyrano de Bergerac 2000: I, 158.

has been done on MONTAIGNE: Screech 1998 provides an edition of Montaigne's annotations to his Lambinus, and Ménager 1989 offers a general assessment of Montaigne's debt to the Roman poet. Several articles are devoted to the 'Apologie de Raimond Sebond' (Ferreyrolles 1976, Hendrick 1975, Wallace 1987), while other contributions deal with the essays more generally (Esclapez 1992, MacPhail 2000, Mathieu-Castellani 1988: 115–32; Moore 1967). Wiesmann 2004 provides a succinct introduction on the topic. Other sixteenth-century writers are dealt with by Morrison 1963 on RONSARD's copy of Lucretius, and Kany-Turpin 1991 on DU BARTAS. For CYRANO DE BERGERAC see Alcover 1970 as well as her introduction to Cyrano de Bergerac 2000. Calder 1996 plays down the importance of Lucretius in MOLIÈRE's *Le Misanthrope*.

15

STUART GILLESPIE

Lucretius in the English Renaissance

Anyone relying on the once standard 1934 study by Thomas Mayo, *Epicurus in England 1650–1725*, might well suppose there is little or nothing to say about the period with which this chapter deals. It was Mayo's understanding that English readers had no more than a general familarity with Epicurean doctrine or Lucretian exposition of it before 1656, the date at which, he held, John Evelyn's partial translation of the *DRN* and Walter Charleton's *Epicurus' Morals* first attracted serious attention to the subject in the wake of French apologists such as Gassendi.[1] Mayo's account posits a *volte-face* where a more gradual development is perceptible. While it may be true that Lucretius had had less impact on English writers than any other major Latin poet by 1650, he had been read and appreciated by an important minority. And while he is not a mainstream figure in English culture before the mid seventeenth century, Dryden is still apologising for translating him in 1685.[2] This discussion will examine the long-standing and diffuse interest in Lucretius as poet and philosopher in Britain before the second half of the seventeenth century and suggest some of the reasons for its previous neglect. The story is taken forward from about 1650 in two further essays in this volume.[3]

To be sure, evidence of neglect of, or hostility towards, Lucretius down to this date can easily be assembled. Some references to the *DRN* are indeed second-hand, some ill-informed, and some hostile. There is a serious dearth of recent editions and commentaries on Lucretius in British libraries and book inventories from this period – scarcely a single documented example of the work of Jansson, or Pareus, or Nardi is to be found.[4] While Lucretius is often included among the lists of authors in the Elizabethan arts of poetry,

---

[1] Mayo 1934: xi.   [2] For Dryden see pp. 250–60, 263–6 below.
[3] Ch. 16 immediately following, and the section of ch. 9 on mid-seventeenth-century England.
[4] For these editions and commentaries see C. A. Gordon 1962. It is possible that more copies of such texts were in circulation than were recorded in contemporary documents.

this counts for little since the usual purpose is merely to exemplify the 'scientific' poet.[5] Sir John Davies pokes fun at atomism in his poem *Orchestra*, 1596; the next year Richard Hooker shakes his head over Lucretius' denial of the soul's immortality; Henry More is still condemning Lucretius' 'putid Muse' half a century later.[6] But it would be unsurprising to find such hostility in many other places and times down to the twentieth century; equally unsurprising is its frequent clerical provenance (Luther and Calvin had already helped to make Epicurus infamous).[7] Even those who condemn Lucretius in one context can regularly be found praising him in another (Henry More is an example). And the common prejudice did not affect all English readers. Hooker condemns not Lucretius alone, but the 'English Saduccees' who accepted his arguments on the mortality of the soul; Lucretius had his supporters, and many more positive references to the *DRN* are in evidence too. In fact, English figures whom we know read Lucretius at first hand, and with interest or explicit approbation, happen to include many of the most eminent writers and thinkers of the early to mid seventeenth century: Sir Thomas Browne, George Chapman, John Donne, Thomas Hobbes, Ben Jonson, John Milton[8] and Thomas Stanley. Edmund Spenser, England's epic poet of the preceding century, also belongs in this category. To these very major literary figures could be added such names as Sir Edward Dering, Abraham Fraunce, Abraham Fleming and George Sandys.[9] Even before Evelyn's English version had made any progress in the world, at least three other translators seem to have purposed or completed – though not published – full English versions of the *DRN*.[10] And, as we shall see, among natural philosophers

---

[5] Ascham is an example, his reference to Lucretius in *The Scholemaster*, Book 2, failing to imply first-hand acquaintance. However, C. T. Harrison 1934: 2n. considers it 'likely' that Puttenham, author of the 1589 *Arte of English Poesie*, read Lucretius.

[6] Hooker, *Ecclesiastical Polity*, 5.2; More, *Psychathanasia*, 1.1.6. For the suggestion that Davies's anti-Epicurean *Nosce Teipsum* was specifically intended as an answer to *DRN* 3, see C. T. Harrison 1934: 13–14.

[7] The attitudes of the preachers Launcelot Andrewes, Joseph Hall and William Perkins are described by C. T. Harrison 1934: 9–10; for a range of other 'ordinary pulpiteers' see Allen 1944: 2.

[8] For Milton see pp. 268–70 below.

[9] Dering's library inventory includes an up-to-date Lucretius edition; a short translation from Lucretius by Fleming appears in Scot 1584: 487–8; Fraunce cites Lucretius several times in *The Third Part of the Countesse of Pembrokes Yuychurche*; Sandys is discussed below.

[10] Evelyn's translation of 1656 was evidently not a fast-moving commodity: in his preface he offered to add the rest to the Book 1 he first published if it received encouragement, but nothing more was printed. Lucy Hutchinson's unpublished translation of the 1650s is discussed in ch. 16 of the present volume. A complete English prose version, probably pre-1650s (*pace* de Quehen 1996a: 237), remains in manuscript in the Bodleian Library, Oxford (MS Rawlinson D.134). A proposed verse translation by Alexander Brome, the translator

and scientists are found collaborative traditions of Lucretianism in the first half of the seventeenth century. Sir Francis Bacon, Lord Herbert of Cherbury, Sir Kenelm Digby and Thomas Hariot all register appreciatively his direct influence.[11]

Something of an epitome of the mixed, and changing, reputation attaching to Epicurean ideas in this period is provided by the history of one book, an introductory work published by an English author in Paris in 1601. Nicholas Hill (1570–c. 1610), a sometime Oxford scholar, college fellow, and Catholic convert once associated with Robert Bassett, a would-be usurper of the English throne, was responsible for only one published volume: his *Philosophia Epicurea, Democritiana, Theophrastica proposita simpliciter non edocta*, printed in Paris in 1601. This disorderly sequence of 509 propositions in natural philosophy may have been intended as a tribute to the memory of Giordano Bruno, who was burned at the stake in 1600, and to whose thinking Hill was committed. It adopted Bruno's (and Lucretius') doctrines of atomism, the eternity of matter, the infinity of the universe and the plurality of worlds. At a more fundamental level it mixed the ideas of the atomists, Aristotle, Hermes Trismegistus and Copernicus. But Hill was careful to deflect attention from his dangerous allegiances, to stress the tentative nature of his observations, and to declare himself willing to destroy his work if anything in it was found contrary to the Catholic faith (Hill's atoms are created and ordered by God). As an extra precaution, 'if he published the book in Catholic Paris, the centre of Lullian studies, he sought safety for himself in protestant Rotterdam'.[12] Hill's work seems at first to have attracted no attention in England except as a target for mockery: Ben Jonson laughed in one of his epigrams (133) at his 'atomi ridiculous'. But following a 1619 reprint the book was taken somewhat more seriously, and condemned by the French monk Marin Mersenne in his attack on Bruno and the deists in the 1620s. Then, with Galileo and Gassendi's promotion of atomism, Hill's reputation staged a posthumous recovery. About 1636, Anthony à Wood tells us, his unpublished papers 'concerning the eternity, infinity, &c of the

---

of Horace, either was never commenced or does not survive (see Norbrook 2000: 192, and p. 256 below).

[11] For the scientific tradition as a whole see Kargon 1966 and C. T. Harrison 1934, who between them cover all the individuals named here.

[12] H. Trevor-Roper, *Oxford Dictionary of National Biography*, s.v. 'Hill, Nicholas'. I draw on Trevor-Roper's biography in the rest of this paragraph. For description of the *Philosophia* volume see C. T. Harrison 1934: 5, or more fully McColley 1940. A copy of Hill's book which seems to have passed through the hands of both Jonson and Donne is preserved in the Middle Temple: see J. Sparrow, *TLS* 5 August 1955: 451, and Keynes 1973: 271.

world' were felt important enough for copies to be made.[13] The famous Bishop Wilkins cited one of his propositions in 1638. About the same year Robert Burton twice discussed Hill's book in his *Anatomy of Melancholy*.[14] Thereafter he was more widely quoted with approval, respected as a precursor (however wayward), and in the 1660s described by John Aubrey as 'one of the most learned men of his time, a great mathematician and philosopher and traveller and poet'.[15]

Alongside the equivocal figure of Hill lies a range of English Lucretians stretching back to the Middle Ages. It is tempting to begin a roll-call of literary names with Chaucer, because the springtime energy of the General Prologue to the *Canterbury Tales* may ultimately derive by indirect routes from Lucretius' Book 1 exordium.[16] The first point at which a Lucretian moment conclusively arrives in a work of English literature, however, is the anonymous 24-line translation from the start of *DRN* 2 printed in the famous 1557 anthology *Tottel's Miscellany* under the title 'The felicitie of a mind imbracing vertue, that beholdeth the wretched desyres of the worlde' and beginning 'When dreadful swelling seas, through boisterous windy blastes | So tosse the shippes, that al for nought, serues ancor sayle and mastes'.[17] This is not quite a mere curiosity: it is not unworthy of its time as a version of the Lucretian text, though most readers would not have recognised the source, and the translator himself would probably have encountered it as an excerpt only. In any case, it pales in significance if placed beside the first major English poet's use of Lucretius – Chaucer excepted – a generation later in the 1590s. Spenser, who as it happens pays his tribute to Chaucer in terms borrowed from Lucretius' praise of Epicurus, notes that even Chaucer drew back from the task of describing Nature.[18] It is in this regard, it has been felt, that Lucretius, the poet of physical law, assumes his main significance for Spenser. Yet Spenser's indebtedness to Lucretius has been hotly disputed, with the English poet's orthodoxy perceived to be at stake.

There is no disputing that as well as many individual local allusions, not necessarily indicative in themselves of any unusual commitment to Lucretius,

---

[13] A. Wood 1815: II, 87.

[14] For details on Wilkins and Burton see McColley 1940: 404–5.

[15] Aubrey 1949: 256.

[16] For Chaucer see Edgecombe 2000, but more sceptically on the Middle Ages in general, ch. 12 above.

[17] Tottel 1557: T4^v. It should be noted that because Tottel collected previously completed works, the date of composition of this translation could easily be pre-1550.

[18] Spenser's praise of Chaucer is at *Faerie Queene* 4.2.34 and the further comment at 7.7.9. This poem is quoted throughout from Smith and de Selincourt 1909–10. For Lucretius' praise of Epicurus see *DRN* 3.1–30.

Spenser draws on the *DRN* as a source in connection with his marked interest in the story of Venus and Adonis. He uses Lucretius for his Garden of Adonis in Canto 3.6 of *The Faerie Queene*, and directly translates or paraphrases the proem to Book 1 in a 36-line passage (4.10.44–7).[19] I shall focus on the latter, which is more than a simple translation since Spenser overgoes or exaggerates Lucretius in his delighted response to the Latin exordium – in his own celebration of the power of Venus. The 'ship-bearing' (*nauigerum*, 3) seas that Lucretius' Venus calms become in Spenser's reworking 'raging seas', which on Venus' arrival do not merely 'laugh' (*rident*, 8) but 'play'. The heavens do more than shine (*diffuso lumine caelum*, 9), they 'laugh'. And 'al the world', Spenser adds emphatically, 'shews ioyous cheare'. This is the first of the four *Faerie Queene* stanzas involved:

> Great *Venus*, Queene of beautie and of grace,
>   The ioy of Gods and men, that vnder skie
> Doest fayrest shine, and most adorne thy place,
>   That with thy smyling looke doest pacifie
>   The raging seas, and makst the stormes to flie;
> Thee goddesse, thee the winds, the clouds doe feare,
>   And when thou spreadst thy mantle forth on hie,
>   The waters play and pleasant lands appeare,
> And heauens laugh, and al the world shews ioyous cheare.
>
>   (4.10.44)

To judge by the feeling of this passage, Spenser's response to Lucretius is warmly and deeply positive, and further probing of his Lucretian allusions would yield more evidence of this warmth. A certain twentieth-century reluctance to recognise this has been associated, in a kind of rerun of the typical Renaissance reaction to the *DRN*, with anxiety about the compatibility of such an attitude on Spenser's part with Christian orthodoxy.[20] But the results of such investigation might point in more than one direction. In the last stanza of this passage Spenser writes:

> So all the world by thee at first was made,
>   And dayly yet thou doest the same repayre:
> Ne ought on earth that merry is and glad,
>   Ne ought on earth that louely is and fayre,

---

[19] See also Esolen 1993 for the suggestion of Lucretian influence on the account of Venus and Mars in the Bower of Bliss episode of *Faerie Queene* 2.

[20] For an account of the controversies sparked by Greenlaw 1920 see Esolin 1994: 49–50, whose summary of the motivation of Greenlaw's opponents is that 'all were determined to save Spenser from heresy'.

But thou the same for pleasure didst prepare.
Great God of men and women, queene of th'ayre,
Mother of laughter, and welspring of blisse,
O graunt that of my loue at last I may not misse.

(4.10.47)

The unusual word in this context, 'repayre', distantly echoes another passage
in the *DRN*: old must give way to new, Lucretius urges, and 'must make
afresh new things out of others' – *ex aliis aliud reparare necessest* (3.965).
These two usages indicate both overlap and distance between the two poets'
portrayals of physical law. For Lucretius, the earth can be 'repaired' but will
eventually die, to create other earths. But this is not part of Spenser's meaning
here. Perhaps his 'repayre' means only 'to supply the means by which the
physical world continues'. But there are signs that, in a fashion not unfamiliar
in Renaissance poetry, Spenser has imaginatively linked his classical deity
with the Christian one. For one thing, there is no reference whatever in
Lucretius to Venus as creator of the world (his Venus merely 'governs' it –
gubernas, 1.21); indeed, Lucretius' denial of the teleological creation was
one of the principal difficulties Christianity had with his poem. If we do
understand the word 'repayre' in a Christian context, then 'it acquires a
theological connotation, since the fact that things fall apart is linked with . . .
sin'.[21] To 'repair the world' thus implies 'to redeem the moral world' – and
the love which created the earth, and which Spenser now prays for, begins to
look assimilable to Christian doctrine. Spenser, clearly, not only uses aspects
of Lucretius that harmonise with Christian teaching, such as mutability, but
also embraces some that do not. However, anxieties about this mixture seem
to be more the property of commentators (of certain eras) than of Spenser
himself.

Among the poets of the earlier seventeenth century, we are told, 'it is
undoubtedly the Spenserians who owe most to the Lucretian strain'.[22] If
so, this is not owing to any example set by Spenser but to an intermediary source which he, like his followers, admired. The route by which this
'strain' travelled was the French poet Du Bartas, the earlier parts of whose
ornate scriptural epic *La Sepmaine* (1578), an enormously learned account
of creation, draw on the *DRN*. Du Bartas mentions Lucretius frequently
and often hostilely. Yet while complaining of the ignorance of Lucretius'
explanation for magnetism, he actually makes use of it; and though he vehe-
mently rejects creation by chance, his description of the warring elements
clearly resembles that of Lucretius. Du Bartas, that is, paraphrases the *DRN*

[21] Esolen 1994: 48.   [22] C. T. Harrison 1934: 14.

freely, and without acknowledgement.[23] *La Sepmaine* was enormously popular in England, partly because of Du Bartas's Protestant convictions, and a complete rendering by Joshua Sylvester (published 1592–1608, under the eventual title *Devine Weekes and Workes*) became the definitive English version, being reprinted for many decades. Its popularity means it can be taken for granted that a number of poets of the earlier seventeenth century would indeed have made indirect contact with Lucretius through Sylvester's Du Bartas, and the minor poets Sir John Davies, Edward Benlowes, William Alexander and Richard James are among those whose links have been traced already.[24] Such names command little attention today. But Milton knew his Sylvester too, as well as his Lucretius, and *Paradise Lost* undoubtedly shows the effects. These lie chronologically outside the scope of the present discussion, but for one example we need venture no further than the opening passage of the poem (1.19–21), invoking the Holy Spirit: 'thou from the first | Wast present, and with mighty wings outspread | Dove-like sat'st brooding on the vast abyss'. Behind this lies Sylvester's rendering of Du Bartas's opening lines, in which the Lucretian void has been dispensed with in favour of the biblical account of how 'the spirit eternal' appeared to 'brood' over chaos (9–10).[25]

Within a few decades of Spenser's *Faerie Queene* there appeared two more extensive, if fragmentary, sets of English translations from Lucretius.[26] John Florio's 1603 translation of Montaigne's *Essays* incorporated English renderings of Montaigne's many quotations from the *DRN*.[27] The second is hardly ever remembered today but deserves a better fate. It came from the hand of George Sandys, the English writer now best known as the early translator of Ovid's *Metamorphoses* (but who also Englished Virgil, the Psalms, the Book of Job and Hugo Grotius). Sandys, who evidently had a close knowledge of the *DRN*, was responsible for translating over two hundred lines of it between 1615 and 1632, but his versions consist of some seventeen dispersed passages appearing incidentally within two other works, the majority in his *Metamorphoses* translation. This, in its final form of 1632, was accompanied by extensive commentaries following each Book, one feature of which is the quotation and accompanying verse translation of other Latin

---

[23] For Du Bartas's response to Lucretius see further p. 229 above, and references there, esp. Whitaker 1936.

[24] C. T. Harrison 1934: 17–18.

[25] For the analogue, supported by repetition of the word 'brood' in Sylvester's preceding lines, see A. Fowler 1998 ad loc.

[26] For a further fragmentary translation of the earlier seventeenth century see P. L. Barbour 1962, who wrongly claims it is the first in English.

[27] For Montaigne see pp. 153–5 and 236–8 above.

authors, in a fashion best demonstrated by an example. Figure 15.1 shows part of a page of the commentary following Book 4 of the *Metamorphoses*. Sandys is led naturally to quote Lucretius in discussing the story of Salmacis and Hermaphroditus. First he glosses it (on the previous page) with the *Remedia Amoris*, then with the analysis of the passion of love in Book 4 of the *DRN*. The Latin text is in the margin, but Sandys's translations are given more prominence typographically. He expresses admiration for Lucretius' accuracy in depicting human emotion: 'Salmacis clinges about the surprized youth like a serpent, till both become one body. The reason why louers so strictly imbrace, is to incorporate with the beloued, which sith they cannot, can neuer be satisfied. Thus with the vanity and vexation thereof to the life expressed by Lucretius.' A wide range of other classical authors is deployed in Sandys's notes – there is nothing exclusive about his interest in the *DRN* – but such expressions of approbation enforce the impression of a marked enthusiasm for the poet. The translation that follows is in decent English verse of which the excessive compression is understandable once we realise it has been composed, as was common in Sandys's time, on a line-for-line principle. So much can be said of all the Lucretian verse translated by Sandys, since there is never more than a single line of discrepancy between the length of the English and of the corresponding Latin passage.

Sandys has recently been called a 'personally enigmatic and generally marginalized' figure.[28] His writings have seldom received much recognition. We know nothing of how or why he developed his knowledge of Lucretius, but it is interesting that Dryden, Lucretius' greatest English translator, came late in life to think of him as 'the ingenious and learned Sandys', 'the best versifier' of the earlier seventeenth century – having condemned his work in earlier comments.[29] At his best Sandys is capable of verse which, if it does not rival Dryden's, is a match for Creech's:

> O wretched minds of men! depriud of light!
> Through what great dangers, o[n] hou dark a night,
> Force you your weary lives! and cannot see
> How Nature onely craues a body free
> From hated paine; a chearefull Mind possest
> Of safe delights, by care nor feare opprest.[30]

---

[28] Andrea 2004: 1.

[29] Dryden, Preface to *Fables Ancient and Modern*, quoted from Hammond and Hopkins (1995–2005): v, 48–9. For Dryden's earlier comments see the Dedication to *Examen Poeticum*.

[30] Sandys 1632: 512, translating *DRN* 2.14–19. For Creech see ch. 16 below.

160   VPON THE FOVRTH BOOKE OF

Salmacis clinges about the surpriz'ed youth like a serpent, till both become one body. The reason why louers so strictly imbrace, is to incorporate with the beloued, which sith they cannot, can neuer be satisfied. Thus with the vanity and vexation thereof to the life expressed by Lucretius.

The louers ardor in inconstancy
Of error strayes, while they their loues inioy.
Their eyes and hands still shift from place to place:
Who hurt what they too eagerly imbrace,
Stifle with kisses, and their soft lips bite
With ravenous teeth, in that no pure delight.
Wherein those stings ly hid which vrge them so
To hurt th'affected whence their furies grow.
But Venus gently mitigates those ills:
And pleasant balme into the wound distills.
For hope, sprung from one fountaine with desire,
Thinks with that beauty to asswage her fire;
Which natures selfe resists: The more possest,
The more desire loue inflames the tortur'd brest.
For meate and drinke into the body ta'ne,
Because in proper places they remaine,
Our thirst and hunger easily subdew:
But in a humane forme and rosiat hew
The aery image is inioyd alone:
Which by our vanisht hopes away is blowne
As those who sleeping striue to drinke, yet get
No water to asswage their inward heat
But seeke the shadow, labour in their dreams;
And thirst amidst th'imaginary streames:
So louers loue deludes with Imagry:
Nor can they satisfie their longing eye;
Nor yet their hands, still griping here and there,
One iot from that beloued body beare.
For this, when first they glow with heat of loue,
And Venus misteries desire to proue;
They greedily imbrace, ioyne mouthes, inspire
Their soules, and bite through ardor of desire:
In vaine; since nothing they can thence translate,
Nor wholy enter and incorporate.
For so sometimes they would, so striue to doe:
And cleaue so close as if no longer two,

Plato recites a fable, how man at the first was created double, and for his arrogancy dissected into male and female: the reason of their affected coniunction, as coueting to returne to their originall: an obscure notion (as we haue formerly written) of Eva's being taken out of the side of Adam. So Hermaphroditus and Salmacis retaine in one person both sexes: of whom the like are called Hermaphrodites. Aristotle writes that they haue the right brest of a man; and the left of a woman, wherewith they nourish their children. They were to choose what sex they would vse, and punished with death if they changed at any time. One not long since burned
for

Figure 15.1. George Sandys, *Ovid's Metamorphoses Englished, Mythologized, and Represented in Figures* (Oxford, 1632), p. 160

As already noted, most of Sandys's translations of the *DRN* are found in his Ovid, but he had also been interested enough in Lucretius to translate him – again in line-for-line pentameter couplets – in his publication of 1615, *A Relation of a Journey begun an. Dom. 1610*. In this memoir of travels through the Ottoman empire it is most often Lucretius on the natural world that engages Sandys's attention. It is this side of the *DRN* that is relevant to the use of Lucretius in natural philosophy in this period, to which this discussion now turns.

The greatest of the Renaissance English 'virtuosi', the wealthy amateurs committed to the advancement of the new philosophy, was Henry Percy (1564–1632), ninth Earl of Northumberland (and descendant of Shakespeare's Hotspur). Possessed of a large fortune at the age of twenty-one, Percy played patron or friend to some highly distinguished scientists: Thomas Hariot, mathematician, physicist and astronomer; Robert Hues, author of *De Globorum Usu*; Walter Warner, mathematician and physicist; Nathaniel Torperley. Nothing of scientific interest was published by the group while still in existence, but inference tells us its members were 'the only English school to combine Copernicanism with that complete rejection of Aristotelianism which accompanies acceptance of the atomic philosophy of Democritus, Epicurus and Lucretius'.[31] Other contacts of Percy's included individuals we have already encountered: John Donne and Nicholas Hall. Sir Walter Ralegh, sometime translator of Epicurus, was another. Unfortunately, Percy's cousin Thomas was deeply implicated in the Gunpowder Plot, and through him, on flimsy evidence, Henry Percy was convicted of treason in 1606. He served sixteen years in the Tower of London, but was not prevented from continuing his studies, and was even able to set up facilities for his scientific friends.

Francis Bacon's relationship to the Percy group is of special interest in the present connection, since the development of Bacon's interests in the ancient atomists around 1605 coincides with close contact with the circle. Whether or not there is a cause-and-effect relationship,[32] Bacon showed himself in the years 1605–12, in the *Cogitationes de natura rerum*, the *De principiis atque originibus*, and in the works added to his *Essays* in 1612, strongly inclined towards atomism, declaring it a 'necessity plainly inevitable', and embraced too the concept of the void.[33] Bacon even felt that atomic theory reinforced religious belief: 'that school which is most accused of Atheisme

---

[31] Kargon 1966: 7; for further discussion of the Northumberland circle see pp. 6–17, to which the present discussion is indebted.

[32] See Kargon 1966: 43–4, who concedes (43) that 'it would be presumptious to claim that either Hariot or the Earl of Northumberland was in any way the cause' of Bacon's atomistic interests.

[33] Bacon, *Cogitationes de Natura Rerum* in Bacon 1857–74: III, 15.

doth demonstrate religion', he claimed in the essay 'Of Atheism', since it is incredible that 'an army of infinite small portions or seeds' could produce order 'without a divine marshal'.[34] Bacon was to discard the atomic view of matter a little later: his main works favouring it – the *Cogitationes* and *De principiis* – went unpublished for many years after his death in 1626. It is significant that they saw the light of day in the 1650s, for this was probably directly owing to continental interest in atomism in the 1640s. Bacon's unprinted manuscripts were left to Sir William Boswell, literary patron and ambassador to the Netherlands from 1633 until his death in 1650. Boswell, who was linked to Descartes and Gassendi through John Pell and other sources, 'in order to further Bacon's good name, and more probably, in order to establish *English* precedence in the revival of atomism . . . publish[ed] Bacon's atomic works in 1653. Hence Bacon, despite his mature opposition to atomism, through the publication of his atomic works at a crucial time contributed to the acceptance of atomism in England'.[35] There is unusual aptness in Abraham Cowley's use of Lucretius' praise of Epicurus (*DRN* 1.62–79) for his eulogy of Bacon ('To the Royal Society').[36]

The further history of English atomism is bound up with another circle of thinkers. Thomas Hobbes and a group of English *emigrés* in the 1640s – the Newcastle circle, so called after William Cavendish, then Marquis of Newcastle – were important mediators for Descartes's and Gassendi's ideas.[37] Yet Sir William Boswell was right to feel that English thinkers had in some ways anticipated continental scholarship. One more individual demands brief mention in this connection, though he seems not to belong very comfortably with either the scientific or the poetic Lucretians of the earlier seventeenth century: Robert Burton.

Burton called himself 'Democritus Junior', and if we consult the index of one of the standard nineteenth-century editions of his *Anatomy of Melancholy* we find some eighteen references to the 'laughing philosopher'. Against Lucretius' name, however, is printed the single word '*passim*'.[38] In the *Anatomy* (first edition 1621, expanded down to 1651) Burton uses Lucretius' phrasing and quotes freely from the *DRN*. He is especially impressed by the depiction of man's miserable state and the follies to which the fear of death

---

[34] Bacon 1857–74: VI, 413.   [35] Kargon 1966: 53.

[36] For other aspects of Bacon's use of Lucretius see C. T. Harrison 1933: 192–200 and ch. 9 above.

[37] This episode is touched upon in ch. 9 above, and recounted more fully in Kargon 1966: 54–78.

[38] So the Bohn library text, Burton 1893. The latest edition of the *Anatomy* (Bamborough and Dodsworth 2000: VI, 379) enumerates some thirty references to Lucretius.

may lead.[39] Like most of the other writers glanced at above, he has not swallowed Lucretius wholesale, and complains of his mortalism. But Burton adds a new element on the other side of the balance sheet too, in observing that the Lucretian-Epicurean tradition has from the start been subject to misrepresentation, and its teaching unfairly caricatured. He is, perhaps, the first English writer to point out that rejecting these falsifications is a necessary precondition for a fair hearing:

> A quiet mind is that *voluptas*, or *Summum bonum* of *Epicurus*, *non dolere*, *curis vacare, animo tranquillo esse*, not to grieve, but to want cares, and have a quiet soule, is the only pleasure of the World, as *Seneca* truly recites his opinion, not that of eating and drinking, which injurious *Aristotle* malitiously puts upon him, and for which he is still mistaken, *malè audit & vapulat*, slandred without a cause, and lashed by all posterity.[40]

The popularity of Burton's *Anatomy* must have meant that at least some ordinary English readers were induced to question the received understanding of Lucretius and Epicurus well before the arrival of Gassendi and Descartes.[41]

Further reading

The nearest approach to a general treatment of the period to 1650 is C. T. Harrison 1934, but this, though useful for individual detail, espouses a view similar to Mayo's, that during the early Restoration period from 1660 Lucretius 'passed within a few years from being quite generally despised or ignored to being studied and esteemed' (72). Cherchi's 1995 narrative begins largely with Evelyn. Kargon 1966 deals with the tradition of atomism in the earlier seventeenth century as far as natural philosophy is concerned. For writers not discussed in any detail above, the following sources may be useful: Hirsch 1991, including suggestions of specific Lucretian echoes in Donne's verse; Herford and Simpson 1925–63: I, 255–8, on Jonson's extensive annotations to his copy of Lucretius; and Allen 1944, on Thomas Stanley's *History of Philosophy* – 'a curious patchwork of Epicurus' letters and Lucretius's poem'.

---

[39] See for example Bamborough and Dodsworth 2000: I, 271, 281, 334, 430–1.
[40] Bamborough and Dodsworth 2000: II, 99; the editors pass no comment on Burton's making Aristotle follow Epicurus in time.
[41] For the suggestion that Burton made an impression on Evelyn, perhaps particularly through his digression 'On the Rational Soul' (*Anatomy* 1.1.2.9), see Repetzki 2000: xxix.

16

DAVID HOPKINS

The English voices of Lucretius from Lucy Hutchinson to John Mason Good

This chapter considers the ways in which writers from the mid seventeenth to the late eighteenth century sought to give Lucretius an English poetic voice. Considerable attention will be paid to translations of the *DRN*, in whole or part, but the discussion will also explore the ways in which specific passages from the *DRN*, or the poem's larger structures and rhetorics, were more obliquely approached by English poets. The focus is thus on specifically literary responses to Lucretius, rather than on the larger role of the *DRN* in disseminating Epicurean ideas in England. A distinction between 'poetic' and 'philosophical' responses to Lucretius can never be absolute, however. English poets and critics regularly affirmed their admiration for Lucretius' 'poetry' while deploring his 'philosophy'. But is it possible to write convincing Lucretian poetry without displaying, or betraying, at least some sympathy for the Roman poet's ideas? And can English poets, whatever their philosophical sympathies, convey anything of Lucretius' poetic quality without being themselves poets of comparable stature?

One leading translator-poet of this period, John Dryden, was convinced that successful translation depends as much on the translator's own poetic gifts as on his knowledge of his original, and that a translator must feel some affinity with what he called the 'genius' or 'soul' of the source-author. But Dryden simultaneously, and paradoxically, stressed the importance of respecting the alterity of one's original by conveying its 'distinguishing character': the individuating features which crucially differentiate it from the productions of other poets, and which must be preserved if a translation is genuinely to resemble its original.[1] For Dryden, successful translation characteristically occurs when the translator feels simultaneously intimate with and at some distance from his source.

---

[1] See Preface to *Sylvae*, Dryden 1956–2000: III, 5–6. All subsequent quotations from Dryden below are taken from this edition, cited as 'Dryden'.

Only three poetic responses to Lucretius in this period, it will be suggested – one (Dryden's rendering of five episodes from the *DRN*) a translation in the normally accepted sense of the term, the other two (John Milton's *Paradise Lost* and Alexander Pope's *Essay on Man*) responses of a more oblique or refracted kind, in which admiration for the Roman poet is balanced by a degree of sceptical distance – attain an artistic quality comparable to their original. And while other poetic responses render, or offer insight into, particular aspects of Lucretius' art, it is only in these three works that Lucretius is given a sustainedly, convincingly English poetic voice – albeit one which is sometimes made to utter sentiments that would have surprised Lucretius himself.

The first near-complete English verse translation of Lucretius – composed in the 1650s, though remaining in manuscript for over three centuries – was that of the Puritan poet and biographer Lucy Hutchinson (1620–81).[2] Some years after completing her translation, Hutchinson firmly dissociated herself from any involvement with Lucretius' 'atheisms and impieties', and repented of the 'youthfull curiositie' which had led her to 'amus[e] [her] selfe with such vaine Philosophy'.[3] But by the 1670s Lucretian Epicureanism had become associated with the (to Hutchinson, repellent) libertinism of the Restoration court, and it seems likely that Hutchinson's remarkable pioneering engagement with Lucretius, the product of a tradition of learned Puritan humanism, had originally been more open-minded than her later remarks suggest.[4] Hutchinson's hostility to Lucretius' theology seems to have been counterbalanced by an attraction to his intellectual radicalism, and particularly his scathing attacks on warmongering, priestcraft, superstition and courtly luxury: she was to recycle some of Lucretius' anti-court sentiments in *Order and Disorder*, the Christian epic poem of her last years.[5] She may also have been motivated by a desire to emulate the neo-Epicurean writing currently fashionable in the royalist Cavendish circle, and had perhaps at one stage conceived of her translation of Lucretius as a tacit rebuke to the royalist writers John Evelyn, who she thought had failed to complete the

---

[2] Hutchinson omitted the treatment of love from *DRN* 4. For the date of her translation see de Quehen 1996a: 10–11.
[3] de Quehen 1996a: 23; the remarks occur in the dedication of her manuscript to Arthur Annesley, first Earl of Anglesey, in 1675.
[4] See Norbrook 2000, on which the discussion below draws.
[5] See L. Hutchinson 2001: xvii–xix.

task, and Alexander Brome, who had apparently ignored the challenge to undertake it.[6]

The translation by the diarist Evelyn, of which Book 1, the only part to be printed in his lifetime, appeared in 1656,[7] was clearly inspired by Pierre Gassendi's recent reassessment of Epicureanism and by the appearance in 1650 of Michel de Marolles's French translation of the *DRN*.[8] But, despite an admiration for Lucretius' descriptive and expository powers, and for some aspects of his moral teaching,[9] Evelyn was from the start openly hostile to Lucretius' religious views. He told Jeremy Taylor that he would use the substantial commentary on his translation to 'provide against all the ill consequences' of Lucretius' opinions,[10] and seems to have had little personal commitment to Lucretius' atomistic view of nature. Some contemporaries were favourably impressed by the translation, the poet Edmund Waller proclaiming that Evelyn's *Essay on the First Book* presented '*Lucretius* whole . . . | His Words, his Musick, and his mind',[11] and another courtly poet, Sir Richard Fanshawe, telling Evelyn in a private letter that his version was '*Lucretius* himself'; it avoids his 'Hayvinesse' yet 'it hath both his Soule and his Lineaments'. [12] But as his work proceeded, Evelyn appears to have become increasingly anxious about the potentially dangerous effects of an English Lucretius on modern morality. In the first of his manuscript comments on *DRN* 3 he expressed his intention of offering 'som Antidote against the Poyson of the Errors, which our Author, here striues to convey vnder all the gildings of Poetry and Arte'.[13] And by 1657–8 he had abandoned any attempt to publish the full version, later telling Meric Casaubon that the manuscript now lay 'in the dust of [his] study, where 'tis likely to be for ever buried'.[14]

The next full-length English Lucretius – and the first to appear in print – was that of the brilliant young Oxford don Thomas Creech (1659–1700), published in 1682. It was an instant success, going through two further editions in the next two years, and becoming the standard full-length English Lucretius throughout the eighteenth century.[15] In the preface to his first edition Creech forthrightly listed the poetic virtues that make Lucretius 'extream difficult to be follow'd':

[6] See Norbrook 2000b: 191–2; Battegli 1998: 40, 49–50; Rees 2000.
[7] The rest remained in manuscript until Repetzki 2000. Book 2 was completed, but is now lost. Like Hutchinson, Evelyn omits the end of *DRN* 4.
[8] See M. Hunter 1995, on which the discussion below draws.
[9] See the notes quoted by M. Hunter 1995: 88, and Repetzki 2000: l–lii.
[10] Letter of 1657, quoted in M. Hunter 1995: 90.   [11] Evelyn 1656: 4.
[12] Fanshawe 1997–9: I, 333–4.   [13] Repetzki 2000: xl–xli.   [14] M. Hunter 1995: 87.
[15] For the bibliographical history see C. A. Gordon 1962: 174–80.

any man ... may perceive that he is *elegant* in his kind; curious and exact in his *images*, happy in *disposition*, flowing, even to *satiety*, in *Instances*, of a brisk and ready Witt, pointed in Satyrs, severe in taunts, grave in precepts, quick and vivacious in his discourses, and every way fitted for his bold attempt.[16]

But, like Evelyn before him, Creech used his preliminaries and notes to repudiate many of Lucretius' sentiments.[17] His own translation was justified, he argued, since 'the best Method to overthrow the *Epicurean Hypothesis* ... is to expose a full System of it to publick view',[18] and Nahum Tate praised Creech precisely for his ability to combine a scrupulous presentation of Lucretius' thought with a salutary correction of his 'Errors', thus providing an effective 'Antidote' 'for his Poyson'.[19] But some commentators thought that Creech sympathised with the sentiments of his original to a greater degree than he was prepared to admit. In the preface to his own Latin edition of the Roman poet (1695), Creech himself admitted to loving Lucretius *fere plus aequo* ('almost more than is right'), and when he committed suicide in 1700, some observers attributed his action, admiringly or contemptuously, to an obsession with Lucretius so intense that it had provoked him to emulate the Latin poet's own fabled end.[20]

Over a century was to pass before the next full verse translation of Lucretius by John Mason Good (1764–1827), a professional physician who supplemented his medical salary with scientific and poetic writing. Encouraged by friends, including Lucretius' editor Gilbert Wakefield, Good began his translation in 1797, composing it 'in the streets of London during [his] extensive walks, to visit his numerous patients'.[21] It was finished by 1799, but the preparation of extensive notes delayed publication until 1805. As a scientist and devoted student of philosophy, Good was clearly attracted by the most celebrated ancient exposition of atomism, a theory which 'at last appears to have obtained an eternal triumph, from its application, by Newton and Huygens, to the department of natural philosophy, and, by Locke and Condillac, to that of metaphysics'.[22] He was, moreover, disposed – in ways that may be coloured by his Unitarian leanings at the time – to see a far greater degree of compatibility than most of his predecessors between Lucretian Epicureanism and Christianity. Though he concedes that 'Epicurus and his disciples disbelieved in a future state', this can, he thinks, 'be no impeachment of [their] wisdom or virtue' since, without the scriptural revelation of

---

[16] Creech 1682: b4[r].   [17] See Mayo 1934: 65–71.
[18] Creech 1682: b2[r].   [19] Creech 1683a: d1[r].
[20] See Mayo 1934: 103; Real 1970: 29. For an admiring response, see Wycherley 1718: 210–11; for contempt, see Anon. 1732: 23–4.
[21] Gregory 1828: 85.   [22] Good 1805: I, cxxx.

Christ's resurrection, they could not have been expected to entertain a belief for which nature alone affords such 'feeble and inconclusive' evidence.[23] Lucretius, moreover, Good argues, is by no means the outright atheist of tradition, since beyond his own serene, detached deities lurks the presence of an *unseen, incomprehensible*, or *mysterious* POWER',[24] the *vis abdita* of *DRN* 5.1233, which underpins and informs the laws of material nature.

In addition to the four full-length versions, a number of translations or adaptations of shorter Lucretian episodes appeared during this period. One of the most popular, Thomas Sprat's *The Plague of Athens* (1659), bears, in fact, only a tenuous relation to *DRN* 6, being effectively a free-standing meditation, more imitative of Abraham Cowley than of Lucretius, on the precariousness and uncertainty of human existence.[25] The rendering of a large section of *DRN* 1 by Sir Edward Sherburne (1616–1702),[26] in contrast, follows Lucretius' Latin closely. Omitting the opening sections of the *DRN*, Sherburne concentrates on Lucretius' exposition (1.162–710) of Epicurean cosmology and mechanistic philosophy. Such an emphasis accords with Sherburne's strong mathematical, scientific and philosophical concerns, and with his interest in Gassendi, a philosopher on whom his own notes survive. Another of the separate versions, 'Of Nature's Changes', by Dryden's brother-in-law Sir Robert Howard (1626–98),[27] renders Lucretius' description (5.235–415) of the processes of cyclical regeneration in the world and its final destruction by the strife of elements. Howard seems to have been fired by Lucretius' grand vision of natural dissolution and rebirth, but just as Sherburne had been careful to omit the overtly anti-religious sentiments near the beginning of *DRN* 1, Howard subtly Christianises Lucretius' account of the warring elements, asserting that water's defeat was brought about by the actions of a 'greater Being', rather than merely *aliqua ratione* ('by some means or other' (5.409)).

The two fragments of Lucretius rendered by the celebrated courtier and rake John Wilmot, Earl of Rochester (1647–80) display, as one might expect, a less inhibited response to Lucretian heterodoxy, one being a sensuously expansive translation of the opening of Lucretius' invocation to Venus (1.1–4), and the other a close rendering of the Roman poet's evocation (2.646–51; 1.44–9) of the perfect peace enjoyed by the gods:

> The *Gods*, by right of Nature, must possess
> An Everlasting Age, of perfect Peace:
> Far off remov'd from us, and our Affairs:

---

[23] Good 1805: I, lxxxii–lxxxiii.   [24] Good 1805: I, lxix.
[25] See Anselment 1996: 13.   [26] Not published until Sherburne 1961.
[27] First published anonymously in *Sylvae*, 1685.

Neither approach'd by *Dangers*, or by *Cares*:
Rich in themselves, to whom we cannot add:
Not pleas'd by *Good* Deeds; nor provok'd by *Bad*.[28]

Among other poets of the period, Thomas Flatman, for whom Lucretius is said to have been 'a favourite',[29] rendered a short fragment from *DRN* 3 on the loss of one's loved ones in death.[30] John Glanvill translated the opening of *DRN* 2,[31] previously rendered by Dryden. And James Beattie made a version of the opening of *DRN* 1, 'written at the particular desire of a Friend, whose commands the Translator hath reason to honour',[32] and apparently designed to temper the surging vigour of Dryden's version with a more measured, Popean elegance and balance.

It is in the versions of John Dryden (1631–1700) that we encounter by far the fullest translatorly engagement with Lucretius, short of a complete rendering.[33] These translations, published in 1685, mark the poet's coming-of-age in verse translation. Though Dryden had a long-standing interest in Epicurean atomic theory, the intensification of his engagement with Lucretius in the 1680s was part of a larger body of religio-philosophical stocktaking in which 'Christian' and 'pagan' elements came into various kinds of complex and paradoxical interaction.[34] From the 1670s Dryden seems to have been associating his own growing reservations about Restoration courtly and theatrical culture with the critique of worldly ambition and libertine morality to be found in the writings of Epicurus and Lucretius, as newly expounded by Gassendi and his English epigones. In the Dedication to his play *Aureng-Zebe* (1676) he had invoked Lucretius in support of his declaration that 'true greatness, if it be any where on Earth, is in a private Virtue; remov'd from the notion of Pomp and Vanity, confin'd to a contemplation of it self, and centring on it self'.[35] But Dryden's interest in Lucretius seems simultaneously to have been motivated by an attraction of opposites: a desire to comprehend and inhabit a poetic mind and temperament which he felt to be, in important respects, very different from his own. The 'distinguishing Character' of Lucretius' 'Soul and Genius', Dryden wrote in the preface to the collection containing the translations,

is a certain kind of noble pride, and positive assertion of his Opinions. He is every where confident of his own reason, and assuming an absolute command not only over the vulgar Reader, but even his patron *Memmius*. For he is always

---

[28] Rochester 1999: 108.   [29] Saintsbury 1905: III, 280.
[30] Flatman 1682: 139–40.   [31] Glanvill 1725: 188–92.
[32] Beattie 1760: x; translation at 77–81.
[33] Dryden renders *DRN* 1.1–40; 2.1–61; 3.830–1094; 4.1052–287; and 5.222–34.
[34] See Hopkins 1986: 90–133.   [35] Dryden IV, 153.

bidding him attend, as if he had the Rod over him; and using a Magisterial authority, while he instructs him.[36]

Lucretius' insistent pursuit of his mission, Dryden declares, sometimes constrained 'the quickness of his Fancy': on occasions, he was 'so much an Atheist, that he forgot to be a Poet'. But in the 'Descriptions, and . . . Moral part of his Philosophy' Lucretius' 'sublime and daring Genius', 'fiery temper' and 'Masculine' 'thoughts' find apt expression in a 'loftiness of . . . Expressions' and a 'perpetual torrent' of verse. In order to convey such qualities in his own translations, Dryden says, he has 'lay'd by [his own] natural Diffidence and Scepticism for a while, to take up that Dogmatical way of his'. Lucretius' 'Opinions concerning the mortality of the Soul', Dryden insists, are morally undesirable and psychologically unsustainable, but there are other arguments in *DRN* 3 'which are strong enough to a reasonable Man, to make him less in love with Life, and consequently in less apprehensions of Death'. These arguments are 'pathetically urg'd', 'beautifully express'd', 'adorn'd' with examples' and 'admirably rais'd by the *Prosopopeia* of Nature, who is brought in speaking to her Children, with so much authority and vigour'. Lucretius' treatment of love in *DRN* 4, moreover, offers 'the truest and most Philosophical account both of the Disease and Remedy which [he] ever found in any Author'. Dryden was confident of the success of his versions: 'I must take the liberty to own, that I was pleas'd with my endeavours, which but rarely happens to me, and that I am not dissatisfied upon the review, of any thing I have done in this Author'.[37]

How successful are the various seventeenth- and eighteenth-century translations of Lucretius in discovering a convincing English poetic voice for the Roman poet? In regard to Lucretius' style, E. J. Kenney observes a striking 'discrepancy in tone and emotional impact' between the grander and more emotionally charged sections of the *DRN* and the 'scientific, or expository' passages which lay out, in systematic detail and with painstaking clarity, the physical basis of Lucretius' larger cosmological, moral and social vision.[38] Lucretius' style in the expository passages, Kenney argues, is carefully calculated for its task. The poet eschews elegant balance and complex periodic structuring in favour of a cogently unfolding verse argument, in which there is a high degree of coincidence between metrical and syntactical structures, and in which thesis-statement, supportive illustration and summative recapitulation follow one another in a clearly differentiated sequence. As a sustained illustration of this expository manner Kenney offers *DRN* 3:323–49. Body

---

[36] Preface to *Sylvae*; Dryden III, 10.
[37] Dryden III, 10–12.   [38] Kenney 1971: 14–29.

and soul, Lucretius argues in this passage, are integrally related and cannot be separated without the destruction of both. Mind and body can no more be divided, or experience feeling separately from one another, than the scent can be separated from a lump of frankincense while still leaving that lump intact. The body is neither born in separation from the soul, nor can the two live separately after death. While water can be heated and then lose that heat without changing its essential nature, human life, from its inception in the womb, involves a mutual, and inseparable, connection of body and soul.

How is the passage rendered by the English translators? Lucy Hutchinson's translation of Lucretius has recently been praised in general terms for the way in which its long compound sentences, heavy enjambement, frequent elisions and comparative lack of parallelism, alliteration and assonance – features which differentiate it strongly from the more polished couplet verse of the eighteenth century – create a forward-surging movement which is particularly suitable for rendering the most urgent and impetuous of Roman poets.[39] But though such qualities may be appropriate for the more impassioned parts of the *DRN*, they are arguably less apt for the more discursive passages, where clarity of exposition is all-important. In the present instance the continuously forward-flowing movement of Hutchinson's verse and the looseness of her sentence structure tend to obscure the clearly articulated contours of Lucretius' argument:

> They in their first beginning are combind
> Nor in lifes tedious voyage ere disjoynd
> Nor can they singly suffer violence
> What either feeles afflicts the others sence
> In all commotions beare an equal share,
> Whatever tumults in the entrailes are.
> The bodie is not borne, nor grows alone,
> Nor after death subsists, the soule being gone.
> Though water heated, when that heate doth goe
> Reteins its being still, yet tis not soe
> With bodies quitted by the vitall heate,
> Corruption there dissolves the empty seate.
>
> (339–50; de Quehen 1996a: 93–4)

But Hutchinson's rendering is a model of elegant lucidity when compared with Evelyn's, in which a regular disjunction of metre and syntax, serving no obvious conceptual or expressive function, makes Lucretius' argument seem clotted and contorted:

---

[39] See de Quehen 1996b.

So from th' whole
Body, to separate the Mind & Soule
Is difficult; but that together all
Dissolve: since from their first original
The Principles so implicated be
And in a life conforme knit mutually.
So that the Mind acts not by't Selfe, nor one
Body, without anothers helpes alone.

(327–34; Repetzki 2000: 67)

Creech's version adds details that have no direct source in the Latin. In his rendering, it is 'with provident care' that the soul protects the 'life and health' of the body; the smell of frankincense is 'ravishing'; embryos spend time in the womb 'Before they pass the confines of the Night'. But Creech is so scrupulously attentive to Lucretius' rhetorical shaping that the reader's mind is led elegantly and effortlessly to a conclusion that seems to emerge convincingly from the examples presented – an effect which is characteristic of his translation, and which makes it, notwithstanding its embroideries and omissions, the most continuously readable of the complete versions:

Besides, the *Body*, is not born alone,
Nor grows, nor lives, when *Mind* and *Soul* are gone;
For tho the water heated o'er the fire
May lose some *Vapours*, yet remain entire;
The *Limbs*, when *Mind* and *Soul* are fled, submit
To the same fate, and die, and rot with it:
Nay more, before the Infants see the light,
Before they pass the confines of the Night,
Whilst yet within their Mothers Womb they lie,
If these *two* separate, they fail and die:
Whence learn, that since the *cause of Life*'s combin'd
And lies in both, their *natures* too are joyn'd.

(Creech 1683b: 78)

Good's version of the passage resembles Creech's both in its embroidery of the original and in its attentiveness to Lucretius' rhetorical shaping. But Good's Miltonic inversions – a regular occupational hazard of eighteenth-century blank verse – sometimes create a stilted effect:

So live they mutual, so, from earliest birth,
In intertwin'd existence, that apart,
Nor this nor that perception can possess

– as does his infelicitous choice of diction ('the tepid lymph | Fly off profuse'):

> This frame, moreo'er, alone can never spring,
> Can never thrive, the dread attack of death
> Can never conquer. For, with aim sublime,
> Though the light vapour from the tepid lymph
> Fly off profuse, while yet the lymph itself
> Exists uninjur'd – the deserted limbs
> Nor harmless, thus, can bear the soul's escape,
> Doom'd to one ruin, and one common grave.
>
> (341–3, 346–53; Good 1805: I, 425–6)

When one turns from the expository sections of the *DRN* to those passages in which Lucretius presents the larger moral, emotional and philosophical upshot of his physical and cosmological convictions, all four full-length versions are clearly outclassed by Dryden.[40] Dryden's ability to offer a more convincing English Lucretius than any other translator may be owing at least in part to the overlap he believed to exist between some of the Roman poet's most passionately held beliefs and his own. Dryden's own disillusionment with the 'wits' of the Restoration court, for example, seems to have fuelled his rendering of Lucretius' scornful denunciation of false hedonists at *DRN* 3.912–15:

> Yet thus the fools, that would be thought the Wits,
> Disturb their mirth with melancholy fits,
> When healths go round, and kindly brimmers[41] flow,
> Till the fresh Garlands on their foreheads glow,
> They whine, and cry, let us make haste to live,
> Short are the joys that humane Life can give.
>
> (*Against the Fear of Death* 97–102; Dryden III, 50)

And Dryden's rendering of Lucretius' portrayal of Sisyphus – a figure, Lucretius insists, to be found not in a mythological Hades but on this side of the grave – is clearly informed by his observation of the destructive ambition of seventeenth-century politicians:

> The *Sisiphus* is he, whom noise and strife
> Seduce from all the soft retreats of life,
> To vex the Government, disturb the Laws;
> Drunk with the Fumes of popular applause,

---

[40] Dryden does not translate *DRN* 3.323–49.

[41] A vogue word for 'brimming cups'.

> He courts the giddy Crowd to make him great,
> And sweats & toils in vain, to mount the sovereign Seat.
> For still to aim at pow'r, and still to fail,
> Ever to strive and never to prevail,
> What is it, but in reasons true account
> To heave the Stone against the rising Mount;
> Which urg'd, and labour'd, and forc'd up with pain,
> Recoils & rowls impetuous down, and smoaks along the plain?
> *(Against the Fear of Death* 200–11; Dryden III, 53)

Dryden's awareness of Lucretius' contemporary resonance is fully matched by his responsiveness to the Roman poet's verbal artistry, here particularly notable in his direct imitation (in the final fourteen-syllable line) of Lucretius' rhythmic mimicry of the ascent and descent of the stone (*DRN* 3.1002).

But Dryden was also able to identify himself in the act of poetic composition with Lucretian sentiments and beliefs to which, in ordinary life, he would have disclaimed any commitment. Consider, for example, the uninhibited relish with which he renders Lucretius' vehement declaration that individual existence ceases at the point of death (3.830–41):

> What has this Bugbear death to frighten Man,
> If Souls can die, as well as Bodies can?
> For, as before our Birth we felt no pain
> When Punique arms infested Land and Mayn,
> When Heav'n and Earth were in confusion hurl'd
> For the debated Empire of the World,
> Which aw'd with dreadful expectation lay,
> Sure to be Slaves, uncertain who shou'd sway:
> So, when our mortal frame shall be disjoin'd,
> The lifeless Lump, uncoupled from the mind,
> From sense of grief and pain we shall be free;
> We shall not feel, because we shall not *Be*.
> *(Against the Fear of Death* 1–12; Dryden III, 48)

Here Dryden combines argumentative cogency with dramatic urgency: the passage culminates in a powerful concluding couplet in which the strong antithesis on the two simple monosyllabic words 'feel' and 'be' acquires greater weight from the cumulative tension built up over the previous eight lines by a continuous flow of sense across line endings. In contrast, the enjambements in Lucy Hutchinson's equivalent passage create a shapeless, rambling effect lacking the point and urgency of Dryden's version or Lucretius' original:

As of past ages we no sence reteine
When the worlds terror the fierce African
Now on his march, the whole earth shooke with feare,
And tumults in th affrighted nations were,
When mankind looking for one suddaine fall,
Doubted which empire should entomb them all.
Whither in Sea-fights or land battailes slaine
The earth or sea should their dead trunkes reteine.
Soe when death shall dissolve that union
By which our soules and bodies now are one,
When we shall cease to be, noe accidents
Shall waken our dead sence, no sad events
Shall moove us then
        (903–15; de Quehen 1996a: 106–7)

The dramatic vividness of Dryden's version is even more strikingly apparent in the diatribe in which Nature rebukes man for squandering her precious gifts:

What does thou mean, ungrateful wretch, thou vain,
Thou mortal thing, thus idly to complain,
And sigh and sob, that thou shalt be no more?
For if thy life were pleasant heretofore,
If all the bounteous blessings I cou'd give }
Thou hast enjoy'd, if thou hast known to live, }
And pleasure not leak'd thro' thee like a Seive, }
Why dost thou not give thanks as at a plenteous feast
Cram'd to the throat with life, and rise and take thy rest?
        (*Against the Fear of Death* 123–31; Dryden III, 51)

Once again, Dryden's masterful control of the interplay between tight metrical form and larger argumentative trajectory throws the emphasis unerringly on the key words, as in the fervently emotional, yet artfully controlled, rhetoric of what Kenney calls Lucretius' 'pathetic' style. 'If thou hast known to live' (128) has no direct equivalent in Lucretius' Latin but perfectly captures the Lucretian Nature's distinction between mere existence and a life lived in full and conscious relish of its goods, leading directly into the triumphant swagger of the final Alexandrine. Evelyn's Nature, by contrast, sounds like a splenetic pedant:[42]

Why Mortal, dos't indulge to sadnesse so?
Why so at death repine, and weeping goe?

[42] Dryden, however, incorporated some details from Evelyn in his own renderings: see Hopkins 2002: 116–18.

> If thy past life so pleasant were to thee
> And that so many ungratefull troubles be
> (As from a Vessell craz'd which doth conteyne
> Them) run out, why sated, dost not refraine
> Retiring from thy life as from a feast?
> And (foole) contentedly take thy safe rest?
>
> (976–83; Repetzki 2000: 86)

Considerations of space preclude further discussion of Dryden's versions.[43] Suffice it to say that the poetic excellence of his version of the closing passage of *DRN* 3 is also evident in his rendering of the opening of *DRN* 1, which combines a hymn-like elegance with a delighted appreciation of the fecundity of the natural processes presided over by Venus, and of the passage on love in *DRN* 4, where Dryden's only rival is the stiff-jointed Good, and where a satirical detachment is miraculously combined with a tumultous depiction of the power of sexual passion which W. B. Yeats described as 'the finest description of sexual intercourse ever written'.[44]

Direct translation, however, only represents part of Lucretius' presence in seventeenth- and eighteenth-century English poetry, since Lucretian form, rhetoric and imagery were deployed by English poets of the period in more partial and indirect ways. The piecemeal use of Lucretius by English poets was in part encouraged by the long-standing tradition of florilegia – thematically organised collections of poetic 'beauties', offered by their publishers both for intrinsic pleasure and as models for poetic composition. In this period collections such as Henry Baker's *Medulla Poetarum Latinorum* (1737), Charles Gildon's *Complete Art of Poetry* (1718), Edward Bysshe's *Art of English Poetry* (1702–18) and *British Parnassus* (1714) included copious selections from Lucretius (usually in the versions of Creech and Dryden) covering the great 'visionary' passages from the *DRN*, complemented by Lucretian descriptions of the physical, natural and human world under such diverse headings as 'Ambition', 'Bird', 'Cloud', 'Disease', 'Dreams', 'Lightning', 'Metals', 'Passions' and 'River'. The miscellaneous influence of such Lucretian 'beauties' is visible in many poems of the period. In some famous lines in his *Elegy written in a Country Churchyard*, for example –

> For them no more the blazing hearth shall burn,
> Or busy housewife ply her evening care:
> No children run to lisp their sire's return,
> Or climb his knees the envied kiss to share.

---

[43] For other analyses see the 'Further reading' section, below.
[44] Jeffares 1962: 267.

– Thomas Gray drew on a celebrated passage in Lucretius (3.894–6) which had previously been translated by Flatman and Dryden, anthologised by Bysshe and Baker, and incorporated thus by James Thomson in *The Seasons*:

> In vain for him th' officious Wife prepares
> The Fire fair-blazing, and the Vestment warm;
> In vain his little Children, peeping out
> Into the mingling Storm, demand their Sire,
> With Tears of artless Innocence. Alas!
> Nor Wife, nor Children, more shall he behold,
> Nor Friends, nor sacred Home.
>
> ('Winter' 311–17; Thomson 1981: 218)

Similarly, Matthew Prior drew on Lucretius' much-anthologised opening invocation to Venus for his own 'Hymn to Venus, upon a Marriage', and Mark Akenside incorporated Lucretius' description of sea shells (*DRN* 2.374–6) in *The Pleasures of the Imagination* (1772):

> thus the pearl
> Shines in the concave of its purple bed,
> And painted shells along some winding shore
> Catch with indented folds the glancing sun.
>
> (1.526–9; Akenside 1996: 190–1)

But in addition to such piecemeal Lucretian borrowings, English poets sometimes displayed a more extensive engagement with the tone and substance of the *DRN*. Lucretius was, for example, frequently invoked in the debates about Newtonian physics found in the scientific poetry of the period, in both English and Latin.[45] Thomson's editor has described the 'shadowy' presence of Lucretius behind the design of *The Seasons*, a poem in which Sir Isaac Newton replaces Epicurus as the leading source of poetic inspiration, and in which 'a Lucretian grandeur and passion' are reoriented to serve very different theological ends.[46] Other poems of the period were more forthrightly – even crudely – explicit in their exploitation of Lucretian form and rhetoric for decidedly unLucretian purposes. The most explicit of all is *Anti-Lucretius* (1766), George Canning's translation of Books 1–5 of the celebrated neo-Latin poem by Cardinal Melchior de Polignac.[47] Just as Polignac had closely imitated Lucretius' style in a point-by-point refutation of the *DRN*'s arguments on the gods and the mortality of the soul, so Canning launches, in English Lucretian style, a lucidly systematic attack

---

[45] See Fara and Money 2004; Spencer 1965.   [46] Thomson 1981: xxiv.
[47] For Polignac see pp. 165, 198–9 above.

on Epicurean teachings about pleasure (Book 1), the void (Book 2), atoms (Book 3), motion (Book 4) and the mind (Book 5).

If *Anti-Lucretius* conducts a systematic imitative refutation of the more technical aspects of Lucretius' poetic teaching, Sir Richard Blackmore's *Creation: a Philosophical Poem* (1712) harnesses Lucretius' tone of lofty and passionate contempt to more emotional, though no less anti-Lucretian, ends, imitating the Roman poet's insistent questions and his passionately enjambed versification to pour scorn on every aspect of his theological and scientific teaching. John Dennis may – like Samuel Johnson, who endorsed his judgement – have been to some extent betraying his own religious bias when he wrote that *Creation* had 'equalled' the *DRN* 'in the Beauty of its Versification, and infinitely surpass'd it, in the Solidity and Strength of its Reasoning'.[48] But modern readers hitherto only acquainted with Blackmore's dismal Arthurian epics might be surprised to encounter the tonal assurance and rhythmic energy of his vehement denunciation of Lucretian teaching about 'the Self-existent, Independent and Eternal Being of Atomes':

> Tell us, fam'd *Roman*, was it e'er deny'd,
> That Seeds for such Productions are supply'd?
> That Nature always must Materials find
> For Beasts and Trees, to propagate their Kind?
> All Generation the rude Peasant knows
> A pre-existent Matter must suppose.
> But what to Nature first her Being gave?
> Tell whence your Atomes their Existence have?
> We ask you whence the Seeds Constituent spring
> Of ev'ry Plant, and ev'ry Living Thing,
> Whence ev'ry Creature should produce its Kind,
> And to its proper Species be confin'd?
> To answer this, *Lucretius*, will require
> More than sweet Numbers and Poetic Fire.
> (Blackmore 1712: 116–17)

The most impressive indirect responses to the *DRN* in the period, however, are to be found, not surprisingly, in the work of two of the period's greatest poets. Milton's response to Lucretius in *Paradise Lost* (1667; revised 1674)[49] forms part of his larger endeavour to forge a new style of epic poetry in which the wisdom and imaginings of the classical world are both assimilated and transcended, and in which elements of long-established poetic genres are fused in new combinations and to new ends. At the heart of

---

[48] Dennis 1939–43: II, 120; S. Johnson 1905: II, 243.
[49] Quotations below are from the 1674 edition.

Paradise Lost (5.469–533) the archangel Raphael discourses to Adam on the nature of God's universe. His 'miniature *De Rerum Natura*'[50] offers, like Lucretius (1.351–7), an analogy from the world of plants to characterise the nature of the material universe, but asserts, in a way markedly different from Lucretian atomism, the divine origins and telos of the primal 'first matter' which constitutes all things and 'which is capable of various degrees of refinement as it nourishes progressively higher forms of life'.[51] Later in his poem Milton remembers Lucretius' account of creation, elaborating the Roman poet's account of the birth of flora from the earth (*DRN* 5.781–91) with even greater sensuousness, as we are told (*Paradise Lost* 7.313–24) how 'Herbs of every leaf' 'sudden flowr'd | Op'ning thir various colours, and made gay | Her bosom smelling sweet', and how 'the clust'ring Vine' 'forth flourish'd thick'. Later still (7.453–70) Milton similarly embellishes Lucretius' account of the earth generating creatures from several wombs (*DRN* 5.795–924) in his own depiction of the earth 'Op'ning her fertile womb' and pouring forth 'Innumerous living Creatures, perfet forms' – such as the lion, who, 'pawing to get free | His hinder parts . . . springs as broke from Bonds, | And Rampant shakes his Brinded mane'. Such animal vigour is for Milton, however, the product not of random atomic collision but of 'the prodigious vitality of a divine Father, who makes his creatures vigorous, active, and potent, and sustains them in continuous processes of growth and generation'.[52] In a similar vein, Milton gives his own distinctively Christian colouring to the Lucretian claim to be leading readers from darkness into light;[53] he offers his inspiring deity Urania (*Paradise Lost* 7.1) as a heavenly alternative to Lucretius' *alma Venus*;[54] and, drawing on the traditional association of Pan with the music of the spheres,[55] he reverses Lucretius' scornful dismissal (*DRN* 4.580–92) of countrymen's superstitious attribution of hillside echoes to the revelling of woodland deities, in his own rapt evocation of the 'Celestial voices' of the 'Millions of spiritual creatures' who in *Paradise Lost* 'walk the earth | Unseen, both when we wake, and when we sleep' (4.677–8, 682). And in his depictions of Satan's Icarus-like fall into Chaos (2.927–38) and Phaethon-like assault on heaven (Book 6), Milton offers an implicit critique of Lucretius' vision of a godless, material universe that is ever falling and decaying, affirming in the process God's role as the preserver and sustainer of cosmic order.[56]

---

[50] Lewalski 1985: 40.   [51] Lewalski 1985: 41.   [52] Lewalski 1985: 135.

[53] *DRN* 1.921–7; 1.146–8 = 2.59–61; 3.91–3; 6.39–41; cf. *Paradise Lost* 3.1–26. See Hardie 1995: 13–15.

[54] See W. B. Hunter 1978–83: V, 39.

[55] See A. Fowler 1998: 260 (on *Paradise Lost* 4.681–4); Hardie 1995:15.

[56] See Quint 2004.

DAVID HOPKINS

Milton's imitation of Lucretius 'through opposition'[57] is strikingly combined in *Paradise Lost* with a unique ability to convey in English some of the
most notable features of Lucretius' poetic style. 'Even at its most prosaic and
ratiocinative', it has been observed, Lucretius' is 'a sublime voice, weighty,
craggy, ponderous, at times even gallumphing'.[58] Milton's responsiveness
to such a voice is nowhere more evident than in his evocation of Chaos,
where specific Lucretian echoes ('a dark | Illimitable Ocean without bound',
'embryon Atoms') are combined with the weighty, heavily enjambed verse
music, markedly reminiscent of Lucretius' sublime manner, in which Milton
evokes a landscape

> where eldest Night
> And *Chaos*, Ancestors of Nature, hold
> Eternal *Anarchie*, amidst the noise
> Of endless Warrs, and by confusion stand.[59]

Another notable 'redirection' of Lucretius' poetic voice in this period
occurs in a poem that some might be surprised to encounter in such a context at all: Alexander Pope's *Essay on Man* of 1733–4. Lucretius' presence
in the poem is in fact well documented.[60] Pope himself referred to his emulation of the Roman poet's 'grave march' in the first two parts of the work,
and the presence has been discerned throughout much of the *Essay* of 'the
hortatory, "magisterial" mode generally associated with Lucretius'.[61] The
'grave' Lucretian 'march' has been heard, for example, in such lines as the
following:[62]

> Oh blindness to the future! kindly giv'n,
> That each may fill the circle mark'd by Heav'n;
> Who sees with equal eye, as God of all,
> A hero perish, or a sparrow fall,
> Atoms or systems into ruin hurl'd,
> And now a bubble burst, and now a world.
> (*Essay on Man* 1.85–90; Pope 1950: 24–5)

Pope told Joseph Spence that he had originally intended to include in the
Essay 'an address to our Saviour, imitated from Lucretius' compliment
to Epicurus',[63] and in one of the manuscripts of the poem its addressee,
Lord Bolingbroke, is twice referred to as 'Memmius'.[64] The beginning of
'Epistle 1' contains prominent echoes of Dryden's version of the opening of

[57] Hardie 1995: 15.   [58] Martindale 2005: 197.
[59] *Paradise Lost* 2.891–2, 900, 894–7. For further discussion of Lucretius' and Milton's Chaos
see J. Leonard 2000.
[60] Fabian 1979, Leranbaum 1977.   [61] Pope 1956: III, 433; Leranbaum 1977: 42.
[62] Spencer 1975: 140–1.   [63] Spence 1966: I, 135.   [64] Mack 1984: 207, 283.

DRN 2.[65] And commentators have also demonstrated the conspicuous presence in Pope's poem of Lucretian satire, and of structural patternings derived from the *DRN*.[66]

But it is equally apparent that, despite some contemporaries' suspicions that *An Essay on Man* was a heterodox, even crypto-pagan work displaying 'strong traces of Infidelity',[67] Pope's poem is no straightforward imitation of Lucretius. Beside his draft of the couplet

> The blest today is as completely so,
> As who began a thousand years ago.
> (*Essay on Man* 1.75–6; Pope 1950: 23)

which clearly echoes Dryden's translation of *DRN 3*:

> The Man as much to all intents is dead,
> Who dyes to day, and will as long be so,
> As he who dy'd a thousand years ago.
> (*Against the Fear of Death* 319–21; Dryden III, 56)

Pope wrote, 'Lucretius of death reverst',[68] a phrase which has been described as 'an appropriate motto not just for this echo but for the entire *Essay*'.[69] And Pope's opening proclamation that the only man capable of plumbing the mysteries of God is

> He, who thro' vast immensity can pierce,
> See worlds on worlds compose one universe,
> (1.23–4; Pope 1950: 15–16)

has been seen as 'implicitly a reply to Lucretius' celebration of Epicurus',[70] an observation supported by the fact that the lines appear in the manuscript as

> He who can all the flaming limits pierce
> Of Worlds on worlds, that form one Universe[71]

– lines which directly echo the *flammantia moenia mundi* of *DRN* 1.73. It has, moreover, been argued that Pope's optimistic assertion of the interdependent order of 'Nature's Chain' is offered as a deliberate *riposte* to Lucretius' depiction of the ultimate dissolution of things.[72]

Should Pope's *Essay* then be seen as a simple 'inversion' of Lucretius, more sophisticated in method but fundamentally similar in intent to Blackmore's

---

[65] See Fabian 1979: 530–1.   [66] See Fabian 1979: 531–3; Leranbaum 1977: 43–6, 55–62.
[67] Pope 1950: xvii.   [68] Mack 1984: 210.
[69] Leranbaum 1977: 50.   [70] Pope 1950: 15.   [71] Mack 1984: 209.
[72] At *DRN* 5.104–9; see Pope 1950: 45–6.

Creation and the Polignac/Canning *Anti-Lucretius*? The *Essay* has often been regarded, both by its admirers and detractors, as a systematising piece of versified philosophy: an attempt to situate the emotional, moral and social nature of man definitively within the larger scheme of things. But an important recent study has drawn attention to the ways in which the poem's local movements complicate its apparently totalising design, subtly counterpointing, without simply contradicting, its tendency to philosophical system-building, with a sceptical resistance that precludes exclusive commitment to any fixed philosophy and finds ultimate satisfaction in a Montaignean surrender to life's flux and inconstancy. According to such an interpretation, Pope's celebrated pronouncement that 'Whatever is, is RIGHT' (*Essay* 1.294) should be seen not so much as an abstract and complacent affirmation of philosophical optimism but as 'the report of an experience . . . in which rational inquiry, through the very process by which it establishes its own inadequacy, finds itself yielding to the current of nature, and finds in that yielding a paradoxical sense of rightness'.[73] Might one see, in Pope's deployment of Lucretius in the *Essay*, an ambivalence or fluidity similar to that which is evident in his attitudes to 'philosophy' in the poem as a whole? On such a reading, Pope is both attracted by Lucretius' dogmatically assertive tone, and, in a complex dialectic of engagement and disengagement, unwilling to align himself with its insistence and evangelical commitment – not merely because it does not accord with his own Christianity, but because he would not align himself wholeheartedly with *any* totalising philosophical certainty. Lucretius is thus appropriated in a manner that hovers ambivalently between sympathetic alignment and sceptical distance, affirmative solidarity and self-conscious self-differentiation. Whereas Dryden had revealed his simultaneous attraction to and distance from Lucretius by assuming a Lucretian voice that would later be complemented by equally empathetic assumptions of other, very different, poetic voices (principally those of Homer, Juvenal, Ovid and Virgil),[74] Pope's *Essay*, like *Paradise Lost* before it, signals its distance from Lucretius *at the same time* as imitating and rendering Lucretius' 'grave march'. Samuel Johnson suggested that Dryden was the first English poet who effectively 'joined argument with poetry'.[75] The evidence presented above suggests that some of the greatest English poets' capacity to 'join argument with poetry' was decisively enhanced by their attempts to assume an English 'Lucretian voice' – even when those

---

[73] Parker 2003: 31.
[74] For this view of Dryden see Hammond 1989, Hopkins 2004: 57–62.
[75] S. Johnson 1905: I, 469.

attempts sometimes served interests distinctly different from, even directly opposed to, Lucretius' own.

Further reading

General surveys of the English reception of Lucretius in the seventeenth and eighteenth centuries are provided by Fleischmann 1964, C. T. Harrison 1933, C. T. Harrison 1934, H. Jones 1989: 186–213 and Mayo 1934. Lucretian influence on, and anti-Lucretian sentiment in, the English scientific poem are surveyed in Spencer 1965, and Fara and Money 2004. There are specialist studies of many of the individual translations and adaptations. On HUTCHIN-SON see R. Barbour 1994, R. Barbour 1997, de Quehen 1996a, de Quehen 1996b, Norbrook 2000. Norbrook's edition of her translation is forthcoming within her complete *Works*; q.v. for full discussion of its date, composition, contexts and artistic strengths. On EVELYN see M. Hunter 1995, Repetzki 2000. On CREECH see Davis 2005, Real 1970; and on SPRAT Anselment 1996. On the relation of DRYDEN'S versions to contemporary discussions of Epicureanism see Hammond 1983, Hammond 2001; on their rhetoric and diction E. Jones 1985; on their relation to the traditions of didactic poetry Davis 2005; on their treatment of love see Mason 1996, Mason 2001. On GOOD see Gregory 1828. On MILTON see Hardie 1995, W. B. Hunter 1978–83, J. Leonard 2000, Lewalski 1985, Martindale 1986, Martindale 2005, Quint 2004. On POPE see Fabian 1979, Leranbaum 1977, Pope 1950.

17

ERIC BAKER

Lucretius in the European Enlightenment

To characterise Lucretius' impact on the age of the Enlightenment is a daunting task. Virtually every major figure of the period was in some way influenced by Lucretius, and many of these engagements represent a complex, often polemically charged dialogue with previous interpretations. However, it is possible to make out three relatively cohesive strands, which might be termed the ameliorist, the radical and the aesthetic.

In the first phase, the Newtonians and deists both English and French (such as Locke, Shaftesbury and Voltaire) seek to reconcile the secular authority of science with the concept of providence. Second comes the inevitable consequence of the tension between these two mutually antagonistic worldviews, for, once science had succeeded in accounting for the order of creation, God, as Laplace remarked to Napoleon, increasingly became an unnecessary hypothesis. Among those who helped to render that hypothesis superfluous, Bayle, Diderot and Hume represent the Lucretian critique of deist arguments from design, while Mandeville and Rousseau illustrate the use of the *DRN* for purposes of a more general social critique. The third strand can be seen as an attempt to negotiate the antagonism between Enlightenment progress and religious value. The focus here will fall chiefly on Kant, but the wider picture includes the work of Burke, Schiller, Rousseau and Goethe.

Common to each of these three aspects of reception are the assumptions of naturalism, a philosophical attitude encompassing three main tenets: '(1) that the bounds of reality are circumscribed by the natural order; (2) that the natural order is the principal object of philosophical study; and (3) that some variety of empiricism is required in order to gain an understanding of the natural order'.[1] Implicit in these tenets are the corollary notions that 'there cannot exist any entities or events which lie, in principle, beyond the scope of scientific explanation'[2] and most importantly 'that the universe as such is neutral to human values and ideals'.[3] Naturalism thus reinstates man

---

[1] Zoll 1972: 210.   [2] Danto 1967: 448.   [3] Lamont 1947: 598.

within the natural world rather than placing him above it. Human beings may be very clever animals, but they are still animals.

The naturalistic outlook of the *DRN* found new relevance in the scientific and philosophical revolutions of the Enlightenment, when philosophers and others debated issues previously thought to fall within the purview of religion. It was in this context that Lucretius acquired a renewed relevance: in H. B. Nisbet's words, 'the Enlightenment's increasing preoccupation with nature to the detriment of theology, and the immense popularity of didactic poetry as a means of disseminating the new knowledge, made his work more accessible than ever before'.[4]

The deist compromise

We are accustomed to think of the eighteenth-century deists as having limited their use of Lucretius to rhetorical purposes. James Thomson's 'To the Memory of Sir Isaac Newton' (1728) deftly transfers Lucretius' sublime characterisation of Epicurus (*DRN* 1.62–79) to his great scientific contemporary:

> He, first of men, with awful wing pursued
> The comet through the long eliptic curve,
> As round innumerous worlds he wound his way;
> Till, to the forehead of our evening sky
> Returned the blazing wonder glares anew,
> And o'er the trembling nations shakes dismay.[5]

But there is no doubting the Christian basis of a poem which finishes by envisaging Newton's resurrection in 'the second life, | When time shall be no more'.[6] Lucretius has been adopted for ornamental effect, not absorbed organically.

On the other hand, the deistic conception of religion bears comparison with that of Lucretius. It is rationally justified and universally true, independent of any specific historical or even, ultimately, any scriptural basis – a religion, in other words, 'without miracles, priestly hierarchies, ritual, divine saviors, original sin, chosen people, and providential history'.[7] The great empiricist philosopher John Locke in his discussion of natural theology in *The Reasonableness of Christianity* (1695) wrote: 'the works of Nature . . . sufficiently evidence a Deity; Yet the World made so little use of their Reason, that they saw him not'. This blindness is attributed in part to 'fearful apprehensions' which 'gave them up into the hands of their priests, to fill their

---

[4] Nisbet 1986: 97.   [5] Thomson 1897: II, 177–8; cf. *DRN* 1.68–77.
[6] Thomson 1897: II, 182.   [7] Gay 1966: 373.

heads with false notions of the Deity, and their worship with foolish rites, as they pleased'. Out of this error grew the later institutional encrustation of religion: 'and what dread or craft once began, devotion soon made sacred, and religion immutable'.[8] Locke's theory of true and false religion turns out, then, to evince strong similarities to Lucretius' theory. I shall return shortly to this derivation of institutionalised religion from fear.

The very different figure of Voltaire was more explicit as to his affiliation with the Roman poet, styling himself a latter-day Lucretius in the *Epître à Uranie* (1722) and making liberal use of Lucretius' arguments against religion throughout his life.[9] He consistently and unequivocally praised *DRN* 3 on the materiality of the mind and the fictionality of the afterlife, and he composed a dialogue (*Entre Lucrèce et Posidonius*, 1756) placing Lucretius' arguments on mortalism in the mouth of his own character. Nevertheless, he still professed a belief in the providential order of Newton's God. He was, however, an empiricist by nature, and when it came to a conflict between doctrine and practice, it was most often the latter that won.

The uneasy alliance of faith and reason of which Newton and Locke were so confident was already beginning to crumble when the great Lisbon earthquake of November 1755 struck. The timing – on the morning of All Saints Day, just as the churches of the city were full, and the city in festive array – was such as to shake the foundations of belief in providence around Europe. Never had a natural catastrophe aroused so much philosophical debate.[10] It immediately called to mind Lucretius' observation that earthquakes are evidence that the walls of the world will crack, and that the universe is devoid of justice and providential order (*DRN* 5.95–109, 1236–40; 6.596–607). In the presence of such suffering, what possible good could come of further debating the theoretical niceties of its causality? That is the question Voltaire posed in *Candide* (1759), and the answer he gave drew heavily, in its substance as well as in its satirical modality, on the *DRN*.

The specific target of Voltaire's satire was the German idealist philosopher Leibniz, who had defended the notion of providence against Bayle's critique in his *Theodicy* (1710). We first encounter Pangloss (i.e. Leibniz) in the opening chapter, delivering a lecture on 'metaphysico-theologico-cosmonigology' which establishes that 'noses were formed to support spectacles', legs 'for the wearing of breeches', and stones to be 'made into castles'. Pangloss concludes: 'those who have argued that all is well have been talking nonsense: they should have said that all is for the best'.[11] Voltaire's satire on

---

[8] Locke 1999: 143.

[9] For a fuller overview of Voltaire's use of Lucretius see Redshaw 1980.

[10] See further Brightman 1919, Ray 2004 and Benjamin 1999.   [11] Voltaire 1991: 2.

providence harks back to Lucretius' stinging critique of anthropomorphism in *DRN* 4, where he cautions against the assumption that nature provided our senses and limbs expressly 'so that we might be able to do what is needful for life' (4.830–1). The shield was designed in order to protect the body in combat, just as the bed and the drinking cup were invented to make life more convenient (4.846–50): such innovations 'may well be supposed to have been invented for the purpose' (4.851–2). But to argue by analogy that just as a clock presupposes a clock-maker, so too with creation, would be what Lucretius calls 'distorted reasoning' (4.832).

The anthropomorphic projection of the logic of cultural invention onto nature recurs with such regularity throughout *Candide* that the reader becomes almost as weary as the protagonists and thus perhaps prepared to accept the bitter lesson with which the story breaks off. The allusion to the garden of Epicurus in the famous concluding line of the novel, 'Il faut cultiver notre jardin', is fairly clear.[12] This particular garden differs from its Epicurean predecessor in some respects,[13] but it is a good example of one of the things that make Enlightenment thought profoundly Lucretian: the notion, as Charles Taylor puts it, 'that the metaphysical views which tie us to a larger moral order destroy our peace of mind . . . in the name of an illusion'.[14] Pangloss is allowed to remain solely on condition that he refrain from all further speculation regarding matters irrelevant to their wellbeing. Martin (a figure based on Pierre Bayle) is the new sage, and his wisdom is predominantly practical in orientation: the pressing concerns are the enjoyment of attainable goods, here and now. There is just a glimmer of hope that tranquillity might still be possible. But we will see much less attenuated promises of *ataraxia* in a later phase of Lucretianism.

Radical critique

Earlier surveys of Lucretius' literary influence[15] tend to assume that rhetorical appropriations of the *DRN* to the end of celebrating the divine book of nature and the feelings of awe and reverence it inspired constituted his major Enlightenment contribution. Today we must accept that 'in their earnest rancour against religion the *philosophes* resembled no one quite so much as Lucretius'[16] and that the basis of that resemblance was methodological and conceptual as well as rhetorical. The deists' attempt to reconcile the dogmas of faith with the demands of reason was no match for the rapidly mounting

---

[12] See Fletcher 1978.   [13] See Redshaw 1980: 40–2.   [14] Taylor 1989: 345.

[15] Fusil 1928, Fusil 1930, Mayo 1934, Hadzsits 1963, Fleischmann 1963.

[16] Gay 1966: 371.

assaults on the notion of design, beginning with the French sceptic Pierre Bayle's *Various Thoughts on the Comet of 1680* (1682), the conceptual basis of which, like 'every psychological discussion of the origins of religion' in the eighteenth century, closely followed Book 5 of the *DRN*, the 'most magnificent ancient expression of the fear-theory'.[17] Bayle was one of the first to take up the Lucretian critique of the anthropomorphic projection of purpose and agency onto the inexplicable events of nature, emphasising not so much the institution of religion as the psychology that made the institution possible.

Bayle continued his assault on design in his *Dictionnaire historique et critique* (1695–7, enlarged 1702). By approaching religion with the same rigour Newton had applied to celestial mechanics, he seemed to pronounce the prophecy that the deists were later unwittingly to fulfil: he made 'the biblical God vanish into the natural world that is in principle subject to the analytical science of physicists and philosophers'.[18] Moreover, Bayle's *Dictionnaire* provided the model – and in many cases, much of the material – on which the later *Encyclopédie* of the *philosophes* was based. This project's chief editor as well as contributor was Denis Diderot, one of the Enlightenment's most outspoken Lucretians. In 1746 he published his *Philosophical Thoughts*, the motto of which is drawn from the *DRN*: *E tenebris autem quae sunt in luce tuemur* ('Now we see out of the dark what is in the light', 4.337). This work, largely a vindication of the Lucretian view of nature devoid of purpose, was one of Diderot's most popular, attracting sufficient attention to be condemned by the Paris parliament to destruction at the hands of the official hangman. Diderot's difficulties with the authorities came to a head with his next publication, *The Letter on the Blind and the Deaf*, 1749. Two weeks after it was issued, Diderot was arrested and imprisoned, and it is not difficult to express the reason in terms of its Lucretianism: 'The *Lettre sur les aveugles* poses a hypothetical universe in undisguisedly Epicurean-Lucretian garb, from which all dogma and the purposeful design of a Christian-Aristotelian universal dualism are excluded.'[19]

The philosophical context of the *Letter* concerns Locke's sensationist notion that all ideas are derived from, and entirely dependent upon, sense experience (as opposed to Descartes' notion of innate ideas). Diderot's heresy consisted in the suggestion that the very idea of God is also a product of the senses, and his demonstration of this thesis relies almost entirely on Lucretius. Towards the close of the *Letter* Diderot stages an encounter between a Protestant minister and the blind Cambridge mathematician, Nicholas Saunderson, set in the circumstances of the latter's impending death. The clergyman begins

---

[17] Manuel 1959: 145–6.   [18] Bartlett 2001: 12.   [19] Schmidt 1982: 200.

by 'haranguing on the wonders of nature', to which the blind mathematician curtly responds: 'Think, if you choose, that the design which strikes you so powerfully has always subsisted, but allow me my own contrary opinion.' Against the minister's deist view, Saunderson asserts that 'if we went back to the origin of things and scenes and perceived matter in motion and the evolution from chaos, we should meet with a number of shapeless creatures, instead of a few creatures highly organized'.[20]

Saunderson's side of the argument is stitched together from several passages in *DRN* 5.[21] His repudiation of purpose and design is clearly Lucretian in origin: 'How many faulty and incomplete worlds have been dispersed and perhaps form again, and are dispersed at every instant in remote regions of space . . . where motion continues and will continue to combine masses of matter until they have found some arrangement in which they may finally persevere?' Against the notion of the immortal soul Saunderson pits the Lucretian notion of the immortality of matter, and against the providence of nature, its monstrosities – monstrosities such as himself: 'Then, turning toward the clergyman, he added, "Look at me, Mr Holmes. I have no eyes. What have we done, you and I, to God, that one of us has this organ while the other has not?"'[22]

Diderot's imprisonment left him understandably inclined to keep to himself productions such as *D'Alembert's Dream* (1769), containing 'more references and similarities to the *De rerum natura* than any other of Diderot's works',[23] and in which the bantering tone and proselytism as well as the subject matter can justly be termed Lucretian. But the use of the *DRN* in undermining the deist notion of design was taken to even greater extremes in David Hume's *Natural History of Religion* (1757), as well as the *Dialogues on Natural Religion* (1777), which like *Le Rêve d'Alembert* was hidden away and unpublished during Hume's lifetime because of its radical implications.

The *Natural History of Religion* expanded Bayle's critique into a thoroughgoing naturalistic, psychological and historico-comparative analysis of the rise of religion. Bishop Warburton was quick to see the implications: Hume's intention was 'to establish *naturalism*, a species of atheism, instead of religion'.[24] In the opening segment Hume unceremoniously dispenses with the notion of a primitive but rational and monotheistic religion: 'The farther we mount up into Antiquity, the more do we find mankind plunged into polytheism. No marks, no symptoms of any more perfect religion.' The common root of both pagan polytheism and Christian monotheism is found to lie in the tendency 'to transfer to every object, those qualities, with which they are

---

[20] Diderot 1999: 70–2.   [21] For full details see Singh 1975.   [22] Diderot 1999: 72–3.
[23] Schmidt 1982: 246. For this work see also Gigandet 2002.   [24] Gay 1966: 409.

familiarly acquainted, and of which they are intimately conscious'. Many of Hume's remarks, moreover, show conspicuous parallels with Diderot's *Letter*. It is the human fear of the inexplicable that leads to religious worship: 'A monstrous birth excites his curiosity, and is deemed a prodigy. It alarms him from its novelty; and immediately sets him a trembling, and sacrificing and praying.' Hence the origin of religion lies precisely in the lack of insight into those 'unknown causes' that are 'the constant object of our hope and fear'.[25]

Throughout Hume's anatomy of the passions and moral sentiments, 'his sources are classical, and mainly Epicurus and Lucretius'.[26] What fuels Hume's animus towards what he ironically characterises as 'comfortable views' is the same scorn of organised religion that animated Lucretius: 'What so pure as some of the morals, included in some theological systems? What so corrupt as some of the practices, to which these systems give rise?' Deism, taken to its logical conclusion, culminates in scepticism: 'Doubt, uncertainty, suspense of judgment appear the only result of our most accurate scrutiny, concerning the subject.' Instead we should 'enlarge our view, and opposing one species of superstition to another, set them a quarrelling; while we ourselves, during their fury and contention, happily make our escape into the calm, though obscure, regions of philosophy'.[27]

The Lucretian strain of Hume's naturalism is more explicit in his *coup de grâce* to deism, the *Dialogues on Natural Religion*. Here, each fictional speaker represents one of three opposed positions: Cleanthes the philosophical deist, Demea the dogmatic theist, and Philo the sceptic (generally assumed to personify Hume). It is Philo who consistently, and often explicitly, uses Lucretius to undermine the religious positions of his opponents. Cleanthes, for instance, presents the conventional deist position: 'The curious adapting of means to ends, throughout all nature, resembles exactly, though it much exceeds, the productions of human contrivance – of human design, thought, wisdom, and intelligence.' It is on the basis of 'the rules of analogy' that Cleanthes asserts 'that the Author of nature is somewhat similar to the mind of man', and Philo is quick to expose the underlying fallacy of anthropomorphism.[28]

Just as Lucretius stresses the faults of the natural world for anti-providentialist purposes (esp. 5.195ff., *tanta stat praedita culpa*), so too Hume: 'This world, for aught he [the providentialist] knows is very faulty and imperfect . . . and was only the first rude essay of some infant deity who afterwards abandoned it, ashamed of his lame performance.'[29] And when

[25] Hume 1956: 23–9.   [26] Taylor 1989: 345.   [27] Hume 1956: 76–9.
[28] Hume 1948: 17–18.   [29] Hume 1948: 18.

Cleanthes has recourse to the standard deist device of revelling in nature's grandeur – 'Look round this universe. What an immense profusion of beings, animated and organised, sensible and active! You admire this prodigious variety and fecundity' – the joyous exclamation immediately collapses when contrasted with the state of man in political society: 'But inspect a little more narrowly these living existences, the only beings worth regarding. How hostile and destructive to each other! How insufficient all of them for their own happiness! How contemptible or odious to the spectator!'[30] It is not surprising that the concluding part of Hume's *Dialogues*, unlike that of the *Natural History*, seems preoccupied with the problem of melancholy.

The contribution of the *DRN* to the Enlightenment critique of religion extended to more general, but equally radical, forms of social critique. The account of the origins of human society and culture in *DRN* 5 played an important role in Bernard de Mandeville's *Fable of the Bees* (first published as *The Grumbling of the Hive*, 1705). The crux of the *Fable*'s lesson is that human nature in the state of political society is driven by greed, ambition and the desire for recognition, rather than rational calculation (as was the case in Locke's social contract theory) or Christian morality. And the basic premiss of this strikingly modern critique – it anticipates in many respects Nietzsche's *Genealogy of Morals* – was Lucretius' derivation of the social contract from the degeneration of the pre-political compact of friendship, caused by avarice and treachery: 'mankind, tired of living in violence, was fainting from its feuds, and so readier to submit to statutes and strict rules of law' (5.1145–7).

The same Lucretian elements that served Mandeville as a means of exposing the hypocrisy of Enlightenment civilisation are taken up by Rousseau in his contribution to the debate occasioned by the Lisbon earthquake, the *Discourse on the Origin and the Foundations of Inequality among Men* (1755), but to very different ends.[31] The dark sarcasm of Mandeville's tone resembles that of Voltaire: he has no illusions regarding human nature, only a desire to force us to acknowledge the inequality on which our way of life is premised, so that it may be better managed. There is, in other words, no hope for change. But change is for Rousseau the entire point of his painful demonstration of the wrong path on which civilisation has set out, and Lucretius' representation of the pre-political state of society serves Rousseau as an ideal. Like Lucretius, Rousseau criticises civilised society as 'the realm of false opinions, unnatural passions, and aggravated fears, all of which

---

[30] Hume 1948: 79.

[31] The influence of Lucretius on this work and others by Rousseau was recognised from early on: for bibliography see Gourevitch 2000: n. 83.

are incompatible with genuine happiness, with natural satisfaction, with unspoiled pleasure'.[32] Indeed, Gordon Campbell's recent characterisation of Epicurean ethics as indicative of 'a deeply ambiguous view of civilisation itself', as being a 'stop-gap' only 'necessary because of present-day human injustice . . . caused by the fear of death and by religion',[33] summarises Lucretius' influence on the *Second Discourse*. Like Rousseau, Lucretius conjured forth the image of 'a naturally occurring just state in the past' which might be recovered, though 'not through the further development of the contrivances of civilization, but through the embracing of Epicureanism'.[34] The source of alienation for Rousseau, as for Lucretius, lies in 'vanity and pride, a concern for and a dependency on the opinions of other men, an ambitious desire for superiority . . . and in consequence the unlimited desire for things that are not by nature good, but are merely goods in the (misguided) opinions of others'.[35] All these points of commonality have been noted also with regard to Mandeville, who in addition adopted a view of the origin of language anticipated in the *DRN*.[36]

Aesthetics and *ataraxia*

By the second half of the eighteenth century the transition was largely complete from Descartes's spiritual self, independent of nature and body and supplied at birth with innate ideas, to Locke's conception of the self as a *tabula rasa* reliant on sensation. The naturalist, Lucretian explanation of the origins of society and religion had rendered deist arguments from design quaint. However, while the *DRN* had served the needs of the Enlightenment in its destructive phase so well, it had little to offer the constructive phase it had helped to usher in by liberating humanity from the shackles of superstition and fear. The ever-increasing speed with which scientific advances were changing the world made Lucretius' quietism seem a dubious proposition. Was the best one could hope for really only peace of mind and freedom from pain? Could we not better achieve that goal by the untrammelled pursuit of science and technology? Indeed, was it not our duty to take the mastery of nature as far as possible in the hope of alleviating suffering and maximising comfort, pleasure and happiness?

As Hans Blumenberg has argued, the persistence of Lucretius' apolitical individualism and passivist ethics came to be perceived as a threat during this time of transition. The original meaning of the Lucretian *topos* of shipwreck, Blumenberg notes, was that seafaring was a violation of nature; 'what drives

---

[32] Nichols 1976: 199.   [33] Campbell 2003: 14.   [34] Campbell 2003: 14.
[35] Nichols 1976: 199.   [36] For the latter see Hundert 1987, Hundert 1995.

man to cross the high seas is at the same time what drives him to go beyond the boundary of his natural needs', and 'the crime of seafaring punishes itself through the fear of mighty powers to which man subjects himself'. In the later, constructive phase of the Enlightenment, by contrast, the shipwreck came to be understood as 'the price that must be paid in order to avoid that complete calming of the sea winds that would make all worldly commerce impossible'. It is trade and technology – not the salvation of the individual through the attainment of *ataraxia* – that is now the goal: 'Shipwreck is no longer the extreme image of the human situation in nature . . . It is the task of technology, of science, to deal with the problem of steering the ship.'[37]

Blumenberg detects a move away from the Lucretian assumptions in Voltaire, culminating in Voltaire's comment on *DRN* 2 in his article on 'Curiosity' in the *Dictionnaire philosophique*. Here Voltaire is concerned to refute Lucretius' claim that the pleasure derives from the gap between one's own security and the peril of others:

> I ask your pardon, Lucretius! I suspect that you are here as mistaken in morals as you are always mistaken in physics. In my opinion it is curiosity alone that induces people to hasten to the shore to see a vessel in danger of being overwhelmed in a tempest.[38]

Voltaire substitutes the pleasure of satisfying curiosity for the pleasure the *DRN* had described, in accordance with the Enlightenment imperative of the acquisition of knowledge, to be understood in the Baconian sense as power. The pleasure of *ataraxia* has yielded to the pleasure of power.

But another shift in the meaning of the shipwreck takes place diametrically opposite to the Enlightenment equation of knowledge with power. For those convinced that science and technology might eventually one day reveal 'the true springs and causes of every event' – not in the Epicurean but in the modern, Newtonian sense of science – the goal is to eradicate not the fear, but the very reality of the threat itself. That is why Voltaire insists that sympathy is motivated by the drive to knowledge: passion is to serve the interests of enlightenment and progress. (For Hume, it was precisely the other way around: 'Reason is, and ought only to be, the slave of the passions.')[39] Lucretius' reception in the latter half of the eighteenth century needs to be understood within the context of these competing paradigms.

Neither the Enlightenment subordination of passion to knowledge nor the consequent degradation of aesthetic experience to a self-indulgent pleasure satisfied those who saw aesthetic experience as a source of value in itself, and

---

[37] Blumenberg 1997: 10–11, 29, 41.
[38] Voltaire 1962: 365.   [39] Hume 1981: 415.

their dissatisfaction took on two opposed forms with respect to Lucretius. For those who looked to literature as a surrogate for moral values, and for anything else that cannot be comprehended from a purely rational perspective – history, tradition, the unique destiny and dignity of the human species – Lucretius was a threat of the first order. Edmund Burke and Friedrich Schiller are prominent representatives of this type of response. By contrast, those who sought to preserve the autonomy of moral as well as literary experience (Kant, Goethe, Schopenhauer) view Lucretius as more a model than a threat.

Burke's *A Philosophical Enquiry into the Origins of Our Ideas of the Sublime and the Beautiful* (1757/9) was written in response to the privileging of theoretical knowledge over feeling (of Locke's *Essay* over Milton's *Paradise Lost*). Burke viewed Lucretius as complicitous in the rationalist tendency to declare everything that cannot be clearly understood and explained – such as the experience of the sublime – to be devoid of all value. But Lucretius was an even greater threat than those who, like Locke, flatly denied the value of literature, for Lucretius had suggested that it was possible to generate the highest and most intense of feelings, the sublime feeling of the *diuina uoluptas* (3.28) traditionally attributed to God, solely by the revelation of nature's law – a nature, moreover, that is completely devoid of purpose or design.

To reassert the authority of the feeling of sympathy over the authority of scientific knowledge, or self-interested pleasure, Burke argues that its true source lies in the theological tradition of Christianity. While he acknowledges that 'Lucretius is a poet not to be suspected of giving way to superstitious terrors', he suggests that his representation of Epicurus as 'overcast with a shade of secret dread and horror' (Lucretius' *diuina uoluptas* is cited as support) testifies not to the greatness of the intellect of man, but to the presence of the divine in nature: 'In the scripture, whenever God is represented as appearing or speaking, every thing terrible in nature is called up to heighten the awe and solemnity of the divine presence. The psalms, and the prophetical books, are crowded with instances of this kind.'[40] We take pleasure in the spectacle of shipwreck, then, because it is part of a providential dispensation that we should feel sympathy with our fellows.

Kant's relationship to Epicurus and Lucretius has received little attention.[41] This is curious considering his open declaration in his first major work, *A General Natural History of the Heavens* (*Allgemeine Naturgeschichte und Theorie des Himmels*, 1755): 'I will . . . not deny that the theory

---

[40] Burke 1968: 69.
[41] But see Aubenque 1969, Fenves 2003, Thouard 2003 and pp. 177–83 above.

of Lucretius or of his predecessors (Epicurus, Leucippus and Democritus) has much similarity to mine.'[42] Since Kant's *Critique of Judgement* is addressed elsewhere in this volume, discussion here will be limited to Kant's early aesthetics in the form of a relatively neglected text, the *Observations on the Feelings of the Sublime and the Beautiful* which appeared in 1764, just a few years after Burke's *Philosophical Enquiry into the Origins of Our Ideas of the Sublime and the Beautiful*. The similarity between the two titles was carefully calculated to draw attention to their dissimilarity: whereas Burke speaks of 'ideas' (presumably in the Lockean, sensationist sense), Kant speaks rather of 'feelings', and the distinction is crucial. In opposition to Burke, Kant seeks to preserve the autonomy of aesthetic feeling, independent of the categories of the understanding as well as the rigorous imperatives of morality. The aesthetic spectator of Kant's early essay relies on the standard not of epistemology nor of morality. Rather, he approaches aesthetic feeling on its own terms: those of pleasure.

Kant had a personal copy of the *Observations* made with interleaved folios in which he collected further notes over the course of several years, the *Notes on the Observations*. These provide the quickest path to his particular kind of aesthetic hedonism. 'The sensitive soul at rest is the greatest perfection in speech and poetry', he writes; 'in society this cannot always be, but it is the final goal. And the same holds true even in marriages.' Kant's understanding of aesthetic pleasure as the 'sensitive soul at rest' is thus clearly bound up with the Epicurean ideal of *ataraxia*: 'The equilibrium of feelings is the soul at rest. This flat surface is only troubled by passion.'[43] Kant even goes so far as to entertain the heretical possibility (as Bayle and Shaftesbury had done before him) that this tranquil equipoise might provide a sufficient basis for morality: 'One wonders if the soul at peace might not provide the basis from which the whole of morality could be deduced'[44] (a notion from which he will later distance himself). The only aesthetic philosopher to have considered the possibility of such a form of the sublime is Santayana, who wrote: 'If we may call the liberation of the self by the consciousness of evil in the world, the Stoic sublime, we may assert that there is also an Epicurean sublime, which consists in liberation by equipoise.'[45]

Although Goethe was inclined to view technically theoretical discourse with suspicion, he did not feel this way about Kant, whose first and third

---

[42] Kant 1968: I, 233 (my translation). For a discussion of this work, see Shea 1986: 95–124.
[43] Kant 1991: 11 (my translation).   [44] Kant 1991: 114 (my translation).
[45] Santayana 1955: 241.

Critiques he read carefully and repeatedly.[46] The assertion of human freedom from divine interference was the subject of his early 'Prometheus' Ode (1774), a poem 'full of the Lucretian spirit of religious defiance' which uses his satirical jibes at the gods (*DRN* 6.396–7, 421–2).[47] Goethe himself conceded that he 'believed more or less in the teachings of Lucretius', and at one time even planned a book on the life of Lucretius.[48] He was instrumental in bringing about the first German translation of the *DRN*, a splendid hexameter work undertaken by Karl Ludwig von Knebel and completed in 1827.[49] Goethe's scientific studies, which stand opposed to the modern, quantitative science of Newton (whose optics he sought to refute with his *Theory of Colours*), also show certain parallels with the *DRN*.[50] Like Lucretius' radical sensualism, Goethe's naturalism aims at the mastery not of nature but of humanity's relationship to nature. It is therefore not surprising that references to the Lucretian *topos* of shipwreck are frequent throughout his literary œuvre as well as his correspondence. These represent variations on the theme of a non-Stoic, hedonistic model of resignation, enabling Goethe to adopt a position of spectatorship with regard to life's randomness.[51] As with Kant and Hume, Goethe's adaptation of the metaphorics of shipwreck consistently expresses a renunciatory stance towards the desire for design or providential order and thus is compatible with the Lucretian presentation itself.

Although a plan to use Knebel's translation as the basis of his own Lucretian poem for the modern age did not come to fruition, as a poet Goethe can be said to have achieved a close approximation to Lucretian verse in the short didactic work probably written at the turn of the century, the 'Metamorphose der Tiere'.[52] Here Goethe passes from zoology to broad generalisation on man and the cosmos, and in the former, much larger section, 'there is scarcely a sentiment that does not have its counterpart in the *DRN*'.[53] Ultimately, however, Goethe parts company with Lucretius, whose poem moves constantly between principles and illustrations rather than concluding with a climactic summation, and whose sombre reflections are not of a piece with Goethe's expression of optimism and faith in mankind.

---

[46] See Molnár 1994. [47] See further Nisbet 1986: 101, also the source of the quotation.
[48] Prandi 1993: 6. [49] For Knebel's translation see Nisbet 1988.
[50] For an in-depth investigation of Goethe's science and its Lucretian leanings, see Tantillo 2002.
[51] See Blumenberg 1997: 58–9.
[52] See the full commentary on this poem in Nisbet 1986, on which the present discussion draws.
[53] Nisbet 1986: 108.

It is clear that secular ways of thinking in later eighteenth-century Europe often constitute responses to Lucretius whether pro or con. Naturally, no major thinker adopted Epicureanism wholesale, but it consistently had the effect of undermining received Christian doctrines. Several more minor figures did become unqualified philosophical materialists, including the French thinkers La Mettrie (*L'Homme machine*, 1748) and Baron d'Holbach (*Système de la nature*, 1770), and in Germany Lucretius' translator Knebel and the eccentric August von Einsiedel (1754–1837), whose unpublished writings on atoms were used by Herder.[54] Moreover, 'when materialism finally came out into the open . . . its classical origins were still evident'.[55] In a later generation, Karl Marx's doctoral dissertation on Democritus and Epicurus would evince considerable attachment to Lucretius.[56] We shall conclude here by glancing at Arthur Schopenhauer's *World as Will and Representation* (1818), which may be said to represent the culmination of the radical as well as aesthetic lines of Lucretius' reception.

G. F. Else characterised the *DRN* as 'an appeal to man to drop his hubris and become a spectator of the tragedy in which he is an actor. To the latter, death and failure in his own designs are terrible; to the former, who stands aside and sees the law as well as the passion, they are beautiful and justified.'[57] That characterisation seems to fit remarkably well with Schopenhauer's characterisation of the duality of the human condition:

> In respect of this withdrawal into reflection, [man] is like an actor who has played his part in one scene, and who takes his place in the audience until he must appear again. In the audience he quietly looks on at whatever may happen, even though it be the preparation of his own death (in the play); but then he again goes on the stage, and acts and suffers as he must.[58]

If the sole means of (temporary) salvation lie in brief respite from the endless cycle of need, want and suffering, then the enduring popular image of Schopenhauer as an inveterate pessimist may be warranted. However, considering what was about to come of all the hopes of the Enlightenment, one might question whether the pessimism was not mixed with prophecy. At a time when the optimistic faith in science was reaching its peak, Schopenhauer's Will, like Lucretius' Nature, stands as a reminder that the control of nature through science and technology – the science of Mars – is always subject to the will, which is to say, to that indifferent and inhuman impulse that is nature.

---

[54] See Dobbok 1957: 11.   [55] Nisbet 1986: 102.   [56] See Prawer 1976: 27.
[57] Else 1930: 165.   [58] Schopenhauer 1969: 85.

Further reading

Though somewhat technical and detailed for the general reader, Lange's classic 1866 study is still a good antidote to the misleading view – prevalent in the works of Hadzsits, Mayo and Fleischmann – that the *DRN* played little or no role in the Enlightenment. Blumenberg 1983 gives a detailed account of the Enlightenment shift regarding Lucretius' image of the detached spectator. W. R. Johnson 2000: 79–102 is restricted to Polignac, Diderot and Voltaire but still represents one of the few more synoptic expositions of Lucretius' role in Enlightenment thought. Nisbet 1986 is an excellent survey of his reception in Germany for the period. Kimmich 1993 provides a more extensive and detailed survey, although it is largely restricted to Epicurus. The rest of the relevant literature on Lucretius' eighteenth-century reception consists of investigations of individual Enlightenment authors.

On DIDEROT, particularly noteworthy for its extensiveness as well as contextualisation is Schmidt 1982. On ROUSSEAU see Masters 1968: chs. 3–4, Vaughan 1982, Scott 1992 and Gourevitch 2000. On GOETHE see Bapp 1926 and Nisbet 1986. LOCKE's relationship to Epicureanism has been discussed by Smock 1946, Tuveson 1955/6, Jackson 1987 and N. Wood 1992. Taylor 1989: 345–9 remarks on HUME's and DIDEROT's reception of Lucretius. For KANT see Aubenque 1969, Shea 1986, Thouard 2003 and especially Fenves 2003: 10–13, 22–9. For VOLTAIRE see Redshaw 1980.

18

MARTIN PRIESTMAN

Lucretius in Romantic and Victorian Britain

The first great Lucretian moment in Britain was the end of the seventeenth century, with Thomas Creech's 1682 translation as its centrepiece. Perhaps because the impact of this moment was so thoroughly absorbed, no new translation appeared until near the end of the eighteenth century; but at its close four appeared within fourteen years of each other: by John Nott (Book 1 only, 1799), John Mason Good (1805), William Hamilton Drummond (Book 1 only, 1808) and Thomas Busby (1813). These were part of what deserves to be called the second British Lucretian moment, from about 1790 to 1820. The exceptionally turbulent period normally tagged with the simplifying label 'Romantic' was marked not only by its partial attempts to transcend the aims of Enlightenment rationalism, but also by many efforts to bring those aims about. In this spirit, 'all that Epicurus and Lucretius have so greatly and convincingly said' was invoked in justification of the first manifesto for atheistic materialism openly published in Britain, Matthew Turner's *Answer to Dr Priestley's Letters to a Philosophical Unbeliever* of 1782.[1] Though not all Romantic Lucretians were such complete unbelievers as Turner, the *DRN*'s role as a scourge of religious orthodoxy was well understood on both sides of an increasingly acerbic debate.

This religious debate cannot be separated from a political context in which Enlightenment ideas were increasingly associated with the French Revolution, whose broad welcome in 1789 was soon followed by horrified revulsion and the declaration in 1793 of an Anglo-French war which continued almost uninterrupted for twenty-two years. For supporters of the increasingly embattled British Enlightenment, this was partly a civil war in which the embrace of progressive rationalism at home was coming under ever more furious attack as godless, pro-French and unpatriotic. Lucretius' twin aim, to proclaim such rationalism while simultaneously retiring from the fray of a horrific present, spoke deeply to a whole intellectual class which had

---

[1] Turner 1782: 48. For Turner's authorship see Berman 1990: 110–15 and Priestman 1999: 15.

supported the French Revolution's original aims but was starting to lose hope of their concrete realisation. Of the *DRN*'s four new translators, Drummond and Good belonged to the rational-dissenting Unitarian sect which had led opposition to war with France under the inspirational guidance of the scientist-preacher Joseph Priestley, who joined the French National assembly, discovered oxygen and asserted the materiality of the soul.[2] Another translator, Thomas Busby, held what the *Dictionary of National Biography* calls 'loose notions on religious subjects' and collaborated in composing the first British melodrama with the notorious atheist Thomas Holcroft, whose 1794 acquittal, alongside others, on a capital charge of treasonable republicanism was a progressive *cause célèbre*.[3] A less fortunate anti-war campaigner than Holcroft was the prominent Unitarian controversialist Gilbert Wakefield, imprisoned on similar charges in 1799, two years after the appearance of his massive new Latin edition of the *DRN*. As translated by Good, there is powerful contemporary resonance in Lucretius' opening plea to Venus – 'Quell, too, the fury of the hostile world, | And lull to peace, that all the strain may hear' – as well as in his closing vision of the victims of a shared catastrophe 'amid th'unhallowed blaze | With blood contending'.[4]

Contemporary with Wakefield's edition, Richard Payne Knight's six-book didactic poem *The Progress of Civil Society*, 1796, is avowedly modelled on *DRN* 5.925–1457, describing the development of human society. Knight wholeheartedly endorses Lucretius' accounts of the misguided construction of religion from human dreams and fears, of class warfare as the guiding force of social change and, despite an added note of Humean scepticism, of the purely material formation of the universe from 'the wild war of elemental strife' and consequent sublimation of 'matter into mind' (1.2–4). Along with Knight's earlier support for the French Revolution and dabblings in the obscener aspects of ancient mythography,[5] all this was enough to attract the attention of the authors of *The Anti-Jacobin* – the government-sponsored periodical which applied the all-purpose smear of pro-French 'Jacobinism'

---

[2] For his views on the materiality of spirit see Priestley 1777. Priestley was inspired to study chemistry by Matthew Turner, whose *Answer* to his rejection of atheism is more of an in-house quarrel among scientific progressives than an attack on Priestley *tout court*.

[3] The melodrama was *A Tale of Mystery* (1802), for which Busby wrote the music. W. R. Johnson 2000: 127–8 quotes Busby's prefatory self-distancing from the *DRN*'s impiety as reflecting the standard anti-Lucretian view, but this underplays the significance of the very act of translating Lucretius at a time when religious 'infidelity' was routinely prosecuted.

[4] Good 1805: I, 15; II, 613 (lines 1.32–3, 6.1340–1). See further on Good's translation ch. 16 above.

[5] See respectively his didactic poem *The Landscape* (1794), 3.415–16, and the graphic illustrations of his mythographic treatise *A Discourse on the Worship of Priapus* (1786).

to a wide range of literature with any kind of radical or progressive tendency. Its spoof 'The Progress of Man: a Didactic Poem' picks out all the Lucretian elements just mentioned, starting with a demonstration of how a materialism that contemplates 'whether, sprung from Chaos' mingling storm, | The mass of matter started into form' leads straight to an atheistic unconcern as to whether 'the joys of earth, the hopes of heaven, | By Man to God, or God to Man, were given'.[6] This attack on modern materialism quite closely echoes that made earlier in the century in Cardinal Melchior de Polignac's *Anti-Lucretius* (1747), whose English translator happened to be the father of the *Anti-Jacobin* team's leading writer, the future Tory Prime Minister George Canning. In Canning Senior's words, Epicurus' philosophy arrogantly 'framd eternal Atoms at his will, | By casual concourse empty Space to fill' and thus 'doomd to death, man's noblest part, the soul, | And gave blind chance the conduct of the whole'.[7]

A similar anti-Lucretianism underlies *The Anti-Jacobin*'s ludicrous account of how earth-generated cabbages supposedly 'by degrees detached themselves from the surface of the earth, and supplied themselves with wings or feet', eventually becoming human and inventing '*language*, and the use of *fire*, with our present and hitherto imperfect system of *Society*'.[8] However, though Knight does touch on the *DRN* 5's proto-evolutionism, this sneer is directed at the protean doctor-scientist-poet Erasmus Darwin, an associate of Priestley's in the Birmingham-based scientific-progressive Lunar Society and the grandfather of Charles Darwin, whose evolutionism he strikingly anticipated. Canning and his associates helped to destroy Darwin's considerable reputation for Lucretian-scientific verse with another *Anti-Jacobin* spoof, 'The Loves of the Triangles', which transposed the vegetable amours of his botanical poem *The Loves of the Plants* to those of polygons. Darwin's *The Botanic Garden*, 1791, comprising *Loves* and a more thoroughgoing survey of cutting-edge science, has an epigraph and numerous detailed echoes from the *DRN*,[9] but his most Lucretian poem was the posthumous *The Temple of Nature, or The Origin of Society*, published in 1803. This began life as a projected imitation of the *DRN* 5's social history, originally titled 'The Progress of Society', but – possibly alerted to Knight's very similar imitation by the *Anti-Jacobin* – Darwin changed course radically to produce his own, full-frontally materialist account 'of the nature of things'.

Opening with an invocation to 'Immortal Love' as the universal principle of gravitational, chemical, sexual and social attraction, Darwin impudently

---

[6] *The Anti-Jacobin*, 1799: I, 525–6, lines 5–6, 13–14.
[7] Canning 1766: 7.   [8] *The Anti-Jacobin*, 1799: II, 172.
[9] See in Darwin 1791 (e.g.) notes on 1.1.193; 1.4.60.

replaces the orthodox creation myth of the Garden of Eden with the epony-
mous Temple, whose position beyond the 'storm' of normal human concerns
(1.65–6) echoes the superior contemplative realm enjoyed by Epicurus and
the gods in the *DRN* (3.14–22). Before copying the former by removing
the goddess Nature's 'mystic veil' (4.522),[10] the first task of Darwin's scientific Muse is to explain the creation of the present universe from a 'flaming
Chaos' of particles and then, astonishingly, that of living, evolving organisms
from inorganic matter: 'Say, MUSE! how rose from elemental strife | Organic
forms, and kindled into life' (1.1–2). Though the idea has a clear precedent in
the *DRN*'s account of the emergence of animal species from the earth (5.795–
808), Darwin takes care to point out that 'spontaneous vitality was only to
be looked for in the simplest organic beings', which only later 'improved
by reproduction'.[11] Elsewhere he distances himself from Epicurus/Lucretius'
attribution of the formation of the universe to blind chance rather than to
ascertainable Newtonian laws,[12] but his overall vision – underpinned by
much cutting-edge geological evidence – of a childish, still-evolving 'Young
Nature' (1.224n) comes directly from the *DRN* (5.330–1).

Both as a poet and as a radical scientist, Erasmus Darwin's influence on
Romantic literature was pervasive,[13] but one particularly striking instance
deserves mention here. In her preface to *Frankenstein*, Mary Shelley describes
how her dream of the home-made monster was partly inspired by her
future husband Percy's discussion with Byron about 'the experiments of
Dr Darwin . . . who preserved a piece of vermicelli in a glass case, till by some
extraordinary means it began to move with voluntary motion'.[14] While she
admits her memory might be garbled, her word 'vermicelli' compresses a
wide range of possible significations. Though Darwin never mentions the
pasta the Shelleys and Byron probably encountered on their travels, he
does refer to microbes spontaneously generated in flour paste, and to others
called 'vorticella'.[15] But Mary's 'vermicelli' point even more directly to the
little worms (*uermiculos*) produced from the rotting of sticks and clods in
the *DRN*'s first discussion of spontaneous generation (2.897–901), which
those devoted Lucretians Shelley and Byron may well have been discussing as
the ancestors of Darwin's microbes. At this junction of three major Romantic
literary minds, which also marked the birth of modern science fiction,
Darwin's Lucretius-tinged contribution was – not untypically – crucial.

Of the major British Romantic poets, it is Wordsworth who gives 'Nature'
the most primacy, in a spirit often taken to be profoundly at odds with

---

[10] Cf. Nature's similar denuding by Epicurus in *DRN* 3.29–30.
[11] Darwin 1803: [2]1; see also 37 (note on 1.417).   [12] Darwin 1803:142 (note on 4.147).
[13] See King-Hele 1986.   [14] M. Shelley 1994: 195.   [15] Darwin 1803: [2]3, [2]7.

scientific materialism. But he was also deeply familiar with Lucretius, putting him first in his list of didactic poets in the *Poems, 1815* preface, wrestling with his shadow in the long discussion of the ultimate reconcilability between the poet and the man of science in the 1802 *Lyrical Ballads* preface, translating his image of birth as shipwreck (*DRN* 5.222–34) in his poem 'To —— upon the Birth of her First-Born Child' (1833) and leading into the early *Descriptive Sketches* (1793) with an epigraph from the *DRN*'s evocation of pastoral simplicity, *Loca pastorum deserta atque otia dia*.[16] Though relating here to a youthful journey through the Alps, the passage clearly sets the tone for Wordsworth's later celebrations of both the emptiness and the countryfolk of the English Lake District.

Lucretius provides the key to another early poem, the anguished, uncompleted *Salisbury Plain* (1793–4), whose opening description of savage life threatened on all sides by storms and wild beasts derives directly from *DRN* 5,[17] as does the ensuing comparison with the present where 'Many thousands weep | Beset with foes more fierce than e'er assail | The savage without home in winter's keenest gale.'[18] Still in virtual nervous breakdown after the collapse of his youthful French Revolutionary hopes, Wordsworth's 'foes' include social inequality as well as Lucretius' prime targets of war and religious superstition, the former of which he excoriates in the account of a poor soldier's destroyed family (226–393) which later became the most politically radical of the 1798 *Lyrical Ballads* poems (as 'The Female Vagrant'), and the latter of which is symbolised by the poem's obsessively recurrent image of Stonehenge, 'that eternal pile which frowns on Sarum's plain' (549) where 'from huge wickers paled with circling fire | . . . horrid shrieks and dying cries | To ears of Daemon-Gods in peals aspire' (424–6). This image of the ancient human sacrifice still lurking behind modern religious practices recalls the *DRN*'s account of the sacrifice of Iphigenia (1.80–101), which Wordsworth regarded as 'worth the whole of Goethe's long poem' on the same subject.[19]

Though this is the early, radical Wordsworth, it is worth noting that he stood by his youthful Lucretianism long after his rebirth as a Christian conservative. Thus as late as 1814 the programmatic 'Prospectus to *The Recluse*', prominently prefaced to *The Excursion* though written in 1800, echoes both Lucretius' description of Epicurus' heroic mental journey and

[16] *DRN* 5.1387. For other echoes see Kelley 1983 and Spiegelman 1985.
[17] Ll. 1–9 in the unfinished first version of *Salisbury Plain*; W. Wordsworth 1986: 13–28. See *DRN* 5.955–87.
[18] *Salisbury Plain*, 34–6; cf. *DRN* 5.999–1000: *at non multa uirum sub signis milia ducta | una dies dabat exitio*.
[19] C. Wordsworth 1851: II, 478; see Kelley 1983: 219.

Figure 18.1. Sir George Beaumont, *Peele Castle in a Storm*

Milton's inversion of it for Satan's flight through Chaos:[20] 'Jehovah with his thunder, and the choir | Of shouting angels, and the empyreal thrones – | I pass them unalarmed'. Wordsworth writes that neither hell nor any other horror scooped out from 'blind vacancy' inspires such awe as 'the Mind of Man – | My haunt, and the main region of my song'.[21]

A final Wordsworth text that must be mentioned in this connection is his 1807 poem 'Elegiac Stanzas, Suggested by a Picture of Peele Castle, in a Storm'. Here Wordsworth's youthful memory of the castle, calmly lit by 'The light that never was, on sea or land' echoes the trouble-free 'high sanctuaries' of *DRN* 2.8, while the 'Hulk which labours in the deadly swell', in the stormy picture he is now admiring (fig. 18.1), ironically evokes both the shipwrecks of others which the *DRN* invites us to enjoy (2.1–2) and his own brother John's recent death at sea. The mismatch between the once-imagined serenity of nature and the realities of personal loss and violent death impels Wordsworth to bid 'Farewell, farewell' to 'the heart that lives alone, | Housed in a dream, at distance from the Kind!' in favour of a grimmer engagement with life's realities, now tempered only by religious hope. But if

[20] *DRN* 1.68–74; *Paradise Lost* 2.920–1055.
[21] 'Prospectus to *The Recluse*', 32–4, 40–1; W. Wordsworth 1950: 590.

this farewell to nature worship is also a farewell to Lucretius, it is not absolute (as many later allusions suggest) and it is coded in completely Lucretian terms.

For the two most committedly Christian of the major Romantic poets, by contrast, summary dismissal of Lucretius' ideas was a clear duty. Given his early Unitarian phase and omnivorous reading habits, Coleridge's lack of regard for the godfather of atheism and uncle of Rational Dissent is striking. His curt remark that 'whatever in Lucretius is poetry is not philosophical, whatever is philosophical is not poetry' is part of his letter-campaign to persuade Wordsworth to compose, in *The Recluse*, 'the *first* and *only* Phil[osophical] poem in existence', exploding 'the absurd notion' of Erasmus Darwin and others that man 'progressed from an Ourang Outan state'.[22] Coleridge's fears that his friend might be wavering in this task seem to arise from *The Excursion*, prefaced as it is with the Lucretian 'Prospectus' quoted above.

More full-bloodedly, William Blake tartly scrawled in his copy of Bacon's *Essays*: 'Every Body Knows that this is Epicurus and Lucretius & Yet Every Body says that it is Christian philosophy; how is this possible? Every Body must be a Liar & deceiver.' And he beautifully dismissed 'The atoms of Democritus' as 'sands upon the Red sea shore | Where Israel's tents do shine so bright'.[23] Nonetheless, Blake's own wildly unorthodox accounts of the creation of 'all Deities' from the imaginations of 'the human breast' are not too far removed from *DRN* 5's derivation of them from dreams.[24]

The *DRN* certainly informs more standard late Enlightenment responses to religion. 'Ode to Superstition' (1786) by Samuel Rogers – a figure almost forgotten now, but placed well above Wordsworth and Coleridge by Byron and other contemporaries[25] – follows a gory description of the sacrifice of Iphigenia, echoing *DRN* 1.84–101, by an acknowledged borrowing from the account of the effects of Superstition at 1.62–5:

> When, with a frown that froze the peopled earth,
>   Thou dartedst thy huge head from high,
>   Night waved her banners o'er the sky,
> And, brooding, gave her shapeless shadows birth.[26]

The same image of a sky-enthroned Superstition crushing earthbound humanity appears in Ann Radcliffe's 'Superstition: an Ode' (1790): 'Involved

---

[22] To Wordsworth, 30 May 1815; Coleridge 1956–71: IV, 969.
[23] Blake 1966: 397, 418.
[24] *The Marriage of Heaven and Hell*; Blake 1966: 418; see *DRN* 5.1169–82. Further on Blake see note 31, below.
[25] See Byron 1973–94: III, 219–20.   [26] Rogers 1891: 146.

in clouds, and brooding future woe, | The demon Superstition Nature shocks, | And waves her sceptre o'er the world below' (ll. 6–8). This poem's context in Radcliffe's gothic novel *A Sicilian Romance* makes it clear that the superstition under primary attack is Roman Catholicism – a common stalking-horse for what might or might not be read as broader challenges to religious orthodoxy. With both Rogers and Radcliffe, the emergence of the 'truth' or 'peace' which replaces Epicurus in vanquishing superstition at the end of the poem could well imply the Protestant Reformation – but the issue is conventionally left open.

In the later Romantic period it was easier to voice open challenges to religion *per se*, at least within certain radical groupings. Though the major figure here is Shelley, the sharing of his kind of atheism by a wider circle is attested in his occasional mentor Leigh Hunt's sonnet 'To Percy Shelley, On the Degrading Notions of Deity' (1818). This attributes the 'jealous rage' of Shelley's attackers to the way in which 'They seat a phantom, swelled into grim size | Out of their own passions and bigotries, | And then, for fear, proclaim it meek and sage!'[27] However, an ensuing sonnet ('To the Same') urges Shelley not to become too embittered to continue worshipping 'The Spirit of Beauty', which 'ever on | Rolls the round day, and calls the starry fires | To their glad watch'. Two years later, Hunt expanded on this image of beauty making the world go round in a translation of *DRN* 1's opening hymn to Venus which begins:

> Parent of Rome, delicious Queen of Love,
> Thou joy of men below and gods above;
> Who in one round of ever-blest increase
> Roll'st the green regions and the dancing seas;
> From whom all beings catch the race they run,
> And leap to life, and visit the dear sun;
> Thee, Goddess, thee, the winds, the winters fly,
> Thee, and the coming of thy suavity: –
> For thee the earth lays forth its flowers: for thee,
> A lustre laughs along the golden sea,
> And lightsome heav'n looks round on all, for thou hast made it free.[28]

The unstilted diction and rich alliteration, and the impudent effectiveness of the direct borrowing 'suavity' (from *DRN* 1.6's *suavis*), give this translation a pleasant insouciance which makes one wish Hunt had attempted more Lucretius.

---

[27] Cf. again *DRN* 1.62–5.
[28] 'Lucretius: To Venus', 1–11; Hunt 1923: 414. Previous Hunt quotations: 242. For contemporary denunciations of the Hunt circle's Lucretianism see Cox 1998: 34.

Shelley's own immersion in Lucretius is too well established to need detailed examination here. It began at Eton, with his conversion to atheism by 'the best of the Latin poets' whom he continued to rank above Virgil as 'in the highest . . . sense, a creator' and whose *DRN* he acclaimed as 'the basis of our metaphysical knowledge'.[29] Lucretius' declaration that he will untie the mental knots of superstition provides an epigraph for the pugnaciously atheistic *Queen Mab*, whose notes spell out the Lucretian sources of its denunciations of money-lust as well as the ill effects of religion.[30] In the poem *Mont Blanc* the phrase 'daedal earth' echoes *DRN* 1.7 in implying the formation of organic from inorganic matter; and 'Ode to the West Wind' derives much of its meteorological imagery from the *DRN*.[31] One recent book-length study, relating Shelley to modern chaos theory by way of the Lucretian *clinamen* or atomic swerve, has argued that the conflicting 'two thoughts' of scepticism and idealism which recent Shelley criticism has struggled to drag into unity are both simply different aspects of his fundamental Lucretianism.[32]

Keats, another writer who exchanged sonnets with Hunt, based his famous sonnet 'On First Looking into Chapman's Homer' on John Evelyn's comparison of Creech's *DRN* translation to Cortez's conquest of the Incas' realms of gold, although otherwise his work has few directly Lucretian echoes.[33] For Byron, on the other hand, the *DRN* was, as poetry, 'the first of Latin poems'.[34] Interestingly – for him – Byron questioned its 'ethics', but this related more to the Epicurean ideal of apolitical disengagement than to the problems presented to schoolteachers by the 'irreligion' which *Don Juan* (1.43) describes with amused irony as 'too strong | For early stomachs, to prove wholesome food'. In a letter to Murray, Byron plays with Lucretius' idea that though we have no immortal souls, the 'surfaces or cases, like the Coats of an onion' that our bodies must constantly throw off to be materially perceptible may somehow survive us: 'I do not disbelieve that we may be *two* . . . I only hope that *t'other me* behaves like a Gemman.'[35] This rather accurately sums up the continuing difficulty Byron still presents to his

---

29 For Eton see Medwin 1913: 50. Quotations from 'A Defence of Poetry' and Preface to *Laon and Cythna*; P. B. Shelley 1988: 287, 319.

30 *Queen Mab*, Epigraph; notes to 5.58, 5.112–13; P. B. Shelley 1907: 754, 794, 796.

31 *Mont Blanc*, 86; for the ode see Edgecombe 1999: 134.

32 Roberts 1997: 411. A more bizarre, but influential, application of the *clinamen* idea to Shelley and, more substantially, to Blake, is made by Bloom 1973: 19–45.

33 See Wagenblass 1937: 539–41; but apart from this derivation of Keats's great sonnet from Creech, Wagenblass's Lucretian 'echoes' in Keats are not specially convincing.

34 'Letter to John Murray, Esq' (1821); Byron 1991: 144.

35 Letter to Murray, 6 October 1820; Byron 1973–94: VII, 192. 'Gemman': i.e. 'gentleman'.

readers, of integrating any poetic interiority his work may contain with the projected, not entirely 'gentlemanly' superstar image.

Elsewhere Byron commented that there is no need to envy Lucretius' 'nonchalant' gods since 'he has excused *us* from damnation':[36] a particularly welcome release in the light of Byron's never-quite-dispelled Calvinism. In return for lifting this anxiety, however, the *DRN* confronts us with another: that since it is only made of a chance confluence of atoms, the world will one day be destroyed – an event arguably prefigured in its closing description of the plague in Athens. The idea that facing such prospects is a necessary though horrendous price to pay for abandoning the old theology of a punitive afterlife is perhaps one explanation of Byron's terrifying poem *Darkness* (1816), in which the sun goes out, mankind perishes in agonies of cold and hunger, and the world becomes 'Seasonless, herbless, treeless, manless, lifeless – | A lump of death – a chaos of hard clay'.[37] A similar motif of universal destruction underlies Mary Shelley's novel *The Last Man* (1826), in which the heroic establishment of an ideal republican world order by heroes clearly based on Byron and her husband sits strangely with the coming of a plague which renders all their efforts futile by annihilating the whole human race. While the novel doubtless has much to do with Mary Shelley's grief and anger at the actual deaths of her husband and Byron just a few years before, it can also be seen as a struggle to work out the contradictions in their circle's twin devotions to political activism and a Lucretian materialism which enjoined apolitical retreat from a world so vulnerable to physical dissolution.

In spite of the slowly darkening image suggested by these last examples, the much-translated Lucretius of the Romantic late Enlightenment was an overwhelmingly bullish, confident figure, authorising a range of challenges to conventional religion, from generalised attacks on excessive 'superstition' to nature worship and the full-blown materialism of the first properly articulated theory of evolution. Despite valuable work on Wordsworth and Shelley in particular, this second Lucretian moment has gone under-recognised partly because the *DRN* does not fit well into the Romantic image of fervent spirituality, and partly thanks to the stealing of the first evolutionary controversy's thunder by Erasmus Darwin's more famous grandson, Charles.

Thus the two best accounts of Lucretius' nineteenth-century influence place its epicentre firmly after *The Origin of Species* in 1859. As Frank M. Turner attests, the challenge to orthodox Christian accounts of creation embodied in Charles Darwin's great work stirred a major mid-Victorian controversy over Lucretius, with Darwinian/atomist materialists led by John Tyndall claiming him as a philosophical forebear, and liberal Christians such

---

[36] Byron 1973–94: III, 210. [37] Ll. 71–2; Byron 1970: 95–6. Cf. *DRN* 5.82–96.

as John Masson, Andrew Veitch and W. H. Mallock using this claimed inheritance to convict modern science for the *DRN*'s demonstrable mistakes, while at the same time recruiting the poet himself for their own side on the grounds that his daring challenge to pagan religion created a perfect Christianity-shaped hole.[38] To make his persuasive case for the liberal-Christian takeover of Lucretius, however, Turner suggests that only in the post-Darwinian 1860s was there any serious interest in the philosophy of 'the Roman poet who during the first half of the century had been judged solely on the artistic merit of his verse'.[39] In another excellent commentary on Lucretius' nineteenth-century impact, W. R. Johnson sums up the whole 'Romantic' response in the single apparent criticism (not borne out by most of Shelley's remarks) from a Shelley supposedly 'agog with Platonic rapture and transcendental yearnings' that Lucretius 'limed the wings of his swift spirit in the dregs of the sensible world', and he uses Byron's quip about Lucretius' irreligion being too strong for the classroom as a proof that Polignac's *Anti-Lucretius* had rendered the *DRN*'s philosophy unreadable in Britain before his high Victorian re-emergence as a gloomy embodiment of tortured 'melancholy'.[40] At his amusing strongest on this compulsion to tie Lucretius hand and foot to 'the "M" word',[41] Johnson completely overlooks his positive importance to many writers of the Romantic period.

It is nonetheless true that a decade or so after Shelley's death Lucretius begins to be read as a tragic figure, whose poetic power is constantly at odds with a philosophy now indeed perceived as 'gloomy' – because without Christian salvation – rather than as enlightened and liberating. In *A Vision of Poets*, 1844, Elizabeth Barrett Browning projects him as one 'nobler than his mood', who 'denied | Divinely the divine' but whose 'Face is stern, | As one compelled, in spite of scorn, | To teach a truth he would not learn'. This shift in focus to Lucretius as a tragic personality is dependent on his philosophy rather than oblivious to it, though that philosophy is now read negatively or ambivalently. The figure of Lucretius as a representative of tormented modernity is embedded throughout Matthew Arnold's work, from his 1837 school verse exercise 'Juvat ire jugis', written at fourteen, to one of his last major poems, *Obermann Once More* (1867), taking in *en route* his most important drama. Expanding on a set Virgilian passage itself influenced by Lucretius, 'Juvat ire jugis' takes this implicit link further in its central image of a solitary poet figure climbing a mountain 'to seek out the secrets of matter'. Lucretius' statement that the hope of poetic renown drives him into the untrodden regions round the Pierian well of knowledge (*DRN*

---

[38] Turner 1993: 270–8. For Masson see also pp. 307–8 below.
[39] Turner 1993: 266.   [40] W. R. Johnson 2000: 84, 104.   [41] W. R. Johnson 2000: 132.

1.926–7) becomes concretised in the image of the lonely mountain ascent, to which Arnold adds the idea of death waiting at the summit (in this case by avalanche), which he later reworked in his major philosophical tragedy, *Empedocles on Etna.*

Published in 1852, *Empedocles* incorporates material from the projected tragedy about Lucretius which Arnold first planned in 1845 and worked on at intervals until abandoning it in 1856.[42] The strong parallels between Lucretius and his suicidal scientist-poet predecessor Empedocles were currently being explored by Arnold's Oxford associate, W. Y. Sellar, whose monograph *The Roman Poets of the Republic* also lends countenance to St Jerome's claim that the former committed suicide – though driven to it by an 'unrelieved intensity of thought and feeling' rather than a love-philtre.[43] It is thus not unlikely that Arnold arrived at the less familiar figure of Empedocles through his interest in Lucretius, finding the first the better subject for his poem on account of his more dramatic and better-attested suicide and his less wholesale rejection of what Sellar calls 'the dreams and sorrows of religious mysticism', the regret at leaving which behind lends Empedocles' awakening rationalism its 'mournful tone'.[44] Arnold's Empedocles is similarly self-divided, between a public self who exhorts his followers to grasp man's position in the material universe without recourse to superstitious hopes or fears, and a private self whose soliloquies agonise over the soul's need for something more. Thus the long Act 1 speech of the public self to his disciples incorporates, alongside many other Lucretian and Epicurean echoes, a passage from the planned Lucretius play, asking if it is 'so small a thing' to have had the pleasure of life,

> That we must feign a bliss
> Of doubtful future date,
> And, while we dream on this,
> Lose all our present state,
> And relegate to worlds yet distant our repose?[45]

It is the other, soliloquising Empedocles of the second act who concludes that the intellectual life is indeed too small a thing, before throwing himself into the crater of Mount Etna.

Arnold gives a more direct view of Lucretius in his lecture 'On the Modern Element in Literature' (1857):

---

[42] See Culler 1966: 217–22.

[43] Sellar 1889: 283. The ideas of Sellar's 1863 (i.e. post-*Empedocles*) study, in which Lucretius is the dominant figure, are likely to have reached Arnold through personal contacts: see Schneider 1981: 191.

[44] Sellar 1889: 301.   [45] 1.ii.402–6; Arnold 1979: 182.

Depression and ennui; these are the characteristics stamped on how many of the representative works of modern times! they are also the characteristics stamped on the poem of Lucretius . . . Yes, Lucretius is modern; but is he adequate? . . . there is no peace, no cheerfulness for him either in the world from which he comes, or in the solitude to which he goes.[46]

This 'depressed' Lucretius, whose retreat from the social world brings him no ultimate solace, does indeed have modern parallels – in Hamlet, Faust, Byron's Manfred and the hero of Senancour's *Obermann*, around whom Arnold twined two key poetic attempts to define his own role as a writer. The second, *Obermann Once More* (1867), can be read as Arnold's farewell to the isolated effort of poetry in favour of the more social communication of prose.[47] Here an image from Lucretius – of a bored nobleman who drives out to the country only to return home the moment he gets there[48] – is used to write off both the irreligious Roman world and the describer, Lucretius himself:

> On that hard Pagan world disgust
> And secret loathing fell,
> Deep weariness and sated lust
> Made human life a hell.[49]

The use of Lucretius to indicate not just the evils of 'pagan' society but also the inadequacy of a purely rationalist solitude seems likewise to characterise Arnold's later plans for a play on the subject of Lucretius himself: as pieced together by A. Dwight Culler, this was to be a busily peopled Shakespearean drama about Roman politics at their most vicious, in which Lucretius seems to stand for the impotent intellectual, incapable of social or emotional commitment.[50]

The long gestation of Arnold's Lucretian project saw it overtaken by several events: a new prose translation of 1851 by John Selby Watson (incorporating a fresh edition of Good's 1805 verse one), a massive new edition by Tennyson's friend H. A. J. Munro in 1864, followed in the same year by the translation which became standard for the rest of the century, and finally Tennyson's poem *Lucretius*, 1868, whose stealing of the march on him Arnold found distinctly annoying.[51] Turner's view that this poem marked 'the beginning of a new appreciation for Lucretius and his philosophy'[52] is somewhat

---

[46] Arnold 1960: 32–3.   [47] See Culler 1966: 285.
[48] *DRN* 3.1060–7, with which Arnold also epitomises Lucretian *ennui* immediately following the prose passage just quoted.
[49] *Obermann Once More*, 93–6; Arnold 1979: 565.   [50] Culler 1966: 218–21.
[51] W. R. Johnson 2000: 109.   [52] Turner 1993: 268.

dubious. Working with Munro at his elbow enabled a skilfully woven net-work of cross-references to the *DRN*, but Tennyson constructs a Lucretius who is plainly wrong – in a tortured, high Victorian way – in almost all his conclusions. The first question the poem raises is why Tennyson chose to refract Lucretius' ideas (or their breakdown) through the lens of St Jerome's unsubstantiated tale of his suicide after a love-potion administered by his wife had driven him mad. At bottom, the poem shares the early Christian apologist's wish to see the unbeliever hoist by the petard of his own supposed self-contradictions: here, the warning against the distractions of sexual love at the end of the *DRN* 4. As reworked by Tennyson, the story also estab-lishes a Lucretius deeply flawed from the start by the sexual impotence which drives his wife to slip the potion into his drink.

Once this background is established, most of the poem consists of Lucretius' tortured, half-mad soliloquy on waking from a dream which min-gles the scarier aspects of his atomic theory with images of sexual orgy, climaxing in a Troy-destroying fire shooting from Helen's naked breasts.[53] Wondering whether all this is Venus' revenge for his critique of monogamous love, Lucretius reminds himself – and the reader – that he does not believe in divine agency, and only uses her 'popular name' to 'shadow forth | The all-generating powers'. This leads to a deeper probing of Epicurus' hitherto-trusted view that the gods do nonetheless exist: if so, 'how then should the Gods | Being atomic not be dissoluble'? Unable to explain this, Lucretius forlornly confesses 'I have forgotten what I meant: my mind | Stumbles.'[54]

Nonetheless, the gods' indifference to human fate is a strong justification for suicide when the body is threatened by illness, or the mind by uncon-trollable sexual images, which are likened to a revolutionary mob breaking down the doors of a wise senate. This idea introduces the most explicit fan-tasy so far, in which a seductively described nymph flees from a repulsive satyr towards the poet himself; despite sharing her loathing for her pursuer, the prospect of her flinging herself 'shameless on me' drives Lucretius to exhort the satyr to catch up and rape her, while he himself is torn between a desire to 'massacre' them both and peer at them through the bushes (203–7). In a passage Freud would have appreciated, he contrasts the long calm picnic of 'settled, sweet, Epicurean life' with the disruption wrought by the id-like 'unseen monster' which, like the satyr, 'lays | His vast and filthy hands upon my will, | Wrenching it backward into his' (218–21). Given all this, and his in any case somewhat lukewarm love of 'our little life' (227), Lucretius deter-mines to die like a Roman, not 'dragged in triumph' (234) by the monster

---

[53] For an extended discussion of this image, see Freeman 1973: 69–75.
[54] A. Tennyson 1987: III, 96–7; ll. 88–9, 114–15; 122–3.

of lust but laying down his life to resist it, like his near-namesake Lucretia after her rape by Tarquin. Glad that, though unfinished, his poem will help mankind by plucking 'the mortal soul from out immortal hell', he expires in the arms of his guilt-stricken wife, pondering the not very Epicurean – but very Victorian – question 'What is duty?' (280).

In turning *DRN* 4's ambivalent rejection of obsessive love (Lucretius has little problem with promiscuity as a cure for this unfortunate state)[55] into a case study in self-repression, Tennyson channels a long British tradition of puritanical figures destroyed by their own inner urges – from Angelo in Shakespeare's *Measure for Measure* to Ambrosio in Matthew Lewis's *The Monk* – into a portrait of sexual neurosis which feels quintessentially British and, indeed, Victorian. As Johnson argues, Tennyson's mixture of fascination and terror over 'the truths about (his) sexuality' as well as the *DRN*'s challenges to his politics and theology led him to produce a poem of unquestionable power which is nonetheless only 'a new version of the Anti-Lucretius, the melancholy suicide who could not be saved by the philosophy that he preached'.[56]

Though Arnold's and Tennyson's depressed, tortured modern marks Lucretius' most striking presence in Victorian literature, there was also a thread of continuity from the Enlightenment/Romantic embrace of the *DRN* as a right-minded guide to the good life. In 1859 Edward FitzGerald prefaced his translation of Omar Khayyám's *Rubáiyát* by pairing the Persian scientist-poet with Lucretius: both were 'men of subtle, strong and cultivated Intellect, fine Imagination, and hearts passionate for Truth and Justice; who justly revolted from their Country's false Religion'.[57] While Omar abandoned all hope of making sense of his godless, deterministic universe except as a pleasurable 'diversion',

> Lucretius . . . composing himself into a Stoical rather than Epicurean severity of Attitude, sat down to contemplate the mechanical Drama of the Universe which he was part Actor in; himself, and all about him (as in his own sublime description of the Roman Theatre) discoloured with the lurid reflex of the Curtain suspended between the Spectator and the Sun.[58]

Though FitzGerald admits the implication that both poets were driven to their extreme positions through lack of access to 'better Revelation', his sympathy with their disabused vision is very plain. While retaining a similar reservation, Walt Whitman also proposed Lucretius' nobility of ambition

---

[55] See *DRN* 4.1062–72.
[56] W. R. Johnson 2000: 122–3. For another useful account of Tennyson's Victorianising of Lucretius see Rudd 1994: 91–116.
[57] FitzGerald 1962: 232.   [58] FitzGerald 1962: 232; cf. *DRN* 4.75–89.

as a model for a future marriage of poetry and science in his classic essay 'Democratic Vistas', 1871:

> What the Roman Lucretius sought most nobly, yet all too blindly, negatively to do for his age and its successors, must be done positively by some great coming literatus, especially poet, who, while remaining fully poet, will absorb whatever science indicates.[59]

Further down the path to the century's end, a distinctly Omaresque Lucretius informs aspects of the emerging Aesthetic Movement, whose presiding figure Walter Pater identifies the *DRN* in *Marius the Epicurean* (1885) with the 'thunder and lightning some distance off, [which] one might recline to enjoy, in a garden of roses'.[60] A more ambivalent range of responses is suggested by W. H. Mallock, an anti-materialist combatant in the Lucretian controversy stirred up by Tyndall's Belfast Address, who helped to dash Pater's hopes of an Oxford University Proctorship with an *ad hominem* portrayal as the Epicurean, moment-hugging and presumably gay 'Mr Rose' in his Peacockian satire *The New Republic* (1877), before himself translating key parts of the *DRN* into the form and idiom of FitzGerald's *Rubáiyát*.[61] A more pugnacious proto-Aesthete than Pater was Algernon Swinburne, whose 'For the Feast of Giordano Bruno', 1878, enthrones Lucretius and Percy Shelley as fit companions for the soul of Bruno, the Renaissance 'philosopher and martyr' whose

> spirit on earth was as a rod
> To scourge off priests, a sword to pierce their God,
> A staff for man's free thought to walk alone.[62]

Swinburne's loud reaffirmation of the atheism that lay at the heart of Victorian nervousness about the *DRN* will serve as a concluding reminder that the robust Lucretius of late Enlightenment Romanticism was not entirely buried.

Further reading

For Lucretius' British reception as a whole, Spencer 1965 surveys the scientific poem and W. R. Johnson 2000 contains the most enjoyable general account to date. For the Romantic period, see Bloom 1973's mysterious thoughts on the *clinamen*, Priestman 1999, and studies of individual writers:

---

[59] Whitman 1964: 2.421.   [60] Pater 1948: 344. See also Hadzsits 1963: 361.
[61] See further Turner 1993: 272–7; Dowling 1991: x–xi; and ch. 19 below.
[62] Ll. 16–18; Swinburne 1905: 3. 48–9. For other Lucretian echoes in Swinburne, see F. W. H. Myers 1893, reprinted in Hyder 1970: 188–97.

on WORDSWORTH, Kelley 1983 (brief but excellent), Spiegelman 1985, Dix 2002; on SHELLEY, at volume length, Roberts 1997. On the Victorian period the most authoritative background account is Turner 1993, while from within that period itself, Sellar 1889 contains a completed version of the speculations about Lucretius which influenced both Arnold and Tennyson. For more on ARNOLD see Culler 1966 and Schneider 1981; on TENNYSON see Rudd 1994, Freeman 1973 and (again) W. R. Johnson 2000. On SWINBURNE see Myers 1893, and on E. B. BROWNING, FITZGERALD, PATER and others see (briefly but instructively) the last pages of Hadzsits 1963, which earlier offers a severe critique of Wakefield's 1796–7 edition.

19

STUART GILLESPIE AND DONALD MACKENZIE

Lucretius and the moderns

Macaulay, in his 1856 *Encyclopedia Britannica* essay on Oliver Goldsmith, proclaimed: 'the finest poem in the Latin language, indeed the finest didactic poem in any language, was written in defence of the silliest and meanest of all systems of natural and moral philosophy'.[1] In the Introduction to his 1976 translation of the *DRN*, C. H. Sisson claims: 'The *De Rerum Natura* is a vision, much as *Piers Plowman* is a vision, though Lucretius is much more powerful as well as more sophisticated. The moments of insight *use* the Epicurean theory as a means of expression, but the vision is of something more terrible than the theory.'[2] The citing of Langland as an analogue is suggestive,[3] the distance opened between Lucretius' vision and the theory it uses, ponderable; and we shall return to both in this account of primarily anglophone responses to Lucretius from about 1890 to the present. But to juxtapose Macaulay and Sisson signals one notable shift in the later twentieth-century reception of Lucretius, from the 1970s on: the response to his poem as offering serious arguments, requiring and rewarding a sustained philosophical engagement. This will be addressed below; but 'philosophical' should be stressed. For the second half of the twentieth century the physical science of the poem is no longer a central focus as it had been in the later nineteenth century, when Lucretius was constantly correlated with contemporary science, whether in enthusiastic appraisal or jaundiced critique.[4] W. R. Johnson supplies a telling overview of the disappearance of this approach in the twentieth century.[5] One might note in passing, however, Sir William Bragg's salute to Lucretius in the opening chapter of his popularising 1925 lectures

---

[1] Macaulay 1860: II, 254. Macaulay's Lucretian marginalia are discussed by Hugh Sykes Davies in Trevelyan 1937: 279–90.
[2] Sisson 1976: 10.
[3] For comparisons with Dante, another medieval poet of 'vision', see Boyde 1981: 1–40.
[4] For examples of enthusiastic appraisal see Mackail 1895: 44–6; of jaundiced critique Mallock 1878: 152–61.
[5] W. R. Johnson 2000: 127–33.

Concerning the Nature of Things – the book which inspired Primo Levi to a scientific career.[6] More recently the possibility has been raised of bringing Lucretius to bear on questions not of cosmology or human evolution as such, but of scientific epistemology. Don and Peta Fowler observe that 'metaphors and models such as the atoms as "seeds" have become in recent years a central concern of scientists and philosophers', and Duncan Kennedy calls on Lucretius in his discussion of epistemological realism versus constructivism.[7]

Images of Lucretius

John Masson's synoptic and summatory two-volume account of *Lucretius: Epicurean and Poet* (1907–9) provides a good vantage point from which to scan approaches to Lucretius near the beginning of the twentieth century. Here we find ourselves in some ways very much in the arena of later nineteenth-century reception of the *DRN*. As has been suggested, the period from 1868 until after the turn of the century is continuous in that 'every major and almost every minor comment, article, or book about Lucretius concentrated on his relationship to contemporary scientific theory and to the conflict between religious and scientific writers'.[8] Masson attends to the rule of universal law as fundamental to a scientific world-view; to Lucretius' place in the history and development of atomic theory; and to the clash between Christian theism and an aggressive materialist naturalism urged by the mathematician William Clifford or the physicist John Tyndall.[9] He expounds in detail Lucretius' own atomic theory, noting in conclusion its anticipation of the doctrine of the conservation of energy. He stresses the conceptual gap between the primordial atoms and the complexity of the world and of consciousness, and he pursues in detail the 1870s controversy on atomic materialism between Tyndall and the Unitarian minister James Martineau, who dismissively characterised Tyndall's Lucretian detachment of the creator from his universe as 'the *new* book of Genesis'. One passage in Masson's narrative vividly illustrates the later nineteenth-century milieu of Lucretius' reception:

> Martineau replied to Tyndall's pamphlet, and the battle was fully fought out. The great controversy was indeed carried out on both sides to its utmost issues, and its progress was watched with an interest of more than mere intellectual curiosity . . . Not a few felt as if convictions in which their lives and hopes were rooted were breaking up and vanishing away . . . If some had at first feared

---

[6] Bragg 1925: 1–4; Levi 2000: 31.   [7] Melville 1997: xxv; Kennedy 2002.

[8] F. M. Turner 1973: 330.

[9] On these topics see further F. M. Turner 1973 and ch. 18 above.

lest insensate Matter should soon become lord of all, they found, when they closely grappled with the phantom, that it collapsed in their grasp.

(1, 188–9)[10]

And the conclusion of this section is interestingly like and unlike later twentieth-century responses to the naturalistic Lucretian universe:

> We have now surveyed the controversy of Matter over all the disputed ground, and what is the result? Is it that the whole world has become disenchanted and dead? or do not the consequences far rather tend the other way, and has not the earth our dwelling-place, with all its mysteries of life and growth, become more wonderful than we before thought it? nay, indeed, is it not more sacred also? (1, 198)

This is part of Masson's overall drive to claim Lucretius for religion, even as clearing the way for a biblical theism. But students of literature and culture will note how his meshing of the *DRN* with contemporary science, theology and anti-theology is framed and balanced, at one end, by a sketch of Lucretius' context in the society of the Republic in its last decades of turmoil, and at the other by a comparison of Lucretius' cosmological poetry with that of Hugo.

The image Masson offers of Lucretius can be flanked by those of the French philosopher Henri Bergson in the introduction to his selection from the *DRN* (1883), and the Harvard thinker George Santayana in his *Three Philosophical Poets* (1910). Bergson concisely informs his readers about text, grammar and vocabulary; he insists on the importance of reading the poem as a whole; and he sketches its achievement and limitation as a work of science, celebrating the role of universal and immutable law as Lucretius' fundamental perception and master concept. He casts Lucretius as following Epicurus very closely, but as nevertheless, and perhaps in spite of himself, 'singularly original'; and this on two counts. First, Lucretius is possessed of a passion for the scientific study of nature in itself, and not only as the (reductive) means to banish the gods; second, he exhibits and evokes a response to human existence very different from the 'unalterable serenity to which the true Epicurean aspires'.[11] The first difference leads us to Lucretius' double vision of nature: 'he perceives in nature at the same instant what interests the geometer and what seduces the painter' (34). The second culminates in the description of the plague at Athens: Lucretius aimed to show us the impotence of gods and men in the face of the laws of nature; he wished the

---

[10] J. Masson 1907–9.

[11] Bergson 1957: 36; subsequent parenthetical citations of Bergson refer to this edition and translations are our own.

spectacle to be terrifying (*effrayant*), and he succeeded. This makes the ending of the poem its proper climax; and it harks back to Bergson's eloquent opening evocation of the poem's essential melancholy, a melancholy whose root cause, though assuredly heightened by Lucretius' political milieu, is that 'we hardly count in the universe' (21). Overall, one might say that Bergson presents a Lucretius with an imaginative vision akin to that of Thomas Hardy – but a Hardy braced by something of the analytic sweep and rigour of Pascal.

Santayana's elegant essay shares at least two features with Bergson's account: a certain disparagement of Epicurus ('the Herbert Spencer of antiquity . . . in his natural philosophy an encyclopaedia of second-hand knowledge'),[12] and the claim that a double vision of nature is central to Lucretius' work. That vision Santayana formulates as an intellectual philosophy of naturalism which

> divines substance behind appearance, continuity behind change, law behind fortune . . . So understood, nature has depth as well as surface, force and necessity as well as sensuous variety. Before the sublimity of this insight, all forms of the pathetic fallacy seem cheap and artificial. Mythology, that to a childish mind is the only possible poetry, sounds like bad rhetoric in comparison.
>
> (35–6)

Naturalism, so conceived, is fundamental to Santayana's account of Lucretius. He claims for him the twin defining features of a naturalist thinker: the 'discarding of final causes on which all progress in science depends', and the tenet that 'Nature is her own standard . . . if she seems to us unnatural, there is no hope for our minds' (28). More radically, he asserts, the fact 'that things have their poetry, not because of what we make them symbols of, but because of their own movement and life, is what Lucretius proves once for all to mankind' (34); and this assertion is worked through in an extended comparison of Lucretius as a poet of nature with Shelley as a 'symbolic landscape poet' (58) and Wordsworth as a poet of human nature in landscape. Comparison with the latter climaxes in the eloquent passage:

> Nature, for the Latin poet, is really nature. He loves and fears her, as she deserves to be loved and feared by her creatures. Whether it be a wind blowing, a torrent rushing, a lamb bleating, the magic of love, genius achieving its purpose, or a war, or a pestilence, Lucretius sees everything in its causes and in its total career. One breath of lavish creation, one iron law of change, runs through the whole, making all things kin in their inmost elements and in their last end . . . Here is the true echo of the life of matter. (61–2)

---

[12] Santayana 1910: 29; subsequent parenthetical citations of Santayana refer to this edition.

Santayana criticises Lucretius on the soul and immortality as 'an imperfect psychologist and an arbitrary moralist' (45); he criticises him for not developing Epicurean piety towards the gods, as Epicurus conceived them, into an aesthetic religion; and for not developing, in comparison with Horace, the Epicurean cult of friendship. Finally he criticises him for too narrow a response to human history. All these complaints issue from Santayana's own version of naturalism, which is not without its danger of a blasé superiority ('Lucretius studies superstition, but only as an enemy; and the naturalistic poet should be the enemy of nothing', 67). And noting that materialism, 'like any system of natural philosophy, carries with it no commandments and no advice' (32), he makes clear his own preference for vitality, with a touch of Nietzschean hardness, against the quietism of Epicurus or the melancholy (perhaps overstated) of Lucretius.

The importance of Lucretius for Santayana is documented elsewhere in his work.[13] *Three Philosophical Poets* brings to bear on the *DRN* a developed philosophical outlook combined with a literary-critical approach which, if tinged at points with the bellettristic, can also, in its ease of comparativist reference and even its phrasing, put one in mind of that Harvard-educated philosopher-critic of the next generation, T. S. Eliot. And Santayana formulates what one might take as the motto for Lucretius' imaginative presence in the modern world:

> A naturalistic conception of things is a great work of imagination, – greater, I think, than any dramatic or moral mythology: it is a conception fit to inspire great poetry, and in the end, perhaps, it will prove the only conception able to inspire it.
>
> (21)

This comprehensive response to Lucretius the cosmological poet, rarer than one might have expected in the twentieth century, finds an echo in two Italian men of letters writing near that century's end. The novelist Italo Calvino offered to undertake for his publisher an Italian translation of the *DRN*; alongside Ovid's *Metamorphoses*, he remarked in 1985, it was his bedside book, and he wished everything he wrote to be related 'to one or the other, or better to both'.[14] His novel *Mr Palomar* was, he concluded, closer to Lucretius: its protagonist experiences a phenomenological desire to observe life and nature from afar. In the opening lecture of his *Six Memos for the Next Millennium* (1988) Calvino salutes the *DRN* as 'the first great work of poetry in which knowledge of the world tends to dissolve the solidity of the world, leading to a perception of all that is infinitely minute,

---

[13] See, e.g., Santayana 1986: 230, 455, 538, 540; Santayana 2003: 370.
[14] Quoted from Weiss 1993: 210. For his offer to translate see McLaughlin 1998: 51.

light, and mobile'.[15] This gives to Lucretius' materialism a new inflection which Calvino uses to illuminate Renaissance syncretism and the inextricable mingling of melancholy and humour in Hamlet or the Jacques of *As You Like It*, as well as a Renaissance sense of 'cosmic excitement' and cosmic precariousness in Cyrano de Bergerac.[16] Near the end of the lecture the cosmic mobility of the atomised modulates into a characteristic modern preoccupation with 'the thread of writing as a metaphor of the powder-fine substance of the world'; 'for Lucretius, letters were atoms in continual motion, creating the most diverse words and sounds by means of their permutations'.[17]

Primo Levi, by contrast, in his personal anthology *The Search for Roots* (first published in Italian in 1981), to which Calvino supplies an afterword, evokes an older image of Lucretius as deliverer from irrational fears and enchaining superstition. The passage of the *DRN* he includes is 2.381–427, his headnote signalling its primal appeal to a professional chemist: 'his materialism, and hence his mechanical reductionism, is naïve and now makes us smile, but here and there appear astonishing intuitions: why is olive-oil viscous, diamond hard, and seawater salty?'[18] The anthology closes with a scientific paper on the search for black holes, from which Levi draws an eloquent summary on the cosmos as alien to man but also comprehensible by science: 'the universe is not made for human beings; it is hostile, violent, alien . . . the heavens are not simple, but neither are they impermeable to our minds'.[19] This interacts most suggestively with a passage from Job with which the anthology opens. Levi's vision includes – can include – no equivalent of the Epicurean gods; but, if even bleaker than that of Lucretius where the latter is at its most ascetically scientific, it is also Lucretian in its power to brace and exhilarate the imagination.

Lucretius among the poets

The American poet Wallace Stevens famously declared that the great poems of Heaven and Hell had already been accomplished, but the great poem of Earth remained to be written. Yet Lucretius has been less seminal for the modern period than might have been expected. There has, of course, been no translation to touch Dryden's classic renderings[20] – classic not only in their quality as translation, but in their engagement with the broad range of the *DRN*: its cosmological poetry that reaches out to Virgil and to the Ovid of the *Metamorphoses*, its satire that has points of contact with Horace and

---

[15] Calvino 1988: 8.   [16] Calvino 1988: 18–22.   [17] Calvino 1988: 26.
[18] Levi 2002: 136.   [19] Levi 2002: 214.   [20] On Dryden see ch. 16, above.

Juvenal, its transmutations of the heroic, its impassioned argument. While one or two of these elements have, as we shall see, appealed to twentieth-century writers, the numerous complete translations of the *DRN*, whether verse or prose, show little special interest in any.[21] W. H. Mallock, it is true, focused on the Epicurean pleasure principle by rendering selections in the stanza of FitzGerald's Omar Khayyám in 1900, but the strain shows: Lucretius' 'epic grandeur and extended argument could not fairly be translated into brief lyrical intensities'.[22] Nor has this period produced a comprehensive icon of the Lucretian such as Tennyson, and in a measure Arnold, were able to fashion for the mid nineteenth century.

Instead there is a series of glancing or minimal engagements with Lucretius; or cases of affinity that involve no specific dependence. William Empson might count as a Lucretian poet *manqué*, imaginatively engaged with science and awed, exhilarated, yet ambivalent in response to an unresponsive cosmos. But there are only a few clear links in his output to particular Lucretian passages.[23] Hugh MacDiarmid's autobiography describes the kind of poetry he himself aspires to write as

> Full of august reverberations of world-literature and world-history,
>   Like the analogies between the Axiochus and the poet's argument
> In the splendours of the close of the Third Book of Lucretius.[24]

And it could be argued that in such a late masterpiece as *On a Raised Beach* MacDiarmid achieves a notably Lucretian poetry: a poetry that ardently expounds the craggily scientific, its cosmological vision austerely decentring the human and achieving a transcendence that is atheist but not irreligious. An earlier Scottish poet, John Davidson (1857–1909) – saluted by MacDiarmid as a forerunner – was aligned with Lucretius by George Bernard Shaw in a suggestive overview of late nineteenth-century materialism.[25] A piece such as *The Testament of John Davidson* and its prose Dedication might be claimed as Lucretian in its monist materialism, its drive to expel all gods from the universe, and its assimilation of science. But the science it assimilates is a contemporary (late nineteenth-century) physics, and its stylistic mixture of the strident and the turgid is very un-Lucretian. Robert Bridges, who referred to his own *Testament of Beauty* as a *De hominum natura*,[26]

---

[21] For translations to 1960 see C. A. Gordon 1962: 185–92. Subsequent verse translators include Humphries 1968 and Sisson 1976.

[22] Vance 1997: 104.

[23] One such is the poem 'Invitation to Juno' which takes off from *DRN* 5.883 onwards.

[24] MacDiarmid 1943: 424.

[25] *Back to Methuselah*, in Shaw 1930–8: xvi, lxiv–v; see also Hadzsits 1963: 360.

[26] Lipscomb 1935: 77.

evokes Lucretius specifically to combat or qualify him. For instance, the proem to *DRN* 1 is evoked in *Testament* 3.245–54, only to incorporate its vision into Bridges' own. But this hardly counts as serious engagement with the Lucretian original.

A. E. Housman, by contrast, reveals a Lucretian substratum through his poetry. William Archer suggested this in an 1898 review of *A Shropshire Lad*;[27] and the latest edition of Housman's poems more fully documents Lucretian echoes and allusions.[28] This demonstrates that the *DRN* counts for Housman's poetry principally in its treatment of death, dissolution and not-being. Housman draws on Lucretius in single phrases and images, or else for an overarching vision of human mortality. A phrase may expand, as *per loca pastorum deserta et otia dia* (*DRN* 5.1387) does in the enchanted pastoral and psychopompic procession of 'The Merry Guide'; or it may be deployed with a deliberate offhandedness, as when *summa rerum* jostles with the mythological and the mundane in 'Epitaph on an Army of Mercenaries':

> Their shoulders held the sky suspended;
> They stood, and earth's foundations stay;
> What God abandoned, these defended,
> And saved the sum of things for pay.

Or the Lucretian can broadly underlie the plangency of a piece such as 'Be still, my soul, be still'.[29] But more potent than such declaimings of a late nineteenth-century pessimism, with its sentimental elaboration, are Housman's responses to Lucretian apocalyptic, the vision of the world running down or hurtling towards a naturalistic ruin. 'I wake from dreams and turning' (*More Poems*, XLIII) fashions this vision into a brocaded cosmological lyric. And 'Parta Quies' subversively marries a Lucretian apocalypse (compare especially *DRN* 3.842) with biblical apocalypse at its most absolute (Revelation 20:11) to achieve an almost toneless transcendence, at once dismissive and releasing:

> When earth's foundations flee,
> Nor sky nor land nor sea
> At all is found,
> Content you, let them burn:
> It is not your concern;
> Sleep on, sleep sound.

[27] Gardner 1992: 76. For more recent discussion see Marlow 1958: 58–9 and Haber 1967: 155–65.

[28] Burnett 1997, from which all subsequent quotations from Housman's poems are drawn.

[29] *A Shropshire Lad* XLVIII; cf. *DRN* 3.972–3 and 5.174–80.

'Proud Songsters' in Thomas Hardy's posthumously published *Winter Words* (1928) provides a coda to the Housman. It is characteristically Hardyesque in its rhythmic spacing, its sense of weather and season, and its imagining of metamorphosis. But whereas in a Hardy poem such as 'Voices from Things Growing in a Churchyard' the last of these elements can be teasingly, hauntingly Ovidian, the close of this one marks it as sparely Lucretian:

> The thrushes sing as the sun is going,
> And the finches whistle in ones and pairs,
> And as it gets dark loud nightingales
>   In bushes
> Pipe, as they can when April wears,
>   As if all Time were theirs.
>
> These are brand-new birds of twelve-months' growing,
> Which a year ago, or less than twain,
> No finches were, nor nightingales,
>   Nor thrushes,
> But only particles of grain,
>   And earth, and air, and rain.[30]

Against such lyric assimilations may be set Robert Frost's, which is expository and mediated through the Bergson of *Creative Evolution*. As with Bergson (see below) Frost engages with Lucretius in an evoking which is also a countering.[31] According to his biographer, Frost 'frequently mentioned his admiration for Lucretius'.[32] Of several Lucretian moments in Frost's work, the fullest comes in the title poem of his 1928 collection *West-Running Brook*, which might be characterised as a georgic dialogue between a husband and wife about a brook which runs west 'when all the other country brooks flow east'. The brook's trusting 'itself to go by contraries' becomes an image of their relationship, and beyond that, of existence which

> seriously, sadly, runs away
> To fill the abyss's void with emptiness . . .
> The universal cataract of death
> That spends to nothingness – and unresisted,
> Save by some strange resistance in itself,
> Not just a swerving, but a throwing back,

---

[30] Hardy 1932: 797–8.
[31] For the Bergson connection see Thompson 1967: 579–81 and 1971: 624–6.
[32] Thompson 1967: 624.

As if regret were in it and were sacred.
It has this throwing backward on itself.
So that the fall of most of it is always
Raising a little, sending up a little.
Our life runs down in sending up the clock.

(Frost is recorded at a 1949 public reading interjecting 'as in Lucretius' after the words 'Not just a swerving', a reference to the *clinamen* of *DRN* 2.216–93.)[33]

These are conscious or extended engagements; elsewhere a passage or element from Lucretius significantly crystallises the vision of an individual text, or provides a point of orientation for an œuvre. Ford Madox Ford exemplifies the former in his *Fifth Queen* trilogy of historical novels (1906–8). As the pivotal second novel, *Privy Seal*, moves to its climax with the overthrow of Cromwell, the plotters against the latter, tensely grouped in a room, overhear Henry VIII quoting Lucretius to Katharine Howard, Cromwell's principled Catholic opponent, who is about to become Henry's fifth wife. The quotation is of *DRN* 5.1233–5:

usque adeo res humanas uis abdita quaedam
obterit, et pulchros fascis saeuasque secures
proculcare ac ludibrio sibi habere uidetur.

So true is it that some hidden power grinds down humanity, and seems to trample upon the noble rods and the cruel axes, and hold them in derision.

In their immediate context those lines mesh with Henry's own capping quotation from Ecclesiastes and with the lines from Horace's decidedly Epicurean Ode 3.29 which supply the novel's epigraph; they underscore equally Cromwell's impending fall and Katharine's ambivalent triumph. In the fuller context of the trilogy they bring to focus the judgement it will pass on the world of Tudor politics with its pageantry, violence and intrigue; as such they can meaningfully be claimed as a subtext for the work as a whole.

Lucretius provides a point of orientation in a passage from the title poem of Edwin Muir's 1949 collection, *The Labyrinth*:

once in a dream or trance I saw the gods
Each sitting on the top of his mountain-isle,
While down below the little ships sailed by,
Toy multitudes swarmed in the harbours, shepherds drove
Their tiny flocks to the pastures, marriage feasts
Went on below, small birthdays and holidays,
Ploughing and harvesting and life and death,

---

[33] Thompson 1967: 624. For further discussion of this poem see Thompson 1971: 299–304.

> And all permissible, all acceptable,
> Clear and secure as in a limpid dream.
> But they, the gods, as large and bright as clouds,
> Conversed across the sounds in tranquil voices
> High in the sky above the untroubled sea,
> And their eternal dialogue was peace
> Where all these things were woven, and this our life
> Was as a chord deep in that dialogue,
> An easy utterance of harmonious words,
> Spontaneous syllables bodying forth a world.[34]

If the opening of this recalls the Homeric gods watching from Mount Ida in Books 13–15 of the *Iliad*, the very un-Homeric tranquillity of Muir's gods, and the dream-clarity with which they are apprehended, fit with Lucretius' decisive reprise of the Homeric Olympians in *DRN* 2.646–50, 3.18–24, 5.1169–82 and 6.73–8. The final lines extend the detached harmony to comprehend and articulate a created cosmos. This seems un- and anti-Lucretian, more akin to a Hebraic concept of the creating divine Word. But such a concept has been crossed with Lucretius' paralleling (*DRN* 2.1013–22; cf. *DRN* 1.823–9) of the letters out of whose combination his own verses are composed, with the elementary particles out of whose combination the cosmos comes into being. And the rippling vision Muir articulates here can link to much that is central in his poetry: to the contrasting Kafkaesque bewilderment or terror of the world-as-labyrinth in this poem itself; to what one might call his poetry of mythic aftermath in pieces like 'Troy' or 'The Grave of Prometheus'; to the heraldic panoramas which feature recurrently in his work. Such features are not, of course, Lucretian as such; but this Lucretian vision of the gods provides one focal point around which they can be ordered.

In the next generation of Scottish poets, Iain Crichton Smith's autobiographical poem *A Life* uses the reading of Lucretius to knit up the thread of his undergraduate studies with the experience of Aberdeen as physical place: its winter brings 'your weather, strict Lucretius . . . | The frost an exhalation of the mind. | The icy planets keep their rectitude. | Religion dies in temperatures like these. | And God the spider shrinks in his crystal web'.[35] Something of this purgative experience may suffuse Crichton Smith's poetry of nature, as in the 1962 meditation 'Deer on the High Hills', which ends:

> The deer step out in isolated air.
> Forgive the distance, let the transient journey
> on delicate ice not tragical appear

---

[34] Muir 1963: 165.   [35] Crichton Smith 1992: 256.

for stars are starry and the rain is rainy,
the stone is stony, and the sun is sunny,
the deer step out in isolated air.[36]

We may recall Santayana on Lucretius against Wordsworth: 'Nature, for the Latin poet, is really nature.'

This kind of Lucretian purification figures more largely in the work of the French poet Francis Ponge, whom Calvino celebrates in his third lecture as perhaps 'the Lucretius of our time, reconstructing the physical nature of the world by means of the impalpable, powder-fine dust of words'.[37] Ponge orientates his own materialist poetics, and its ethical thrust to cleanse the world, towards the work of Lucretius, for whom his admiration is unbounded ('I re-read Lucretius and say to myself that no-one has ever written anything more beautiful; that nothing of what he urged, in any category, seems to me to have been seriously refuted').[38] But though he proclaims a wish 'to write a kind of *De Rerum Natura* . . . not poems . . . but a single cosmogony',[39] the fact that his poetic is most distinctively realised in the often densely textured prose poems of *Le Parti pris des choses*, with the strenuous repristination of objects to which they summon their readers, may say something about Lucretian writing in the modern world. So likewise does his reversal of the Lucretian analogy between atoms and letters: 'whereas Lucretius developed his analogies in order to illustrate the workings of nature . . . in [Ponge's] work, they are used to explain the nature of the poetic text'.[40]

In English, while Ezra Pound waxed cool about Lucretius ('I suppose men can still read Lucretius. I prefer to respect him'),[41] some of his followers felt differently. Basil Bunting thought he had not 'read anything finer for twenty or thirty lines than the opening of the *De Rerum Natura*'[42] – and rendered it into English verse in 1927. Lucretius on the gods inspired the self-described 'Quaker atheist' Bunting more generally at this time. In an ode of the following year he wrote of

The distant gods enorbed in bright indifference
whom we confess creatures or abstracts of our spirit,
unadored, absorbed into the incoherence.[43]

---

[36] Crichton Smith 1992: 46.   [37] Calvino 1988: 76.

[38] Ponge 1999: 498; our translation. For an extended exposition see Meadows 1997: 73–154.

[39] Quoted in Meadows 1997: 27.   [40] Meadows 1997: 87.

[41] Pound 1978: 119. However, as Gilonis 1995: 161 n. 7 points out, there are some indications that Pound used the *DRN* more than this remark might suggest.

[42] Letter quoted by Gilonis 1995: 148.   [43] 'Ode 1. 8'; Bunting 1994: 86.

And, in his masterpiece *Briggflatts*, Bunting gave as the 'motto' of a central section Lucretius' line 1.73, *extra processit longe flammantia moenia mundi*.[44] In the later American Poundian Louis Zukofsky's understanding, Lucretius, 'who generates a world of atoms, [cannot] help proving his reason by dedicating it to the visible goodness of generative, bodily Venus'.[45] Zukofsky strips down, in his long poem *"A"*, the celebration of Venus in *DRN* 5.737ff.:

> Dear Spring goes her way with Venus.
> Before them –
> Inevitable wonders of winds,
> After – the west wind,
> Flowers run down the lanes.
> Next, heat parches
> Fullgrown grain blown dusty
> In annual gusts of the North.
> And it is autumn.
> Dancing step by step
> With Euhius Euan.[46]

More recently one can point to a range of more tangible, if small-scale, engagements on the part of, for example, Alistair Elliot or Derek Mahon.[47] But no poet currently writing in English seems quite so well matched with Lucretius the poet of the physical world as the contemporary German Raoul Schrott, whose work combines sharp sensory apprehension of natural phenomena with a marked interest in natural science. This affinity has led (to date) to a sequence of four short poems in imitation of moments in the *DRN*. We close this section with Iain Galbraith's English translation of the first:

> the way we squeeze a bay leaf
> between our fingers and the scent remains the rind
>   of green twigs easily peels the locusts
> shed their slender shells in summer
>   and snakes slough skin and leave the torn
> shreds flying on the thorns so too before
>   our eyes the images scale off things

---

44 See further Gilonis 1995: 157.   45 Zukofsky 1963: I, 88.

46 *"A"*, Part 12; Zukofsky 1966: 171. Here Zukofsky's Lucretius can be seen to be mediated through Cyril Bailey's 1910 prose translation.

47 See Elliot's poem 'An Old Theory of Vision' in his *Turning the Stones* (1993), which explicitly deploys the Lucretian notion of 'films'. For Mahon see the translation from *DRN* 6.451–523, 'Lucretius on Clouds', in his *Harbour Lights* (2005).

in countless outmost layers and carried by the wind
they come upon us waking or in sleep
and torture us as thoughts on a soul[48]

Lucretian arguments

Among twentieth-century engagements with Lucretius' thought which integrate the imaginative with the philosophical can be numbered those of Santayana at various points in the development of his thinking; of Bergson in his *Creative Evolution* of 1907; and, more recently, of Martha Nussbaum in her *Therapy of Desire*. Santayana recurrently professes himself 'a Naturalist in general philosophy'.[49] 'My naturalism', he claims, 'was never like Dewey's, without the realm of matter in the background, but was like Spinoza's or like that of Lucretius, who gives an admirable sketch of "the phases of human progress"' (370). Some implications of that materialist naturalism are set out, with an eloquent salute to Lucretius, in the Preface to his *Realm of Matter*, one of whose epigraphs is from the *DRN*:

> Weight and figure are not more characteristic of matter than explosiveness, swiftness, fertility, and radiation. Planters and breeders of animals, or poets watching the passing generations of mankind, will feel that the heart and mystery of matter lie in the seeds of things, *semina rerum*, and in the customary cycles of their transformation. It is by its motion and energy, by its fidelity to measure and law, that matter has become the substance of our world, and the principle of life and of death in it . . . Even those who, partly for dialectical reasons, reduced matter to impenetrable atoms, attributed all its fertility to the play of collisions which swept perpetually through the void and drove those dead atoms into constellations and vortices and organisms. This endless propulsion and those fated complications were no less material, and far more terrible, than any monumental heap into which matter might sometimes be gathered, and which to a gaping mind might seem more substantial. If any poet ever felt the life of nature in its truth, irrepressible, many-sided, here flaming up savagely, there helplessly dying down, that poet was Lucretius, whose materialism was unqualified.[50]

That resonates with Santayana's 1910 essay, but may resonate too with Sisson's remark on the Lucretian vision quoted at the opening of this chapter.

---

[48] Translation published *PN Review*, May–June 2004. Cf. *DRN* 4.54ff., 4.33ff.
[49] Santayana 2003: 106. Subsequent references to this edition parenthetically in the text.
[50] Santayana 1930: ix–x.

In the case of Bergson, his concept of the life force *might* be correlated with the Lucretian Venus of *DRN* 1. Also approximating to Lucretian protocols are his emphases on evolutionary discords and retrogressions,[51] on animal and human vulnerability (137–9), or – perhaps drawing him closer to the *DRN* – his emphasis on an unending process which overrides individual existences: 'It is as if the organism itself were only an excrescence . . . The essential thing is the *continuous progress* indefinitely pursued, an invisible progress, on which each visible organism rides during the short interval of time given it to live' (28–9; cf. 94–102, 104–7). But these remain affinities too general to illuminate very precisely. A closer kinship can be found when Bergson deploys Lucretian formulations, such as the parallel between the composition of a poem and the coming into being of the cosmos, to achieve conclusions that are un- or counter-Lucretian:

> Consider the letters of the alphabet that enter into the composition of everything that has ever been written: we do not conceive that new letters spring up and come to join themselves to the others in order to make a new poem. But that the poet creates the poem and that human thought is thereby made richer, we understand very well . . . that the number of atoms composing the material universe at a given moment should increase, runs counter to our habits of mind, contradicts the whole of our experience; but that a reality of quite another order, which contrasts with the atom as the thought of the poet with the letters of the alphabet, should increase by sudden additions, is not inadmissible; and the reverse of each addition might indeed be a world, which we then represent to ourselves, symbolically, as an assemblage of atoms.
>
> (253; cf. 220–2)

Fundamental to Bergson's philosophic vision in *Creative Evolution* is the opposition between the geometric, logical, or intellectual, and their kinship with the material; and on the other hand the (complementary, and more than complementary) reality of life as process. This opposition recalls his praise, quoted earlier, of Lucretius as perceiving 'in nature at the same instance what interests the geometer and what seduces the painter'.[52] A later passage, expanding this opposition, again evokes Lucretius (on the fall of atoms through the void) to a counter-Lucretian end:

> All our analyses show us, in life, an effort to remount the incline that matter descends . . . The life that evolves on the surface of our planet is indeed attached to matter. If it were pure consciousness, *a fortiori* if it were supraconsciousness, it would be pure creative activity. In fact, it is riveted to an organism that

---

[51] See, e.g., Bergson 1911: 108–10. Subsequent references to this edition parenthetically in the text.

[52] Bergson 1957: 34.

subjects it to the general laws of inert matter. But everything happens as if it
were doing its utmost to set itself free from these laws. (259)

This brings us within sight of the perfervid, and wildly anti-Lucretian, climax
of the third chapter:

The animal takes its stand on the plant, man bestrides animality, and the whole
of humanity, in space and in time, is one immense army galloping beside and
before and behind each of us in an overwhelming charge able to beat down
every resistance and clear the most formidable obstacles, perhaps even death.
(285–6)

This vision was, incidentally, one of the sources of the cosmic imperialism that C. S. Lewis pilloried in his first two science fiction romances
Out of the Silent Planet and *Perelandra*. In his late *Experiment in Criticism* Lewis robustly rejects the notion that literary evaluation requires credal
agreement – once, he says, he largely agreed with Lucretius whereas now he
largely agrees with Dante, but this has not 'at all altered my evaluation, of
either'.[53] But the engagement with Lucretius, incidental though it be, across
the span of his work, exemplifies the continuation into our own times of the
propensity prominent Christians have long had to ponder and react towards
or against the *DRN*. In *The Allegory of Love* Lucretius, the atheist poet
who, as atheist, can see a purely aesthetic beauty in the gods, is evoked as
a nodal figure in the account of the role of myth and religion in Romantic poetry – an account that might reach out to German as well as English
Romanticism.[54] In *Surprised by Joy*, writing of his own adolescent atheism,
Lewis picks out three elements, all with Lucretian affinities or origins, and
mapping, interestingly, the outlook of the Edwardian schoolboy onto later
nineteenth-century responses. There is, first, the (over-)reaction to the element of fear in his previous period of faith; second the negative attraction of
a materialist universe ('no strictly infinite disaster could overtake you in it');
and finally the fundamental tension of imagination and intellect involved:

Any conception of reality which a sane mind can admit must favour some of its
wishes and frustrate others. The materialistic universe had one great, negative
attraction to offer me. It had no other. And this had to be accepted; one had to
look out on a meaningless dance of atoms (remember, I was reading Lucretius),
to realise that all the apparent beauty was a subjective phosphorescence, and
to relegate everything one valued to the world of mirage.[55]

From Lewis's later Christian perspective, the Lucretian insistence on an alien
cosmos not designed for us can serve as a backdrop or a polemical corrective

[53] Lewis 1961: 86.   [54] Lewis 1936: 83.   [55] Lewis 1955: 162–3.

to humanist arrogance.[56] The materialist universe as ultimately a meaningless dance of atoms becomes a fundamental feature of his argument that
naturalism is self-refuting.[57]

Professional philosophers have also engaged with Lucretius more systematically (sometimes simply as Epicurean exponent or explicator).[58] As
Martha Nussbaum observes, the Epicurean argument against the fear of
death 'has been, in recent years, the subject of intense philosophical debate.
In fact, there is no aspect of Hellenistic ethics that has generated such wide
philosophical interest, and produced work of such high philosophical quality.'[59] This readiness to take Lucretius seriously as a thinker can be located
in a larger revaluation of Hellenistic philosophy.[60] But it is not confined to
students of the Hellenistic period: both Thomas Nagel and Bernard Williams
evoke and discuss Lucretius in the context of a general philosophical consideration of human mortality.[61] And wider claims are made – sometimes
slackly – for the contemporary value of an Epicurean philosophy.[62] Nussbaum, more astringently, noting that 'all of Lucretius' assaults on traditional
belief now look like a part of our own traditions of belief' (142), also notes
the challenge that his critique of sexual desire poses to the high valuation of
erotic love in our secular culture, and she goes on to argue for the validity of
much of that critique. She devotes three chapters of her *Therapy of Desire* to
an examination of Lucretius on sexuality, on mortality, and on violence in its
relation to human vulnerability. Discussing him in a larger context of Hellenistic philosophy as therapeutic – dedicated to the eradication and transformation of deep-seated structures of mistaken beliefs and values – takes her
beyond generalisations about Lucretius as versifying Epicurean philosophy,
or achieving passages of superlative poetry amid much arid argumentation.
Although she can pay precise attention to verbal detail, she concentrates illu-
minatingly on the poem's large-scale strategies. Yet careful and persuasive as
much of her discussion is, one can find it sometimes in danger of a certain
bien-pensant pedestrianism. Is Lucretius' extraordinary evocation in *DRN*
4 of compulsive passion, of the lover's desire for a total interpenetration, to
be viewed only as therapeutic? (One recalls Yeats's pungent dictum, apropos
of Dryden's version of Lucretius on love: 'the tragedy of sexual intercourse

[56] See Lewis 1942: 1–4; Lewis 1984: 88–9.
[57] Most fully developed in Lewis 1947: 15–81.
[58] See recently, for example, O'Keefe 2005, or the range of essays in Gordon and Suits 2003.
[59] Nussbaum 1994: 204; subsequent parenthetical citations of Nussbaum refer to this work.
[60] See, for example, Barnes in Boardman, Griffin and Murray 1991: 422.
[61] B. Williams 1973: 82–100; Nagel 1979: 1–10.
[62] See, for example, Dane Gordon in Gordon and Suits 2003: 14–15.

is the perpetual virginity of the soul'.)[63] But Nussbaum does finally question (190–1) the limitations of Lucretius' therapeutic account, citing the importance of vulnerability in 'much of the most powerful erotic writing in the Western tradition'.

This judgement opens onto a wider tension that Nussbaum finds in Lucretius' Epicureanism: 'a deep attachment to godlike self-sufficiency that pulls against the injunction to live in accordance with nature, accepting the limits of a finite life' (276). Her discussion of Lucretius on the fear of death and violence makes that tension central, and to explore it she deploys a variety of resources: skilfully switching her own stylistic registers, testing and sifting Lucretian arguments, suggestively reading the history of civilisation in Book 5 as an analytic myth and evoking the Homeric gods as an experiment in imagining immortality and its consequences. This leads on – significantly, via the citation of Wallace Stevens's poem 'Sunday Morning' – to Nussbaum's own final proposal of a therapy for the fear of death which is 'the appropriate development of the naturalistic portions of Lucretius' argument, separated loose from its conflicting commitment to transcendence' (232).

Sisson's judgement as to the affinity of the *DRN* with *Piers Plowman* could be glossed in terms of its interweaving of sharply observed mundane detail with the ontological, and the way it makes that interweaving the vehicle of a cosmic vision urged on the reader with an imperious evangelising energy against which generic classifications such as 'didactic' or 'expository' pale. What it is that he finds 'terrible' in the Lucretian vision Sisson does not specify: the endless rain of atoms through the infinite void? the insistence on human mortality? on human vulnerability? the snatches of apocalypse? the comprehensive vision of human life within a cosmos *tanta . . . praedita culpa*? We have seen how a number of powerful modern minds have responded to these elements, though not always finding them terrible. Perhaps this chapter, and this book, should conclude with not the least powerful of those minds, Santayana, whose remarks on vision in philosophy and poetry restate for the moderns some of the most fundamental questions about Lucretius and the kind of poem the *DRN* is:

> If his philosophy had been wormwood to him, he could not have said . . .
> 'It is joy . . . that I teach sublime truths and come to free the soul from the
> strangling knots of superstition' . . . The vision of philosophy is sublime. The
> order it reveals in the world is something beautiful, tragic, sympathetic to the
> mind, and just what every poet, on a small or on a large scale, is always trying

[63] Jeffares 1962: 267.

to catch . . . A philosopher who attains it is, for the moment, a poet; and a poet who turns his practised and passionate imagination on the order of all things, or on anything in the light of the whole, is for that moment a philosopher.[64]

Further reading

Recent reports on the continuing dialogues between modern thinkers and Lucretian/Epicurean ideas include Gordon and Suits 2003 and W. R. Johnson 2000. We are, however, aware of no other synoptic discussions of Lucretius' twentieth-century presence on the literary-cultural scene. All references to work on individual writers and thinkers will be found at the appropriate points above.

[64] Santayana 1910: 9–11; the quotation/translation is of *DRN* 1.931–2.

DATELINE

In date ranges, a hyphen indicates continuous activity whereas an oblique denotes first completion or publication/later revision or supplement.

BC

432	Death of Empedocles
322	Death of Aristotle
270	Death of Epicurus
169	Death of Ennius
106	Birth of Cicero
c. 94	Birth of Lucretius
70	Birth of Virgil
65	Birth of Horace
60	First triumvirate of Pompey, Crassus and Caesar
59	Catullus active
58	Praetorship of C. Memmius
55 or later	Death of Lucretius (possibly leaving *DRN* incomplete)
51	Cicero, *De re publica*
49	Civil war begins
43	Birth of Ovid
c. 40	Death of Philodemus
37–29	Composition of Virgil's *Georgics*
29–19	Composition of Virgil's *Aeneid*; death of Virgil
8	Death of Horace

AD

14	Death of Augustus; Manilius' *Astronomica* being written
17	Death of Ovid
303–13	Lactantius, *Divinae institutiones*
1417	Poggio rediscovers text of *DRN*
1473	First printed edition of *DRN*

c. 1478	Botticelli, *Primavera*
1535	Aonio Paleario, *De animorum immortalitate*
1563	Denis Lambin's edition of *DRN* published
1572–80/88	Michel de Montaigne, *Essais*
1590/96	Edmund Spenser, *The Faerie Queene*
1591	Giordano Bruno, *De immenso*
1650s	Lucy Hutchinson's translation of *DRN* composed
1656	John Evelyn's translation of *DRN* 1 published
1657	Walter Charleton, *The Immortality of the Human Soul*
1658	Pierre Gassendi, *Syntagma philosophicum*
1667/74	John Milton, *Paradise Lost*
1682	Thomas Creech's translation of complete *DRN* published
1685	John Dryden's selected translations from *DRN* published
1718	Isaac Newton, *Optics*, 2nd edn
1733/4	Alexander Pope, *An Essay on Man*
1747	Melchior de Polignac, *Anti-Lucretius*
1790	Immanuel Kant, *Critique of Judgement*
1805	John Mason Good's translation of *DRN* published
1827	Karl Ludwig von Hebel's translation of *DRN* completed
1850	Karl Lachmann's edition of *DRN*
1852	Matthew Arnold, *Empedocles on Etna*
1864	H. A. J. Munro's edition and commentary on *DRN*
1868	Alfred, Lord Tennyson, *Lucretius*
1910	George Santayana, *Three Philosophical Poets*
1947	Cyril Bailey's edition and commentary on *DRN*

WORKS CITED

Adkins, A. W. H. (1977) 'Lucretius 1.16–139 and the problems of writing *versus Latini*', *Phoenix* 31: 145–58.

Adler, E. (2003) *Vergil's Empire. Political Thought in the Aeneid*. Lanham, Md. and Oxford.

Aicher, P. J. (1992) 'Lucretian revisions of Homer', *Classical Journal* 87: 139–58.

Akenside, M. (1996) *Poetical Works*, ed. R. Dix. Cranbury, N.J.

Albury, W. R. (1978) 'Halley's Ode on the *Principia* of Newton and the Epicurean revival in England', *Journal of the History of Ideas* 39: 24–43.

Alcover, M. (1970) *La Pensée philosophique et scientifique de Cyrano de Bergerac*. Geneva.

Aldington, R. (transl.) (1927) *Letters of Voltaire and Frederick the Great*. New York.

Alfonsi, L. (1978) 'L'avventura di Lucrezio nel mondo antico . . . e oltre', in Gigon (1978), 271–321.

Algra, K. A., Barnes, J., Mansfeld, J. and Schofield, M. (eds.) (1999) *The Cambridge History of Hellenistic Philosophy*. Cambridge.

Algra, K. A., Koenen, M. H. and Schrijvers, P. H. (eds.) (1997) *Lucretius and His Intellectual Background*. Amsterdam.

Allen, D. C. (1944) 'The rehabilitation of Epicurus and his doctrine of pleasure in the early Renaissance', *Studies in Philology* 41: 1–15.

Andrade, E. N. da C. (1928) 'The scientific significance of Lucretius', in *T. Lucreti Cari de Rerum Natura Libri Sex*, ed. H. A. J. Munro, 4th edn (3 vols.). Cambridge: ii, v–xxii.

André, J.-M. (1980) 'La notion de *Pestilentia* à Rome: du tabou religieux à l'interprétation préscientifique', *Latomus* 39: 3–16.

Andrea, B. (2004) Review of J. Ellison, *George Sandys: Travel, Colonialism and Tolerance in the Seventeenth Century*, *Early Modern Literary Studies*, 9.iii: 1–4.

Andreoni, E. (1979) 'Sul contrasto ideologico fra il *De re publica* di Cicerone e il poema di Lucrezio (La genesi della società civile)', in *Studi di poesia latina in onore di A. Traglia* (2 vols.). Rome: i, 281–321.

Annas, J. (1992) *Hellenistic Philosophy of Mind*. Berkeley.

Anon. (1732) *The War with Priestcraft*. London.

Anon. (1988) *La venuta del Cristianissimo Re in Italia*, in *Guerre in ottava rima*, ed. M. Beer and D. Diamanti (4 vols.). Modena.

Anselment, R. A. (1996) 'Thomas Sprat's *The Plague of Athens*: Thucydides, Lucretius, and the "Pindaric way"', *Bulletin of the John Rylands University Library of Manchester* 78: 3–20.

Anstey, P. (2002) 'Boyle on seminal principles', *Studies in History and Philosophy of Biological and Biomedical Sciences* 33: 597–630.

Appel, G. (1909) *De Romanorum precationibus*. Giessen, reprinted New York, 1975.

Arnold, M. (1960) *The Complete Prose Works*, vol. I: *On the Classical Tradition*, ed. R. H. Super. Ann Arbor.

(1979) *Poems*, ed. K. Allott and M. Allott, 2nd edn. London.

Arrighetti, G. (1997) 'Lucrèce dans l'histoire de l'Epicurisme: quelques réflexions', in Algra, Koenen and Schrijvers (1997), 21–33.

Asmis, E. (1982) 'Lucretius' Venus and Stoic Zeus', *Hermes* 110: 458–70.

(1983) 'Rhetoric and reason in Lucretius', *American Journal of Philology* 104: 36–66.

(1995) 'Epicurean poetics', in *Philodemus and Poetry: Poetic Theory and Practice in Lucretius, Philodemus, and Horace*, ed. D. Obbink. Oxford and New York: 15–34.

Asper, M. (1997) *Onomata allotria: zur Genese, Struktur und Funktion poetologischer Metaphern bei Kallimachos*. Stuttgart.

Atherton, C. (ed.) (1997) *Form and Content in Didactic Poetry*. Bari.

Aubenque, P. (1969) 'Kant et l'épicurisme', *Actes du VIIe congrès Association Guillaume-Budé, Paris, 5–10 avril 1968*. Paris: 293–303.

Aubrey, J. (1949) *Brief Lives*, ed. O. M. Dick. London.

Austin, R. G. (1977) *P. Vergili Maronis Aeneidos liber sextus, with a Commentary*. Oxford.

Axelson, B. (1945) *Unpoetische Wörter: ein Beitrag zur Kenntnis der lateinischen Dichtersprache*. Lund.

Bacon, F. (1857–74) *Works*, ed. R. L. Ellis, J. Spedding and D. Heath (14 vols.). London.

(1905) *The Philosophical Works*, ed. J. M. Robertson. New York.

(1985) *The Essayes*, ed. M. Kiernan. Oxford.

(2000) *The Advancement of Learning*, ed. M. Kiernan. Oxford.

Bailey, C. (1947) *Lucretius: De Rerum Natura. Edited, with Prolegomena, Critical Apparatus, Translation and Commentary* (3 vols.). Oxford.

Bamborough, J. B. and Dodsworth, M. (eds.) (2000) *Robert Burton: the Anatomy of Melancholy* (6 vols.). Oxford.

Bapp, K. (1926) 'Goethe und Lukrez', *Jahrbuch der Goethe-Gesellschaft* 12: 47–67.

Barbaro, F. (1999) *Epistolario*, ed. C. Griggio. Florence.

Barbour, P. L. (1962) 'Captain John Smith and the Bishop of Sarum', *Huntingdon Library Quarterly* 26: 11–29.

Barbour, R. (1994) 'Between atoms and the spirit: Lucy Hutchinson's translation of Lucretius', *Renaissance Papers* 1–16.

(1997) 'Lucy Hutchinson, atomism, and the atheist dog', in *Women, Science, and Medicine, 1500–1700*, ed. L. H. Hutton and S. Hutton. Stroud: 122–37.

(1998) *English Epicures and Stoics: Ancient Legacies in Early Stuart Culture*. Amherst, Mass.

(2005) 'Bacon, atomism, and imposture', in *Francis Bacon and the Refiguring of Early Modern Thought*, ed. J. Solomon and C. Martin. Aldershot: 17–44.

Barnes, J. and Griffin, M. (eds.) (1997) *Philosophia Togata II: Plato and Aristotle at Rome*. Oxford.

Bartlett, R. C. (2001) 'On the politics of faith and reason: the Enlightenment project in Pierre Bayle and Montesquieu', *Journal of Politics* 63: 1–28.

Basile, B. (1984) 'Tasso lettore di Lucrezio', in *Poëta Melancholicus – Tradizione classica e follia nell'ultimo Tasso*. Pisa: 65–101.

Battegli, A. M. (1998) *Margaret Cavendish and the Exiles of the Mind*. Lexington.

Bausi, F. (ed.) (1996) *Angelo Poliziano. Sylvae*. Florence.

Beard, M., North, J. and Price, S. (1998) *Religions of Rome*, vol. 1: *A History*. Cambridge.

Beattie, J. (1760) *Poems*. London.

Beer, G. (1983) *Darwin's Plots: Evolutionary Narrative in Darwin, George Eliot, and Nineteenth-Century Fiction*. London.

Benjamin, W. (1999) 'The Lisbon earthquake', in *Selected Writings*, transl. R. Livingstone, ed. M. W. Jennings, H. Eiland and G. Smith. Cambridge: 536–40.

Bergson, H. (1884) *Extraits de Lucrèce, avec un commentaire, des notes et une étude sur la poésie, la philosophie, la physique, le texte et la langue de Lucrèce*, 11th edn. Paris.

(1911) *Creative Evolution*, transl. Arthur Mitchell. London.

(1957) *Ecrits et paroles*, vol. 1. Paris.

Berman, D. (1990) *A History of Atheism in Britain from Hobbes to Russell*. London.

Bertelli, S. (1964) 'Noterelle machiavelliane: ancora su Lucrezio e Machiavelli', *Rivista Storica Italiana* 76: 774–92.

Beye, C. R. (1963) 'Lucretius and progress', *Classical Journal* 58: 160–9.

Bignone, E. (1913) 'Per la fortuna di Lucrezio e dell'epicureismo nel medio evo', *Rivista di Filologia e d'Istruzione Classica* 41: 230–62.

Billanovich, Guido (1958) '"Veterum uestigia uatum" nei carmi dei preumanisti padovani', *Italia Medioevale e Umanistica* 1: 155–243.

Bischoff, B. (1998) *Katalog der festländischen Handschriften des neunten Jahrhunderts (mit Ausnahme der wisigothischen), Teil I: Aachen-Lambach*. Wiesbaden.

(2004) *Katalog der festländischen Handschriften des neunten Jahrhunderts (mit Ausnahme der wisigothischen), Teil II: Laon-Paderborn*. Wiesbaden.

Blackmore, Sir R. (1712) *Creation. A Philosophical Poem*. London.

Blake, W. (1966) *Complete Writings*, ed. G. Keynes. London.

Blanning, T. C. W. (1990) 'Frederick the Great and enlightened absolutism', in *Enlightened Absolutism: Reform and Reformers in Later Eighteenth-Century Europe*, ed. H. Scott. London: 265–88.

Blickman, D. R. (1989) 'Lucretius, Epicurus, and prehistory', *Harvard Studies in Classical Philology* 92: 157–91.

Bloom, H. (1973) *The Anxiety of Influence: a Theory of Poetry*. New York.

Blumenberg, H. (1983) *The Legitimacy of the Modern Age*. Cambridge.

(1997) *Shipwreck with Spectator: Paradigm of a Metaphor for Existence*, transl. S. Rendall. Cambridge, Mass. and London.

Boardman, J., Griffin, J. and Murray, O. (eds.) (1991) *The Oxford History of Greece and the Hellenistic World*. Oxford.

Boccuto, G. (1984) 'L'influsso di Lucrezio negli inni naturali di Michele Marullo', *Rivista di Cultura Classica e Medioevale* 26: 117–33.

Bohr, N. (1934) 'The atomic theory and the fundamental principles underlying the description of nature' (lecture read 1929), in *Atomic Theory and the Description of Nature*. Cambridge: 102–19.

Bollack, J. (1965) *Empédocle* (3 vols.). Paris.

Borghini, V. (1971) *Scritti inediti o rari sulla lingua*, ed. J. R. Woodhouse. Bologna.

Bottari, G. (1991) *Guglielmo da Pastrengo De uiris illustribus et De originibus*. Padua.

Boyancé, P. (1963) *Lucrèce et l'Epicurisme*. Paris.

Boyde, P. (1981) *Dante, Philomythes and Philosopher: Man in the Cosmos*. Cambridge.

Boyle, R. (1999–2000) *Works*, ed. M. Hunter and E. B. Davis (14 vols.). London.

Bradner, L. (1940) *Musae Anglicanae: a History of Anglo-Latin Poetry, 1500–1925*. New York and London.

Bragg, Sir W. (1925) *Concerning the Nature of Things*. London.

Bramble, J. C. (1974) *Persius and the Programmatic Satire. A Study in Form and Imagery*. Cambridge.

Brandt, S. (1891) 'Lactantius und Lucretius', *Neue Jahrbücher für Philologie* 143: 225–59.

Bretone, M. (1998) *I fondamenti del diritto romano. Le cose e la natura*. Rome and Bari.

Bright, D. F. (1971) 'The plague and the structure of *De rerum natura*', *Latomus* 30: 607–32.

Brightman, E. S. (1919) 'The Lisbon earthquake: a study in religious valuation', *American Journal of Theology* 23: 500–18.

Brillenburg Wurth, C. A. W. (2002) 'The musically sublime: infinity, indeterminacy, irresolvability'. Diss. Groningen.

Brody, J. (1958) *Boileau and Longinus*. Geneva.

Brown, A. (1979) *Bartolomeo Scala, Chancellor of Florence: the Humanist as Bureaucrat*. Princeton.

(2001) 'Lucretius and the Epicureans in the social and political context of Renaissance Florence', *I Tatti Studies* 9: 11–62.

Brown, R. D. (1982) 'Lucretius and Callimachus', *Illinois Classical Studies* 7: 77–97.

(1987) *Lucretius on Love and Sex. A Commentary on De Rerum Natura IV, 1030–1287, with Prolegomena, Text and Translation*. Leiden and New York.

Browne, I. H. (1745) *De animi immortalitate*. London.

Bruno, G. B. (1997–) *Œuvres latines*, ed. Rita Sturlese (8 vols., in progress). Paris.

Bunting, B. (1994) *Complete Poems*, ed. R. Caddel. Oxford.

Burke, E. (1968) *A Philosophical Enquiry into the Origin of Our Ideas of the Sublime and Beautiful*, ed. J. T. Boulton. Notre Dame, reprint edn. (first pub. 1958).

Burnett, A. (ed.) (1997) *The Poems of A. E. Housman*. Oxford.

Burnyeat, M. F. (1978) 'The upside-down back-to-front sceptic of Lucretius IV 472', *Philologus* 122: 197–206.

Burton, R. (1893) *The Anatomy of Melancholy*, ed. A. R. Shilleto (3 vols.). London.

Busby, T. (1813) *The Nature of Things, A Didascalic Poem; Translated from the Latin of Titus Lucretius Carus*. London.

Byron (George Gordon), Lord (1970) *Poetical Works*, ed. F. Page and J. Jump, 3rd edn. London.

(1973–94) *Letters and Journals*, ed. L. A. Marchand (13 vols.). London.

(1991) *The Complete Miscellaneous Prose*, ed. A. Nicholson. Oxford.

Cabisius, G. (1984) 'Social metaphor and the atomic cycle in Lucretius', *Classical Journal* 80: 109–20.

Cagnetta, M. (2001) 'La peste e la *stasis*', *Quaderni di Storia* 53: 5–37.

Calder, R. (1996) 'Molière, misanthropy and forbearance: Eliante's "Lucretian" diatribe', *French Studies* 50: 138–43.

Calvino, I. (1988) *Six Memos for the Next Millennium*. Cambridge, Mass.

Cambiano, G. (1982) 'Patologia e metafora politica. Alcmeone, Platone, *Corpus Hippocraticum*', *Elenchos* 3: 219–36.

Cameron, A. (1995) *Callimachus and His Critics*. Princeton.

Campbell, G. (1999) Review of Sedley 1998, *Bryn Mawr Classical Review* 1999.10.29, online at: http://ccat.sas.upenn.edu/bmcr/ 1999/1999-10-29.html.
(2003). *Lucretius on Creation and Evolution. A Commentary on De Rerum Natura Book Five, lines 772–1104*. Oxford.

Campbell, S. J. (2003) 'Giorgione's *Tempest*, *studiolo* culture, and the Renaissance', *Renaissance Quarterly* 56.2: 299–332.

Canfora, L. (1993a) *Studi di storia della storiografia romana*. Bari.
(1993b) *Vita di Lucrezio*. Palermo.

Canning, G. (1766) *A Translation of Anti-Lucretius*. London.

Capasso, M. (2003) 'Filodemo e Lucrezio', in Monet (2003), 77–107.

Castner, C. (1988) *Prosopography of Roman Epicureans from the Second Century BC to the Second Century AD*. New York.

Caston, V. (1997) 'Epiphenomenalisms, ancient and modern', *Philosophical Review* 106: 309–63.

Catrein, C. (2003). *Vertauschte Sinne. Untersuchungen zur Synästhesie in der römischen Dichtung*. Munich and Leipzig.

Ceva, T. (1704) *Philosophia novo-antiqua*. Milan.

Charleton, W. (1926) *Epicurus. His Morals*, ed. F. Manning. London.
(1985) *The Immortality of the Human Soul*, ed. J. M. Armistead. New York.

Cherchi, G. (1995) 'Poesia, scienza, filosofia: Epicuro e Lucrezio in Inghilterra fra sei e settecento', *Lettore di Provincia* 26: 3–30.

Clark, S. H. (1991) '*Pendet homo incertus*: Gray's response to Locke', *Eighteenth-Century Studies* 24: 237–91, 484–503.

Classen, C. J. (1968) 'Poetry and rhetoric in Lucretius', *Transactions of the American Philological Association* 99: 77–118, reprinted in Classen (1986), 331–73.
(ed.) (1986) *Probleme der Lukrezforschung*. Hildesheim, Zurich and New York.

Clausen, W. (1987) *Virgil's Aeneid and the Tradition of Hellenistic Poetry* (Sather Classical Lectures 51). Berkeley, Los Angeles and London.
(1994) *A Commentary on Virgil Eclogues*. Oxford.

Clay, D. (1983) *Lucretius and Epicurus*. Ithaca.

Clericuzio, A. (1984) 'Le trasmutazioni in Bacon e Boyle', in *Francis Bacon: Terminologia e fortuna nel XVII secolo*, ed. M. Fattori. Rome: 29–42.

Clucas, S. (1994) 'The atomism of the Cavendish circle: a reappraisal', *The Seventeenth Century* 9: 247–73.

Cohen, I. B. (1964) '"Quantum in se est": Newton's concept of inertia in relation to Descartes and Lucretius', *Notes and Records of the Royal Society* 19: 131–55.

Cole, T. (1990) *Democritus and the Sources of Greek Anthropology*, 2nd edn. Atlanta.

Coleridge, S. T. (1965–71) *Collected Letters*, ed. E. L. Griggs (6 vols.). Oxford.

Commager, H. S., Jr. (1957) 'Lucretius' interpretation of the plague', *Harvard Studies in Classical Philology* 62: 105–18.

Conte, G. B. (1965) 'Il trionfo della morte e la galleria dei grandi trapassati in Lucrezio III, 1024–1053', *Studi Italiani di Filologia Classica* 37: 114–32.

(1966) 'Hypsos e diatriba nello stile di Lucrezio: De Rer. Nat. II 1–61', *Maia* 18: 338–68.

(1992) 'Proems in the middle', in *Beginnings in Classical Literature*, ed. F. Dunn and T. Cole. Cambridge: 147–59.

(1994) *Genres and Readers: Lucretius, Love Elegy, Pliny's Encyclopedia*, transl. G. W. Most. Baltimore and London.

Conti, M. (1982) 'Spunti politici nell'opera di Lucrezio', *Rivista di Cultura Classica e Medioevale* 24: 27–46.

Copley, F. O. (1956) *Exclusus Amator: a Study in Latin Love Poetry*. Baltimore.

Coppini, D. (ed.) (1995) *Michele Marullo Tarcaniota: Inni Naturali*. Florence.

Costa, C. D. N. (ed.) (1984) *Lucreti De Rerum Natura V*. Oxford.

Courtine, J.-F. et al. (1993) *Of the Sublime: Presence in Question*, transl. J. Librett. Albany.

Courtney, E. (1995) *Musa Lapidaria. A Selection of Latin Verse Inscriptions*. Atlanta.

Cowley, A. (1905), *The English Writings*, ed. A. R. Waller (2 vols.). Cambridge.

Cox, J. N. (1998) *Poetry and Politics in the Cockney School: Keats, Shelley, Hunt and Their Circle*. Cambridge.

Creech, T. (1682) *T. Lucretius Carus the Epicurean Philosopher, His Six Books De Natura Rerum Done into English Verse, with Notes*. Oxford.

(1683a) *T. Lucretius Carus. The Epicurean Philosopher, His Six Books De Natura Rerum Done into English Verse*, 2nd edn. Oxford.

(1683b) *Titus Lucretius Carus His Six Books of Epicurean Philosophy, Done into English Verse*, 3rd edn. London.

(1714) *T. Lucretius Carus Of the Nature of Things, In Six Books, Translated into English Verse*, ed. J. Digby (2 vols.). London.

Crichton Smith, I. (1992) *Collected Poems*. Manchester.

Crowther, N. B. (1979) 'Water and wine as symbols of inspiration', *Mnemosyne* 32: 1–11.

Cucchiarelli, A. (ed.) (2003) *La veglia di Venere: Pervigilium Veneris*. Milan.

Culler, A. D. (1966) *Imaginative Reason: the Poetry of Matthew Arnold*. London.

Cyrano de Bergerac, S. (2000) *Œuvres complètes*, ed. M. Alcover (3 vols.). Paris.

D'Addario, A. (1972) *Aspetti della Controriforma a Firenze*. Rome.

Daiber, H. (1992) 'The *Meteorology* in Syriac and Arabic translation', in *Theophrastus: His Psychological, Doxographical, and Scientific Writings*, ed. W. W. Fortenbaugh and D. Gutas. New Brunswick: 166–293.

Dalton, J. (1808) *A New System of Chemical Philosophy*. Manchester.

Dalzell, A. (1996) *The Criticism of Didactic Poetry: Essays on Lucretius, Virgil, and Ovid*. Toronto and London.

Danto, A. C. (1967) 'Naturalism', in *The Encyclopedia of Philosophy*, ed. P. Edwards (8 vols.). New York: 448–50.

Darwin, E. (1791) *The Botanic Garden; A Poem*. London.

(1803) *The Temple of Nature, or The Origin of Society*. London.

Davidson, J. (1973) *The Poems of John Davidson*, ed. A. Turnbull (2 vols.). Edinburgh.

Davies, M. C. (1995) *Aldus Manutius, Printer and Publisher of Renaissance Venice.* London.

Davis, P. (2005) 'Classical Greek and Latin literature: didactic poetry', in *The Oxford History of Literary Translation in English,* vol. III: *1660–1790,* ed. S. Gillespie and D. Hopkins. Oxford: 191–203.

De Lacy, P. H. (1964) 'Distant views: the imagery of Lucretius 2', *Classical Journal* 60: 49–55, reprinted in Gale (forthcoming).

Delattre, D. (2003) 'Présence ou absence d'une copie du *De rerum natura* à Herculaneum?', in Monet (2003), 109–16.

Del Nero, V. (1985–6) 'Filosofia e teologia nel commento di Giovan Battista Pio a Lucrezio', *Interpres* 6: 156–99.

Delon, M. (1988) 'Naufrages vus de loin: les développements narratifs d'un thème lucrétien', *Rivista di Letterature Moderne e Comparate* 41: 91–119.

de Man, P. (1996) *Aesthetic Ideology,* ed. A. Warminski. Minneapolis.

Dempsey, C. (1968) 'Mercurius Ver: the sources of Botticelli's Primavera', *Journal of the Warburg and Courtauld Institutes* 31: 251–73.

(1992) *The Portrayal of Love: Botticelli's 'Primavera' and Humanist Culture at the Time of Lorenzo the Magnificent.* Princeton.

Dennis, J. (1939–43) *Critical Works,* ed. E. N. Hooker (2 vols.). Baltimore.

de Quehen, H. (ed.) (1996a) *Lucy Hutchinson's Translation of Lucretius: De Rerum Natura.* London.

(1996b) 'Ease and flow in Lucy Hutchinson's Lucretius', *Studies in Philology* 93: 288–303.

Derrida, J. (1984) 'My chances/*mes chances*: a rendezvous with some Epicurean stereophonies', in *Taking Chances: Derrida, Psychoanalysis, and Literature,* ed. J. H. Smith and W. Kerrigan. Baltimore: 1–32.

Desmouliez. A. (1958) 'Cupidité, ambition et crainte de la mort chez Lucrèce (*de R. N.,* III, 59–93)', *Latomus* 17: 317–23.

Deufert, M. (1998) 'Die Lukrezemendationen des Francesco Bernardino Cipelli', *Hermes* 126: 370–9.

(1999) 'Lukrez und Marullus: ein kurzer Blick in die Werkstatt eines humanistischen Interpolators', *Rheinisches Museum* 142: 210–23.

DeWitt, N. W. (1954). *Epicurus and His Philosophy.* Minneapolis.

D'Holbach, B. (1970) *The System of Nature,* transl. H. Robinson. New York.

Diderot, D. (1995) *The Salon of 1767,* in *Diderot on Art,* ed. and transl. John Goodman. New Haven.

(1999) *Thoughts on the Interpretation of Nature, and Other Philosophical Works,* transl. L. Sandler. Manchester.

Diels, H. (1923) *T. Lucreti Cari De Rerum Natura libri sex.* Berlin.

(transl.) (1924) *Lukrez, Von der Natur.* Berlin.

Dionigi, I. (1985) 'Marullo e Lucrezio: tra esegesi e poesia', *Res publica litterarum* 8: 47–69.

(1988). *Lucrezio: Le parole e le cose.* Bologna.

(1997) 'Lucrezio', in *Enciclopedia oraziana,* vol. II. Rome: 15–22.

d'Ippolito, F. (1988) 'Le XII Tavole: il testo e la politica', in *Roma in Italia,* vol. I: *Storia di Roma,* ed. A. Momigliano and A. Schiavone. Turin: 397–413.

Dix, R. (2002) 'Wordsworth and Lucretius: the psychological impact of Creech's translation', *English Language Notes* 39: 25–33.

Dobbek, W. (ed.) (1957) *August von Einsiedel: Ideen.* Berlin.

Donno, F. (1979) *L'amorosa Clarice*, ed. G. Rizzo. Lecce.

Donohue, H. (1993) *The Song of the Swan: Lucretius and the Influence of Callimachus.* Lanham, Md.

Douglas, A. E. (ed.) (1966) *M. Tulli Ciceronis Brutus.* Oxford.

Dowling, L. (1991) 'Foreword' to *Pater in the 1990s*, ed. L. Brake and I. Small. Greensboro, N.C.

Droz-Vincent, G. (1996) 'Les *foedera naturae* chez Lucrèce', in *Le Concept de Natura à Rome*, ed. C. Lévy. Paris: 191–211.

Drummand, W. H. (1808) *The First Book of T. Lucretius Carus on the Nature of Things. Translated into English Verse.* London.

Dryden, J. (1956–2000) *The Works of John Dryden*, ed. H. T. Swedenberg *et al.* (20 vols.). Berkeley, Los Angeles and London.

Du Bartas, G. de S. (1994) *La Sepmaine (texte de 1581)*, ed. Y. Bellenger. Paris.

Du Bellay, J. (1908–31) *Œuvres poétiques*, ed. H. Chamard (6 vols.). Paris.

Dudley, D. R. (ed.) (1965a) *Lucretius.* London.

(1965b) 'The satiric element in Lucretius', in Dudley (1965a), 115–30.

Due, O. S. (1974) *Changing Forms. Studies in the Metamorphoses of Ovid.* Copenhagen.

Duhem, P. (2002) *Mixture and Chemical Combination and Related Essays*, transl. P. Needham. Dordrecht.

Dyck, A. R. (2004) *A Commentary on Cicero, De legibus.* Ann Arbor.

Dyson, J. T. (1996) 'Dido the Epicurean', *Classical Antiquity* 15: 203–21.

Eatough, G. (1984) *Fracastoro's Syphilis. Introduction, Text, Translation and Notes.* Liverpool.

Edgecombe, R. S. (1999) 'Lucretius, Shelley and "Ode to the West Wind"', *Keats–Shelley Review* 13: 134.

(2000) 'Chaucer, Lucretius and the prologue to *The Canterbury Tales*', *Classical and Modern Literature* 20.ii: 61–5.

Else, G. F. (1930) 'Lucretius and the aesthetic attitude', *Harvard Studies in Classical Philology* 41: 149–82.

Equicola, M. (1999) *Libro de natura de amore*, ed. L. Ricci. Rome.

Esclapez, R. (1992) 'La Nature et la mort: présence de Lucrèce dans le livre 1 des *Essais* de Montaigne', *Littératures* 27: 21–44.

Esolen, A. (1993) 'Spenser's "Alma Venus": energy and economics in the Bower of Bliss', *English Literary Renaissance* 23: 267–86.

(1994) 'Spenserian chaos: Lucretius in *The Faerie Queene*', *Spenser Studies* 11: 31–51.

(transl.) (1995) *On the Nature of Things.* Baltimore.

Esposito, P. (1996) 'Lucrezio come intertesto lucaneo', *Bollettino di Studi Latini* 26: 517–44.

Evelyn, J. (1656) *An Essay on the First Book of T. Lucretius Carus De Rerum Natura.* London.

Fabian, B. (1979) 'Pope and Lucretius: observations on *An Essay on Man*', *Modern Language Review* 74: 524–37.

Fallot, J. (1977) *Il piacere e la morte nella filosofia di Epicuro: la liberazione epicurea.* Turin.

Fanshawe, Sir R. (1997–9) *The Poems and Translations*, ed. P. Davidson (2 vols.). Oxford.

Fantuzzi, M. and Hunter, R. L. (2004) *Tradition and Innovation in Hellenistic Poetry.* Cambridge.

Fara, P. and Money, D. (2004) 'Isaac Newton and Augustan Anglo-Latin poetry', *Studies in the History and Philosophy of Science* 34: 549–71.

Farrell, J. (1991) *Vergil's Georgics and the Traditions of Ancient Epic: the Art of Allusion in Literary History.* New York.

——— (2001) *Latin Language and Latin Culture from Ancient to Modern Times.* Cambridge.

Farrington, B. (1939) *Science and Politics in the Ancient World.* London.

Fenves, P. (2003) *Late Kant: Toward Another Law of the Earth.* New York.

Fermor, S. (1993) *Piero di Cosimo: Fiction, Invention and Fantasia.* London.

Ferrari, M. (1972) '"In Papia conveniant ad Dungalum"', *Italia Medioevale e Umanistica* 15: 1–52.

Ferreyrolles, G. (1976) 'Les citations de Lucrèce dans l'*Apologie de Raimond Sebond*', *Bulletin de la Société des Amis de Montaigne* 17: 49–63.

Ferri, R. (1993) *I dispiaceri di un epicureo: uno studio sulla poetica oraziana delle Epistole (con un capitolo su Persio).* Pisa.

Feynman, R. (1963) *The Feynman Lectures on Physics* (3 vols.). London.

Ficino, M. (1576) *Opera.* Basle.

——— (1987) *El libro dell'amore*, ed. S. Niccoli. Florence.

Fiesoli, G. (2004) 'Percorsi di classici nel Medioevo: il Lucrezio bobiense. Raterio lettore di Plauto e di Catullo', *Medioevo e Rinascimento* 18: 1–37.

Figala, K. (1992) 'Newton's alchemical studies and his idea of the atomic structure of matter', in *Isaac Newton, Adventurer in Thought*, ed. A. R. Hall. Oxford: 381–7.

Finch, C. E. (1967) 'Lucretius in codex Vat. Reg. Lat. 1587', *Classical Philology* 62: 261–2.

Finley, J. H. (1967) *Three Essays on Thucydides.* Cambridge, Mass.

FitzGerald, E. (1962) *Selected Works*, ed. J. Richardson. London.

Fitzgerald, W. (1995) *Catullan Provocations: Lyric Poetry and the Drama of Position.* Berkeley.

Flatman, T. (1682) *Poems and Songs*, 3rd edn. London.

Fleischmann, W. B. (1963) 'The debt of the Enlightenment to Lucretius', *Studies on Voltaire and the Eighteenth Century* 25: 631–43.

——— (1964) *Lucretius and English Literature, 1680–1740.* Paris.

——— (1971) 'Lucretius' in *Catalogus Translationum et Commentariorum – Medieval and Renaissance Latin Translations and Commentaries: Annotated Lists and Guides*, vol. II, ed. P. O. Kristeller and F. E. Cranz. New York: 349–65.

Fletcher, D. J. (1978) '*Candide* and the philosophy of the garden', *Trivium* 13: 18–30.

Flores, E. (1984–5) 'Lessico politico di Lucrezio (su *avarities* 3,59) e Sallustio', in *Sodalitas: Scritti in onore di Antonio Guarino.* Naples: 1505–13.

——— (ed.) (2002) *Titus Lucretius Carus, De rerum natura*, vol. I: *Libri I–III.* Naples.

Fontaine, J. (1966) 'Le Songe de Scipion premier Anti-Lucrèce?', in *Mélanges d'Archéologie et d'histoire offerts à André Piganiol*, ed. R. Chevallier (3 vols.). Paris: III, 1711–29.

Ford, P. (1999) 'Claude Quillet's *Callipaedia* (1655): Eugenics treatise or pregnancy manual?', in Haskell and Hardie (1999), 125–40.

Foscolo, V. U. (1990) *Letture di Lucrezio: dal De rerum natura al sonetto Alla sera*, ed. F. Longoni. Milan.

Fowler, A., ed. (1998) *John Milton: Paradise Lost*, 2nd edn. London.

Fowler, D. P. (1989) 'Lucretius and politics', in Griffin and Barnes (1989), 120–50.

(2000) 'Philosophy and literature in Lucretian intertextuality', in *Roman Constructions: Readings in Postmodern Latin*. Oxford: 138–55.

(2002) *Lucretius on Atomic Motion. A Commentary on De Rerum Natura 2.1–332*. Oxford.

Fowler, P. G. (1997) 'Lucretian conclusions', in *Classical Closure: Reading the End in Greek and Latin Literature*, ed. D. H. Roberts, F. M. Dunn and D. Fowler. Princeton: 112–38.

Fraisse, S. (1962) *L'Influence de Lucrèce en France au seizième siècle*. Paris.

Frederick II, Emperor of Prussia (1789) *Posthumous Works* (13 vols.). London.

Freeman, J. A. (1973) 'Tennyson, "Lucretius" and the "breasts of Helen"', *Victorian Poetry* 11: 69–75.

Furley, D. J. (1966) 'Lucretius and the Stoics', *Bulletin of the Institute of Classical Studies* 13: 13–33, reprinted in Furley (1989), 183–205.

(1970) 'Variations on themes from Empedocles in Lucretius' proem', *Bulletin of the Institute of Classical Studies* 17: 55–64.

(1978) 'Lucretius the Epicurean, on the history of man', in Gigon (1978), 1–27, reprinted in Furley (1989), 206–22.

(1989) *Cosmic Problems: Essays on Greek and Roman Philosophy of Nature*. Cambridge.

Fusil, C. A. (1928) 'Lucrèce et les philosophes du XVIIIᵉ siècle', *Revue d'Histoire Littéraire de la France* 37: 194–210.

(1930) 'Lucrèce et les littérateurs, poètes et artistes du XVIIIe siècle', *Revue d'Histoire Littéraire de la France* 39: 461–76.

Gale, M. (1994a) *Myth and Poetry in Lucretius*. Cambridge.

(1994b) 'Lucretius 4.1–25 and the proems of the *De rerum natura*', *Proceedings of the Cambridge Philological Society* 40: 1–17.

(2000) *Virgil on the Nature of Things: the Georgics, Lucretius and the Didactic Tradition*. Cambridge.

(forthcoming) *Oxford Readings in Lucretius*. Oxford.

Galinsky, G. K. (1969) *Aeneas, Sicily and Rome*. Princeton.

Gambino Longo, S. (2004) *Savoir de la nature et poésie des choses: Lucrèce et Epicure à la Renaissance italienne*. Paris.

Gantner, J. (1958) *Leonardos Visionen von der Sintflut und vom Untergang der Welt: Geschichte einer künstlerischen Idee*. Bern.

Ganz, D. (1996) 'Lucretius in the Carolingian age: the Leiden manuscripts and their Carolingian readers', in *Medieval Manuscripts of the Latin Classics: Production and Use*, ed. C. A. Chavannes-Mazel and M. M. Smith. Los Altos Hills: 91–102.

Garani, M. (2007) *Empedocles redivivus: Poetry and Analogy in Lucretius*. London and New York.

(forthcoming) 'Cosmological oaths in Empedocles and Lucretius', in *Horkos*, ed. A. H. Sommerstein and J. Fletcher. Bristol.

Gardner, P. (ed.) (1992) *A. E. Housman: the Critical Heritage*. London.

Gassendi, P. (1972) *Selected Works*, ed. and transl. C. Brush. New York.

Gay, P. (1966) *The Enlightenment, an Interpretation: the Rise of Modern Paganism*. London, reprinted Baltimore 1995.

Gee, E. (forthcoming) 'Astronomy and philosophical orientation in classical and Renaissance didactic poetry', in *What Nature Does Not Teach: Didactic Literature in the Medieval and Early Modern Periods*, ed. J. Ruys. Turnhout.

Gemelli, B. (1996) *Aspetti dell'atomismo classico nella filosofia di Francis Bacon e nel seicento*. Florence.

Gervais, A. (1972) 'A propos de la "Peste" d'Athènes: Thucydide et la littérature de l'épidémie', *Bulletin de l' Association G. Budé* 31: 395–427.

Giesecke, A. (2000) *Atoms, Ataraxy, and Allusion: Cross-Generic Imitation of the De Rerum Natura in Early Augustan Poetry*. Hildesheim, Zurich and New York.

Gigandet, A. (2002) 'Lucrèce vu en songe: Diderot, Le Rêve d'Alembert et le De rerum natura', *Revue de Métaphysique et de Morale* 2002: 427–39.

Gigante, M. (1988) 'Ambrogio Traversari interprete di Diogene Laerzio', in *Ambrogio Traversari nel VI centenario della nascita*, ed. G. C. Garfagnini. Florence: 367–459.

(2002) *Philodemus in Italy: the Books from Herculaneum*, transl. D. Obbink, 2nd edn. Ann Arbor.

Gigon, O. (ed.) (1978) *Lucrèce* (Entretiens sur l'Antiquité Classique 24, Fondation Hardt). Geneva.

Gilonis, H. (1995) 'The forms cut out of the mystery: Bunting, some contemporaries, and Lucretius's "poetry of facts"', *Durham University Journal* 89: 147–62.

Giussani, C. (1896–8) *T. Lucreti Cari De Rerum Natura libri sex* (4 vols.). Turin.

Glanvill, J. (1725) *Poems*. London.

Glei, R. F. (1995) 'Über Gott und die Welt. Kardinal Melchior de Polignacs lateinisches Lehrgedicht *Anti-Lucretius*', *Forschung an der Universität Bielefeld* 12: 36–40.

(forthcoming) 'Novus orbis. Melchior de Polignac über das Mikroskop', in *Acta Conventus Neo-Latini Abulensis*, ed. R. Schnur. Tempe, Ariz.

Goddard, C. P. (1991a) 'Epicureanism and the poetry of Lucretius in the Renaissance'. Diss. Cambridge.

(1991b) 'Pontano's use of the didactic genre: rhetoric, irony and the manipulation of Lucretius in *Urania*', *Renaissance Studies* 5: 250–62.

(1993) 'Lucretius and Lucretian science in the works of Fracastoro', *Res Publica Litterarum* 16: 185–92.

Goetschel, W. (1994), *Constituting Critique: Kant's Writing as Critical Practice*, transl. E. Schwab. Durham.

Goldschmidt, V. (1977) *La Doctrine d'Epicure et le droit*. Paris.

Gombrich, E. (1972) 'Botticelli's mythologies. A study in the Neo-platonic symbolism of his circle', in *Symbolic Images. Studies in the Art of the Renaissance*, vol. II, London: 31–81.

Good, J. M. (1805) *The Nature of Things: a Didactic Poem. Translated from the Latin of Titus Lucretius Carus* (2 vols.). London.

Gordon, C. A. (1962) *A Bibliography of Lucretius*. London, reprinted 1985.

Gordon, D. R. and Suits, D. B. (2003) *Epicurus: His Continuing Influence and Contemporary Relevance*. New York.

Gottschalk, H. B. (1971) 'Soul as *harmonia*', *Phronesis* 16: 179–98.

Gourevitch, V. (2000) 'Rousseau on providence', *Review of Metaphysics* 53: 565–611.

Gransden, K. (1976) *Virgil. Aeneid VIII*. Cambridge.

Grant, E. (1981) *Much Ado about Nothing: Theories of Space and Vacuum from the Middle Ages to the Scientific Revolution*. Cambridge.

Gray, T. (1775) *Poems*, 2nd edn. London.

Greenlaw, E. (1920) 'Spenser and Lucretius', *Studies in Philology* 17: 439–64.

Gregory, O. (1828) *Memoirs of the Life, Writings, and Character, Literary, Professional and Religious, of the Late John Mason Good, M.D.* London.

Griffin, J. (1986) *Virgil*. New York.

Griffin, M. (1989) 'Philosophy, politics and politicians at Rome', in Griffin and Barnes (1989), 1–38.

Griffin, M. and Barnes, J. (eds.) (1989) *Philosophia Togata: Essays on Philosophy and Roman Society*. Oxford.

Grimal, P. (1978) 'Le poème de Lucrèce en son temps', in Gigon (1978), 233–70.

Gutzwiller, K. (1998) *Poetic Garlands: Hellenistic Epigrams in Context*. Berkeley, Los Angeles and London.

Haber, T. B. (1967) *A. E. Housman*. Boston, Mass.

Hadot, P. (1995) 'The view from above', in *Philosophy as a Way of Life: Spiritual Exercises from Socrates to Foucault*, ed. A. I. Davidson. Malden, Mass.: 238–50.

Hadzsits, G. D. (1963) *Lucretius and His Influence*. New York.

Hagendahl, H. (1958) *Latin Fathers and the Classics*. Göteborg.

Hammond, P. (1983) 'The integrity of Dryden's Lucretius', *Modern Language Review* 78: 1–23.

(1989) 'John Dryden: the classicist as sceptic', *The Seventeenth Century* 4: 165–87.

(2001) 'Dryden, Milton, and Lucretius', *The Seventeenth Century* 16: 158–76.

Hammond, P. and Hopkins, D. (eds.) (1995–2005) *The Poems of John Dryden* (5 vols.). London.

Hardie, P. (1986) *Virgil's 'Aeneid': Cosmos and Imperium*. Oxford.

(1992) 'Augustan poets and the mutability of Rome', in *Roman Poetry and Propaganda in the Age of Augustus*, ed. A. Powell. Bristol: 59–82.

(1995) 'The presence of Lucretius in *Paradise Lost*', *Milton Quarterly* 29: 13–35.

(2002) *Ovid's Poetics of Illusion*. Cambridge.

(2006) 'Cultural and historical narratives in Virgil's *Eclogues* and Lucretius', in *Brill's Companion to Greek and Latin Pastoral*, ed. M. Fantuzzi and T. Papanghelis. Leiden and Boston: 275–300.

(2008) 'Horace's sublime yearnings: Lucretian ironies', *Papers of the Langford Latin Seminar* 13.

(forthcoming a) 'Lucretian multiple explanations and their tradition', in *Lucrezio, la natura e la scienza*, ed. M. Beretta and F. Citti. Florence.

(forthcoming b) 'Lucretian visions in Virgil'.

Hardy, T. (1932) *Collected Poems of Thomas Hardy*. London.

Harrison, C. T. (1933) 'Bacon, Hobbes, Boyle, and the ancient atomists', *Harvard Studies and Notes in Philology and Literature* 15: 191–219.

(1934) 'The ancient atomists and English literature of the seventeenth century', *Harvard Studies in Classical Philology* 45: 1–79.

Harrison, J. (1978) *The Library of Isaac Newton*. Cambridge.

Harrison, S. J. (1990) 'Lucretius, Euripides and the philosophers: *De Rerum Natura* 5.13–21', *Classical Quarterly* 40: 195–8.

(2002) 'Ennius and the prologue to Lucretius *DRN* 1 (1.1–148)', *Leeds International Classical Studies* 1.iv, online at www.leeds.ac.uk/classics/lics.

Haskell, Y. (1998a) 'The masculine muse: form and content in the Latin didactic poetry of Palingenius and Bruno', in *Form and Content in Didactic Poetry*, ed. C. Atherton. Bari: 117–44.

(1998b) 'Renaissance Latin didactic poetry on the stars: wonder, myth, and science', *Renaissance Studies* 12: 495–522.

(1998c) 'The *Tristia* of a Greek refugee: Michael Marullus and the politics of Latin subjectivity after the fall of Constantinople', *Proceedings of the Cambridge Philological Society* 44: 110–36.

(1999) 'Between fact and fiction: the Renaissance didactic poetry of Fracastoro, Palingenio and Valvasone', in Haskell and Hardie (1999), 77–103.

(2003) *Loyola's Bees: Ideology and Industry in Jesuit Latin Didactic Poetry*. Oxford.

(forthcoming a) 'Latin poet-doctors of the eighteenth century: the German Lucretius (Johann Ernst Hebenstreit) versus the Dutch Ovid (Gerard Nicolaas Heerkens)', in *Humanism and Medicine in the Early Modern Period*, ed. S. Broomhall and Y. Haskell. London.

(forthcoming b) 'Sleeping with the enemy: Tommaso Ceva's use and abuse of Lucretius in the *Philosophia Novo-antiqua*', in *What Nature Does Not Teach: Didactic Literature in the Medieval and Early Modern Periods*, ed. J. Ruys. Turnhout.

Haskell, Y. and Hardie, P. (eds.) (1999) *Poets and Teachers: Latin Didactic Poetry and the Didactic Authority of the Latin Poet from the Renaissance to the Present*. Bari.

Hastie, W. (1900) *Kant's Cosmogony*. New York.

Heilen, S. (ed.) (1999) Lorenzo Bonincontri, *De rebus naturalibus et divinis: Zwei Lehrgedichte an Lorenzo de' Medici und Ferdinand von Aragonien; Einleitung und kritische Edition*. Stuttgart.

Heisenberg, W. (1958) *Physics and Philosophy*. New York.

Hellegouarc'h, J. (1963) *Le Vocabulaire latin des relations et des partis politiques sous la République*. Paris.

Henderson, A. A. R. (1969) 'Tibullus, Elysium and Tartarus', *Latomus* 28: 649–53.

Hendrick, P. (1975) 'Lucretius in the *Apologie de Raimond Sebond*', *Bibliothèque d'Humanisme et Renaissance* 37: 457–66.

Herford, C. H., Simpson, P. and Simpson, E. (eds.) (1925–63) *Ben Jonson* (11 vols.). London.

Herrmann, L. (1956) 'Catulle et Lucrèce', *Latomus* 15: 465–80.

Hinds, S. E. (1987) 'Language at the breaking point: Lucretius 1. 452', *Classical Quarterly* 37: 450–3.

Hirsch, D. A. H. (1991) 'Donne's atomies and anatomies: deconstructed bodies and the resurrection of atomic theory', *Studies in English Literature 1500–1900* 31: 69–94.

Hollis, A. S. (1990) 'Nicander and Lucretius', *Papers of the Leeds International Latin Seminar* 10: 169–84.

Holton, G. J. (1978) *The Scientific Imagination: Case Studies*. Cambridge, Mass.
(1993) *Science and Anti-Science*. Cambridge, Mass.

Hooley, D. M. (1997) *The Knotted Thong. Structures of Mimesis in Persius*. Ann Arbor.

Hopkins, D. (1986) *John Dryden*. Cambridge.
(2002) Review of Repetzki 2000, *Translation and Literature* 11: 114–18.
(2004) *Writers and their Work: John Dryden*. Tavistock.

Hornblower, S. (1991) *A Commentary on Thucydides*, vol. 1: *Books I–III*. Oxford.

Hume, D. (1948) *Dialogues Concerning Natural Religion*. New York and London.
(1956) *The Natural History of Religion*. Stanford.
(1981) *A Treatise of Human Nature*. Oxford.

Humphries, R. (transl.) (1968) *The Way Things Are: the De Rerum Natura*. Bloomington.

Hundert, E. J. (1987) 'The thread of language and the web of dominion: Mandeville to Rousseau and back', *Eighteenth-Century Studies* 21: 169–91.
(1995) 'Bernard Mandeville and the Enlightenment's maxims of modernity', *Journal of the History of Ideas* 56: 577–93.

Hunt, L. (1923) *The Poetical Works of Leigh Hunt*, ed. H. S. Milford. London.

Hunter, M. (1995) *Science and the Shape of Orthodoxy: Intellectual Change in Late Seventeenth-Century Britain*. Woodbridge.

Hunter, W. B. (1978–83) *A Milton Encyclopedia* (5 vols.). Lewisburg.

Hutchinson, G. (2001) 'The date of *De Rerum Natura*', *Classical Quarterly* 51: 150–62.

Hutchinson, L. (2001) *Order and Disorder*, ed. D. Norbrook. Oxford.

Hyder, C. K. (ed.) (1970) *Swinburne: the Critical Heritage*. London.

Ingalls, W. B. (1971) 'Repetition in Lucretius', *Phoenix* 25: 227–36.

Ingegno, A. (1985) *La sommersa nave della religione: studio sulla polemica anticristiana di Bruno*. Naples.

Innes, D. C. (1979) 'Gigantomachy and natural philosophy', *Classical Quarterly* 29: 165–71.

Inwood, B. and Gerson, L. (eds. and transl.) (1994) *The Epicurus Reader*. Cambridge.

Jackson, G. B. (1987) 'From essence to accident: Locke and the language of poetry in the eighteenth century', *Criticism* 29: 27–66.

Jal, P. (1963) *La Guerre civile à Rome: étude littéraire et morale*. Paris.

Jameson, F. (1973) 'The vanishing mediator: narrative structure in Max Weber', *New German Critique* 1: 52–89.

Jankélévitch, V. (1980) *Le je-ne-sais-quoi et le presque-rien* (3 vols.). Paris.
(1986) *L'Imprescriptible: pardonner? dans l'honneur et la dignité*. Paris.

Janko, R. (ed.) (2000) *Philodemus: On Poems Book 1*. Oxford.

Jeffares, A. N. (1962) *W. B. Yeats: Man and Poet*, 2nd edn. London.

Jenkyns, R. (1998) *Virgil's Experience. Nature and History; Times, Names, and Places*. Oxford.

Jocelyn, H. (1977) 'The ruling class of the Roman republic and Greek philosophers', *Bulletin of the John Rylands University Library* 59: 323–66.

Johnson, M. R. (2003) 'Was Gassendi an Epicurean?', *History of Philosophy Quarterly* 20: 339–59.

Johnson, S. (1905) *Lives of the English Poets*, ed. G. B. Hill (3 vols.). Oxford.

Johnson, W. R. (2000) *Lucretius and the Modern World*. London.

Jones, E. (1985) 'A "perpetual torrent": Dryden's Lucretian style', in *Augustan Studies: Essays in Honor of Irvin Ehrenpreis*, ed. D. L. Patey and T. Keegan. Newark, Del.: 47–63.

Jones, H. (1989) *The Epicurean Tradition*. London, reprinted 1992.

(1991) 'An eighteenth-century refutation of Epicurean physics: the *Anti-Lucretius* of Melchior de Polignac (1747)', *Acta Conventus Neo-Latini Torontonensis*, ed. A. Dalzell *et al.* Binghamton, N.Y.: 393–401.

Kandinsky, W. (1955) *Rückblick*. Baden-Baden.

Kant, I. (1902) *Gesammelte Schriften* (29 vols. in 34). Berlin.

(1928) *The Critique of Judgement*, transl. J. C. Meredith. Oxford, reprinted 1982.

(1968) *Vorkritische Schriften*, vol. I: *Werkausgabe*, ed. Wilhelm Weischedel (12 vols.). Stuttgart.

(1991) *Kant-Forschungen*, vol. III: *Bemerkungen in den 'Beobachtungen über das Gefühl des Schönen und Erhabenen'*, ed. M. Rischmüller. Hamburg.

(2004) *Metaphysical Foundations of Natural Science*, transl. M. Friedman. Cambridge.

Kany-Turpin, J. (1991) 'Une réinvention de Lucrèce par Guillaume du Bartas', in *La Littérature et ses avatars: discrédits, déformations et réhabilitations dans l'histoire de la littérature*, ed. Y. Bellenger. Paris: 31–9.

Kargon, R. H. (1966) *Atomism in England from Hariot to Newton*. Oxford.

Kelley, P. (1983) 'Wordsworth and Lucretius' *De rerum natura*', *Notes & Queries* 228: 219–22.

Kennedy, D. F. (2002) *Rethinking Reality: Lucretius and the Textualization of Nature*. Ann Arbor.

Kenney, E. J. (1970) '*Doctus Lucretius*', *Mnemosyne* 23: 366–92, reprinted with addenda in Classen (1986), 237–65.

(ed.) (1971) *Lucretius De Rerum Natura Book III*, Cambridge, reprinted with corrections and addenda 1984.

(1972) 'The historical imagination of Lucretius', *Greece & Rome* 19: 12–24.

(1973) 'The style of the Metamorphoses' in *Ovid*, ed. J. W. Binns. London: 116–53, reprinted with modifications in *Brill's Companion to Ovid*, ed. B. W. Boyd (2002). Leiden, Boston and Cologne: 28–89.

(1974) '*Viuida uis*: Polemic and pathos in Lucretius 1.62–101', in *Quality and Pleasure*, ed. T. Woodman and D. West. Cambridge: 18–30.

(1981) Review of E. Ackermann, *Lukrez und der Mythos* (1979). *Classical Review* 31: 19–21.

(1995) *Lucretius* (Greece and Rome: New Surveys in the Classics 11), rev. edn with addenda by M. Gale. Oxford.

Kerferd, G. B. (1971) 'Epicurus' doctrine of the soul', *Phronesis* 16: 80–96.

Kerson, A. L. (1988) 'Enlightened thought in Diego José Abad's *De Deo, Deoque Homine Heroica*', in *Acta Conventus Neo-Latini Guelpherbytani*, ed. S. Revard *et al.* Binghamton, N.Y.: 617–23.

Keynes, G. (1973) *A Bibliography of Dr John Donne*, 4th edn. Oxford.

Kimmich, D. (1993) *Epikureische Aufklärung. Philosophische und poetische Konzepte der Selbstsorge*. Darmstadt.

King, J. (1998) 'Erotodidaxis: *iucunda uoluptas* in Lucretius 2.3 and Propertius 1.10.3', in *Qui miscuit utile dulci: Festschrift Essays for Paul Lachlan MacKendrick*, ed. G. Schmeling and J. D. Mikalson. Wauconda, Ill.: 201–22.

King-Hele, D. (1986) *Erasmus Darwin and the Romantic Poets*. London and Basingstoke.

Kleve, K. (1978) 'The philosophical polemics in Lucretius: a study in the history of Epicurean criticism', in Gigon (1978), 39–76.

(1989) 'Lucretius in Herculaneum', *Cronache Ercolanesi* 19: 5–27.

(1997) 'Lucretius and Philodemus', in Algra, Koenen and Schrijvers (1997), 49–66.

(2007) 'Lucretius' Book II in P.Herc. 395', in *Akten des 23. Internationalen Papyrologenkongresses*, ed. B. Palme. Vienna: 347–54.

Knox, P. E. (1999) 'Lucretius on the narrow road', *Harvard Studies in Classical Philology* 99: 275–87.

Knust, H. (1886) *Liber de vita et moribus philosophorum*. Tübingen.

Kristeller, P. O. (1937) *Supplementum Ficinianum* (2 vols.). Florence.

(1943) *The Philosophy of Marsilio Ficino*, transl. V. L. Conant. New York.

(1956) 'Marsilio Ficino and his circle', in *Studies in Renaissance Thought and Letters*, vol. I. Rome: 35–247.

Kristeva, J. (1974) *La Révolution du langage poétique: l'avant-garde à la fin du XIXe siècle, Lautréamont et Mallarmé*. Paris.

Kroll, R. (1991) *The Material Word: Literate Culture in the Restoration and Early Eighteenth Century*. Baltimore.

Kronenberg, L. (2005) 'Mezentius the Epicurean', *Transactions of the American Philological Association* 135: 403–31.

Kyriakidis, S. (2004) 'Middles in Lucretius' *De rerum natura*: the poet and his work', in *Middles in Latin Poetry*, ed. S. Kyriakidis and F. De Martino. Bari: 27–50.

Lacan, J. (1986) *L'Ethique de la psychanalyse, 1959–1960: Le Séminaire Livre VII*, ed. J.-A. Miller. Paris.

Laird, A. (2006) *The Epic of America: an Introduction to Rafael Landívar and the Rusticatio Mexicana*. London.

Lamont, C. (1947) 'Naturalism and the appreciation of nature', *Journal of Philosophy* 44: 597–608.

Landolfi, L. (1992) '*Caeli cavernae*: fortuna di uno stilema', *Vichiana*, 3rd series 1–2: 208–19.

Langdon, H. (2004) 'A theatre of marvels: the poetics of Salvator Rosa', *Konsthistorisk Tidskrift*, 73.iii: 179–92.

Lange, F. A. (1866) *Geschichte des Materialismus*. Iserlohn (transl. E. C. Thomas as *The History of Materialism*, 1925).

Lasswitz, K. (1890) *Geschichte der Atomistik vom Mittelalter bis Newton* (2 vols.). Hamburg.

Latham, R. E. (1994) *On the Nature of the Universe*, rev. J. Godwin. London.

Lattimore, R. (1962) *Themes in Greek and Latin Epitaphs*. Urbana.

Lehnerdt, M. (1904) *Lucretius in der Renaissance*. Königsberg.

Lennon, T. (1993) *The Battle of the Gods and Giants: the Legacies of Descartes and Gassendi, 1655–1715*. Princeton.

Lentin, A. (ed.) (1985) *Enlightened Absolutism (1760–1790): a Documentary Sourcebook*. Woking.

Leonard, J. (2000) 'Milton, Lucretius, and "the void profound of unessential light"', in *Living Texts: Interpreting Milton*, ed. K. A. Pruitt and C. W. Durham. Selinsgrove, Penn.: 198–217.

Leonard, W. E. and Smith, S. B. (eds.) (1965) *T. Lucreti Cari De Rerum Natura libri sex*. Madison.

Leonhardt, J. (1989) *Dimensio syllabarum*. Göttingen.

Leranbaum, M. (1977) *Alexander Pope's 'Opus Magnum', 1729–1744*. Oxford.

Levi, P. (2002) *The Search for Roots: a Personal Anthology*, transl. P. Forbes. Harmondsworth.

Lévy, C. (1997) 'Lucrèce avait-il lu Enésidème?', in Algra, Koenen and Schrijvers (1997), 115–24.

(2005) 'Le philosophe et le légionnaire: l'armée comme thème et métaphore dans la pensée romaine, de Lucrèce à Marc Aurèle', in *Politica e cultura in Roma antica*, ed. F. Bessone and E. Malaspina. Bologna: 59–79.

Lewalski, B. K. (1985) *Paradise Lost and the Rhetoric of Literary Forms*. Princeton.

Lewis, C. S. (1936) *The Allegory of Love*. Oxford.

(1942) *The Problem of Pain*. London.

(1947) *Miracles: a Preliminary Study*. London.

(1955) *Surprised by Joy: the Story of My Early Life*. London.

(1961) *An Experiment in Criticism*. Cambridge.

(1984) *Of This and Other Worlds*, ed. W. Hooper. London.

Lipscomb, H. C. (1935) 'Lucretius and *The Testament of Beauty*', *Classical Journal* 31: 77–88.

Litman, T. A. (1971) *Le Sublime en France (1660–1714)*. Paris.

Locke, J. (1959) *An Essay Concerning Human Understanding*, ed. A. C. Fraser (2 vols.). New York.

(1999) *The Reasonableness of Christianity: As Delivered in the Scriptures*, ed. J. C. Higgins-Biddle. Oxford.

Long, A. A. (1977) 'Chance and natural law in Epicureanism', *Phronesis* 22: 63–88.

(1997), 'Lucretius on nature and the Epicurean self,' in Algra, Koenen and Schrijvers (1997), 128–32.

Long, A. A. and Sedley, D. N. (1987) *The Hellenistic Philosophers* (2 vols.). Cambridge.

Lonsdale, R. (ed.) (1969) *Poems of Thomas Gray, William Collins and Oliver Goldsmith*. London.

Lotito, G. (1981) 'Modelli etici e base economica nelle opere filosofiche di Cicerone', in *Modelli etici, diritto e trasformazioni sociali*, ed. A. Giardina and A. Schiavone. Rome and Bari: 79–126.

Ludwig, W. (1988) 'Neulateinische Lehrgedichte und Vergils *Georgica*', in *Litterae Neolatinae: Schriften zur neulateinischen Literatur*. Munich: 100–27.

Luhr, F.-F. (1969) *Ratio und Fatum: Dichtung und Lehre bei Manilius*. Frankfurt.

Lüthy, C., Murdoch, J. E. and Newman, W. R. (eds.) (2001) *Late Medieval and Early Modern Corpuscular Matter Theories*. Leiden.

Lyne, R. O. A. M. (1994) 'Subversion by intertextuality: Catullus 66.39–40 and other examples', *Greece & Rome* 41: 187–203.

Lyotard, J.-F. (1991) *The Inhuman: Reflections on Time*, transl. G. Bennington and R. Bowlby. Cambridge.

Maas, H. (ed.) (1971) *The Letters of A. E. Housman*. London.

Macaulay, T. B. (1860) *The Miscellaneous Writings of Lord Macaulay* (2 vols.). London.

McColley, G. (1940) 'Nicholas Hill and the *Philosophia Epicurea*', *Annals of Science* 4: 390–405.

MacDiarmid, H. (1943) *Lucky Poet: a Self-Study in Literature and Political Ideas: Being the Autobiography of Hugh MacDiarmid (Christopher Murray Grieve)*. London.

MacDonogh, G. (1999) *Frederick the Great: a Life in Deed and Letters*. London.

McGuire, J. E. and Rattansi, P. M. (1966) 'Newton and the Pipes of Pan', *Notes and Records of the Royal Society* 21: 108–34.

McGuire, J. E. and Tamny, M. (eds.) (1983) *Certain Philosophical Questions: Newton's Trinity Notebook*. Cambridge.

McGushin, P. (1980) *Sallust. Bellum Catilinae*. Bristol.

Mack, M. (ed.) (1984) *The Last and Greatest Art: Some Unpublished Poetic Manuscripts of Alexander Pope*. Newark, Del.

Mackail, J. W. (1895) *Latin Literature*. London.

Mackenzie, D. (2007) 'Two versions of Lucretius: Arnold and Housman', *Translation and Literature* 16: 160–77.

McLaughlin, M. (1988) *Italo Calvino*. Edinburgh.

MacPhail, E. (2000) 'Montaigne's new Epicureanism', *Montaigne Studies* 12: 91–103.

Maguinness, W. S. (1965) 'The language of Lucretius', in Dudley (1965a), 69–93.

Mallock, W. H. (1878) *Lucretius*. Edinburgh.

Maltby, R. (1991) *A Lexicon of Ancient Latin Etymologies*. Leeds.

Manitius, M. (1931) *Geschichte der lateinischen Literatur des Mittelalters*, vol. III. Munich.

Mansfeld, J. (1992) 'A Theophrastean excursus on god and nature and its aftermath in Hellenistic thought', *Phronesis* 37: 314–35.

Manuel, F. E. (1959) *The Eighteenth Century Confronts the Gods*. Cambridge, Mass.

Manuwald, B. (1980) *Der Aufbau der lukrezischen Kulturentstehungslehre (De rerum natura 5, 925–1457)*. Mainz.

Marlow, N. (1958) *A. E. Housman: Scholar and Poet*. London.

Martha, C. (1884) *Le Poème de Lucrèce. Morale – Religion – Science*, 3rd edn. Paris (first pub. 1867).

Martin, J. (1934) *T. Lucreti Cari De Rerum Natura libri sex*. Leipzig.

Martindale, C. (1986) *John Milton and the Transformation of Ancient Epic*. London.

(2005) *Latin Poetry and the Judgement of Taste: an Essay in Aesthetics*. Oxford.

Marullus, M. (1995a) *Hymnes naturels*, ed. and transl. J. Chomarat. Geneva.

(1995b) *Inni Naturali con testo a fronte*, ed. D. Coppini. Florence.

Mason, T. (1996) 'Is there a classical tradition in English poetry?', *Translation and Literature* 5: 203–19.

(2001) '"Et versus digitos habet": Dryden, Montaigne, Lucretius, Virgil and Boccaccio in praise of Venus', *Translation and Literature* 10: 89–109.

Masson, A. (2004) 'Introduction' to *Sur L'Anti-Lucrèce de monsieur le cardinal de Polignac*, in Voltaire (1968–), vol. xxxc: 321–35.

Masson, J. (1907–9) *Lucretius: Epicurean and Poet* (2 vols.). London.

Masters, R. D. (1968) *The Political Philosophy of Rousseau*. Princeton.

Mathieu-Castellani, G. (1988) *Montaigne et l'écriture de l'essai*. Paris.

Maxwell, J. C. (1873) 'Molecules', *Nature* 8: 437–41.

Mayer, R. G. (1990) 'The epic of Lucretius', *Papers of the Leeds Latin Seminar* 6: 35–43.

Mayo, T. F. (1934) *Epicurus in England (1650–1725)*. Dallas.

Mazzoli, G. (1970) *Seneca e la poesia*. Milan.

— (1996) 'Orazio e il sublime', in *Doctus Horatius: Atti del Convegno di Studi per Virginio Cremona (Brescia 9–10 febbraio 1995)*, ed. P. V. Cova. Milan: 21–40.

Meadows, P. A. (1997) *Francis Ponge and the Nature of Things: From Ancient Atomism to a Modern Poetics*. Lewisberg.

Medwin, T. (1913) *The Life of Percy Bysshe Shelley*, ed. H. B. Forman. London.

Meinel, C. (1988) 'Early seventeenth century atomism: theory, epistemology, and the insufficiency of experiment', *Isis* 79: 86–103.

Mellinghoff-Bourgerie, V. (1990) *Les Incertitudes de Virgile: contributions épicuriennes à la théologie de l'Enéide*. Brussels.

Mellor, R. (1981) 'The goddess Roma', *Aufstieg und Niedergang der römischen Welt* 2.17.2: 950–1030.

Melville, Sir R. (1997) *On the Nature of the Universe: a New Verse Translation*, ed. D. Fowler and P. Fowler. Oxford.

Ménager, D. (1989) 'Les citations de Lucrèce chez Montaigne', in *Montaigne in Cambridge*, ed. P. Ford and G. Jondorf. Cambridge: 25–38.

Mercuriale, G. (1588) *Hieronymi Mercurialis Variarum Lectionum in medicinae scriptoribus et alijs libri sex*. Venice.

Michael, E. (2001) 'Sennert's Sea Change: Atoms and Causes', in Lüthy *et al.* (2001): 331–62.

Milanese, G. (1989) *Lucida carmina: comunicazione e scrittura da Epicuro a Lucrezio*. Milan.

— (2005) *Censimento dei manoscritti noniani*. Genoa.

Miles, G. (1980) *Virgil's 'Georgics': a New Interpretation*. Berkeley.

Miller, J. F. (1997) 'Lucretian moments in Ovidian elegy', *Classical Journal* 92: 384–98.

Minadeo, R. (1965) 'The formal design of the *De rerum natura*', *Arion* 4: 444–61.

— (1969) *The Lyre of Science: Form and Meaning in Lucretius' De rerum natura*. Detroit.

Minyard, J. D. (1978) *Mode and Value in the De Rerum Natura: a Study in Lucretius' Metrical Language*. Wiesbaden.

— (1985) *Lucretius and the Late Republic: an Essay in Roman Intellectual History*. Leiden.

Mitsis, P. (1988) *Epicurus' Ethical Theory: the Pleasures of Invulnerability*. Ithaca and London.

— (1993) 'Committing philosophy on the reader: didactic coercion and reader autonomy in *De rerum natura*', in Schiesaro *et al.* (1993), 111–28.

Molnár, G. v. (1994) *Goethes Kantstudien: eine Zusammenstellung nach Eintragungen in seinen Handexemplaren der "Kritik der reinen Vernunft" und der "Kritik der Urteilskraft"*. Weimar.

Momigliano, A. (1960) Review of Farrington (1939) in *Secondo contributo alla storia degli studi classici*. Rome: 375–88, originally in *Journal of Roman Studies* 31 (1941) 149–57.

Monet, A. (ed.) (2003) *Le Jardin romain. Epicurisme et poésie à Rome. Mélanges offerts à Mayotte Bollack*. Lille.

Money, D. (1999) 'A symphony in Gray and Browne: was eighteenth-century didactic poetry off colour?', in Haskell and Hardie (1999), 141–54.

Montaigne, M. de (1987) *The Complete Essays*, ed. and transl. M. A. Screech. London.

(1978) *Les Essais*, ed. P. Villey and V.-L. Saulnier (3 vols.). Paris.

Monti, C. (1991) 'Lukrezianismus und Neuplatonismus. Versuch einer theoretischen Synthese in den lateinischen Gedichten Giordano Brunos', in *Die Frankfurter Schriften Giordano Brunos und ihre Voraussetzungen*, ed. K. Heipke, W. Neuser and E. Wicke. Weinheim: 163–79.

Monti, R. C. (1981) 'Lucretius on greed, political ambition and society, *de rer. nat.* 3,59–86', *Latomus* 40: 48–66.

Moore, W. G. (1967) 'Lucretius and Montaigne', *Yale French Studies* 38: 109–14.

More, H. (1998) *A Platonick Song of the Soul*, ed. A. Jacobs. London.

Morgan, L. (1999) *Patterns of Redemption in Virgil's 'Georgics'*. Cambridge.

Morrison, M. (1963) 'Another book from Ronsard's library: a presentation copy of Lambin's Lucretius', *Bibliothèque d'Humanisme et Renaissance*, 25: 561–6.

Muir, E. (1963) *Collected Poems*. London.

Munk Olsen, B. (1979) 'Les classiques latins dans les florilèges médiévaux antérieurs au XIIIe siècle', *Revue d'Histoire des Textes* 9: 47–121.

Munro, H. A. J. (ed.) (1886) *T. Lucreti Cari De Rerum Natura libri sex*, 4th edn (3 vols.). Cambridge and London, with later reprintings.

Murley, C. (1939) 'Lucretius and the history of satire', *Transactions of the American Philological Association* 70: 380–95.

(1947) 'Lucretius, *De rerum natura*, viewed as epic', *Transactions of the American Philological Association* 78: 336–46.

Myers, F. W. H. (1893) 'Modern poets and the meaning of life', *The Nineteenth Century* 33: 93–111.

Myers, K. S. (1994) *Ovid's Causes: Cosmogony and Aetiology in the Metamorphoses*. Ann Arbor.

Nagel, T. (1979) *Mortal Questions*. London.

(1986) *The View from Nowhere*. New York and Oxford.

Naiden, J. (ed.) (1952). *The Sphera of George Buchanan (1506–1582): a Literary Opponent of Copernicus and Tycho Brahe*. Philadelphia.

Nardi, G. (ed.) (1647) *Titi Lucretii Cari De Rerum Natura libri sex*. Florence.

Narducci, E. (2004) *Cicerone e i suoi interpreti: studi sull'opera e la fortuna*. Pisa.

Newman, J. K. (1967) *The Concept of Vates in Augustan Poetry*. Brussels.

Newton, I. (1718) *Opticks: Or, A Treatise of the Reflections, Refractions, Inflections and Colours of Light*, 2nd edn. London.

(1962) *Unpublished Scientific Papers*, ed. A. R. Hall and M. B. Hall. Cambridge.

Nichols, J. H., Jr. (1976) *Epicurean Political Philosophy: the 'De Rerum Natura' of Lucretius*. Ithaca.

Nietzsche, F. W. (1933–42) *Historisch-kritische Gesamtausgabe: Werke*. ed. H. J. Mette, K. Schlechta and C. Koch (5 vols.). Munich.

Nightingale, A. (2007) 'Night-vision: Epicurean eschatology', *Arion* 14: 61–98.

Nisbet, H. B. (1986) 'Lucretius in eighteenth-century Germany with a commentary on Goethe's "Metamorphose der Tiere"', *Modern Language Review* 81: 97–115.

(1988) 'Karl Ludwig von Knebel's hexameter translation of Lucretius', *German Life and Letters* 44: 413–25.

Norbrook, D. (2000) 'Margaret Cavendish and Lucy Hutchinson: identity, ideology and politics', *In-Between: Essays and Studies in Literary Criticism*, 9: 179–203.

Nosei, A. P. (1927) 'Marcello Palingenio Stellato e Lucrezio', *Studi Italiani di Filologia Classica*, n.s. 5: 111–23.

Nott, J. (1799) *The First Book of Titus Lucretius Carus, on the Nature of Things. In English Verse, with the Latin Text*. London.

Novara, V. A. (1983) *Les Idées romaines sur le progrès d'après les écrivains de la République: essai sur le sens latin du progrès*. Paris.

Noyes, A. (1925–30) *The Torch-Bearers* (3 vols.). Edinburgh.

Nugent, S. G. (1994) 'Mater matters: the female in Lucretius' *De rerum natura*', *Colby Quarterly* 30: 179–205.

Nünlist, R. (1997) 'Zu den Lukrez-Buchrollen aus Herculaneum', *Zeitschrift für Papyrologie und Epigraphik* 116: 19–20.

Nussbaum, M. (1994) *The Therapy of Desire: Theory and Practice in Hellenistic Ethics*. Princeton.

Nüssel, A. (1999), '"Sed quid ego hic Musas"? On invocations in Aonio Paleario, *De animorum immortalitate* (1535) and Scipione Capece, *De principiis rerum* (1546)', in Haskell and Hardie (1999), 35–56.

Obbink, D. (1989) 'The atheism of Epicurus', *Greek, Roman and Byzantine Studies* 30: 187–223.

(ed.) (1995) *Philodemus and Poetry: Poetic Theory and Practice in Lucretius, Philodemus and Horace*. New York and Oxford.

O'Daly, G. (1991) *The Poetry of Boethius*. London.

O'Keefe, T. (2005) *Epicurus on Freedom*. Cambridge.

Osler, M. (2002) 'Gassendi', in *A Companion to Early Modern Philosophy*, ed. S. Nadler. Oxford: 80–95.

(2003) 'Early modern uses of Hellenistic philosophy: Gassendi's Epicurean project', in *Hellenistic and Early Modern Philosophy*, ed. J. Miller and B. Inwood. Cambridge: 30–44.

Otis, B. (1964) *Virgil: a Study in Civilized Poetry*. Oxford.

Owen, W. H. (1968–9) 'Structural patterns in Lucretius' *De rerum natura*', *Classical World* 62: 121–7, 166–72.

'Palingenius' (1996) *Le Zodiaque de la vie*, ed. and transl. J. Chomarat. Geneva.

Panofsky, E. (1962) *Studies in Iconology. Humanistic Themes in the Art of the Renaissance*. New York.

Parker, F. (2003) *Scepticism and Literature: an Essay on Pope, Hume, Sterne, and Johnson*. Oxford.

Partington, J. R. (1939) 'The origins of the atomic theory', *Annals of Science* 4: 245–82.

Pater, W. (1948) *Selected Works*, ed. Richard Aldington. London.

Patin, M. (1868) *Etudes sur la poésie latine* (2 vols.). Paris.

Pauly, A. F. von and Wissowa, G. (1894–1963) *Paulys Real-encyclopädie der classischen Altertumswissenschaft*. Stuttgart.

Pease, A. S. (1920–3) *M. Tulli Ciceronis De diuinatione* (2 vols.). Urbana.

(1935) *Publi Vergili Maronis Aeneidos liber quartus*. Cambridge, Mass.

Penwill, J. L. (1995) 'Image, ideology and action in Cicero and Lucretius', in *Roman Literature and Ideology: Roman Essays for J. P. Sullivan*. Bendigo: 68–91.

(1996) 'The ending of sense: death as closure in Lucretius book 6', *Ramus* 25: 146–69.

Perkell, C. (1989) *The Poet's Truth. A Study of the Poet in Virgil's Georgics.* Berkeley, Los Angeles and London.

Perret, J. (1940) 'L'amour de l'argent, l'ambition et la crainte de la mort (Lucrèce, III, 59–86)', in *Mélanges de philologie, de littérature et d'histoire anciennes offerts à Alfred Ernout.* Paris: 277–84.

Perutelli, A. (1980) 'Scipione ed Epicuro. Sul proemio al V di Lucrezio', *Atene & Roma* 25: 23–8.

Pianezzola, E. (1977) 'Lucrezio: sopravvivenza e potere', *Rivista di Cultura Classica e Medioevale* 19: 609–24.

Piazzi, L. (2005) *Lucrezio e i presocratici: un commento a De Rerum Natura 1: 635–920.* Pisa.

Pieri, A. (1977) *Lucrezio in Macrobio.* Florence.

Pizzani, U. (1986) 'Dimensione cristiana dell'umanesimo e messaggio lucreziano: la *Paraphrasis in Lucretium* di Raphael Francus', in *Validità perenne dell'Umanesimo*, ed. G. Tarugi. Florence: 313–33.

(1990) 'L'erramento ferino e lo sviluppo della società nei *Nutricia* di Angelo Poliziano: La presenza di Lucrezio', in *Homo sapiens, homo humanus*, vol. II: *Letteratura, arte e scienza nella seconda metà del'400*, ed. G. Tarugi. Florence: 389–406.

Poignault, R. (ed.) (1999) *Présence de Lucrèce. Actes du colloque tenu à Tours (3–5 décembre 1998).* Tours.

Polignac, M. de (1757) *Anti-Lucretius*, transl. W. Dobson. London.

Ponge, Francis (1999) *Œuvres complètes*, tome premier. Paris.

Pope, A. (1950) *The Twickenham Edition of the Poems of Alexander Pope*, vol. III.1: *An Essay on Man*, ed. M. Mack. London.

(1956) *Correspondence*, ed. G. Sherburn (5 vols.). Oxford.

Porter, J. I. (1992) 'Hermeneutic lines and circles: Aristarchus and Crates on Homeric exegesis', in *Homer's Ancient Readers: the Hermeneutics of Greek Epic's Earliest Exegetes*, ed. R. Lamberton and J. J. Keaney. Princeton: 67–114.

(2001) 'Des sons qu'on ne peut entendre: Ciceron, les "kritikoi" et la tradition du sublime dans la critique littéraire', in *Cicéron et Philodème: la polémique en philosophie*, ed. C. Auvray-Assayas and D. Delattre. Paris: 315–41.

(2003) 'Lucretius and the poetics of void', in *Le Jardin romain: Epicurisme et poésie à Rome. Mélanges offerts à Mayotte Bollack*, ed. A. Monet. Villeneuve d'Ascq: 197–226.

(2004) 'Vergil's voids', *Helios* 31.i–ii: 123–51.

(2005) 'Love of life: Lucretius to Freud', in *Erotikon: Essays on Eros, Ancient and Modern*, ed. S. Bartsch and T. Bartscherer. Chicago: 113–41.

Possevino, A. (1595) *Antonii Possevini Societatis Iesu Tractatio De Poësi et Pictura ethnica, humana, et fabulosa collata cum vera, honesta, et sacra.* Lyons.

Pound, E. (1978) *Guide to Kulchur.* London.

Powell, J. G. F. (1995a) 'Introduction: Cicero's philosophical works and their background', in *Cicero the Philosopher*, ed. J. G. F. Powell. Oxford: 1–35.

(1995b) 'Cicero's translations from Greek', in *Cicero the Philosopher*, ed. J. G. F. Powell. Oxford: 273–300.

Prandi, J. D. (1993) *Dare to be Happy! A Study of Goethe's Ethics.* Lanham.

Prawer, S. S. (1976) *Karl Marx and World Literature.* Oxford.

Previtera, C. (ed.) (1943) *Giovanni Pontano: I Dialoghi.* Florence.

Priestley, J. (1777) *Disquisitions relating to Matter and Spirit*. London.

Priestman, M. (1999) *Romantic Atheism: Poetry and Freethought, 1780–1830*. Cambridge.

Prosperi, V. (2004) *Di soave licor gli orli del vaso: la fortuna di Lucrezio dall'umanesimo alla controriforma*. Turin.

Pucci, G. C. (1966) 'Echi lucreziani in Cicerone', *Studi Italiani di Filologia Classica* 38: 70–132.

Pullman, B. (1998) *The Atom in the History of Human Thought*, transl. A. Reisinger. Oxford.

Putnam, M. (1979) *Virgil's Poem of the Earth: Studies in the 'Georgics'*. Princeton.

Quadlbauer, F. (1958) 'Die genera dicendi bis Plinius d. J.', *Wiener Studien* 71: 55–111.

Quinn, K. (1963) *Latin Explorations*. London.

(ed.) (1973) *Catullus: the Poems*, 2nd edn. London.

Quint, D. (2004) 'Fear of falling: Icarus, Phaethon, and Lucretius in *Paradise Lost*', *Renaissance Quarterly* 57: 847–81.

Radcliffe, A. (1790) *A Sicilian Romance*. London.

Raimondi, E. (1974) 'Il primo commento umanistico a Lucrezio', in *Tra latino e volgare: per Carlo Dionisotti*. Padua: 641–74.

Rapisarda, E. (1951) *Introduzione alla lettura di Prudenzio*, vol. I: *Influssi Lucreziani*. Catania.

Ray, G. (2004) 'Reading the Lisbon earthquake: Adorno, Lyotard, and the contemporary sublime', *Yale Journal of Criticism* 17: 1–18.

Real, H. J. R. (1970) *Untersuchungen zur Lukrez-Übersetzung von Thomas Creech*. Bad Homburg.

Redshaw, A. (1980) 'Voltaire and Lucretius', *Studies on Voltaire and the Eighteenth Century* 189: 19–43.

Rees, E. L. (2000) '"Sweet honey of the muses": Lucretian resonances in *Poems, and Fancies*', *In-Between: Essays and Studies in Literary Criticism* 9: 3–16.

Reeve, M. D. (1980) 'The Italian tradition of Lucretius', *Italia Medioevale e Umanistica* 23: 27–48.

(2005) 'The Italian tradition of Lucretius revisited', *Aevum* 79: 115–64.

(2006) 'Lucretius from the 1460s to the 17th century: seven questions of attribution', *Aevum* 80: 165–84.

Rehmann, R. (1969) 'Die Beziehungen zwischen Lukrez und Horaz'. Diss. Freiburg.

Repetzki, M. M. (ed.) (2000) *John Evelyn's Translation of Titus Lucretius Carus De Rerum Natura: an Old-Spelling Critical Edition*. Frankfurt.

Reynolds, L. D. (1983) *Texts and Transmission*. Oxford.

Roberts, H. (1997) *Shelley and the Chaos of History: a New Politics of Poetry*. University Park, Penn.

Rochester (John Wilmot), Earl of (1999) *Works*, ed. H. Love. Oxford.

Rogers, S. (1891) *Poetical Works*, ed. E. Bell. London.

Roller, D. W. (1970) 'Gaius Memmius: patron of Lucretius', *Classical Philology* 65: 246–8.

Rollins, H. E. (ed.) (1958) *The Letters of John Keats* (2 vols.). Cambridge, Mass.

Ronca, I. and Curr, M. (transl.) (1977) *William of Conches: a Dialogue on Natural Philosophy*. Notre Dame.

Ronsard, P. de (1924–75) *Œuvres complètes*, ed. P. Laumonier (20 vols.). Paris.

Roscoe, H. E. and Harden, A. (1896) *A New View of the Origin of Dalton's Atomic Theory*. London.

Rosenmeyer, T. G. (1969) *The Green Cabinet. Theocritus and the European Pastoral Lyric*. Berkeley and Los Angeles.

(2000) 'Seneca and nature', *Arethusa* 33: 99–119.

Rosivach, V. J. (1980) 'Lucretius 4.1123–40', *American Journal of Philology* 101: 401–3.

Rösler, W. (1973) 'Lukrez und die Vorsokratiker', *Hermes* 101: 48–64.

Ross, D. (1987) *Virgil's Elements: Physics and Poetry in the 'Georgics'*. Princeton.

Rousseau, J.-J. (1979) *Emile, or, On Education*, transl. A. Bloom. New York.

(1994) *The First and Second Discourses, together with Replies to Critics and Essay on the Origin of Languages*, transl. V. Gourevitch. New York.

Rudd, N. (1994) *The Classical Tradition in Operation*. Toronto.

Runia, D. T. (1997) 'Lucretius and doxography', in Algra, Koenen and Schrijvers (1997), 93–103.

Russell, D. A. (ed.) (1964) *'Longinus' on the Sublime*. Oxford.

Russell, D. A. and Winterbottom, M. (1972) *Ancient Literary Criticism: the Principal Texts in New Translations*. Oxford.

Saccenti, M. (1966) *Lucrezio in Toscana: Studio su Alessandro Marchetti*. Florence.

Sacré, D. (ed.) (1992), *Aonio Paleario: De animorum immortalitate libri 3*. Brussels.

(1999) 'Le premier Anti-Lucrèce de l'époque moderne?', in Poignault (1999), 345–59.

Saint-Denis, E. de (ed.) (1966) *Virgil: Géorgiques*. Paris.

Saintsbury, G. (1924) *A Last Scrap-Book*. London.

(ed.) (1905) *Minor Poets of the Caroline Period* (3 vols.). Oxford.

Salvatore, M. (2003a) 'Giordano Bruno, Lucrezio e l'entusiasmo per la vita infinita', *Studi Rinascimentali* 1: 111–18.

(2003b) 'Immagini lucreziane nel *De immenso* di Giordano Bruno', *Vichiana* 5: 123–35.

S[andys], G. (transl.) (1632) *Ovid's Metamorphoses Englished, Mythologiz'd, and Represented in Figures*. London.

Santayana, G. (1910) *Three Philosophical Poets: Lucretius, Dante, and Goethe*. Cambridge, Mass., reprinted 1947.

(1930) *The Realm of Matter: Book Second of Realms of Being*. London.

(1955) *The Sense of Beauty, Being the Outline of Aesthetic Theory*. New York.

(1986) *Persons and Places*. Cambridge, Mass.

(2003) *Letters*, vol. iv: *1933–1936*, ed. W. G. Holzberger, Cambridge, Mass.

Schaefer, D. (1990) *The Political Philosophy of Montaigne*. Ithaca.

Schiesaro, A. (1987) 'Lucrezio, Cicerone e l'oratoria', *Materiali e Discussioni* 19: 29–61.

(1990) *Simulacrum et imago: gli argomenti analogici nel De rerum natura*. Pisa.

(1994) 'The palingenesis of *De rerum natura*', *Proceedings of the Cambridge Philological Society* 40: 81–107.

(1996) 'La "palingenesi" nel *De rerum natura* (iii 847–869)', in *Epicureismo greco e romano: atti del congresso internazionale, Napoli, 19–26 maggio 1995*, ed. G. Giannantoni and M. Gigante (3 vols.). Naples: ii, 795–804.

(2007) 'Didaxis, rhetoric and the law in Lucretius', in *Classical Constructions: Papers in Memory of Don Fowler, Classicist and Epicurean*, ed. S. J. Heyworth, P. G. Fowler and S. J. Harrison. Oxford 63–90.

(forthcoming) 'La Peste a Roma', in *Lucrezio, la natura e la scienza*, ed. M. Beretta and F. Citti. Florence.

Schiesaro, A., Mitsis, P. and Clay, J. S. (eds.) (1993) *Mega Nepios: il destinatario nell'epos didascalico (Materiali e Discussioni 31)*. Pisa.

Schindler, C. (2000) *Untersuchungen zu den Gleichnissen im römischen Lehrgedicht: Lucrez, Vergil, Manilius*. Göttingen.

Schmidt, A.-M. (1970) *La Poésie scientifique en France au XVIe siècle*. Paris.

Schmidt, J. W. (1982), 'Diderot and Lucretius: the *De rerum natura* and Lucretius's legacy in Diderot's scientific, aesthetic, and ethical thought', *Studies on Voltaire and the Eighteenth Century* 208: 183–294.

Schneider, M. W. (1981), 'The Lucretian background of "Dover Beach"', *Victorian Poetry* 19: 190–5.

Schofield, M. (1975) 'Doxographica Anaxagorea', *Hermes* 103: 1–24.

(1995) 'Cicero's definition of *Res Publica*', in *Cicero the Philosopher: Twelve Papers*, ed. J. G. F. Powell. Oxford: 63–83.

(2000) 'Epicurean and Stoic political thought', in *The Cambridge History of Greek and Roman Political Thought*, ed. C. Rowe and M. Schofield. Cambridge: 435–56.

Schopenhauer, A. (1969) *World as Will and Representation*, transl. E. F. J. Payne (2 vols.). New York.

Schrijvers, P. H. (1970) *Horror ac divina voluptas: études sur la poétique et la poésie de Lucrèce*. Amsterdam.

(1978) 'Le regard sur l'invisible: étude sur l'emploi de l'analogie dans l'œuvre de Lucrèce', in Gigon (1978), 77–114, English translation in Gale (forthcoming).

(1992) 'Lucrèce et les sceptiques (*DRN* IV 962–1036)', in *La Langue latine, langue de la philosophie* (Collection de l'Ecole Française de Rome 161). Rome: 125–40, reprinted in Schrijvers (1999), 167–82.

(1996) 'Lucretius and the origin and development of political life (*De rerum natura* 5.1105–1160)', in *Polyhistor: Studies in the History and Historiography of Ancient Philosophy, Presented to Jaap Mansfeld on his Sixtieth Birthday*, ed. K. A. Algra, P. W. Van der Horst and D. T. Runia. Leiden, New York and Cologne: 220–30.

(1999) *Lucrèce et les sciences de la vie*. Leiden.

(2004) 'Silius Italicus en het Romeins Sublieme', *Lampas* 37.ii: 86–101.

Schrödinger, E. (1954) *Nature and the Greeks*. Cambridge.

Schroeder, F. M. (2004) 'Philodemus: *avocatio* and the pathos of distance in Lucretius and Virgil', in *Vergil, Philodemus, and the Augustans*, ed. D. Armstrong *et al.* Austin: 139–56.

Schuh, F. (1974) *Franz Hebenstreit, 1747–1795: Mensch unter Menschen*. Trier.

Scodel, J. (2002) *Excess and Mean in Early Modern Literature*. Princeton.

Scot, R. (1584) *The Discoverie of Witchcraft*. London.

Scott, J. T. (1992) 'The theodicy of the second discourse: the "pure state of nature" and Rousseau's political thought', *American Political Science Review* 86: 696–711.

Screech, M. A. (1998) *Montaigne's Annotated Copy of Lucretius*. Geneva.

Sedley, D. N. (1976) 'Epicurus and his professional rivals', in *Etudes sur l'épicurisme antique*, ed. J. Bollack and A. Laks. Lille: 121–59.

  (1997a) 'The ethics of Brutus and Cassius', *Journal of Roman Studies* 87: 41–53.

  (1997b) 'The sequence of argument in Lucretius I', in Atherton (1997), 37–55.

  (1998) *Lucretius and the Transformation of Greek Wisdom*. Cambridge.

  (1999) 'Lucretius' use and avoidance of Greek', in *Aspects of the Language of Latin Poetry*, ed. J. N. Adams and R. G. Mayer. Oxford: 227–46.

  (2003) 'Philodemus and the decentralization of philosophy', *Cronache Ercolanesi* 33: 31–41.

Segal, C. (1990) *Lucretius on Death and Anxiety: Poetry and Philosophy in De rerum natura*. Princeton.

Sellar, W. Y. (1877) *The Roman Poets of the Augustan Age: Virgil*. Oxford.

  (1889) *The Roman Poets of the Republic*, 3rd edn. Oxford.

Sennert, D. (1660) *Thirteen Books of Natural Philosophy*, transl. A. Cole and N. Culpeper. London.

Shackleton Bailey, D. R. (ed.) (1980) *Cicero: Epistulae ad Quintum Fratrem et M. Brutum*. Cambridge.

Shaw, B. D. (1985) 'The divine economy: Stoicism as ideology', *Latomus* 64: 16–54.

Shaw, G. B. (1930–8) *Works* (33 vols.). London.

Shea, W. R. (1986) 'Filled with wonder: Kant's cosmological essay, the *Universal Natural History and Theory of the Heavens*', in *Kant's Philosophy of Physical Science*, ed. R. Butts. Boston, Mass: 95–124.

Shelley, M. (1994) *Frankenstein, or The Modern Prometheus: the 1818 Text*, ed. M. Butler. Oxford.

Shelley, P. B. (1907) *The Complete Poetical Works of Percy Bysshe Shelley*, ed. Thomas Hutchinson. London.

  (1988) *Shelley's Prose, or The Trumpet of a Prophecy*, ed. D. L. Clark, revised edn. London.

Sherburne, Sir E. (1961) *The Poems and Translations of Sir Edward Sherburne (1616–1702), Excluding Seneca and Manilius*, ed. F. J. Van Beeck, SJ. Assen.

Shulman, J. (1980/1) '*Te quoque falle tamen*: Ovid's anti-Lucretian didactics', *Classical Journal* 76: 242–53.

Sider, D. (ed.) (1997) *The Epigrams of Philodemus*. New York and Oxford.

  (2005) *The Library of the Villa dei Papiri at Herculaneum*. Los Angeles.

Singh, C. M. (1975) 'The *Lettre sur les aveugles*: its debt to Lucretius', *Studies in Eighteenth-Century French Literature presented to Robert Niklaus*, ed. J. H. Fox, M. H. Waddicor and D. A. Watts. Exeter: 233–42.

Sisson, C. H. (transl.) (1976) *Lucretius De Rerum Natura: the Poem on Nature*. Manchester.

Sivo, V. (1988) '"Fortuna" medievale di un verso lucreziano (da Micone di Saint-Riquier a Giovanni Balbi)', *Invigilata Lucernis* 10: 305–25.

Smith, J. (1978) *Select Discourses [1660]* (facs. reprint). New York.

Smith, J. C. and Sélincourt, E. de (eds.) (1909–10) *The Poetical Works of Edmund Spenser* (3 vols.). Oxford.

Smith, M. F. (1993) *Diogenes of Oinoanda: the Epicurean Inscription*. Naples.

  (ed.) (1992) *Lucretius De Rerum Natura with an English Translation by W. H. D. Rouse*. Cambridge, Mass. and London.

Smock, G. E. (1946) 'John Locke and the Augustan age of Literature', *Philosophical Review* 55: 264–81.

Snyder, J. M. (1980) *Puns and Poetry in Lucretius' De Rerum Natura*. Amsterdam.

Solaro, G. (1993) *Pomponio Leto, 'Lucrezio'*. Palermo.

(1997) 'Lucrezio in Inghilterra agli inizi del secolo XIII?', *Eikasmos* 8: 241–4.

(2000) *Lucrezio: biografie umanistiche*. Bari.

Sommariva, G. (1980) 'La parodia di Lucrezio nell'*Ars* e nei *Remedia* ovidiani', *Atene & Roma* 25: 123–48.

Sottili, A. (1984) 'Il Laerzio latino e greco e altri autografi di Ambrogio Traversari', in *Vestigia: studi in onore di Giuseppe Billanovich*, ed. R. Avesani *et al.* (2 vols.). Rome: II, 699–745.

Soubiran, J. (ed.) (1972) *Cicéron Aratea. Fragments poétiques*. Paris.

Spence, J. (1966) *Anecdotes of Books and Men*, ed. J. M. Osborn (2 vols.). Oxford.

Spencer, T. J. B. (1965) 'Lucretius and the scientific poem in English', in Dudley (1965a): 131–64.

Speroni, S. (1988) *Opere*, ed. M. Pozzi. Rome.

Spiegelman, W. (1985) 'Some Lucretian elements in Wordsworth', *Comparative Literature* 37: 27–49.

Spink, J. S. (1960) *French Free-Thought from Gassendi to Voltaire*. London.

Stephan, C. (1885) 'Das prosodische Florilegium der S. Gallener Handschrift nr. 870 und sein Werth für die Iuvenalkritik', *Rheinisches Museum* 40: 263–82.

Stewart, S. (1993) *On Longing: Narratives of the Miniature, the Gigantic, the Souvenir, the Collection*. Durham (1st pub. 1984).

Suerbaum, W. (1994) 'Herculanensische Lukrez-Papyri', *Zeitschrift für Papyrologie und Epigraphik* 104: 1–21.

Swinburne, A. C. (1905) *The Poems of Algernon Charles Swinburne* (6 vols.). London.

Symonds, J. A. (1875) 'Lucretius', *Fortnightly Review* 17: 44–62.

Tantillo, A. O. (2002) *The Will to Create: Goethe's Philosophy of Nature*. Pittsburgh.

Tasso, T. (1979) *Gerusalemme liberata*, ed. L. Caretti. Milan.

Tatum, W. (1984) 'The Presocratics in book one of Lucretius' *De rerum natura*', *Transactions of the American Philological Association* 114: 177–89, reprinted in Gale (forthcoming).

Taylor, C. (1989) *Sources of the Self: the Making of the Modern Identity*. Cambridge.

Tennyson, A. (Lord) (1987) *The Poems of Tennyson*, ed. C. Ricks (3 vols.). London.

Tennyson, H. (Baron) (1897). *Alfred Lord Tennyson: a Memoir by His Son* (2 vols.). London.

Thomas, R. F. (1988) *Virgil: Georgics* (2 vols.). Cambridge.

Thompson, L. (1967) *Robert Frost: the Early Years 1874–1915*. London.

(1971) *Robert Frost: The Years of Triumph 1915–1938*. New York.

Thomson, J. (1897) *The Poetical Works*, ed. D. C. Tovey (2 vols.). London.

(1981) *The Seasons*, ed. J. Sambrook. Oxford.

Thouard, D. (2003) 'Kant et Lucrèce', in *Le Jardin Romain: Epicurisme et poésie à Rome; mélanges offerts à Mayotte Bollack*, ed. A. Monet. Lille: 265–80.

Timpanaro, S. (1988) 'Epicuro, Lucrezio e Leopardi', *Critica Storia* 25: 359–402.

Tosi, M. (1984–5) 'Documenti riguardanti l'abbaziato di Gerberto a Bobbio', *Archivum Bobiense* 6–7: 91–172.

Tottel, R. (ed.) (1557) *Songes and Sonettes, written by the Ryght Honorable Lorde Henry Haward Late Earle of Surrey, and Other*. London.

Townend, G. B. (1979) 'The original plan of Lucretius' *De rerum natura*', *Classical Quarterly* 29: 101–11.

Traina, A. (1975) 'Lucrezio e la "congiura del silenzio"', in *Poeti latini (e neolatini): note e saggi filologici*. Bologna: 81–91.

Trépanier, S. (2004) *Empedocles: an Interpretation*. New York.

Trevelyan, R. C. (transl.) (1937) *De Rerum Natura*. Cambridge.

Tsakiropoulou-Summers, T. (2004) '*Tantum potuit suadere libido*: religion and pleasure in Polignac's *Anti-Lucretius*', *Eighteenth-Century Thought* 2: 165–205.

Turnbull, H. W., Scott, J. F., Hall, A. R. and Tilling, L. (eds.) (1959–77) *The Correspondence of Isaac Newton* (7 vols.). Cambridge.

Turner, F. M. (1973) 'Lucretius among the Victorians', *Victorian Studies* 16: 329–48.
  (1993) 'Ancient materialism and modern science: Lucretius among the Victorians', in *Contesting Cultural Authority: Essays in Victorian Intellectual Life*. Cambridge: 262–83.

[Turner, M.] (1782) *Answer to Dr Priestley's Letters to a Philosophical Unbeliever, Part I*, ed. W. Hammon. London.

Tuveson, E. L. (1955/6) 'Locke and the "dissolution of the ego"', *Modern Philology* 52: 159–74.

Valla, L. (1990) *L'arte della grammatica*, ed. P. Casciano. Milan.

Vance, N. (1997) *The Victorians and Ancient Rome*. Oxford.

Vander Waerdt, P. A. (1988) 'Hermarchus and the Epicurean genealogy of morals', *Transactions of the American Philological Association* 118: 87–106.
  (1989) 'Colotes and the Epicurean refutation of scepticism', *Greek, Roman and Byzantine Studies* 30: 225–67.

Vasoli, C. (1997) 'Ficino, Marsilio', *Dizionario biografico degli Italiani* 47: 378–95.

Vaughan, F. (1982) *The Tradition of Political Hedonism from Hobbes to J. S. Mill*. New York.

Vegetti, M. (1983) 'Metafora politica e immagine del corpo nella medicina greca', in *Tra Edipo e Euclide*. Milan: 41–58.

Verde, A. (1998) 'Il secondo periodo de Lo Studio Fiorentino (1504–1528)', in *L'Università e la sua storia: Origini, spazi istituzionali e pratiche didattiche dello Studium cittadino. Atti del Convegno di Studi (Arezzo, 15–16 novembre 1991)*, ed. P. Renzi. Arezzo: 105–31.

Vettori, P. (1586) *Petri Victorii epistolarum libri X. Orationes XIIII. Et liber De laudibus Ioannae Austriacae*. Florence.

Vida, M. G. (1976) *De arte poetica*, ed. and transl. R. G. Williams. New York.

Volk, K. (2002) *The Poetics of Latin Didactic. Lucretius, Vergil, Ovid, Manilius*. Oxford.

Voltaire (1877–85) *Œuvres*, ed. L. Moland (52 vols.). Paris.
  (1962) *Philosophical Dictionary*, ed. and transl. P. Gay. New York.
  (1968–) *Complete Works*, ed. T. Bestermann *et al.* (68 vols. to date). Geneva.
  (1991) *Candide, or Optimism*, ed. and transl. R. M. Adams. New York.

Wagenblass, J. H. (1937) 'Keats and Lucretius', *Modern Language Review* 32: 537–52.

Wakefield, G. (ed.) (1796–7) *T. Lucretii Cari de Rerum Natura* (3 vols.). London.

Wallace, N. O. (1987) 'Montaigne, Lucretius, and intertextuality in *Essais* II. xii ("Apologie de Raimond Sebond")', *Spiegel der Letteren: Tijdschrift voor Nederlandse Literatuurgeschiedenis en voor Literatuurwetenschap* 29: 79–85.

Wallach, B. P. (1975) 'Lucretius and the Diatribe. *De rerum natura* II.1–61', in *Gesellschaft – Kultur – Literatur. Rezeption und Originalität im Wachsen einer europäischen Literatur und Geistigkeit. Beiträge Luitpold Wallach gewidmet*, ed. K. Bosl. Stuttgart: 49–77.

(1976) *Lucretius and the Diatribe against the Fear of Death: De Rerum Natura III, 830–1094*. Leiden.

Wardy, R. (1996) 'Atomism', in *Oxford Classical Dictionary*, 3rd edn. Oxford.

Warren, J. (2002) *Epicurus and Democritean Ethics: an Archaeology of Ataraxia*. Cambridge.

(2004) *Facing Death: Epicurus and his Critics*. Oxford.

(2006) 'Psychic disharmony: Philoponus and Epicurus on Plato's *Phaedo*', *Oxford Studies in Ancient Philosophy* 30: 233–57.

(ed.) (forthcoming) *The Cambridge Companion to Epicureanism*. Cambridge.

Wehrli, F. (1946) 'Der erhabene und der schlichte Stil in der poetisch-rhetorischen Theorie der Antike', *Phyllobolia für Peter von der Mühll zum 60. Geburtstag am 1. August 1945*, ed. O. Gigon *et al*. Basel: 9–34.

Weinberg, S. (1983) *The Discovery of Subatomic Particles*. New York.

Weiskel, T. (1976) *The Romantic Sublime: Studies in the Structure and Psychology of Transcendence*. Baltimore.

Weiss, B. (1993) *Understanding Italo Calvino*. Columbia, S.C.

West, D. (1969) *The Imagery and Poetry of Lucretius*. Bristol.

(1970) 'Virgilian multiple-correspondence similes and their antecedents', *Philologus* 114: 262–75.

(1995) *Horace Odes I. Carpe Diem*. Oxford.

Wheeler, S. M. (1995) '*Imago mundi*: another view of the creation in Ovid's *Metamorphoses*', *American Journal of Philology* 116: 95–121.

Whitaker, V. K. (1936) 'Du Bartas' use of Lucretius', *Studies in Philology* 33: 134–46.

Whitman, W. (1964) *Prose Works 1892*, ed. F. Stovall (2 vols.). New York.

Wick, C. [paper forthcoming in] '*The Best of Nature'*: *Naturphänomene und Naturkatastrophen in hellenistischen Epigrammen*.

Wiesmann, M. (2004) 'Lucrèce', in *Dictionnaire de Michel de Montaigne*, ed. P. Desan. Paris: 610–12.

Wilding, M. (1987) *Dragon's Teeth: Literature in the English Revolution*. Oxford.

Williams, B. (1973) *Problems of the Self: Philosophical Papers, 1956–1972*. London.

Williams, G. (2006) 'Greco-Roman seismology and Seneca on earthquakes in *Natural Questions* 6', *Journal of Roman Studies* 96: 124–46.

Wilson, A. (1985) 'The prologue to Manilius 1', *Papers of the Liverpool Latin Seminar* 5: 283–98.

Wilson, C. (1982) 'Leibniz and atomism', *Studies in the History and Philosophy of Science* 15: 175–99.

(2003) 'Epicureanism in early modern philosophy: Leibniz and his contemporaries', in *Hellenistic and Early Modern Philosophy*, ed. B. Inwood and J. Miller. Cambridge: 90–115.

Winbolt, S. E. (1903) *Latin Hexameter Verse: an Aid to Composition*. London.

Winkler, L. (1995) *Salus vom Staatskult zur politischen Idee: eine archäologische Untersuchung.* Heidelberg.

Wiseman, T. P. (1974) *Cinna the Poet and Other Roman Essays.* Leicester.

(1982) '*Pete nobiles amicos*: poets and patrons in late Republican Rome', in *Literary and Artistic Patronage in Ancient Rome*, ed. B. K. Gold. Austin: 28–49.

Wood, A. (1815) *Athenae Oxonienses* (3 vols.). London.

Wood, N. (1992) '*Tabula Rasa*, social environmentalism, and the "English Paradigm"', *Journal of the History of Ideas* 53: 647–68.

Woodman, A. J. (1988) *Rhetoric in Classical Historiography: Four Studies.* London.

Wordsworth, C. (1851) *Memoirs of William Wordsworth* (2 vols.). London.

Wordsworth, W. (1950) *Poetical Works.* London.

(1986) *The Oxford Authors: William Wordsworth*, ed. Stephen Gill. Oxford.

Wray, D. (2001) *Catullus and the Poetics of Roman Manhood.* Cambridge.

Wright, M. R. (1997) 'Philosopher poets: Parmenides and Empedocles', in Atherton (1997), 1–22.

Wycherley, W. (1718) *Posthumous Works.* London.

Zetzel, J. E. G. (1977) 'Lucilius, Lucretius, and Persius 1.1', *Classical Philology* 72: 40–2.

(1998) '*De re publica* and *De rerum natura*', in *Style and Tradition: Studies in Honor of Wendell Clausen*, ed. P. E. Knox and C. Foss. Stuttgart and Leipzig: 230–47.

Zimmerman, M. (2006) 'Awe and opposition: the ambivalent presence of Lucretius in Apuleius' *Metamorphoses*', in *Authors, Authority, and Interpreters in the Ancient Novel: Essays in Honor of Gareth L. Schmeling*, ed. S. N. Byrne, E. P. Cueva and J. Alvares. Groningen: 317–39.

Žižek, S. (1989) *The Sublime Object of Ideology.* London and New York.

(1991) *For They Know Not What They Do: Enjoyment as a Political Factor.* London.

Zoll, D. A. (1972) 'Naturalism and political philosophy', *Review of Politics* 34: 210–22.

Zukofsky, L. (1963) *Bottom: On Shakespeare* (2 vols.). Austin, Tx.

(1966) *"A" 1–12.* London.

INDEX OF MAIN LUCRETIAN PASSAGES DISCUSSED

See also under individual authors for translations

Cambridge Companions to Literature

AUTHORS

Edward Albee edited by Stephen J. Bottoms

Margaret Atwood edited by Coral Ann Howells

W. H. Auden edited by Stan Smith

Jane Austen edited by Edward Copeland and Juliet McMaster

Beckett edited by John Pilling

Aphra Behn edited by Derek Hughes and Janet Todd

Walter Benjamin edited by David S. Ferris

William Blake edited by Morris Eaves

Brecht edited by Peter Thomson and Glendyr Sacks (second edition)

The Brontës edited by Heather Glen

Byron edited by Drummond Bone

Albert Camus edited by Edward J. Hughes

Willa Cather edited by Marilee Lindemann

Cervantes edited by Anthony J. Cascardi

Chaucer, edited by Piero Boitani and Jill Mann (second edition)

Chekhov edited by Vera Gottlieb and Paul Allain

Coleridge edited by Lucy Newlyn

Wilkie Collins edited by Jenny Bourne Taylor

Joseph Conrad edited by J. H. Stape

Dante edited by Rachel Jacoff (second edition)

Charles Dickens edited by John O. Jordan

Emily Dickinson edited by Wendy Martin

John Donne edited by Achsah Guibbory

Dostoevskii edited by W. J. Leatherbarrow

Theodore Dreiser edited by Leonard Cassuto and Claire Virginia Eby

John Dryden edited by Steven N. Zwicker

George Eliot edited by George Levine

T. S. Eliot edited by A. David Moody

Ralph Ellison edited by Ross Posnock

Ralph Waldo Emerson edited by Joel Porte and Saundra Morris

William Faulkner edited by Philip M. Weinstein

F. Scott Fitzgerald edited by Ruth Prigozy

Flaubert edited by Timothy Unwin

E. M. Forster edited by David Bradshaw

Brian Friel edited by Anthony Roche

Robert Frost edited by Robert Faggen

Elizabeth Gaskell edited by Jill L. Matus

Goethe edited by Lesley Sharpe

Thomas Hardy edited by Dale Kramer

Nathaniel Hawthorne edited by Richard Millington

Ernest Hemingway edited by Scott Donaldson

Homer edited by Robert Fowler

Horace edited by Stephen Harrison

Ibsen edited by James McFarlane

Henry James edited by Jonathan Freedman

Samuel Johnson edited by Greg Clingham

Ben Jonson edited by Richard Harp and Stanley Stewart

James Joyce edited by Derek Attridge (second edition)

Kafka edited by Julian Preece

Keats edited by Susan J. Wolfson

Lacan edited by Jean-Michel Rabaté

D. H. Lawrence edited by Anne Fernihough

Lucretius edited by Stuart Gillespie and Philip Hardie

David Mamet edited by Christopher Bigsby

Thomas Mann edited by Ritchie Robertson

Christopher Marlowe edited by Patrick Cheney

Herman Melville edited by Robert S. Levine

Arthur Miller edited by Christopher Bigsby

Milton edited by Dennis Danielson (second edition)

Molière edited by David Bradby and Andrew Calder

Toni Morrison edited by Justine Tally

Nabokov edited by Julian W. Connolly

Eugene O'Neill edited by Michael Manheim

George Orwell edited by John Rodden

Ovid edited by Philip Hardie

Harold Pinter edited by Peter Raby

Sylvia Plath edited by Jo Gill

Edgar Allan Poe edited by Kevin J. Hayes

Ezra Pound edited by Ira B. Nadel

Proust edited by Richard Bales

Pushkin edited by Andrew Kahn

Philip Roth edited by Timothy Parrish

Salman Rushdie edited by Abdulrazak Gurnah

Shakespeare edited by Margareta de Grazia and Stanley Wells

Made in the USA
San Bernardino, CA
26 January 2013